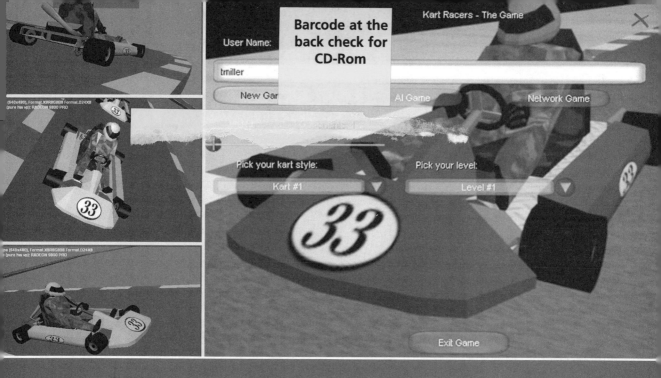

Kart Racers - The Game

User Name:

tmiller

Barcode at the back check for CD-Rom

New Game   AI Game   Network Game

Pick your kart style: Pick your level:

Kart #1 ▼   Level #1 ▼

33

Exit Game

BEGINNING

3D

GAME PROGRAMMING

Tom Miller

SAMS 800 East 96th St., Indianapolis, Indiana, 46240 USA

Beginning 3D Game Programming

Copyright © 2005 by Sams Publishing

International Standard Book Number: 0-672-32661-2

Library of Congress Catalog Card Number: 2004095062

Printed in the United States of America

First Printing:

07   06   05   4   3   2

Trademarks

All terms mentioned in this book that are known to be trademarks or service marks have been appropriately capitalized. Sams Publishing cannot attest to the accuracy of this information. Use of a term in this book should not be regarded as affecting the validity of any trademark or service mark.

Warning and Disclaimer

Every effort has been made to make this book as complete and as accurate as possible, but no warranty or fitness is implied. The information provided is on an "as is" basis. The author and the publisher shall have neither liability nor responsibility to any person or entity with respect to any loss or damages arising from the information contained in this book.

Bulk Sales

Sams Publishing offers excellent discounts on this book when ordered in quantity for bulk purchases or special sales. For more information, please contact

> **U.S. Corporate and Government Sales**
> 1-800-382-3419
> corpsales@pearsontechgroup.com

For sales outside of the United States, please contact

> **International Sales**
> international@pearsoned.com

Associate Publisher
Michael Stephens

Acquisitions Editor
Neil Rowe

Development Editor
Mark Renfrow

Managing Editor
Charlotte Clapp

Project Editor
George Nedeff

Copy Editor
Kris Simmons

Indexer
Erika Millen

Proofreader
Wendy Ott

Technical Editors
Mitch Walker

David Weller

Rick Hoskinson

Team Coordinator
Cindy Teeters

Interior Designer
Gary Adair

Cover Designer
Aren Howell

Page Layout
Kelly Maish

Contents at a Glance

Part V: Advanced Graphics, Client/Server Networking, Game 3

Part VI: Appendix

Table of Contents

About the Author

Tom Miller is the designer and development lead for the Managed DirectX API. He has worked at Microsoft since 1997 where he started on the Visual Basic team before his love of games and game programming took him to the DirectX team. He has been with the DirectX team since late 1999, and has worked to bring the DirectX API (and game programming in general) to a wider audience. He has also written the definitive book on the Managed DirectX libraries to date.

Acknowledgments

To my wife Tanya, my son Lucas, and my daughter Samantha: I know it wasn't easy with me being constantly busy. I couldn't have done this without your support. Jason Kepner and Greg Loker: Each of whom helped out with both reviewing and user interface art. Wes Greene: Created all of the great 3D art you see in the applications. My managers at Microsoft: Andy Glaister, Bob Gaines, Rod Toll, and Drew Johnston, without their support I wouldn't be in the position I am today. To the Managed DirectX Test team: Rick Hoskinson, Adam Lonnberg, and Rich Sauer. To my mom Vicki, and my sister Jessica. I put them in the last one, and that set a trend that's probably unbreakable now. All of the beta testers and users of Managed DirectX for the great feedback. You, for reading this book! Finally, I was watching the ESPY awards one day, and after receiving an award Carmello Anthony said as part of his acceptance speech: "I also want to thank myself, I put a lot of hard work day in and day out." It was the highlight of the show, and I love the fact he was proud enough of his work to say it. I feel the same way.

We Want to Hear from You!

As the reader of this book, *you* are our most important critic and commentator. We value your opinion and want to know what we're doing right, what we could do better, what areas you'd like to see us publish in, and any other words of wisdom you're willing to pass our way.

As an associate publisher for Sams, I welcome your comments. You can email or write me directly to let me know what you did or didn't like about this book—as well as what we can do to make our books better.

Please note that I cannot help you with technical problems related to the topic of this book. We do have a User Services group, however, where I will forward specific technical questions related to the book.

When you write, please be sure to include this book's title and author as well as your name, email address, and phone number. I will carefully review your comments and share them with the author and editors who worked on the book.

Email: feedback@samspublishing.com

Mail: Michael Stephens
         Associate Publisher
         Sams Publishing
         800 East 96th Street
         Indianapolis, IN 46240 USA

Reader Services

For more information about this book or others from Sams Publishing, visit our website at http://www.samspublishing.com. Type the ISBN (excluding hyphens) or the title of the book in the Search box to find the book you're looking for.

Introduction

So You Want to be a Game Developer

Just about every developer I've ever met has at one time or another wanted to be involved in game development. Video games are more than just an idle interest to most: they can be a downright obsession. People become immersed in these virtual worlds and often begin to fantasize about creating such rich fantasy lands themselves.

Don't be fooled by the pretty graphics, the wonderful stories, and the moving musical score. Writing a game is hard work, and it takes a special type of developer to be successful. Aside from the obvious technical talent required, a good game developer should possess other intangibles, such as actually being a gamer. It's not impossible to write great games as a nongamer, but it certainly makes the job more challenging.

Becoming a game developer is certainly no easy task either. Virtually no game development company will hire you without experience, and it's hard to get experience when no one will hire you. There are a few courses and even some schools dedicated to teaching game development. However, the best way to get your foot in the door is to make a demo reel. It shows the prospective employer what you are capable of doing and how you go about doing it.

Reading this book will get you well on your way to producing a compelling demo reel.

Who Should Read This Book?

The most common question I'm asked is why anyone would want to write a game using the .NET framework. Other questions include, "Isn't that just for web server applications?" "Isn't it slow?" These are naturally important questions to the game developer (or prospective game developer, as the case may be), but they come from misconceptions about what the .NET framework is.

The .NET framework is *not* the latest version of the web server, nor is it an extension of any of the server components. It is certainly true that you can create powerful web server applications using the .NET framework; however, there is so much more. It includes a capable client-side Application Programming Interface (API), and with the release of Managed DirectX, virtually the entire DirectX API is now exposed to the .NET developers. It opens up an entirely new array of applications that can be written, including games. To think the .NET framework limits you to server applications is somewhat naïve. It can produce complex client-side applications as well.

The lingering question of performance still remains, and it's not one that I can simply write off. Anytime a "new" language or runtime is introduced, developers are naturally hesitant to adopt it. It wasn't long ago that many games were still written in Assembly because the game developers didn't believe that the C or C++ language was fast enough to do the things they needed to do. The .NET framework is no exception to this rule. Until someone actually proves the performance of the .NET framework, the game developers will look at it with a suspicious eye. Throughout this book are a number of games developed using the .NET runtime exclusively. It's been said that actions speak louder than words, so rather than speak at length about how the performance of the .NET runtime compares to the native world, I let the real-world games in this book make the point.

Why Would I Want to Use the .NET Framework

Anyone who's ever written Windows programs both with and without the .NET Framework recognizes the difficulties of writing even simple Windows applications using the Win32 API. The .NET framework was designed to provide a simpler way to do the common things you need to do in a Windows program and to eliminate many of the things that the average developer doesn't want to worry about, such as memory management.

With developers freed from some of the more mundane tasks, such as spending three days trying to track down a memory leak bug, they can actually add features to the games they are writing. Too many times, great features are cut from a game because of the amount of time dedicated to solving problems that the .NET framework solves for you.

Another interesting feature of the .NET framework is that it is language agnostic. As long as the features being used are Common Language Specification (CLS) compliant, any language that can use CLS-compliant features will work. In the past, the developer who only knew Visual Basic would have a difficult time transitioning to code using strictly C++. Now, the developer using Visual Basic .NET can transition to C# more easily because there are only minor syntax differences between the two languages. The code in this book is written in C#.

Why This Book?

I wrote this book to meet the needs of a development community that has been sorely lacking information on this topic. Too many potential game developers have been turned away because they couldn't find the information they needed. The majority of game development books on the market today cover 2D graphics, which is a nice place to start, but the majority of games written today are fully 3D, and gamers expect that now. It's not that you can't still write a great 2D game, but if that's all you can do, you're limiting yourself needlessly.

This book will not teach you how to write a multimillion-dollar game. This book will give you all the tools and information for you to teach yourself how to develop in-depth, fully 3D games. You will be implementing two complete 3D games during the course of this book, and by the end of this book, you will be able to design and implement your own 3D games and call yourself a game developer. The final game in the book is left as an exercise for you to complete.

PART I

Introduction to Microsoft .NET

CHAPTER 1

Game Development and Managed Code

If you're already familiar with writing code that takes advantage of the CLR (Common Language Runtime), you're probably already aware of the choices you have when it comes to development languages. With the latest version of the Visual Studio .NET product, four languages are available to use when writing managed code: C#, Visual Basic .NET, Managed C++, and J#. This doesn't even take into consideration the languages that may be available from other third-party vendors outside of the Visual Studio .NET product, such as COBOL or FORTRAN.

Although the concepts that will be discussed in this book should be easily transferable to any language that is fully CLS (Common Language Specification)-compliant, the actual code included will only cover the first two languages mentioned; namely C# and Visual Basic. NET. The text of the book will cover the C# code, but the accompanying CD will include the code in each language.

In this chapter, you'll learn

- ▶ Defining .NET
- ▶ Managed Code
- ▶ Using the Visual Studio .NET IDE
- ▶ Compiling Managed Code on the Command Line
- ▶ The Developers
- ▶ The Process
- ▶ The Tools

What Is .NET?

Since Microsoft first announced and released .NET, people have been trying to figure out what exactly this new 'thing' is. According to the marketing that Microsoft was pushing, it would revolutionize computing as we know it. That's an awfully big promise to keep, and it's still too early to tell if it really will accomplish its goals. However, it is well on its way to doing so.

When people talk about .NET, you can never be sure which "component" of .NET they're talking about. No other "product" or "idea" released by Microsoft has taken on so many different forms. There are products, services, and even concepts that are tagged with the .NET moniker, so it's hard to figure out what exactly .NET is.

When .NET is discussed in this book, it will be in reference to the new development languages and runtime available with the .NET Framework SDK (which is included on the accompanying CD). This SDK includes the .NET Runtime, which contains everything you need to run applications written for the .NET environment. You can think of the .NET Runtime as consisting of several components. The components of the CLR reside in the Global Assembly Cache (GAC). The compilers for the Microsoft .NET languages are also included (C#, VB .NET, VJ#, and so on). You can see the GAC in Figure 1.1.

FIGURE 1.1
The Global
Assembly Cache.

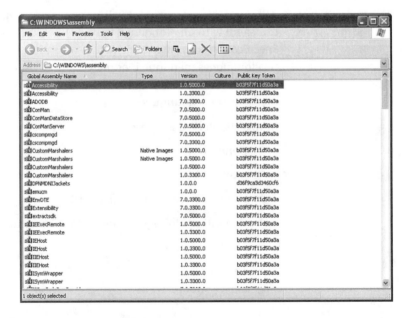

One of the most common misconceptions people have about running .NET code is that the code being executed is "interpreted," much like Java byte code or the old visual basic runtimes are. The truth is that code written for .NET is compiled natively before it is ever executed. When a .NET application is compiled, it is compiled into an *intermediary language (IL)*. This IL is actually what is stored in the executable or library that has been created.

This IL will be compiled into native code at one of two points. At the installation time of the code, a process called *ngen* (short for *native generation*) can be performed. This compiles the IL directly into native code, and stores the compiled native code in a special place in the GAC—the native assembly cache. Assuming the code wasn't compiled at installation time, it must be compiled before the first execution. During startup of the application, a special feature of the .NET Runtime called the JIT (Just In Time) compiler performs the compilation in the background.

You can imagine that in the latter case, the startup time of your application could be negatively affected because of this compilation happening behind the scenes. If startup time is important to your application (which it should be if you're writing games), it would be wise to ensure that your installation includes the ngen step. However, some optimizations can't be made during this step that can be made if the code is compiled via the JIT, so if the startup time isn't important, feel free to let the .NET Runtime do what it was designed to do.

What Is Managed Code?

Managed code will be mentioned quite often during the course of this book. The API that will be used throughout the book is called Managed DirectX, and it's not uncommon at all to hear the .NET languages called the *managed languages*. The *managed* term comes from the fact that the .NET Runtime has a built-in memory manager.

In the "old days" (you remember, just a few years ago), developers who were writing code in C and C++ would have to do their own memory management. Allocated memory would have to be freed when it was no longer necessary, unless you wanted that memory to "leak," which could be the cause of horrible performance later on down the line. Even worse, because you were dealing directly with pointers, it's quite easy to corrupt the memory your project is using. In many cases, this leads to long debugging sessions because in the majority of cases where you actually see the error occurring is nowhere near where the memory originally became corrupt.

The C and C++ languages have a reputation of being "hard" mainly because of many of these types of issues. Many developers were reluctant to try out C or C++

because of this reputation, and thus tried out some other high-level languages that could eliminate these headaches, such as Visual Basic. Although these new languages did have the benefits of being easy to use and learn, they also had drawbacks. The performance of these other languages wasn't competitive with C and C++, at most times noticeably slow. Also, because the underlying operating system was developed using C++, not all of the features were available in these other languages. Although you could do quite a bit of good work using them, if you wanted all the power, performance, and features available with the operating system, you were on your own, if it was possible at all.

With the release of the first version of the .NET Runtime, much of this changed. Microsoft went back to the drawing board, designed an entirely new API, and tried to make sure developers' concerns were addressed. This new Runtime had to be easy to use, it had to be fast, and it had to eliminate the headaches of memory management. Throughout this book, you will see how well they actually achieved these goals.

Writing Code with the Microsoft Visual Studio .NET 2003 IDE

Construction Cue

> This book will assume that you're writing your code inside the Visual Studio .NET IDE (integrated development environment). Although this isn't a requirement for writing games using .NET, nor of using .NET itself, it is the IDE of choice for this book. You can see the Visual Studio .NET 2003 IDE in Figure 1.2.

The IDE is the one-stop shop for everything you need to write .NET applications. It not only includes the editors you will need for writing your code, but a host of other features designed to make the development of .NET applications easy. It has designers to allow you to easily create rich content, such as Windows applications. It also has a built-in compiler and debugger, with everything integrated seamlessly. Throughout this book, it will be assumed that you are using the IDE to do your development.

The best way to familiarize yourself with the IDE is to use it to write a simple application. Classic computer programming tradition would have you write a simple "Hello World" application that really does nothing more than output that text to the screen. In all honesty, that application couldn't be any more boring, so instead you should try to write something slightly more in-depth. No need for anything fancy, because this is just an introduction to the IDE, but how about something with a little user interaction? Let's write an application that asks for the user's name and year of birth, and then outputs the current age.

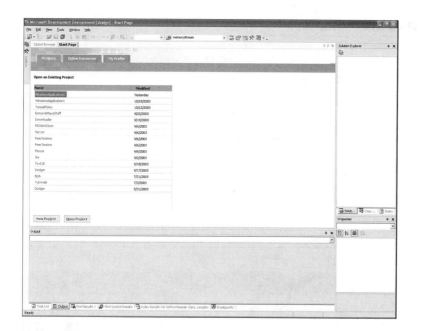

FIGURE 1.2
The Visual Studio
.NET IDE.

The C# Code

Go ahead and start up the Visual Studio .NET 2003 IDE now. When it first starts up, it should default to the start page you saw in Figure 1.2. Click the New Project button on this page to start a new project. If this page isn't shown, you can also click the New, Project selection from the File menu or use the Ctrl+Shift+N keyboard shortcut. This brings up a New Project dialog, such as that in Figure 1.3.

You should try the C# code first, so in the New Project dialog, select the Visual C# Projects item from the left-hand list box, and the Console Application item from the right-hand list box. Select any name and click the OK button to create the project. This creates a new console application that currently does nothing. Replace the code that's automatically generated for you with the code found in Listing 1.1.

LISTING 1.1   A Simple C# Console Application

```
using System;
class ConsoleApp
{
 static void Main()
 {
 Console.Write("Hello World C#!\r\nPlease enter your name:");
 string name = Console.ReadLine();
 Console.Write("Hello {0}, please enter the year you were born: ", name);
 int year = int.MaxValue;
 while(year == int.MaxValue)
```

LISTING 1.1   Continued

```
{
try
{
year = int.Parse(Console.ReadLine());
}
catch (FormatException)
{
Console.Write("You did not enter a valid number. ");
Console.WriteLine("Please enter an integer, such as 1975.");
}
}
Console.WriteLine("You must be approximately {0} years old!",
    DateTime.Now.Year-year);
Console.WriteLine("Press the <Enter> key to exit the application");
Console.Read();
}
}
```

FIGURE 1.3
The New Project
dialog.

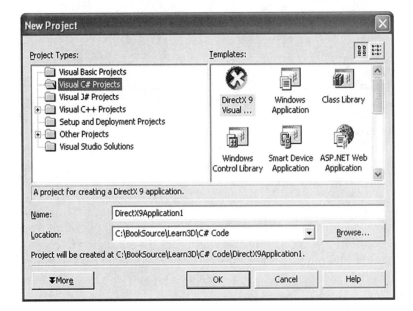

If you are already fluent in C, C++, or Java, the syntax of the C# language is probably quite similar to what you've been accustomed to. Although the underlying runtime of C# is still the CLR, the syntax is definitely derived from these languages, and developers familiar with them normally have no difficulty making the switch. As you can see here, the code isn't overly complex. It uses the Console class first to write out a simple message (including the ubiquitous "Hello World") before asking the user's name and year of birth. Notice that the application will continue to ask for a year of birth until a valid numeric value has been entered. It finally outputs the user's current age based on the simple formula. You can see the expected output of this application in Figure 1.4.

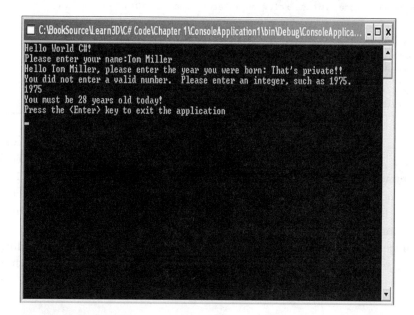

```
C:\BookSource\Learn3D\C# Code\Chapter 1\ConsoleApplication1\bin\Debug\ConsoleApplica...
Hello World C#!
Please enter your name:Tom Miller
Hello Tom Miller, please enter the year you were born: That's private!!
You did not enter a valid number.  Please enter an integer, such as 1975.
1975
You must be 28 years old today!
Press the <Enter> key to exit the application
```

FIGURE 1.4
Your first application!

The VB .NET Code

If you are more familiar with Visual Basic syntax, you will likely still be able to follow the preceding code for the most part. The syntactical difference between the two languages isn't that great, but you should try to write a Visual Basic .NET version anyway. Once again, you will need to start a new project and follow the same instructions as you did with the C# code, with the natural exception being the project type you are creating. Instead of selecting Visual C# Projects from the left-hand list, you should choose Visual Basic Projects instead. After the project has been created, replace the automatically generated code with the code you find in Listing 1.2.

LISTING 1.2 A Simple VB .NET Console Application

```vbnet
Module Module1
 Sub Main()
 Console.Write("Hello World C#!" + vbCr + vbLf + "Please enter your name:")
 Dim name As String = Console.ReadLine()
 Console.Write("Hello {0}, please enter the year you were born: ", name)
 Dim year As Integer = Integer.MaxValue
 While year = Integer.MaxValue
 Try
```

LISTING 1.2   Continued

```
year = Integer.Parse(Console.ReadLine())
Catch fe As FormatException
Console.Write("You did not enter a valid number. ")
Console.WriteLine("Please enter an integer, such as 1975.")
End Try
End While
Console.WriteLine("You must be approximately {0} years old!",
    DateTime.Now.Year - year)
Console.WriteLine("Press the <Enter> key to exit the application")
Console.Read()
End Sub 'Main
End Module ' Module1
```

As you can see, the translation of the code from C# to VB .NET isn't overly complicated. Because each language is running on top of the same runtime, there are
only minor syntactical differences between the two pieces of code. You should also
notice that each code produces the same results. This is a powerful feature of .NET
because it frees the developer up to write code in whichever language he is most
comfortable with. There's no longer the worry that if you use programming
language X, you won't be able to take advantage of feature Y in programming
language Z. Because each of the managed languages use the same underlying
runtime, they all have similar feature sets.

Compiling .NET Code on the Command Line

Using the Visual Studio .NET IDE is by far the easiest way to develop .NET applications, but it is certainly not the only way. The .NET Runtime ships with the compilers for C#, VB .NET, and VJ# as part of the runtime itself, so as long as you have a
text editor and the .NET Runtime, you can create any .NET applications you want.

Construction Cue

> To actually develop and use the .NET applications, you will naturally need the .NET
> Runtime. If you do not have it installed already, you may install it from the included
> CD or download it from the Microsoft website at http://www.microsoft.com/net.

Open up your favorite text editor (Notepad, for instance) and enter the code from
one of the previous listings, depending on your language preference. After you
have written the code, save it and open up a command prompt. Before you can
actually use the compilers that are part of the .NET Runtime, you will need to set
your path to point to the location of the underlying .NET Framework. In your
command window, enter the following command to update your path:

```
set path=%path%;C:\WINDOWS\Microsoft.NET\Framework\v1.1.4322
```

If your Windows folder is not located at `C:\windows`, make sure you enter the location of your Windows folder when updating the path variable.

The command-line compilers are located in the folder listed here, along with the assemblies that comprise the .NET Runtime itself. The C# compiler is found in the `csc.exe`, and the VB .NET compiler is found in `vbc.exe`. Each of these executables takes a similar set of command-line arguments, and you can use a single argument of `/?` to display the list of all arguments for each of these compilers.

Assuming you used the C# version of the code and saved the file as `class1.cs`, you can do the following to compile the application to an executable named `app.exe`. First navigate to the folder where your code file was stored and then run the following command:

```
csc /out:app.exe /target:exe Class1.cs
```

The output should be similar to the following:

```
Microsoft (R) Visual C# .NET Compiler version 7.10.3052.4
for Microsoft (R) .NET Framework version 1.1.4322
Copyright (C) Microsoft Corporation 2001-2002. All rights reserved.
```

Running the application now produces the exact same output you saw when using the IDE as your development environment.

Introducing Game Development

In 2001, revenue from the video game industry surpassed box office receipts from the movie industry for the first time. The industry is thriving, and the need for good developers is strong. Given that companies can spend millions of dollars on one of the top-of-the-line games, they are naturally quite particular about the team they hire to develop the games for them. Throughout this chapter, we will discuss the game development process, and the teams that make these great games.

The Developers

As a member of the DirectX team for the last few years, I've had the pleasure of speaking with quite a few game developers. Although each of the developers is naturally unique, they all have similar traits. One of the most obvious traits they share is an absolute love of games. However, this should be expected. Game development is a tough job, with long hours, tight schedules, and immense pressure. Anyone without a strong devotion to the gaming world should go write software without these pressures.

Although it's not common for a game studio today to actually announce how much it spends on the games being developed, many titles cost millions of dollars during development, a substantial investment for the company publishing the game. Many of the games are in development for years, which requires extreme confidence in the game itself and the developers, artists, designers, and everyone else involved in making it. Many times publishers succumb to the pressure and release games before they are ready. On the other end of the spectrum are cases such as *Duke Nukem Forever*, which is being published by 3D Realms. The game has been in development for well over five years, and the publisher maintains that it won't be released "until it's done."

Back in the old days of video game development (early arcades and the Atari home system), games were commonly written by one or two individuals in a matter of weeks, not years. You can chalk this up to the huge strides that have been made in the video game world today. Back then you could make an extremely simple game such as *Galaga* that essentially had a single level you played over and over. The graphics were simple, the game was fun and addicting, but was it hard to write? Any developer who's ever seen the game should recognize that it wasn't.

By contrast, today's games feature huge, expansive worlds that must be designed, developed, and have art assets created. Most include multiple levels and much more in-depth game play than the simple move-back-and-forth-and-fire seen in earlier games. All of these advanced features require more and more development time, and as players today expect these advanced features, it seems unlikely that any big-budget titles will be written in a matter of a few short weeks.

Today's big games also add a layer of complexity for the blossoming game developer because games that capture the attention of the masses can no longer be written single-handedly. It's also virtually impossible to get a game written by a single person (or even a small group) onto store shelves because of the extremely high cost of getting the computer stores to stock your title.

Most beginning game developers release the titles they write as shareware, or even freeware. There are quite a few sites out there devoted to shareware game development, and the community consists of many other game developers who provide valued feedback, testing, and a forum in which to express new ideas and show off your latest creations. Burgeoning game developers aren't likely to become wealthy creating these small shareware games, but it does allow them to develop the all important "demo reel" that can be used when applying for a game development position on one of the big-budget titles.

As mentioned in the introduction, this book will start you on your way to growing the skills you need to develop a high-performance, fully 3D game that you can turn into your own demo reel some day. Before that, you need to ask yourself: Are you ready to become a game developer? Ask yourself a few of these questions:

▶ Do you love playing video games?

▶ Have you ever found yourself so immersed in a game that you lose track of time?

▶ Do you often stop to wonder how these worlds were created?

▶ Do you believe you have the idea that could be turned into the next great video game?

▶ Are you tired of all the same old games out there today? Do you have the idea for a genre-redefining video game?

▶ Do you wish I would just shut up and tell you how to write your own video games?

If you answered yes to one or more of these questions, chances are you already have the desire to be a game developer. Perhaps you already have the ideas, but you just don't have the skills to make the ideas in your head actually come to life through code. This book will help you teach yourself these skills quickly, and by using actual games to do so.

The Process

All games start out as an idea. Without an idea, what would you write? Just random code in the hope that sometime in the future it might turn into a masterpiece? Although this might work for abstract painters, software developers can't do anything without a plan. However, just because you have the idea doesn't mean it's time to start writing code.

One of the biggest mistakes I've seen and continue to see no matter how many times I tell them otherwise is developers who jump right into coding. Unless the code you're writing is so brain-dead simple that you can do it in minutes, it is *never* a good idea to begin writing code with just an idea. Jumping right into coding without a plan will cause you nothing but pain, rewrites, and a longer development time.

Before you write your first line of code, you should develop a *design specification* (*spec* for short). This document should contain specific information on how your code will be designed, how the objects will interact, and the various properties your objects may have. Starting coding directly without this step will most times lead you to solve the wrong problems in most cases. Although it may be possible to solve these problems quickly, it doesn't do you any good if you're not solving the correct problems. You'll end up spending more time making your solutions work for the real problems later.

You should also spend the time to commit the idea to paper (or computer file, if that suits you better). You don't want your idea for the next great computer game to be so vague that you can't figure out what problems need to be solved for your design specification. Try to make sure your idea is completely fleshed out. Show your friends, have them ask questions, and ensure they are answered by your document. If your idea is something like "Write an awesome first-person shooter game," chances are you haven't done enough thinking about your idea. What kinds of weapons will you have? What kinds of game modes will be available? Will it be multiplayer? You need to have your idea well thought-out before proceeding.

If you are attempting to develop a game for a commercial publisher, you will also need to develop a game proposal. Although it is important to have the documentation mentioned previously for this proposal, in the majority of cases you will also need a demo that is pretty far along. It is rare for a publisher to give you the green light on a project based only on an idea (unless you already have the reputation as a top-notch game developer, in which case, you probably don't need to teach yourself the beginning 3D programming this book covers).

The Tools

Writing great games isn't all about writing good code, either. Although I don't want to imply that the code writing isn't important (because it most certainly is), there are quite a few things that go into creating these games. One thing all games need is a good set of tools that are used to create the game.

The majority of the games created today (even the strictly 2D ones) have most of the art created for them from a 3D modeling software package. These tools are invaluable to the artists who are working on your game, and make the ideas floating around in your head a reality. Although we won't be discussing how to actually create the necessary artwork in this book, the tools used need to be mentioned. Two of the more popular digital content creation applications used today are Maya and 3D Studio MAX, which you can see in Figures 1.5 and 1.6.

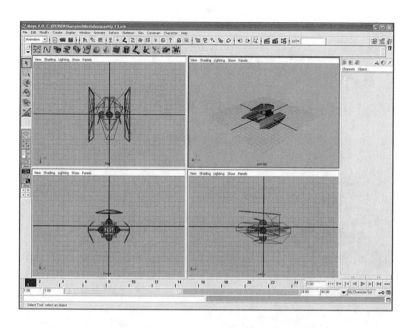

FIGURE 1.5
Using Maya to model a spaceship.

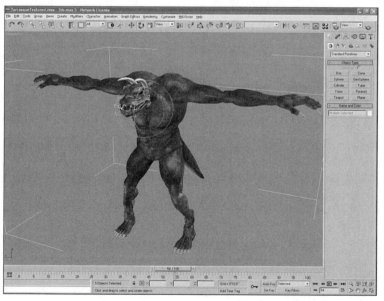

FIGURE 1.6
Using 3D Studio MAX to model a monster.

Creating art isn't all about the 3D models, though. Even a model with millions of polygons looks bland if it isn't textured. There are quite a few tools you can use for creating textures, such as Photoshop (seen in Figure 1.7) and Paint (which ships with Windows and is seen in Figure 1.8).

FIGURE 1.7
Using Photoshop to manipulate textures.

FIGURE 1.8
Using Paint to manipulate textures.

Development and art tools are pretty obvious tools that you would be using to help your game development. There are other types of tools that can be just as important that many people don't even consider, such as a good source control management tool.

Assuming your game will have sound, you will probably need a tool for manipulating sound files as well. This can be as simple as using the Sound Recorder that ships with Windows (seen in Figure 1.9) or as complex as WaveStudio, which ships as part of Creative Labs' Audigy software (seen in Figure 1.10).

FIGURE 1.9
Using the Sound Recorder.

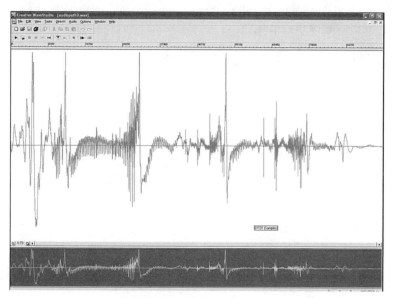

FIGURE 1.10
Using Creative Lab's WaveStudio.

With all these tools creating content for your game, you will probably need a tool that can also *store* that content for your entire team. You will likely have quite a bit of information that needs to be stored and hopefully backed up periodically. Even better is a record of changes and additions that have been made. Most source control management tools provide at least some of this functionality.

Visual Source Safe is a tool that first started shipping with Visual Studio quite a few years ago, and it's designed to be a simple source control management tool for a team with very few people. This tool doesn't include many of the powerful features a large team would need, such as the capability to allow multiple people to work on a file and to auto-merge conflicting changes, but for a small project on a small team, it's normally adequate. There are plenty of other source control tools out there (such as Perforce), so do a little investigating and find out which tool is right for you and your group. Just about any tool you use is better than nothing.

Summary

During this chapter, you have been introduced to .NET. You had an overview on what exactly .NET and managed code is, and wrote a simple application in the two languages this book will cover. You also learned to compile these applications outside the integrated development environment. The basics for getting started in game development were covered, and you learned about the developers that want to do game development (all of them), some of the processes that need to be followed, and tools of the trade.

The next chapter introduces game development.

PART II

Introducing Graphics, Game 1

CHAPTER 2

Planning Your First Game

With the simple introductory items out of the way, now would be the perfect time to jump right into what this book is designed to help you teach yourself: 3D game programming. Obviously, this topic is quite complex, so your first game won't be anything that you'll be able to turn around and publish, but it will introduce the fundamentals that you should use for every game.

Turning your idea for a game into a reality is one of the more rewarding experiences you can have. Sculpting the thoughts racing through your brain into something tangible that other people can enjoy is the goal of any developer, but when those thoughts are about games, the rewards seem to be amplified. Hopefully you're ready to be rewarded.

In this chapter, you'll learn

- ▶ Coming up with a game idea
- ▶ Differences between 2D and 3D programming
- ▶ Detailing your specifications

Coming Up with the Game Idea

Everything that has ever been created started out as an idea, and games are no different. Game ideas can come from just about any source you can think of. Perhaps you saw another game that you enjoyed, but thought it would be so much better if it did something differently. Maybe you had a dream that would make the perfect game. Perhaps you realized two unrelated games could be combined to create the ultimate game. Wherever your inspiration comes from, you'll need to tap into that before you can start making your game.

Unfortunately, as no one has yet invented a mind-reading book, you'll have to trust my ideas for this game. I chose the games in this book for a variety of reasons, mainly concerning the level of development difficulty. However, each is in a different genre to cover the wide variety of topics you'll encounter in your game development coding.

The first genre is the puzzle game. It's probably safe to assume you have seen or played puzzle games before. *Tetris* is a classic puzzle game that just about everyone has either heard of or lost tons of hours of sleep playing. Everyone it seems has also written a *Tetris* clone, so it likely wouldn't be the best choice for the puzzle game you will be writing. Also, *Tetris* is a 2D sprite game (although there have been 3D *Tetris*-type games), so you will probably want to skip it for that reason as well.

Instead, you should write something somewhat unique. The game will have a single character that is on a *board*. This board will be made up of a series of cubes in an undetermined pattern, with each cube having at least one other cube directly adjacent to it. A chess board would be an example of a board that meets these criteria. Each cube will be a particular color, and when the player steps on one of these cubes, it will change to the next predetermined color. The level will end when every cube in the level is on the correct color for that level.

Detailing the Proposal

Like you learned in the previous chapter, once the basic idea for the game is laid out, you should spend some time coming up with the game proposal, ensuring you answer as many questions as possible. For this game, here is a bulleted list of items to help detail the proposal:

- ▶ Puzzle game called *Blockers*
- ▶ Single-player only
- ▶ Fully 3D environment
- ▶ Score based on time to complete level
- ▶ Each level consists of a series of adjacent cubes, such as found on a chess board
- ▶ Each cube is always a single solid color
- ▶ Each level will end when every cube in the level is the same color, and that color is the predetermined "end" color for that level
- ▶ Each level will have a maximum time limit
- ▶ Each cube will have a "list" of colors assigned to it—his list will have a minimum of two colors, with a maximum of six

▶ Players move by "bouncing" on a cube, which will change the color of the cube to the next available in the list

▶ Beginning levels will have the minimum list of two colors per cube

▶ Difficulty will be raised by adding more colors per cube in more advanced levels

▶ If player can finish these levels, difficulty will be raised once more by allowing the color list to "wrap" back to the beginning

▶ Game is over if player cannot complete level within maximum time limit

Is this an exhaustive list of every feature of the game? Probably not, but it does answer the majority of questions that you need to answer before you can start planning the game. It's important to understand that the planning phase isn't designed to detail every feature of the game before you begin development, but more to get you thinking about the features your game will require. Jumping in and coding without considering the features you really want will lead to more difficult work later in trying to fix the things you missed or did incorrectly because of a rushed plan.

With a plan in place, you can now start designing the object model you will use for this game. Look at the basic program layout diagram shown in Figure 2.1.

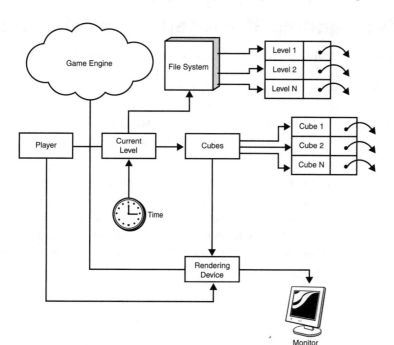

FIGURE 2.1
A high-level object diagram for the game.

As you see here, the object diagram isn't overly complex. You have the mysterious game engine, which maintains information about the player, the current level, and the rendering device. The rendering device is used to display the fancy graphics for the game onto the monitor. The player will need some type of visual representation, and the rendering device will handle this as well.

Much of the game requires information about the current level. The current time is important because it will be used to determine both the high scores and when the game is over (when it runs out), so the current level must have access to it.

The actual levels themselves will be stored in the file system, in the media folder of the application. Because the current level will need to load one of the existing levels, it will of course need access to those as well. The only thing the level really needs to keep track of is the list of cubes that comprise the level. Each level will have at least two cubes, but can add many more to accommodate larger levels.

This game won't be easy to write, but as you can see, there aren't many objects that you will need to create to ensure that the goals of the game are met. The game has the potential to be quite fun as well, as long as the more difficult levels don't become so difficult that they end up frustrating the player. A game can do nothing worse than annoy the player. If the game isn't fun, no one will play it, and the game cannot be considered successful.

Understanding the Need for a 3D Game

It's important to realize that this game (actually, any game) does not "need" to be rendered as a fully 3D world. Considering that your monitor is most likely a rectangular flat plane, even your fancy 3D rendered images will be displayed on a 2D plane. It would be entirely possible to create a set of 2D sprites that cover every possible scenario that would need to be displayed in your world, but the art assets required for something like this would be enormous. Look at this experiment as an example.

Assuming you have the DirectX SDK Summer 2004 Update installed, load the DirectX Sample Browser (see Figure 2.2) and make sure the Managed option is the only item checked on the left. Click the Direct3D heading, scroll down to find the Empty Project item, and click the Install Project link, following the steps of the wizard (naming the project "Teapot"). Once the project has been created, load it into the IDE.

This will create a new "empty" project. (It actually renders some user interface controls, but for now, those can be ignored.) However, there isn't anything 3D in this project yet, and because the point of this exercise is to show why you'd want to write 3D games, it might be a good idea to add some now.

You'll need to add a few lines to this project to make it render a slowly spinning teapot. You'll be adding a few lines of code to make this application do the rendering, although for this chapter the explanations of what exactly is going on will be skipped. There will be plenty of time throughout the rest of the book for these explanations, but they are not necessary for this demonstration. Assuming you named the project "Teapot," open up the code file teapot.cs and add these two variables to the class file:

```
private Mesh teapotMesh = null; // Mesh for rendering the teapot
private Material teapotMaterial; // Material for rendering the teapot
```

Now you'll want to create the teapot and material you'll be using to render the scene, so find the OnCreateDevice method in this class and add the following code to the end of the method:

```
// Create the teapot mesh and material
device = e.Device();
teapotMesh = Mesh.Teapot(device);
teapotMaterial = new Material();
teapotMaterial.DiffuseColor = new ColorValue(1.0f, 1.0f, 1.0f, 1.0f);
```

To make the teapot look better, you'll want to have a light (these will be explained in much greater detail later), so for now, find the OnResetDevice method in your class and add this code to the end of it:

```
// Setup lights
device.Lights[0].DiffuseColor = new ColorValue(1.0f, 1.0f, 1.0f, 1.0f);
device.Lights[0].Direction = new Vector3(0,-1,0);
device.Lights[0].Type = LightType.Directional;
device.Lights[0].Enabled = true;
```

You're just about ready now. Find the OnFrameRender method in your class and add this code directly following the BeginScene call:

```
device.Transform.View = camera.ViewMatrix;
device.Transform.Projection = camera.ProjectionMatrix;
device.Transform.World = Matrix.RotationX((float)appTime);
device.Material = teapotMaterial;
teapotMesh.DrawSubset(0);
```

Running this application renders a teapot. Teapots have quite a storied history in the world of 3D rendering. One of the first "free" models available for rendering was a teapot, and considering that back then the complex modeling packages that we have today didn't exist, creating an actual 3D model was complicated. Anything free was welcomed. The teapot also has plenty of properties that make it an excellent test model: it has curved surfaces, can shadow itself, and is recognized easily.

The application that you created renders this teapot and slowly rotates i so you can see varying views. See Figure 2.3 for an example.

As the application runs, watch as the teapot rotates slowly. It's important to realize that the only media required for this application is the teapot model. No media is actually required for this model because you used a method in the Mesh class (which will be discussed in a subsequent chapter) that created the teapot for you. So, you get a nice looking teapot at a minimal media cost.

Now let's compare this to rendering a teapot in the 2D world. Create a new project using the DirectX wizard once more.

If you install the code found on the included CD, you'll notice a media folder that actually contains all the media for every example you will be writing during the course of this book. One of the pieces of media you will notice is the 2dteapot.bmp file, which is an example of what you'd need to render your teapot in a 2D environment. The biggest difference between the 2D and 3D world is the media requirements. The bitmap is currently only showing one view of the teapot, whereas the 3D version can show the teapot from any angle. To show this teapot at any angle in the 2D version, you would need a separate piece of media for each position the teapot can be in. Imagine that you need one image of the teapot for each degree of rotation (360 total images). Now imagine that you want to rotate the teapot around any axis (X, Y, Z). You'll need a whopping 46,656,000 different images of the teapot. Imagine a graphically intensive game such as *Unreal Tournament* rendered with nothing but 2D sprites. You would need entire DVDs-worth of content, and an army of artists would take years to create something that massive.

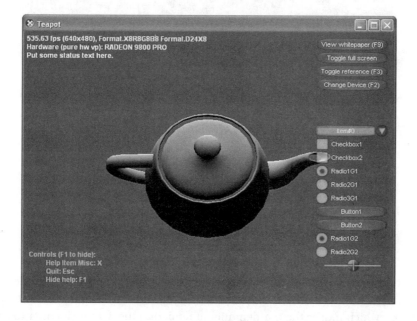

FIGURE 2.3
A spinning 3D teapot.

If you have an artist capable of creating highly detailed 3D models, you obviously have much more freedom in the scenes you can create with much more "limited" media. A single model can be rendered in so many ways, with various lighting, scaling, positions, rotations, that it is so impractical to create this artwork in 2D, it is essentially impossible to do. This power doesn't come free, though.

The freedom that the 3D applications bring takes quite a bit of processing power, so much so that an entire industry has been formed based on providing it. Although there are quite a few companies in the business, the clear leaders as of this writing are nVidia and ATI. There have been so many innovations in graphics cards recently that they are even evolving quicker and becoming faster than the more generalized CPU.

Modern cards (cards that are DirectX 9-compliant, meaning they have support for at least shader model 2.0) are capable of rendering millions of triangles per second. Don't worry; shaders will be discussed later in this book. If you are wondering where triangles came from, it should be mentioned that they are the basic polygon used to create a 3D model. See Figure 2.4 for a view of the teapot that was seen earlier using only triangles to do the rendering.

FIGURE 2.4
A wireframe teapot.

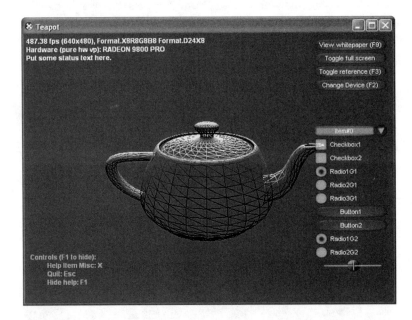

As you can see, the entire teapot is made up of hundreds of triangles. Triangles are used because they are the only closed polygon that can be guaranteed to be coplanar, which makes the mathematics of rendering the 3D much easier to calculate. Any 3D shape can be simulated with enough triangles.

So, does this game need to be written in 3D? Of course not, you could write it entirely with sprites and without rendering any 3D content, but what's the fun in that? The majority of "teach yourself"-type game development books always cover rendering 2D content, and very few concentrate on the 3D worlds that make today's games great. Although 2D game development hasn't died yet (and may never completely die), if you are in the market for a development job in the games industry, you must have 3D experience.

The Specification

With much of the busywork out of the way, you can start working on one of the most important sections of the game—the specification. I cannot stress enough the need for you to spend time thinking about the problems you need to solve before you write a single line of code. Virtually every budding game developer I know has started the first game by jumping in and writing some code. You'll only be making more work for yourself later when you realize your quick working solution doesn't quite work the way you intended.

So for this game, what problems need to be solved? Look at the diagram shown in Figure 2.1 earlier. Obviously you will need some type of game engine that will be the brains of the operation. You will need a player object, a rendering device, and a way to maintain the level information. A common way to display development specifications is with UML (unified modeling language). You will find a Visio UML document in the media folder on the included CD, and also in Figure 2.5.

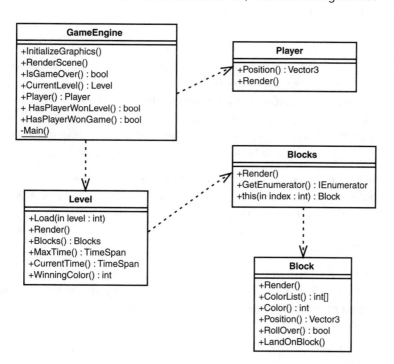

FIGURE 2.5
A simple UML diagram of the game objects.

If you're familiar with UML, the figure probably looks familiar enough. If you're not, perhaps you should understand what the point of this document is. First, it breaks down the problem into the logical components that will make up the game. In this case, those objects are the main game engine, the player, the level, the list of blocks, and each individual block. The public properties and methods for each object are listed within that object's box, so you can have a quick overview of the size and scope of each of the objects themselves.

Fancy diagrams aside, what really needs to be done for the game? You will obviously need to have a central area where everything is controlled. In this case, it will be the game engine. If you notice in the UML, the game engine will also maintain the graphics rendering device and code as well (which is implied through the InitializeGraphics method). The major things the game engine needs to know are:

- ▶ The player object
- ▶ The current level
- ▶ Is the game over?
- ▶ If so, has the player won the level?
- ▶ If so, has the player won the game?

The game engine will also need to store other information, such as the rendering device, plus maintain the game's objects, but these will occur in private methods and are not shown in the UML from Figure 2.5. The next object is the player, which is actually quite simple. The only information needed for the player is the position it's currently in, and the capability to render itself in the scene. In our game engine, the player is really more of an abstract concept than a development object. The object here is mainly used to control how the player is shown visually.

Everything else in the game engine comes from the levels object. In reality, this object is quite simple as well, because it just maintains a few other objects, notably the blocks collection. Each block maintains all of the information needed to control itself within the level, including the list of possible colors, and whether the colors will roll over.

With the basic specification out of the way, it's time to start coding. You can rest assured that most likely the specification will change slightly between now and the completion of the game, but this gives you a perfect opportunity to start writing some code.

Summary

During this chapter you were introduced to a few new principles of writing games. You learned about the game idea, the object design, and the specification.

In the next chapter, we will begin writing code to initialize the graphics device.

CHAPTER 3

Understanding the Sample Framework

Now that the idea is complete, the object model has enough information, and you've laid out the specification, you're almost ready to jump into what you've been waiting for: actually writing the code for the game. Normally, you would need to write a lot of "boilerplate" code before you begin this development, which would include such things as enumerating through the devices on your system and picking the most appropriate one to render your scene, as well as creating and maintaining this device. Because the DirectX SDK Summer 2004 Update now includes a robust sample framework that is designed to be used directly by your code and that handles much of this work for you, you can save yourself a lot of time and hassle by simply using that.

The examples in this book use this sample framework, so you will spend this chapter examining it.

In this chapter, you'll learn

- How to create your project
- How to use the sample framework to enumerate devices

Creating Your Project

Construction Cue

For the rest of this book, I assume that you are using Visual Studio .NET 2003 for all your development needs. If you do not want to use this environment, you can look back to Chapter 1, "Game Development and Managed Code," to see the discussion on compiling code on the command line, which allows you to use any text editor or integrated development environment (IDE) you want. All the sample code included with the CD has an accompanying Visual Studio .NET 2003 project and solution file for easy loading.

Go ahead and load up Visual Studio .NET 2003, and click the New Project button on the start page. If you do not use the start page, click the Project item under the New submenu on the File menu, or use the shortcut Ctrl+Shift+N. Choose the Windows Application item under the Visual C# Projects section. (See Figure 1.3 in Chapter 1 for a reminder of what this dialog looks like.) Name this project Blockers because that is what the name of the game will be.

Before you start looking at the code that was automatically generated, first add the code files for the sample framework into your project. Normally, I put these files into a separate folder by right-clicking on the project in the solution explorer and choosing New Folder from the Add menu. Call this folder Framework. Right-click on the newly created folder and this time choose Add Existing Item from the Add menu. Navigate to the DirectX SDK folder, and you will find the sample framework files in the Samples\Managed\Common folder. Select each of these files to add to your project.

With the sample framework added to the project now, you can get rid of the code that was automatically generated. Most of it is used to make fancy Windows Forms applications, so it's irrelevant to the code you will be writing for this game. Replace the existing code and class (named Form1) with the code in Listing 3.1.

LISTING 3.1   The Empty Framework

```
using System;
using System.Configuration;
using Microsoft.DirectX;
using Microsoft.DirectX.Direct3D;
using Microsoft.Samples.DirectX.UtilityToolkit;

public class GameEngine : IDeviceCreation
{
    /// <summary>
    /// Entry point to the program. Initializes everything and goes into a
    /// message processing loop. Idle time is used to render the scene.
    /// </summary>
    static int Main()
    {
        using(Framework sampleFramework = new Framework())
        {
            return sampleFramework.ExitCode;
        }
    }
}
```

Three things should stand out from this new code. First, you'll notice that every-thing was removed, with the exception of the static main method, which was modified. The rest of the code was support code for the Windows Form designer.

Because you won't be using that designer for this application, the code isn't relevant and can be removed. Second, this code won't compile because the two interfaces the game engine class is supposed to implement haven't been implemented yet. Third, the code doesn't actually do anything.

Before you begin fixing those last two problems, you'll need to add some references. Because you will be rendering fancy 3D graphics during this project, you probably need to add references to an assembly capable of doing this rendering. This book focuses on using the Managed DirectX assemblies to do this work, so in the Project menu, click Add Reference. It brings up a dialog much like you see in Figure 3.1.

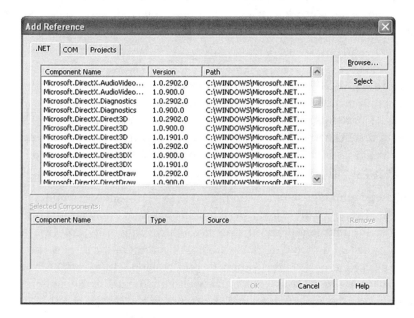

FIGURE 3.1
The Add Reference dialog.

If you have the Summer 2004 SDK update of DirectX 9 installed (which you should because the code in this book requires it), you notice that there might be more than one version of each of the Managed DirectX assemblies. Pick the latest version (marked with version 1.0.2902.0). For this project, you add three different assemblies to your references:

- ▶ Microsoft.DirectX
- ▶ Microsoft.DirectX.Direct3D
- ▶ Microsoft.DirectX.Direct3DX

The root `DirectX` assembly contains the math structures that help formulate any computations needed for the rendering. The other two assemblies contain the functionality of Direct3D and D3DX, respectively. With the references added, you should look briefly at the `using` clause you added in Listing 3.1 to make sure that the namespaces referenced as well. This step ensures that you don't have to fully qualify your types. For example, without adding the `using` clause, to declare a variable for a Direct3D device, you would need to declare it as

```
Microsoft.DirectX.Direct3D.Device device = null;
```

The using clauses allow you to eliminate the majority of this typing. (No one wants to type all that stuff for every single variable you would be declaring.) Because you've already added the using clauses, you could instead declare that same device in this way:

```
private Device device = null;
```

As you can see, declaring the device in this way is much easier. You've saved yourself an immense amount of typing. With these few things out of the way, now you begin to fix the compilation errors in the application and get ready to write your first 3D game. The only interface you've currently got to implement is `IDeviceCreation`, which is designed to let you control the enumeration and creation of your device.

You might be thinking, "Enumerating devices? I've only got one monitor!" Although most top-of-the-line, modern graphics cards actually do support multiple monitors (multimon for short), even if you have only a single device, you still have many different modes to choose from. The format of the display can vary. (You might have even seen this variety in your desktop settings on the Windows desktop, as in 16-bit or 32-bit colors.) The width and height of the full-screen modes can have different values, and you can even control the refresh rate of the screen. All in all, there are quite a few things to account for.

To fix the compilation errors in the application, add the code in Listing 3.2.

LISTING 3.2   Implementing the Interface

```
/// <summary>
/// Called during device initialization, this code checks the device for a
/// minimum set of capabilities and rejects those that don't pass by
/// returning false.
/// </summary>
public bool IsDeviceAcceptable(Caps caps, Format adapterFormat,
 Format backBufferFormat, bool windowed)
{
    // Skip back buffer formats that don't support alpha blending
```

LISTING 3.2   Continued

```
    if (!Manager.CheckDeviceFormat(caps.AdapterOrdinal, caps.DeviceType,
        adapterFormat, Usage.QueryPostPixelShaderBlending,
        ResourceType.Textures, backBufferFormat))
        return false;

    // Skip any device that doesn't support at least a single light
    if (caps.MaxActiveLights == 0)
        return false;

    return true;
}


/// <summary>
/// This callback function is called immediately before a device is created
/// to allow the application to modify the device settings. The supplied
/// settings parameter contains the settings that the framework has selected
/// for the new device, and the application can make any desired changes
/// directly to this structure. Note however that the sample framework
/// will not correct invalid device settings so care must be taken
/// to return valid device settings; otherwise, creating the device will fail.
/// </summary>
public void ModifyDeviceSettings(DeviceSettings settings, Caps caps)
{
    // This application is designed to work on a pure device by not using
    // any get methods, so create a pure device if supported and using HWVP.
    if ( (caps.DeviceCaps.SupportsPureDevice) &&
        ((settings.BehaviorFlags & CreateFlags.HardwareVertexProcessing) != 0 ) )
        settings.BehaviorFlags |= CreateFlags.PureDevice;
}
```

Look at the first method you declared, the IsDeviceAcceptable method. While
the sample framework is busy enumerating the devices on the system, it calls this
method for every combination it finds. Notice how the method returns a bool
value? This is your opportunity to tell the sample framework whether you consider this device acceptable for your needs. Before you look at the code in that first
method, however, notice the second method that's been declared,
ModifyDeviceSettings. This method is called by the sample framework immediately before the device is created, allowing you to tweak any options you want. Be
careful with the options you choose because you could cause the device creation
to fail.

Now, back to that first method: first take a look at the parameters that it accepts.
First, it takes a type called Caps, which is short for capabilities. This structure has
an amazing amount of information about the particular device that will help you
decide whether this is the type of device you want to use. The next two parameters are formats that are specific to the device: one for the back buffer and the
other the device's format.

The back buffer is where the actual rendered data (the pixels) is stored before that data is sent to the video card to be processed and put onscreen. The back buffer formats determine how many colors can be displayed. Most of the formats follow a particular naming convention, each character followed by a number, such as A8R8G8B8. The component specified by the character has a number of bits equal to the number. In A8R8G8B8, the format can contain 32 bits of information for color, with 8 each for alpha, red, green, and blue. The most common components are

A Alpha

R Red

G Green

B Blue

X Unused

You can look in the DirectX SDK documentation for more information on formats.

Because it's also important to know whether this device can render to a window, that is the last parameter to this method. Although the majority of games run in full-screen mode, it can be difficult to write and debug a game running in full-screen mode. During debugging, this application renders in windowed mode rather than full-screen mode.

Windowed mode is how most of the applications you run are opened. Many of them have a border and the control menu, the minimize and maximize buttons, and a close button in the upper-right corner. In full-screen mode, the application covers the entire screen and in most cases does not have a border. You can change the desktop resolution if the full-screen mode is using a different screen size from your currently running desktop.

You'll notice that the default behavior is to accept the device, but before it is accepted, two specific checks happen. The first check ensures that the device passed in can perform alpha blending (the user interface for the game will require this), and if it cannot, it returns false to signify that this device is not acceptable. Next, the capabilities are checked to see whether there is support for active lights. Scenes with no lighting look flat and fake, so you always want at least a single light.

There's also code that actually modifies the device before creation, and even though you won't be creating the device in this chapter, you'll want to know what this code is for. Devices can do the processing required to render vertices in various ways, by either performing the calculations in hardware, performing them in software, or doing a mixture of both. If the processing happens entirely in hardware, another mode, called a *pure hardware device*, allows potentially even greater performance. This code checks whether you are currently going to create a hardware processing device; if you are and the pure device is available, it switches to using that instead. The only time you cannot create a pure device (if it is available) is if you are planning to call one of the many get methods or properties on a device. Because you won't be doing that in any of the applications in this book, you're free to use this more powerful device.

There is one last thing to do before you're ready to go on. The sample framework has some unsafe code in it, so you need to update your project to handle it. See Figure 3.2.

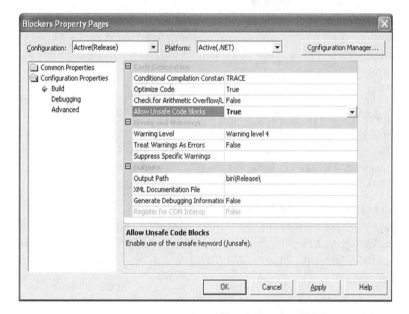

FIGURE 3.2
Allowing unsafe code.

Enumerating All Device Options

Now you're ready to have the framework start enumerating the devices on your system. First, declare a constructor for the game engine class, and pass in the sample framework's instance you've created from main. See Listing 3.3.

LISTING 3.3   Adding a Constructor

```
private Framework sampleFramework = null; // Framework for samples
/// <summary>Create a new instance of the class</summary>
public GameEngine(Framework f)
{
    // Store framework
    sampleFramework = f;
}
```

The constructor doesn't do anything other than store the sample framework instance because that is required for almost everything that happens within the game. One of the first things the sample framework does after you invoke it is try to enumerate all the devices on your system. In your project file, you'll see a file dxmutenum.cs in the Framework folder you created earlier. This file contains all the necessary code to enumerate the devices on your system. Because it is important that you understand the how and why of the device enumeration, open that file now.

One of the first things you should notice is that the Enumeration class itself cannot be created, and every member variable and method is declared as static. Because it is (at least currently) extremely unlikely that your graphics hardware would change while your application is running (and the computer is on), it is reasonable to have the enumeration code run only once at the beginning of the application.

The bulk of the enumeration works starts from the Enumerate method, which is called by the sample framework before device creation. Notice that the only parameter this method accepts is the interface you've implemented in the game engine class so far. This interface is stored because later, as the device combinations are enumerated, the IsDeviceAcceptable method is called to determine whether the device should be added to the list of valid devices.

So how are the devices actually enumerated? The bulk of the functionality resides in the Manager class from Managed DirectX. If you're familiar with the unmanaged DirectX Application Programming Interface (API), this class mirrors the IDirect3D9 Component Object Model (COM) interface. Notice the first loop in the Enumerate method in Listing 3.4.

LISTING 3.4 Enumerating Devices

```
// Look through every adapter on the system
for each(AdapterInformation ai in Manager.Adapters)
{
    EnumAdapterInformation adapterInfo = new EnumAdapterInformation();
    // Store some information
    adapterInfo.AdapterOrdinal = (uint)ai.Adapter; // Ordinal
    adapterInfo.AdapterInformation = ai.Information; // Information

    // Get list of all display modes on this adapter.
    // Also build a temporary list of all display adapter formats.
    adapterFormatList.Clear();

    // Now check to see which formats are supported
    for(int i = 0; i < allowedFormats.Length; i++)
    {
```

LISTING 3.4   Continued

```
        // Check each of the supported display modes for this format
        for each(DisplayMode dm in ai.SupportedDisplayModes[allowedFormats[i]])
        {
            if ( (dm.Width < minimumWidth) ||
                 (dm.Height < minimumHeight) ||
                 (dm.Width > maximumWidth) ||
                 (dm.Height > maximumHeight) ||
                 (dm.RefreshRate < minimumRefresh) ||
                 (dm.RefreshRate > maximumRefresh) )
            {
                continue; // This format isn't valid
            }

            // Add this to the list
            adapterInfo.displayModeList.Add(dm);

            // Add this to the format list if it doesn't already exist
            if (!adapterFormatList.Contains(dm.Format))
            {
                adapterFormatList.Add(dm.Format);
            }
        }
    }

    // Get the adapter display mode
    DisplayMode currentAdapterMode = ai.CurrentDisplayMode;
    // Check to see if this format is in the list
    if (!adapterFormatList.Contains(currentAdapterMode.Format))
    {
        adapterFormatList.Add(currentAdapterMode.Format);
    }

    // Sort the display mode list
    adapterInfo.displayModeList.Sort(sorter);

    // Get information for each device with this adapter
    EnumerateDevices(adapterInfo, adapterFormatList);

    // If there was at least one device on the adapter and it's compatible,
    // add it to the list
    if (adapterInfo.deviceInfoList.Count > 0)
    {
        adapterInformationList.Add(adapterInfo);
    }
}
```

The Adapters property on the Manager class is a collection that contains information about every "adapter" on your system. The term *adapter* is somewhat of a misnomer, but the basic definition is anything a monitor can connect to. For example, let's say you have an ATI Radeon 9800 XT graphics card. There is only a single graphics card here, but it is possible to hook up two different monitors to it (via the video graphics adapter [VGA] port and the Digital Visual Interface [DVI] port on the back). With the two monitors hooked up, this single card would have two adapters, and thus two different devices.

Construction Cue

> There is a way to have a single card share resources among all "different" devices by creating the device as an adapter group. There are several limitations to this approach. See the DirectX documentation for more information on this topic.

Depending on your system, this loop has at least a single iteration. After storing some basic information about the currently active adapter, the code needs to find all the possible display modes this adapter can support in full-screen mode. You'll notice here that the supported display modes can be enumerated directly from the adapter information you are currently enumerating, and that's exactly what this code is doing.

The first thing that happens when a display mode is enumerated is it's checked against a set of minimum and maximum ranges. Most devices support a wide range of modes that nothing would actually want to render at today. A number of years ago, you might have seen games running in a 320x200 full-screen window, but today it just doesn't happen (unless you happen to be playing on a handheld such as Gameboy Advance). The default minimum size the sample framework picks is a 640x480 window, and the maximum isn't set.

Construction Cue

> Just because the sample framework picks a minimum size of 640x480, that doesn't mean in full-screen mode the sample framework will choose the smallest possible size. For full-screen mode, the framework picks the best available size, which is almost always the current size of the desktop (which most likely is *not* 640x480).

After the supported modes that meet the requirements of the framework are added to the list, the current display mode is then added because it is naturally always supported. Finally, the modes themselves are sorted by an implementation of the IComparer interface. See Listing 3.5.

LISTING 3.5   Sorting Display Modes

```
public class DisplayModeSorter : IComparer
{
    /// <summary>
    /// Compare two display modes
    /// </summary>
    public int Compare(object x, object y)
    {
        DisplayMode d1 = (DisplayMode)x;
```

LISTING 3.5 Continued

```
        DisplayMode d2 = (DisplayMode)y;

        if (d1.Width > d2.Width)
            return +1;
        if (d1.Width < d2.Width)
            return -1;
        if (d1.Height > d2.Height)
            return +1;
        if (d1.Height < d2.Height)
            return -1;
        if (d1.Format > d2.Format)
            return +1;
        if (d1.Format < d2.Format)
            return -1;
        if (d1.RefreshRate > d2.RefreshRate)
            return +1;
        if (d1.RefreshRate < d2.RefreshRate)
            return -1;

        // They must be the same, return 0
        return 0;
    }
}
```

The IComparer interface allows a simple, quick sort algorithm to be executed on an array or collection. The only method the interface provides is the Compare method, which should return an integer—namely, +1 if the left item is greater than the right, -1 if the left item is less than the right, and 0 if the two items are equal. As you can see with the implementation here, the width of the display mode takes the highest precedence, followed by the height, format, and refresh rate. This order dictates the correct behavior when comparing two modes such as 1280x1024 and 1280x768.

Once the modes are sorted, the EnumerateDevices method is called. You can see this method in Listing 3.6.

LISTING 3.6 Enumerating Device Types

```
private static void EnumerateDevices(EnumAdapterInformation adapterInfo,
    ArrayList adapterFormatList)
{
    // Ignore any exceptions while looking for these device types
    DirectXException.IgnoreExceptions();
    // Enumerate each Direct3D device type
    for(uint i = 0; i < deviceTypeArray.Length; i++)
    {
        // Create a new device information object
        EnumDeviceInformation deviceInfo = new EnumDeviceInformation();
```

LISTING 3.6　Continued

```
        // Store the type
        deviceInfo.DeviceType = deviceTypeArray[i];

        // Try to get the capabilities
        deviceInfo.Caps = Manager.GetDeviceCaps(
            (int)adapterInfo.AdapterOrdinal, deviceInfo.DeviceType);

        // Get information about each device combination on this device
        EnumerateDeviceCombos( adapterInfo, deviceInfo, adapterFormatList);

        // Do we have any device combinations?
        if (deviceInfo.deviceSettingsList.Count > 0)
        {
            // Yes, add it
            adapterInfo.deviceInfoList.Add(deviceInfo);
        }
    }
    // Turn exception handling back on
    DirectXException.EnableExceptions();
}
```

When looking at this code, you should notice and remember two very important things. Can you guess what they are? If you guessed the calls into the DirectXException class, you win the grand prize. The first one turns off exception throwing in virtually all cases from inside the Managed DirectX assemblies. You might wonder what benefit that would give you, and the answer is performance. Catching and throwing exceptions can be an expensive operation, and this particular code section could have numerous items that normally throw these exceptions. You would expect the enumeration code to execute quickly, so any exceptions that occur are simply ignored, and after the function finishes, normal exception handling is restored. The code itself seems pretty simple, though, so you're probably asking, "Why would this code be prone to throwing exceptions anyway?"

Well, I'm glad you asked, and luckily I just happen to have a good answer. The most common scenario is that the device doesn't support DirectX 9. Maybe you haven't upgraded your video driver and the current video driver doesn't have the necessary code paths. It could be that the card itself is simply too old and incapable of using DirectX 9. Many times, someone enables multimon on his system by including an old peripheral component interconnect (PCI) video card that does not support DirectX 9.

The code in this method tries to get the capabilities and enumerate the various combinations for this adapter, and it tries to get this information for every device type available. The possible device types follow:

▶ *Hardware*—The most common device type created. The rendering is processed by a piece of hardware (a video card).

▶ *Reference*—A device that can render with any settings supported by the Direct3D runtime, regardless of whether there is a piece of hardware capable of the processing. All processing happens in software, which means this device type is much too slow in a game.

▶ *Software*—Unless you've written a software rasterizer (in which case, you're probably beyond this beginners' book), you will never use this option.

Assuming some combination of device settings was found during the enumeration, it is stored in a list. The enumeration class stores a few lists that the sample framework uses later while creating the device. See Listing 3.7 for the EnumerateDeviceCombos method.

LISTING 3.7   Enumerating Device Combinations

```
private static void EnumerateDeviceCombos(EnumAdapterInformation adapterInfo,
    EnumDeviceInformation deviceInfo, ArrayList adapterFormatList)
{
    // Find out which adapter formats are supported by this device
    for each(Format adapterFormat in adapterFormatList)
    {
        for(int i = 0; i < backbufferFormatsArray.Length; i++)
        {
            // Go through each windowed mode
            bool windowed = false;
            do
            {
                if ((!windowed) && (adapterInfo.displayModeList.Count == 0))
                    continue; // Nothing here

                if (!Manager.CheckDeviceType((int)adapterInfo.AdapterOrdinal,
                    deviceInfo.DeviceType,  adapterFormat,
                    backbufferFormatsArray[i], windowed))
                        continue; // Unsupported

                // Do we require post pixel shader blending?
                if (isPostPixelShaderBlendingRequired)
                {
                    if (!Manager.CheckDeviceFormat(
                            (int)adapterInfo.AdapterOrdinal,
                            deviceInfo.DeviceType, adapterFormat,
                            Usage.QueryPostPixelShaderBlending,
                            ResourceType.Textures, backbufferFormatsArray[i]))
                        continue; // Unsupported
                }

                // If an application callback function has been provided,
                // make sure this device is acceptable to the app.
                if (deviceCreationInterface != null)
```

LISTING 3.7   Continued

```
                {
                    if
(!deviceCreationInterface.IsDeviceAcceptable(deviceInfo.Caps,
                        adapterFormat, backbufferFormatsArray[i],windowed))
                        continue; // Application doesn't like this device
                }

                // At this point, we have an adapter/device/adapterformat/
                // backbufferformat/iswindowed DeviceCombo that is supported
                // by the system and acceptable to the app. We still need
                // to find one or more suitable depth/stencil buffer format,
                // multisample type, and present interval.

                EnumDeviceSettingsCombo deviceCombo = new
                 EnumDeviceSettingsCombo();

                // Store the information
                deviceCombo.AdapterOrdinal = adapterInfo.AdapterOrdinal;
                deviceCombo.DeviceType = deviceInfo.DeviceType;
                deviceCombo.AdapterFormat = adapterFormat;
                deviceCombo.BackBufferFormat = backbufferFormatsArray[i];
                deviceCombo.IsWindowed = windowed;

                // Build the depth stencil format and multisample type list
                BuildDepthStencilFormatList(deviceCombo);
                BuildMultiSampleTypeList(deviceCombo);
                if (deviceCombo.multiSampleTypeList.Count == 0)
                {
                    // Nothing to do
                    continue;
                }
                // Build the conflict and present lists
                BuildConflictList(deviceCombo);
                BuildPresentIntervalList(deviceInfo, deviceCombo);

                deviceCombo.adapterInformation = adapterInfo;
                deviceCombo.deviceInformation = deviceInfo;

                // Add the combo to the list of devices
                deviceInfo.deviceSettingsList.Add(deviceCombo);
                // Flip value so it loops
                windowed = !windowed;
            }
            while (windowed);
        }
    }
}
```

Much like earlier methods, this one goes through a list of items (in this case, formats) and creates a new list of valid data. The important item to take away from this method is the call into the IsDeviceAcceptable method. Notice that if false is returned from this method, the device combination is ignored.

Summary

During this chapter, you started your first game project and took your first look at the sample framework. You looked through quite a bit of code that enumerates the device combinations that your system might support. This sample framework is a great starting point for just about any game that you will write in the future.

In the next chapter, you will actually create the device and start rendering something.

CHAPTER 4

Show Something Onscreen!

So far, the code you've written hasn't been all that exciting. In the Chapter 3, "Understanding the Sample Framework," you spent time examining a lot of the sample framework code. Although it's important to have this code written, you don't get the great excitement of seeing your creation onscreen as you would with the graphical portions of the game.

The framework code examined in the last chapter was leading you to the position of being able to render fancy 3D graphics, so get ready. You're about to write your first 3D rendering code.

In this chapter, you'll learn

- ▶ How to create the Direct3D device
- ▶ How to render onscreen
- ▶ How to load a mesh
- ▶ How to create your camera

Creating Your Device

For the rest of the development of this game, you should still be working with the project you started in the last chapter. One of the first things you want to do now is set up the project to actually work with the sample framework. In the Main method you created in the last chapter, add the code in Listing 4.1 immediately following the creation of the GameEngine class.

LISTING 4.1   Hooking Events and Callbacks

```
// Set the callback functions. These functions allow the sample framework
// to notify the application about device changes, user input, and Windows
// messages. The callbacks are optional so you need only set callbacks for
// events you're interested in. However, if you don't handle the device
// reset/lost callbacks, then the sample framework won't be able to reset
// your device since the application must first release all device resources
// before resetting. Likewise, if you don't handle the device created/destroyed
// callbacks, then the sample framework won't be able to re-create your device
// resources.
sampleFramework.Disposing += new EventHandler(blockersEngine.OnDestroyDevice);
sampleFramework.DeviceLost += new EventHandler(blockersEngine.OnLostDevice);
sampleFramework.DeviceCreated +=
  new DeviceEventHandler(blockersEngine.OnCreateDevice);
sampleFramework.DeviceReset +=
  new DeviceEventHandler(blockersEngine.OnResetDevice);

sampleFramework.SetKeyboardCallback(new KeyboardCallback(
blockersEngine.OnKeyEvent));
// Catch mouse move events
sampleFramework.IsNotifiedOnMouseMove = true;
sampleFramework.SetMouseCallback(new MouseCallback(blockersEngine.OnMouseEvent));

sampleFramework.SetCallbackInterface(blockersEngine);
```

A lot of things are happening in this small section of code. A total of four events are being hooked to let you know when the rendering device has been created, lost, reset, and destroyed. You'll need to add the implementations for these handlers in a moment from Listing 4.2. After that, you'll notice that you're hooking two callbacks the sample framework has for user input, namely the keyboard and mouse (Listing 4.3). Finally, you call the SetCallbackInterface method passing in the game engine instance; however, you might notice that the instance doesn't implement the correct interface. You'll need to fix that as well.

LISTING 4.2   Framework Event Handlers

```
/// <summary>
/// This event will be fired immediately after the Direct3D device has been
/// created, which will happen during application initialization and
/// windowed/full screen toggles. This is the best location to create
/// Pool.Managed resources since these resources need to be reloaded whenever
/// the device is destroyed. Resources created here should be released
/// in the Disposing event.
/// </summary>
private void OnCreateDevice(object sender, DeviceEventArgs e)
{
    SurfaceDescription desc = e.BackBufferDescription;
}

/// <summary>
/// This event will be fired immediately after the Direct3D device has been
```

LISTING 4.2   Continued

```
/// reset, which will happen after a lost device scenario. This is the best
/// location to create Pool.Default resources since these resources need to
/// be reloaded whenever the device is lost. Resources created here should
/// be released in the OnLostDevice event.
/// </summary>
private void OnResetDevice(object sender, DeviceEventArgs e)
{
    SurfaceDescription desc = e.BackBufferDescription;
}
/// <summary>
/// This event function will be called fired after the Direct3D device has
/// entered a lost state and before Device.Reset() is called. Resources created
/// in the OnResetDevice callback should be released here, which generally
/// includes all Pool.Default resources. See the "Lost Devices" section of the
/// documentation for information about lost devices.
/// </summary>
private void OnLostDevice(object sender, EventArgs e)
{
}
/// <summary>
/// This callback function will be called immediately after the Direct3D device
/// has been destroyed, which generally happens as a result of application
/// termination or windowed/full screen toggles. Resources created in the
/// OnCreateDevice callback should be released here, which generally includes
/// all Pool.Managed resources.
/// </summary>
private void OnDestroyDevice(object sender, EventArgs e)
{
}
```

LISTING 4.3   User Input Handlers

```
/// <summary>Hook the mouse events</summary>
private void OnMouseEvent(bool leftDown, bool rightDown, bool middleDown,
    bool side1Down, bool side2Down, int wheel, int x, int y)
{
}

/// <summary>Handle keyboard strokes</summary>
private void OnKeyEvent(System.Windows.Forms.Keys key, bool keyDown,
    bool altDown)
{
}
```

Now, the SetCallbackInterface method you called earlier expects a variable of type IFrameworkCallback, and you passed in the game engine class, which does not implement this type. You can fix this easily by changing the game engine class declaration:

```
public class GameEngine : IFrameworkCallback, IDeviceCreation
```

Of course, now you need to add the implementation of the two methods this interface defines (Listing 4.4).

LISTING 4.4   Framework Callback Interface

```
/// <summary>
/// This callback function will be called once at the beginning of every frame.
/// This is the best location for your application to handle updates to the
/// scene but is not intended to contain actual rendering calls, which should
/// instead be placed in the OnFrameRender callback.
/// </summary>
public void OnFrameMove(Device device, double appTime, float elapsedTime)
{
}

/// <summary>
/// This callback function will be called at the end of every frame to perform
/// all the rendering calls for the scene, and it will also be called if the
/// window needs to be repainted. After this function has returned, the sample
/// framework will call Device.Present to display the contents of the next
/// buffer in the swap chain
/// </summary>
public void OnFrameRender(Device device, double appTime, float elapsedTime)
{
}
```

With that boilerplate code out of the way, you're ready to start doing something interesting now. First, you should tell the sample framework that you're ready to render your application and to start the game engine. Go back to the Main method, and add the code in Listing 4.5 immediately after your SetCallbackInterface call.

LISTING 4.5   Starting the Game

```
try
{
#if (!DEBUG)
    // In retail mode, force the app to fullscreen mode
    sampleFramework.IsOverridingFullScreen = true;
#endif
    // Show the cursor and clip it when in full screen
    sampleFramework.SetCursorSettings(true, true);

    // Initialize the sample framework and create the desired window and
    // Direct3D device for the application. Calling each of these functions
    // is optional, but they allow you to set several options that control
    // the behavior of the sampleFramework.
    sampleFramework.Initialize( false, false, true );
    sampleFramework.CreateWindow("Blockers - The Game");
    sampleFramework.CreateDevice( 0, true, Framework.DefaultSizeWidth,
        Framework.DefaultSizeHeight, blockersEngine);
```

LISTING 4.5   Continued

```
    // Pass control to the sample framework for handling the message pump and
    // dispatching render calls. The sample framework will call your FrameMove
    // and FrameRender callback when there is idle time between handling
    // window messages.
    sampleFramework.MainLoop();

}
#if(DEBUG)
catch (Exception e)
{
    // In debug mode show this error (maybe - depending on settings)
    sampleFramework.DisplayErrorMessage(e);
#else
catch
{
// In release mode fail silently
#endif
    // Ignore any exceptions here, they would have been handled by other areas
    return (sampleFramework.ExitCode == 0) ? 1 : sampleFramework.ExitCode;
    // Return an error code here
}
```

What is going on here? The first thing to notice is that the entire code section is wrapped in a try/catch block, and the catch block varies depending on whether you're compiling in debug or release mode. In debug mode, any errors are displayed, and then the application exits. In release mode, all errors are ignored, and the application exits. The first thing that happens in the block is that the sample framework is told to render in full-screen mode if you are not in debug mode. This step ensures that while you're debugging, the game runs in a window, allowing easy debugging, but when it's complete, it runs in full-screen mode, as most games do.

The next call might seem a little strange, but the basic goal of the call is to determine the behavior of the cursor while in full-screen mode. The first parameter determines whether the cursor is displayed in full-screen mode, and the second determines whether the cursor should be clipped. Clipping the cursor simply ensures that the cursor cannot leave the area of the game being rendered. In a single monitor scenario, it isn't a big deal either way, but in a multimon scenario, you wouldn't want the user to move the cursor to the other monitor where you weren't rendering.

The Initialize call sets up some internal variables for the sample framework. The three parameters to the call determine whether the command line should be parsed (no), whether the default hotkeys should be handled (no again), and whether message boxes should be shown (yes). You don't want the game to parse the command line or handle the default hotkeys because they are normally reserved for samples that ship with the DirectX SDK. The `CreateWindow` call is relatively self-explanatory; it creates the window where the rendering occurs with the title listed as the parameter.

Finally, the `CreateDevice` call is created. Notice that this is where you pass in the instance of the game engine class for the `IDeviceCreation` interface. Before the device is created, every combination is enumerated on your system, and the `IsDeviceAcceptable` method that you wrote in the last chapter is called to determine whether the device is acceptable to you. After the list is created, the `ModifyDevice` method is called to allow you to modify any settings right before the device is created. The constructor that you use for the device creation looks like this:

```
public Device ( System.Int32 adapter ,
    Microsoft.DirectX.Direct3D.DeviceType deviceType ,
    System.IntPtr renderWindowHandle ,
    Microsoft.DirectX.Direct3D.CreateFlags behaviorFlags ,
    params Microsoft.DirectX.Direct3D.PresentParameters[]
    presentationParameters )
```

The *adapter* parameter is the ordinal of the adapter you enumerated earlier. In the majority of cases, it is the default parameter, which is 0. The *deviceType* parameter can be one of the following values:

▶ `DeviceType.Hardware`—A hardware device. This is by far the most common device type created. The hardware device will most likely not support every feature of the Direct3D runtime. You need to check the capabilities of the device for specific features. This option is naturally the fastest option.

▶ `DeviceType.Reference`—A device using the reference rasterizer. The reference rasterizer performs all calculations for rendering in software mode. Although this device type supports every feature of Direct3D, it does so very, very slowly. You should also note that the reference rasterizer only ships with the DirectX SDK. End users will most likely not have this rasterizer installed.

▶ `DeviceType.Software`—A software rendering device. It is extremely uncommon to use this option. Unless you have written a software rendering library, and you have it pluggable with Direct3D, you will not be using this device type.

Obviously, because you are dealing with graphics, you need someplace to actually show the rendered image. In this overload of the device constructor, the sample framework uses the window it has created, but you could pass in any control from the `System.Windows.Forms` library that comes with the .NET framework.

Although it won't be used in this game, you could use any valid control, such as a picture box.

The next parameter is the behavior of the device. You might remember from the last chapter when you determined the best set of flags, including whether the device supported transforming and lighting in hardware and whether the device can be pure. You find the possible value of this parameter by combining the values in Table 4.1.

TABLE 4.1   Possible Behavior Flags

CreateFlags.AdapterGroupDevice	Used for multimon-capable adapters. Specifies that a single device will control each of the adapters on the system.
CreateFlags.DisableDriverManagement	Tells Direct3D to handle the resource management rather than the driver. In most cases, you will not want to specify this flag.
CreateFlags.MixedVertexProcessing	Tells Direct3D that a combination of hardware and software vertex processing will be used. This flag cannot be combined with either the software or hardware vertex processing flags.
CreateFlags.HardwareVertexProcessing	Tells Direct3D that all vertex processing will occur in hardware. This flag cannot be combined with the software or mixed vertex processing flags.
CreateFlags.SoftwareVertexProcessing	Tells Direct3D that all vertex processing will occur in software. This flag cannot be combined with the hardware or mixed vertex processing flags.
CreateFlags.PureDevice	Specifies that this device will be a pure device.
CreateFlags.Multithreaded	Specifies that this device may be accessed for more than one thread simultaneously. Because the garbage collector runs on a separate thread, this option is turned on by default in Managed DirectX. Note that there is a slight performance penalty for using this flag.
CreateFlags.FpuPreserve	Tells Direct3D to preserve the current floating-point unit precision.

For this game, you should stick with either software or hardware vertex processing only, which is what the enumeration code picked during the last chapter. The final parameter of the device constructor is a parameter array of the PresentParameters class. You only need more than one of these objects if you are using the CreateFlags.AdapterGroupDevice flag mentioned earlier, and then you need one for each adapter in the group.

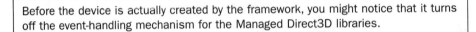

Construction Cue

Before the device is actually created by the framework, you might notice that it turns off the event-handling mechanism for the Managed Direct3D libraries.

Before you go on, it's important to understand why turning off the event-handling model is a good idea. The default implementation of the Managed DirectX classes hooks certain events on the Direct3D device for every resource that is created. At a minimum, each resource (such as textures or a vertex buffer) hooks the Disposing event and more likely also hooks other events, such as the DeviceLost and DeviceReset events. This step happens for maintaining object lifetimes. Why wouldn't you want this great benefit in your application?

The main reason is that this benefit comes at a cost, and that cost could potentially be quite large. To understand this point, you must first have a sense of what is going on behind the scenes. You can look at this simple case, written here in pseudo-code:

```
SomeResource res = new SomeResource(device);
device.Render(res);
```

As you can see, this code looks harmless enough. You simply create a resource and render it. The object is obviously never used again, so the garbage collector should be smart enough to clean up the object. This thought is common, but this thought is incorrect. When the new resource is created, it hooks a minimum of one event on the device to allow it to clean up correctly. This hooking of the event is a double-edged sword.

One, there is an allocation of the EventHandler class when doing the actual hook. Granted, the allocation is small, but as you will see in a moment, even small allocations can add up quickly. Second, after the event is hooked, the resource has a hard link to the device. In the eyes of the garbage collector, this object is still in use and will remain in use for the lifetime of the device or until the events are unhooked. In the pseudo-code earlier, imagine if this code were run once every frame to render something. Imagine that your game was pushing around a thousand frames per second, and imagine it was running for two minutes. You've just created 120,000 objects that will not be collected while the device is around, plus another 120,000 event handlers. All these created objects can cause memory consumption to rise quickly, as well as extra garbage collections to be performed, which can hurt performance. If your resources are in video memory, you can be assured you will run out quickly.

This scenario doesn't even consider what happens when the device is finally disposed. In the preceding example, when the device is disposed, it fires the Disposing event, which has been hooked by 120,000 listeners. You can imagine that this cascading list of event handlers which must be called will take some time, and you'd be correct. It could take literally minutes and cause people to think the application has locked up.

You only want to use the event handling that is built in to Managed Direct3D in the simplest of cases. At any point where you care about memory consumption or performance (for example, in games), you want to avoid this process, as you've done in this example (or at the very least ensure that you are disposing of objects properly). The sample framework gives you the opportunity to do so.

You'll notice that last method you called in the Main method is the MainLoop method from the sample framework. This point is where you are telling the sample framework that you're ready to run your application now. This method will run and process Windows messages as well as call your rendering methods constantly until the application exits. This method will not return until it happens. From now on, all interaction with the sample framework comes from the events it fires and the callbacks it calls into.

A few times throughout the course of the code, you might need to know the name of the game. You can simply add this constant to your game engine class:

```
public const string GameName = "Blockers";
```

Time to Render

Well, you have your device created now, so you can start getting something rendered onscreen. You already have the rendering method where you can write all the code needed to render your scene, so add the code in Listing 4.6.

LISTING 4.6   The Render Method

```
bool beginSceneCalled = false;

// Clear the render target and the zbuffer
device.Clear(ClearFlags.ZBuffer | ClearFlags.Target, 0, 1.0f, 0);
try
{
    device.BeginScene();
    beginSceneCalled = true;

}
finally
{
    if (beginSceneCalled)
        device.EndScene();
}
```

Before you can do any actual rendering, you most likely want to clear the device to prepare it for a new frame. In this case, clear the render target (`ClearFlags.Target`) to a particular color and the depth buffer (`ClearFlags.ZBuffer`) to a particular depth. The second parameter is the color you want to clear the device with. It can be either a member of the `System.Drawing.Color` object (or any of its many built-in colors) or an integer value in the format of `0xAARRGGBB`. In this case, each component of the color (alpha, red, green, and blue) can be represented by two hexadecimal digits, ranging from 00 to FF, where 00 is completely off and FF is completely on. The preceding call uses 0, which is the same as `0x00000000`, or everything completely off or black. If you want to clear to blue using an integer value, you use `0x000000ff`; for green, `0x0000ff00`; or any other combination you feel appropriate.

The third parameter is the new value of every member of the depth buffer. A common value here is to reset everything to a depth of `1.0f`. The last parameter is for clearing a stencil, which hasn't been created for this game, so I do not discuss it at this time. After the device is cleared, you want to inform Direct3D that you are ready to begin drawing, which is the purpose of the `BeginScene` call. Direct3D sets up its internal state and prepares itself for rendering your graphics. For now, you don't have anything to render, so you can simply call `EndScene` to let Direct3D know you're done rendering. You must call `EndScene` for every call to `BeginScene` in your application, and you cannot call `BeginScene` again until after you've called `EndScene`. This is why the `try/finally` block ensures that the `EndScene` method is called for every `BeginScene` call.

Just because you've notified Direct3D that you're done rendering doesn't actually mean Direct3D updates the display. It's entirely possible for you to have multiple render targets, and you don't want the display updated until you've rendered them all. To handle this scenario, Direct3D splits up the ending of the scene and the updating of the display. The Present call handles updating the display for you; it is called automatically by the sample framework. The overload used in the framework updates the entire display at once, which is the desired behavior for your game. The other overload allows you to update small subsections of the entire display; however, for your beginning simple games, you never need this flexibility.

If you run the application now, you should notice that the window is cleared to a black color, and that's really about it. You can have the "background" of the game be this single color if you want, but that's not exciting. Instead, you should make the background of the game be something called a "sky box." In the simplest terms, a sky box is simply a large cube with the inside six walls of the cube textured to look like the sky or whatever background your scene should have. It allows you to look around your scene from any direction and see a valid view of your background image.

Loading and Rendering a Mesh

1. Determine the media path.
2. Declare the mesh variables.
3. Load the mesh and textures from files.
4. Render the mesh.

Step 1 is determining the media path. In the included CD, you will notice a Blockers folder in the media folder. This folder includes all the game media, so you need to copy it onto your hard drive somewhere (or use the installation application from the CD). After you copy the media to your hard drive, you need to add an application configuration file to your project, much as you did in previous chapters. Choose Project, Add New Item, and add an application configuration file to your project. Replace the Extensible Markup Language (XML) that was automatically generated with the following:

```
<?xml version="1.0" encoding="utf-8" ?>
<configuration>
  <appSettings>
    <add key="MediaPath" value="..\..\..\..\Media\Blockers\" />
  </appSettings>
</configuration>
```

Obviously, you want the MediaPath value to match wherever you have copied the media on your hard drive. If you used the installation program, the value shown here will work for you. With the configuration file in your project, you need a variable to actually access this key, so add this variable to your game engine class:

```
public static readonly string MediaPath =
 ConfigurationSettings.AppSettings.Get("MediaPath");
```

For Step 2, you declare the mesh variables. One of the media files in the folder is an X file called level.x. The X files are used to store geometry data, which can then be easily rendered with DirectX. This particular X file is simply your sky box, with a series of textures, marking each wall of the "level." In Direct3D, the Mesh class will be used to hold the actual geometry data, and the Texture class will be used to hold each texture. A single mesh can have 0 to many textures, so you want to declare the following variables in your game engine class:

```
// The information for the mesh that will display the level
private Mesh levelMesh = null;
private Texture[] levelTextures = null;
```

As you can see, you have a single Mesh object that will be used to store the geometry and an array of textures to store the texture for the walls. Before continuing, however, you might find yourself wondering, what exactly is a mesh? When rendering 3D graphics, everything that is rendered onscreen consists of one to many triangles. A triangle is the smallest closed polygon that will always be coplanar. (Rendering primitives that are not coplanar isn't very efficient.) You can build virtually any object by using a large number of triangles. A **mesh** is simply a data store for this triangle (or geometry) data.

Step 3 is loading the mesh and textures from files. You are now ready to load your mesh data into the variables you just created. Take the code in Listing 4.7, and include it in the OnCreateDevice method you've already written.

LISTING 4.7 Loading the Sky Box Mesh

```
// Create the mesh for the level
ExtendedMaterial[] mtrls;
levelMesh = Mesh.FromFile(MediaPath + "level.x", MeshFlags.Managed, device,
                          out mtrls);

// Store the materials for later use, and create the textures
if ((mtrls != null) && (mtrls.Length > 0))
{
    levelTextures = new Texture[mtrls.Length];
```

LISTING 4.7 Continued

```
    for (int i = 0; i < mtrls.Length; i++)
    {
        // Create the texture
        levelTextures[i] = TextureLoader.FromFile(device, MediaPath +
            mtrls[i].TextureFilename);
    }
}
```

For the mesh you are creating, you want to load this from a file, using the media path variable that was declared earlier in this chapter. The second parameter of this call is any flag you might want to pass in. Because this mesh is simply static, you can use the MeshFlags.Managed flag, which informs Direct3D that it should manage the mesh. You also need the created device when creating this mesh, so that is what you pass in as the third parameter. The final parameter is extended material information about the mesh. Because a mesh can have more than one set of material information, it is returned as an array.

After the mesh is created, ensure that the extended material array has members. If it does, you can create the texture array, scroll through each of the members of the extended material array, and load the appropriate texture from a file. Notice that the texture loading method has only two parameters: the rendering device and the location of the file. The texture filename normally doesn't include path information, so to ensure that it loads the texture from the correct location, it's a good idea to include the media path here as well.

Step 4 is rendering the mesh. The actual rendering of this mesh is pretty simple. Take the code in Listing 4.8, and include it in your render method. Place the code between the calls to BeginScene and EndScene to ensure that it is rendered correctly.

LISTING 4.8 Rendering the Sky Box Mesh

```
// First render the level mesh, but before that is done, you will need
// to turn off the zbuffer. This isn't needed for this drawing
device.RenderState.ZBufferEnable = false;
device.RenderState.ZBufferWriteEnable = false;

device.Transform.World = Matrix.Scaling(15,15,15);
device.RenderState.Lighting = false;
for(int i = 0; i < levelTextures.Length; i++)
{
    device.SetTexture(0, levelTextures[i]);
    levelMesh.DrawSubset(i);
}
```

LISTING 4.8   Continued

```
// Turn the zbuffer back on
device.RenderState.ZBufferEnable = true;
device.RenderState.ZBufferWriteEnable = true;

// Now, turn back on our light
device.RenderState.Lighting = true;
```

There's actually quite a bit of new stuff in here. First, if you remember the discussion on depth buffers earlier in this chapter, you learned that the depth buffer stores the depth of each of the objects in a scene. Because the sky box is a single object that will *always* be behind any other objects in the scene, you can simply turn off the depth buffer and render it first. In many cases, simply turning the depth buffer off (setting the ZBufferEnable render state to false) is adequate; however, in some cases, drivers still write to the depth buffer even if it is off. To handle this case, you can simply turn off writing to the depth buffer as well.

Next, you want to actually size the sky box. The mesh that has been loaded has all the triangle information stored in what is called **object space**. The mesh itself has no knowledge of any other objects that might or might not be in a scene. To enable you to render your objects anywhere in your scene, Direct3D provides a transform, which allows you to move from one coordinate system to another. In this case, you want to scale the sky box 15 units for each of the axes. (I discuss transforms more in depth in later chapters.)

Because the sky box is textured, you don't want any lighting calculations that the scene might need to affect the box. To ensure that no lighting calculations are used when rendering the sky box, you simply set the Lighting render state to false. Next, you are ready to draw your mesh.

You'll notice here that you want to go through each texture in your array. First, call the SetTexture method to let Direct3D know which texture you expect to be using for rendering this portion of the mesh. Then, you call DrawSubset on the mesh itself, passing in the index to the texture inside the array you are currently rendering.

Adding a Camera to Your Scene

If you run the application, you notice that nothing looks different. You still see a black screen and nothing else. You have all the code in to load and render your sky box mesh, so why isn't it rendering? Direct3D doesn't know exactly what it can render yet. In a 3D scene, you need to include a camera so Direct3D knows which areas of the world it should render. Add the code in Listing 4.9 to the OnDeviceReset method now.

LISTING 4.9   Setting Up a Camera

```
// Set the transformation matrices
localDevice.Transform.Projection = Matrix.PerspectiveFovLH(
    (float)Math.PI / 4,
    (float)this.Width / (float)this.Height, 1.0f, 1000000.0f);
localDevice.Transform.View = Matrix.LookAtLH(new Vector3(0,0,-54),
    new Vector3(), new Vector3(0,1,0));
```

Here you set two transforms on the device that control the camera. The first is the projection matrix, which determines how the camera's lens behaves. You can use PespectiveFovLH method to create a projection matrix based on the field of view for a left-handed coordinate system (which is described later in Chapter 10, "A Quick 3D-Math Primer").

By default, Direct3D uses a left-handed coordinate system, so it is assumed from here on that you are as well. Direct3D can render in a right-handed coordinate system as well, but that topic isn't important for this book. Here is the prototype for the projection matrix function:

```
public static Microsoft.DirectX.Matrix PerspectiveFovLH (
    System.Single fieldOfViewY ,
    System.Single aspectRatio ,
    System.Single znearPlane ,
    System.Single zfarPlane )
```

The projection transform is used to describe the viewing frustum of the scene. You can think of the **viewing frustum** as a pyramid with the top of it cut off; the inside of the pyramid is what you can actually see inside your scene. The two parameters in the preceding function, the near and far planes, describe the limits of this pyramid, with the far plane making up the "base" of the pyramid structure and the near plane where you would cut off the top. (See Figure 4.1.) The field-of-view parameter describes the angle between the point of the pyramid. (See Figure 4.2.) You can think of the aspect ratio as you do the aspect ratio of your television; for example, a wide-screen television has an aspect ratio of 1.85. You can normally figure out this parameter by dividing the width of your viewing area by the height. Only objects that are contained within this frustum are drawn by Direct3D.

FIGURE 4.1
Viewing frustum.

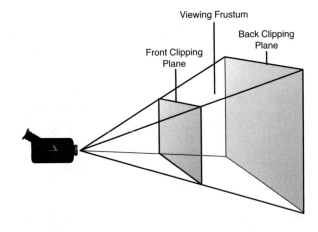

FIGURE 4.2
Field of view.

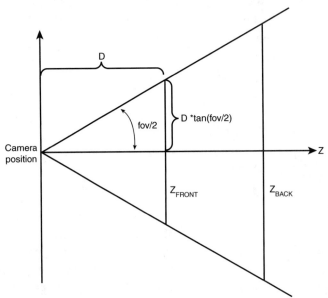

The second transform is the view transform, which describes the actual camera's position in your scene. You'll notice that you can once again use the left-handed function off the Matrix object to construct this transform for you. The prototype for the method is

```
public static Microsoft.DirectX.Matrix LookAtLH (
    Microsoft.DirectX.Vector3 cameraPosition ,
    Microsoft.DirectX.Vector3 cameraTarget ,
    Microsoft.DirectX.Vector3 cameraUpVector )
```

You'll notice this method is simple. You have a position where you want the camera to be located, a position where you want the camera to be looking, and finally a vector describing which way "up" is to this camera. In most normal cases, up is simply the positive Y axis. With the camera transforms set up, you might be wondering why you add the code to the OnDeviceReset method. The reason is that any time the device is reset (for any reason, such as being lost), all device-specific state is lost. This state includes the camera transformations. As a result, the OnDeviceReset method (which is called after the device has been reset) is the perfect place for the code.

You might also be wondering why you are using events, and why they would work, because earlier in this chapter you disabled the event handling. The event handling that you disabled was only the internal Direct3D event handling. The events are still fired and are available for you to consume if needed.

Running the application shows you part of the sky box that will be used for your levels. (See Figure 4.3.)

FIGURE 4.3
A rendered sky box.

Remember from earlier, you can't rely on the event handlers to automatically clean up your objects for you. You need to make sure you dispose of these new items you've created when the application shuts down. It's important to clean up these objects because failure to do so results in **memory leaks**, which can cause system instability and poor performance. Although the garbage collector can (and does) handle much of this memory management for you, doing this cleanup here will give you much finer control over the resources the system is using. Add the following code to your OnDestroyDevice method:

```
// Clean up the textures used for the mesh level
if ((levelTextures != null) && (levelTextures.Length > 0))
{
    for(int i = 0; i < levelTextures.Length; i++)
    {
        levelTextures[i].Dispose();
    }
    // Clean up the mesh level itself
    levelMesh.Dispose();
}
```

This code ensures each of the textures and the mesh are cleaned up. You must add any resource that you create to this method for cleanup.

Summary

During this chapter, you actually got something rendered. You set up your rendering device, loaded and rendered a sky box model, and set up the cameras for use in your scene. With those items finally handled, you could actually see the work you've done so far when running the application.

CHAPTER 5

Finishing Up the Support Code

Before you can get into the intricacies of this game, you first need to add some utility functionality to the application. You need to include a high-resolution timer in your application, and it would be a good idea to add some debug output that you can see when running the game.

Also, because the default project configuration is to run in debug mode, more than likely you've only seen your scene being rendered in windowed mode. Because running in full screen might behave slightly differently, it would be wise to run the game in release mode as well.

Finally, you want to display some type of user interface (UI) in the game rather than use the "ugly" graphics device interface (GDI) controls that Windows provides.

In this chapter, you'll learn

- ▶ How to use a high resolution timer
- ▶ How to display debug output
- ▶ How to handle lost devices
- ▶ How to design UI screens and buttons

Understanding the High-Resolution Timer

All games today require at least some semblance of a timer. Back in the "early days" of game development, using a timer wasn't considered important. Computer systems were still all relatively the same speed (slow), and any calculations that needed to be performed could be based on the number of frames that had passed. If the code was only ever going to run on a single computer system, or if every system it was running on was identical, this *might* be a valid way to perform these calculations—but even in that case, it's not normally the best-case scenario.

Imagine the situation where you are designing a physical limit on a car. Does it make more sense to think "The maximum speed of the car is 250 units per 6 frames," or instead, "The maximum speed of the car is 250 miles per hour (0.7 miles per second)?" Most calculations for things like physics are based on values over time, so it makes more sense to actually use time.

Another reason to avoid using frame-based calculations concerns the vast differences in computing systems nowadays. Imagine developing your game on a 2GHz processor. Through some trial and error, you've got your car physics perfect. Now, you give your game to your two buddies, one of whom has a 1GHz machine, the other a 3GHz machine. The one with the slower machine complains that everything goes too slow; the other complains about how things move too fast to control. It's never a good idea to rely on processing speed for any important calculations. Even on identical systems, other running applications could affect the running speed of your application.

Construction Cue

> The .NET runtime comes with a property, `System.Environment.Tickcount`, which you can use to calculate time. This property returns the number of ticks (milliseconds) that have elapsed since the computer was last restarted. At first glance, it probably looks like the perfect answer; however, it has a pretty glaring drawback, which is that the property isn't updated every millisecond.
>
> How often the property is updated is often referred to as the **resolution** of the timer. In this case, the resolution of the tick-count property is on average 15 milliseconds (ms). If you access this property continuously in a loop, it returns the same value for 15ms before updating, and then it returns that new value for another 15ms before updating again. In modern computers that can perform unheard-of amounts of calculations per second, a 15ms resolution can cause your calculations to appear "jerky." No one wants to play a game like that.

Caution

> If you decide that using the `TickCount` property is what you want to do, make sure you realize that it will return a signed integer value. Because the property is the number of ticks since the computer was started, if the computer is on for an extremely long time (say more than 25 days), you start getting negative numbers returned from the property. If you do not take this into account, it can mess up the formulas you're using. After an even longer period of time, the values "wrap" and go back to 0.

What you need here is a timer that has a much higher resolution. A resolution of 1ms would be perfect. The sample framework has such a timer built in, located in the dxmutmisc.cs code file. Because it is an important topic, I briefly discuss this timer now.

Because there is no high-resolution timer built into the .NET runtime, and you need it for your game, you need to use the DllImport attribute to call two particular Win32 APIs, QueryPerformanceFrequency and QueryPerformanceCounter. You see the declarations for these two external methods in the NativeMethods class, such as what appears in Listing 5.1.

LISTING 5.1   Declaring External Functions

```
[System.Security.SuppressUnmanagedCodeSecurity] // We won't use this maliciously
[DllImport("kernel32")]
private static extern bool QueryPerformanceFrequency(
ref long PerformanceFrequency);
[System.Security.SuppressUnmanagedCodeSecurity] // We won't use this maliciously
[DllImport("kernel32")]
private static extern bool QueryPerformanceCounter(ref long PerformanceCount);
```

You'll notice that not only are you using the DllImport attribute, but you are also using the SuppressUnmanagedCodeSecurity attribute. Because you are calling a method that isn't controlled by the .NET runtime, in the default case it does a stack walk and ensures that your process has enough privileges to run unmanaged code (which is what the Win32 API calls are)—and it performs this check every time you call this method. This security check is expensive and time-consuming, and this attribute ensures that the check happens only once. Aside from that fix, this is a simple case where you declare a call into a Win32 API. Also notice a few instance variables in the FrameworkTimer class so that it can calculate the total time or the time elapsed since the last update:

```
private static bool isUsingQPF;
private static bool isTimerStopped;
private static long ticksPerSecond;
private static long stopTime;
private static long lastElapsedTime;
private static long baseTime;
```

Here you can see that you want to store the time the timer has started, the amount of time that has elapsed, and the time that was stored at the last update. Because the high-resolution timer can have a varying number of ticks per second, you also want to store that as well. Finally, you store the actual state of the timer. Notice that all the variables are marked static. This move ensures that there is only one high-resolution timer per application domain. (You can read more about application domains in the .NET documentation.) With the state variables declared, you now need to initialize your data in the constructor for this class, as shown in Listing 5.2.

LISTING 5.2   Initializing the High-Resolution Timer

```
private FrameworkTimer() { } // No creation
/// <summary>
/// Static creation routine
/// </summary>
static FrameworkTimer()
{
    isTimerStopped = true;
    ticksPerSecond = 0;
    stopTime = 0;
    lastElapsedTime = 0;
    baseTime = 0;
    // Use QueryPerformanceFrequency to get frequency of the timer
    isUsingQPF = NativeMethods.QueryPerformanceFrequency(ref ticksPerSecond);
}
```

There are two things to see in the initialization here. First, there is a static constructor where the real initialization takes place, and second, the normal constructor is private. Because this class is going to contain only static methods, you don't want anyone to be able to create an instance of the class. The only initialization you need here is to determine the amount of ticks per second. If this function returns `false`, the system does not support a high-resolution timer. You could spend the time writing code to fall back to the less reliable `TickCount` property, but that work goes beyond the scope of this book. Now you add the code in Listing 5.3 to the timer code, which finishes up the timer class.

LISTING 5.3   Implementation of the High-Resolution Timer

```
public static void Reset()
{
    if (!isUsingQPF)
        return; // Nothing to do

    // Get either the current time or the stop time
    long time = 0;
    if (stopTime != 0)
        time = stopTime;
    else
        NativeMethods.QueryPerformanceCounter(ref time);

    baseTime = time;
    lastElapsedTime = time;
    stopTime = 0;
```

LISTING 5.3   Continued

```
      isTimerStopped = false;
}

public static void Start()
{
    if (!isUsingQPF)
        return; // Nothing to do

    // Get either the current time or the stop time
    long time = 0;
    if (stopTime != 0)
        time = stopTime;
    else
        NativeMethods.QueryPerformanceCounter(ref time);

    if (isTimerStopped)
        baseTime += (time - stopTime);
    stopTime = 0;
    lastElapsedTime = time;
    isTimerStopped = false;
}

public static void Stop()
{
    if (!isUsingQPF)
        return; // Nothing to do

    if (!isTimerStopped)
    {
        // Get either the current time or the stop time
        long time = 0;
        if (stopTime != 0)
            time = stopTime;
        else
            NativeMethods.QueryPerformanceCounter(ref time);

        stopTime = time;
        lastElapsedTime = time;
        isTimerStopped = true;
    }
}

public static void Advance()
{
    if (!isUsingQPF)
        return; // Nothing to do

    stopTime += ticksPerSecond / 10;
}

public static double GetAbsoluteTime()
{
    if (!isUsingQPF)
        return -1.0; // Nothing to do
```

LISTING 5.3   Continued

```
        // Get either the current time or the stop time
        long time = 0;
        if (stopTime != 0)
            time = stopTime;
        else
            NativeMethods.QueryPerformanceCounter(ref time);

        double absoluteTime = time / (double)ticksPerSecond;
        return absoluteTime;
}

public static double GetTime()
{
    if (!isUsingQPF)
        return -1.0; // Nothing to do

    // Get either the current time or the stop time
    long time = 0;
    if (stopTime != 0)
        time = stopTime;
    else
        NativeMethods.QueryPerformanceCounter(ref time);

    double appTime = (double)(time - baseTime) / (double)ticksPerSecond;
    return appTime;
}

public static double GetElapsedTime()
{
    if (!isUsingQPF)
        return -1.0; // Nothing to do

    // Get either the current time or the stop time
    long time = 0;
    if (stopTime != 0)
        time = stopTime;
    else
        NativeMethods.QueryPerformanceCounter(ref time);

    double elapsedTime = (double)(time - lastElapsedTime) /
  (double)ticksPerSecond;
    lastElapsedTime = time;
    return elapsedTime;
}

public static bool IsStopped
{
    get { return isTimerStopped; }
}
```

This is a relatively simple implementation. Everything you need to know about the state of the timer you have here, including starting, stopping, and getting the elapsed time or the total time. Each of these properties returns a float value based in seconds; for example, `1.0f` is exactly 1 second, and `1.5f` is exactly a second and a half. With that, you have a generic high-resolution timer available for your games.

Handling Lost Devices

Before you start using that timer, you need to take care of something more pressing. To see the problem in action, change your project to run in release mode. You can do so by selecting Build, Configuration Manager. For the Active Solution Configuration, choose Release. (See Figure 5.1.)

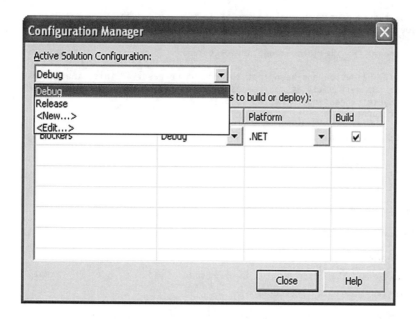

FIGURE 5.1
The Configuration Manager dialog.

Running the application now renders the fledgling game in full-screen mode. On the surface, everything should appear the same; however, you might notice quickly that with the window border no longer around, you can't close the application. Luckily, you are using the sample framework; otherwise, if you decided to minimize the window (for example, by using the Alt+Tab key combination to switch to the next application) or close the window, the game would throw an exception as soon as it lost focus. Even though you don't have this problem because you're using the sample framework, it's important to know what causes this.

When you are running the application in full-screen mode, Direct3D takes exclusive mode over the monitor that is being used to render the full screen image.

When you switch to a different application, that exclusive mode must be released to allow the other application to run, so the current application is minimized and the device is lost. Once a device is lost, you cannot render to it any longer, and trying to do so throws an exception (specifically the DeviceLostException).

Because this is a common problem that every game has to solve, you wouldn't want to clutter your rendering method with code to handle the situation, which is why the sample framework handles it for you. Look at the code snippet in Listing 5.4 for more information.

LISTING 5.4 Handling Lost Devices

```
int result;
// Check the cooperative level to see if it's ok to render
if (!device.CheckCooperativeLevel(out result))
{
    if (result == (int)ResultCode.DeviceLost)
    {
        // The device has been lost but cannot be reset at this time.
        // So wait until it can be reset.
        System.Threading.Thread.Sleep(50);
        return;
    }
    // Other code snippets
}
// Other code snippets
// Show the frame on the primary surface
try
{
    device.Present();
}
catch (DeviceLostException)
{
    // Whoops, device is lost now
    State.IsDeviceLost = true;
}
catch (DriverInternalErrorException)
{
    // When DriverInternalErrorException is thrown from Present(),
    // the application can do one of the following:
    //
    // - End, with the pop-up window saying that the application cannot continue
    //   because of problems in the display adapter and that the user should
    //   contact the adapter manufacturer.
    //
    // - Attempt to restart by calling Device.Reset, which is essentially the
    //   same path as recovering from a lost device. If Device.Reset throws the
    //   DriverInternalErrorException, the application should end immediately
    //   with the message that the user should contact the adapter manufacturer.
    //
    // The framework attempts the path of resetting the device
    //
    State.IsDeviceLost = true;
}
```

You'll notice immediately that this method updates the variable `IsDeviceLost` on the `State` class. In this method, you check to see whether the device is currently lost, and if it is, you call the `CheckCooperativeLevel` method on the device. This call returns a Boolean value, `true` if the device is available and ready to use and `false` otherwise. Notice that an integer value is returned as an out parameter, which is the reason why the device is still not available.

After this call (assuming it returned `false`), you want to check the reason why the device is not available to render. The two likely reasons are that the device is still lost (the application still doesn't have focus) or that the application has regained focus, but the device hasn't been reset. If the device is still lost, there's nothing you can do right now, so you simply return from the method. However, if the device needs to be reset (which it always does after regaining focus), you simply call the `Reset` method, which should return the device back to the exclusive mode and be ready for rendering (the framework handles this for you).

Assuming you made it past that section, either the device was never lost to begin with or it is reset and ready to use now. Next, you are ready to render your scene. The framework calls the render method you have written and then makes the `Present` call. This call is the one that throws the exception when the device is lost, so after the render method is called, Present is called, wrapped in a `try/catch` block. Notice that the only exceptions caught are `DeviceLostException` and `DriverInternalErrorException` and the only action taken is to set the Boolean variable to `true` to start the check of the current cooperative level.

Adding Frame Rate Output

One more of the many things the sample framework does is keep track of the game's frame rate. Frame rate is something that most 3D games closely track because it deals directly with the performance of the game. It is simply the number of frames rendered in any given second, and the framework calculates it using the high-resolution timer discussed earlier in this chapter.

The code included on the CD only displays the frame rate in debug mode so it doesn't clutter the screen in full-screen mode. Therefore, the code in this section assumes this behavior as well. Add the following variable to your game engine class declarations:

```
#if (DEBUG)
private Direct3D.Font debugFont = null;
#endif
```

The first thing you'll notice here is that you've declared a new type of variable, the Direct3D.Font object. This object is used to render text onscreen as part of your scene.

> You'll also notice the 'alias' for the Direct3D namespace used here. It allows you to reference the items in the Direct3D namespace without having to type the full Microsoft.DirectX.Direct3D namespace (which is **fully qualified**). Using this alias is required for the Font class because more than one Font class exists, the one you just declared and another in the System.Drawing namespace. Make sure that you add the using alias at the top of your game engine code file:
>
> ```
> using Direct3D = Microsoft.DirectX.Direct3D;
> ```

Now that the variable is declared, in your OnCreateDevice method add the following code to create a new font object:

```
#if (DEBUG)
debugFont = new Direct3D.Font(device, new System.Drawing.Font("Arial", 12));
#endif
```

The only parameters you need for this object are the rendering device and the font you want to render with. Using a default font is adequate for this scenario. Because the font object here is also a resource, make sure that you clean up that object in your OnDestroyDevice method. Add this code to that method now:

```
#if (DEBUG)
if (debugFont != null)
{
    // Clean up the font
    debugFont.Dispose();
    debugFont = null;
}
#endif
```

One thing you might notice on the font object is that it has two "special" methods for use when a device has just been reset or is about to be lost, OnDeviceReset and OnDeviceLost, respectively. You already have methods to handle when the device has just been reset and lost, so you want to call these font methods there. Add this section of code to the beginning of your OnResetDevice method to make sure that the font behaves correctly during a device reset:

```
#if (DEBUG)
// Make sure the debug font resets correctly
debugFont.OnResetDevice();
#endif
```

You want to handle the lost case as well, so add this section of code to the
OnLostDevice method:

```
#if (DEBUG)
if (debugFont != null)
{
    // Make sure the debug font gets rid of any resources
    debugFont.OnLostDevice();
}
#endif
```

Now that your font is created, you can look at the implementation of the
UpdateFrameStats method from the framework, which is called every frame and
calculates the current frame rate. See the code in Listing 5.5 from the framework.

LISTING 5.5   Calculating Frame Rate

```
private void UpdateFrameStats()
{
    // Keep track of frame count
    double time = FrameworkTimer.GetAbsoluteTime();
    State.LastStatsUpdateFrames++;

    if (time - State.LastStatsUpdateTime > 1.0)
    {
        float fps = (float)(State.LastStatsUpdateFrames /
            (time - State.LastStatsUpdateTime));
        State.CurrentFrameRate = fps;
        State.LastStatsUpdateFrames = 0;
        State.LastStatsUpdateTime = time;

        State.FrameStats = string.Format(State.StaticFrameStats,
            fps.ToString("f2",
            System.Globalization.CultureInfo.CurrentUICulture));
    }
}
```

Now that you know how the frame rate is calculated, the last thing you need to
do is actually update your scene by rendering this text. Add this code to the end
of your render method, directly before your EndScene call (but not inside the
finally block).

```
#if (DEBUG)
// Show debug stats (in debug mode)
debugFont.DrawText(null, sampleFramework.FrameStats,
    new System.Drawing.Rectangle(2,0,0,0),
    DrawTextFormat.NoClip, unchecked((int)0xffffff00));
debugFont.DrawText(null, sampleFramework.DeviceStats,
    new System.Drawing.Rectangle(2,15,0,0),
    DrawTextFormat.NoClip, unchecked((int)0xffffff00));
#endif
```

Look at the prototype for the DrawText call; it is more or less self-explanatory. The prototype looks like this:

```
public System.Int32 DrawText ( Microsoft.DirectX.Direct3D.Sprite sprite ,
    System.String text , System.Drawing.Rectangle rect ,
    Microsoft.DirectX.Direct3D.DrawTextFormat format ,
    System.Drawing.Color color )
```

Because the first parameter is null, you are specifying that you want to draw directly onscreen. Sprites are used to render 2D images onto the screen, and you use them for rendering the UI of the game later. For now, however, because you are just rendering debug information, you want it rendered directly to the screen. The second parameter is the string you will be rendering, and the third parameter is the rectangle you want to render the text into. The client rectangle is perfect here, even though you wouldn't need to use it all. The last parameter is the color you want the text to be rendered. It really is as simple as that.

Designing a UI Screen

Undoubtedly you've seen some type of UI before while using your computer. Windows has plenty of resources built into the GDI, which ships as part of the operating system to build rich graphical user interfaces (GUIs). However, these interfaces don't translate well into the full-screen DirectX applications. When running your game in full screen, you don't want an extra window (that looks nothing like the rest of your application) popping up. At best, it's not appealing; at worst, it can cause your main application to minimize or have other problems.

To present a consistent look and feel throughout an application, most game developers actually design a completely new UI to meld with the rest of the games they are developing. Because the goal of this book is for you to learn to be a 3D game developer, you should do what they do. For this game, you will design some overly simple UI screens, consisting only of buttons and a background image. Because the game will have multiple screens (the main screen to start a new game, a select character screen, and a quit confirmation screen), create a base class that encompasses the major functionality of your screens. To do so, add a new code file to your project named gui.cs. This code file will contain all your UI screens when the game is complete.

Because this first class you are writing in this file will be the base for all subsequent UI screens, you should make it abstract so you don't attempt to accidentally create an instance of it yourself. Add the code in Listing 5.6 to your new code file now.

LISTING 5.6 The Abstract UI Class

```
public abstract class UiScreen : IDisposable
{
    // Constants
    public static readonly Vector3 ObjectCenter = new Vector3();
    public static readonly int SpriteColor = unchecked((int)0xffffffff);

    protected const int SmallButtonWidth = 128;
    protected const int SmallButtonHeight = 64;
    protected const int LargeButtonWidth = 256;
    protected const int LargeButtonHeight = 64;

    protected Sprite renderSprite = null;
    protected Texture backgroundTexture = null;
    protected Rectangle backgroundSource;

    // Screen size
    protected int screenWidth = 0;
    protected int screenHeight = 0;

    // Should the object be centered?
    private bool isCentered = false;
    protected Vector3 centerUpper;

    #region IDisposable Members
    /// <summary>
    /// Clean up in case dispose isn't called
    /// </summary>
    ~UiScreen()
    {
        Dispose();
    }
    /// <summary>
    /// Clean up any resources
    /// </summary>
    public virtual void Dispose()
    {
        GC.SuppressFinalize(this);
        // Dispose the sprite
        if (renderSprite != null)
        {
            renderSprite.Dispose();
        }
        renderSprite = null;
    }

    #endregion
}
```

You will need to add more to this class soon, but this section is the initial code that can actually be compiled successfully. You'll notice that first you need to declare two constants. They will be used during the rendering of your UI. The first one is the rotation center of your texture, but because you do not need to rotate it, an empty vector will suffice. The next parameter is the color you want to render the texture to—a slightly misleading description because it's not the only factor determining color.

Construction Cue

> The value specified in the color constant is equivalent to the solid color white; however, this doesn't mean that when you render your texture it will appear entirely in white.
>
> The integer value of this constant has four separate color components, each a single byte, ranging from 0x0 to 0xff. The components are alpha, red, blue, and green, and in this constant, you are specifying "full power" to each. When the texture is rendered, the colors are not affected at all because you are specifying the full power for each. Say, however, that you declare the constant as 0xff00ffff instead. In this case, there is no red component, so when you render your textures, they have no red in them either. You can use this constant to add varying effects, but for this game, you want the images rendering as they are, with no changes.

The last of the constants are the sizes (both width and height) of the buttons you need for your UI. The two different sizes of buttons, large and small, are represented via these constants. The screens you create will have buttons and will use these constants to determine where (and how) to place them onscreen.

The first three nonconstant variable declarations deal directly with the items you will be rendering for the UI screens. The first is a Sprite object, which is a built-in object to Managed DirectX that greatly simplifies the process of rendering 2D images (sprites) in a 3D scene. This object is generic enough that it can render many different sprites, from many different textures in a single scene. Therefore, you need to include a texture that will be the background of your UI screen. If you do not want one, it can obviously be null. Finally, you might want more than one texture inside the same texture file. The rectangle variable stored here allows you to specify the location of the texture inside the main texture file. For UI screens, it will almost certainly be the same size as the main texture itself. The object is listed as protected, however, so any of the deriving classes can change it if they need to.

You also need to know the screen width and height for your UI screens. This information is mainly so you can calculate the position of various items on the screen (such as buttons) and have them appear in a similar location regardless of the resolution.

The last two variables determine whether the background of the UI screen should be centered onscreen or "stretched" to encompass the entire screen. You only need to know whether the centering should happen (the Boolean variable) and, if so, where the upper-left corner of the texture should go onscreen. This value is calculated during the object's construction, which you get to in just a moment.

Finally, this object needs a way to release the objects that it has created. Notice that the object implements the IDisposable interface, which is a convenient way to mark an object has resources it needs to clean up at a deterministic time. The only object that you actually create for this object is the Sprite class, so that is the only object you need to clean up when you call the Dispose method. You also notice that a SuppressFinalize method is called when you clean up the object. In C#, the Finalize method is declared with the destructor syntax from C/C++, as you saw in Listing 5.6 earlier. The only thing the destructor does is call the Dispose method. When an object goes out of scope and it is ready to be collected by the garbage collector, it first detects whether that object needs to be "finalized." If it does, it places the object on a separate queue, and the object survives the collection. Calling the SuppressFinalize method eliminates this scenario and is more efficient. A good rule of thumb is that if you implement IDisposable, you must always implement a destructor that calls your Dispose method and always call SuppressFinalize in your Dispose method.

Now then, how should you actually create an instance of this class? Well, because it is marked as abstract, you won't be able to do so directly; however, you should still add a constructor because your derived classes will call into the constructor of its base class. Add the constructor (and supporting method) in Listing 5.7 to your class.

LISTING 5.7   Creating the UI Screen Class

```
/// <summary>
/// Create a new UI Screen
/// </summary>
public UiScreen(Device device, int width, int height)
{
    // Create the sprite object
    renderSprite = new Sprite(device);

    // Hook the device events to 'fix' the sprite if needed
    device.DeviceLost += new EventHandler(OnDeviceLost);
    device.DeviceReset += new EventHandler(OnDeviceReset);

    StoreTexture(null, width, height, false);
}
/// <summary>
/// Store the texture for the background
/// </summary>
protected void StoreTexture(Texture background, int width, int height,
    bool centerTexture)
{
```

LISTING 5.7   Continued

```
    // Store the background texture
    backgroundTexture = background;

    if (backgroundTexture != null)
    {
        // Get the background texture
        using (Surface s = backgroundTexture.GetSurfaceLevel(0))
        {
            SurfaceDescription desc = s.Description;
            backgroundSource = new Rectangle(0, 0,
                desc.Width, desc.Height);
        }
    }

    // Store the width/height
    screenWidth = width;
    screenHeight = height;

    // Store the centered texture
    isCentered = centerTexture;

    if (isCentered)
    {
        centerUpper = new Vector3((float)(width - backgroundSource.Width) / 2.0f,
            (float)(height - backgroundSource.Height) / 2.0f, 0.0f);
    }
}
```

The constructor for the object takes the device you are rendering with as well as the size of the screen. The rendering device is needed to create the sprite object and to hook some of the events. Before the device is lost, and after the device has been reset, you need to call certain methods on the sprite object so the sprite behaves correctly. You can add these event-handling methods to your class now:

```
private void OnDeviceLost(object sender, EventArgs e)
{
    // The device has been lost, make sure the sprite cleans itself up
    if (renderSprite != null)
        renderSprite.OnLostDevice();
}
private void OnDeviceReset(object sender, EventArgs e)
{
    // The device has been reset, make sure the sprite fixes itself up
    if (renderSprite != null)
        renderSprite.OnResetDevice();
}
```

These methods are entirely self-explanatory. When the device is lost, you call the OnLostDevice method on the sprite. After the device is reset, you call the OnResetDevice method. If you were allowing Managed DirectX to handle the event handling for you, this would happen automatically. Because you are not, you need to ensure that it happens. Without this code, when you try to switch from full-screen mode or return back to full-screen mode after switching, an exception is thrown because the sprite object is not cleaned up correctly.

The call to StoreTexture in the constructor isn't actually necessary because each derived class needs to call this method on its own—but I use it so you can visualize the process. Obviously, the first thing you want to do in this method is store the texture. Then (assuming you really do have a texture), you want to calculate the full size of the texture. The default for the background textures of a UI screen is to use the entire texture. Notice here that you get the actual surface the texture is occupying and then use the width and height from the surface description to create a new rectangle. Next, you simply store the remaining variables and calculate the upper-left corner of the screen if you will be centering the background texture. You calculate the center by taking the full size of the screen, subtracting the size of the texture, and dividing that in half.

The last thing you do to finish your UI class is to have a method actually render the screen. Add the code in Listing 5.8 to your class to handle the rendering.

LISTING 5.8   Rendering the UI Screen

```
/// <summary>
/// Start drawing with this sprite
/// </summary>
protected void BeginSprite()
{
    renderSprite.Begin(SpriteFlags.AlphaBlend);
}
/// <summary>
/// Stop drawing with this sprite
/// </summary>
protected void EndSprite()
{
    renderSprite.End();
}
/// <summary>
/// Render the button in the correct state
/// </summary>
public virtual void Draw()
{
    // Render the background if it exists
    if (backgroundTexture != null)
    {
        if (isCentered)
        {
            // Render to the screen centered
            renderSprite.Draw(backgroundTexture, backgroundSource,
                ObjectCenter, centerUpper, SpriteColor);
```

LISTING 5.8 Continued

```
        }
        else
        {
            // Scale the background to the right size
            renderSprite.Transform = Matrix.Scaling(
                (float)screenWidth / (float)backgroundSource.Width,
                (float)screenHeight / (float)backgroundSource.Height,
                0);

            // Render it to the screen
            renderSprite.Draw(backgroundTexture, backgroundSource,
                ObjectCenter, ObjectCenter, SpriteColor);
            // Reset the transform
            renderSprite.Transform = Matrix.Identity;
        }
    }
}
```

The first thing you'll probably notice here is that the BeginSprite and EndSprite methods are separate and not part of the main Draw call. I did this intentionally because the sprite object is shared with the derived UI screens, as well as the buttons. Rather than let each separate object have its own sprite class and do its own begin and end calls (which isn't overly efficient), each UI screen will share the same sprite and do all the drawing between a single begin/end block. To facilitate this step, you need these protected methods so the derived classes can control the beginning and ending of the sprite drawing. The begin call ensures that the sprites will be rendered with alpha blending—which means that the backgrounds of your UI and the buttons will be rendered with transparency. You'll see this effect in action in later chapters.

The Draw call itself isn't overly complicated either. Assuming you have a texture to render, you simply need to draw the sprite onscreen, either centered or not. If the sprite should be centered, it's one simple call to the Draw method on the sprite. The prototype for this method is as follows:

```
public void Draw ( Microsoft.DirectX.Direct3D.Texture srcTexture ,
    System.Drawing.Rectangle srcRectangle ,
    Microsoft.DirectX.Vector3 center ,
    Microsoft.DirectX.Vector3 position ,
    System.Drawing.Color color )
```

The first parameter is the texture you want to render, in this case the background of the screen. The second parameter is the location of the data inside that texture. As you can see, you are passing in the rectangle that was calculated in the

`StoreTexture` method, and it encompasses the entire texture. If there were multiple items per texture (as you will see with the buttons soon), this rectangle would only cover the data needed for that texture. The third parameter is the "center" of the sprite, and it is only used for calculating rotation, which is why it uses the constant you declared earlier. You won't be rotating your sprites. The position vector is where you want this sprite to be rendered onto the screen, in screen coordinates, and the last parameter is the "color" of the sprite. (I already discussed this parameter when you declared the constants earlier in this chapter.)

For the centered case, you simply use the "default" parameters for the `Draw` call, and for the position, you use the vector you calculated earlier. The `Draw` call for the stretched case is virtually identical; the exception is that the position vector you are using is the same constant you used for the center vector. That vector resides at 0,0,0, which is where you want the upper-left corner of the sprite to be rendered for your stretched image. Why create a whole new instance of the same data when you can simply reuse the existing one?

The stretched case has an extra call before the `Draw` call, however—namely, setting the transform that should be used when rendering this sprite. Because you want to ensure that the sprite is "stretched" across the entire screen, you want to scale the image. Notice that the calculation takes the size of the texture you will be rendering and divides it by the actual size of the screen to determine the correct scaling factor. Each of these items is first cast to a float before the calculations are performed. The question here is "Do you know why?"

You do so because the items are originally integers, which can produce strange results. For example, in C#, what do you think the following statement will display?

`Console.WriteLine(2/3);`

If you didn't guess 0, well, this caution is for you because you would be wrong. Both operands are integers, so the runtime will take 2/3 (0.3333) and then cast it back to an integer (0). To preserve the fraction, you need to ensure that both of the operands are floats, which is why you do the cast.

**Caution**

Also notice that after the draw is done, the transform is set once more back to the default `Identity`. Because the sprite object is shared, any subsequent calls to `Draw` would have the same scaling effect without it, which isn't the behavior you desire.

With that, the UI abstract class is complete. In the next chapter, you create a UI screen, but before you can do that, you first need a way to render a button.

Designing a Button

You can keep the code for your button in the same `gui.cs` code file you've been using up to this point (which is what the code on the included CD does), or you can put it in its own code file, which you would need to add to your project. Either way, add the class in Listing 5.9 to your code file.

LISTING 5.9   The `UiButton` Class

```
/// <summary>
/// Will hold a 'button' that will be rendered via DX
/// </summary>
public class UiButton
{
    private Sprite renderSprite = null;
    private Texture buttonTextureOff = null;
    private Texture buttonTextureOn = null;
    private Rectangle onSource;
    private Rectangle offSource;
    private Vector3 location;
    private bool isButtonOn = false;
    private Rectangle buttonRect;

    // The click event
    public event EventHandler Click;

    /// <summary>
    /// Create a new instance of the Button class using an existing sprite
    /// </summary>
    public UiButton(Sprite sprite, Texture on, Texture off,
        Rectangle rectOn, Rectangle rectOff, Point buttonLocation)
    {
        // Store the sprite object
        renderSprite = sprite;

        // Store the textures
        buttonTextureOff = off;
        buttonTextureOn = on;

        // Rectangles
        onSource = rectOn;
        offSource = rectOff;

        // Location
        location = new Vector3(buttonLocation.X, buttonLocation.Y, 0);

        // Create a rectangle based on the location and size
        buttonRect = new Rectangle((int)location.X, (int)location.Y,
            onSource.Width, onSource.Height);

    }

    /// <summary>
```

LISTING 5.9   Continued

```
/// Render the button in the correct state
/// </summary>
public void Draw()
{
    if (isButtonOn)
    {
        renderSprite.Draw(buttonTextureOn, onSource, UiScreen.ObjectCenter,
            location, UiScreen.SpriteColor);
    }
    else
    {
        renderSprite.Draw(buttonTextureOff, offSource, UiScreen.ObjectCenter,
            location, UiScreen.SpriteColor);
    }
}
}
```

You'll notice initially that this class is somewhat similar to the UI abstract class you just wrote. There are some important differences, though. First, you should see that there are two textures to store. One is used to render the button in the "off" state, and the other is used to render the button in the "on" state. It's entirely possible (and in this case, probable) that these textures will be the same file, simply with different source rectangles.

The constructor takes as arguments the sprite used to render the button, the textures for both the on and off states of the button, the rectangle sources of each of these states, and the location onscreen where the button will be rendered. Each of these items is stored for later use in the related class variable. The class itself has three other variables it will need, however. One, it needs to know what state the button is in. Because the button will either be on or off, a Boolean value is the natural selection here, with a default of off. Two, you also need to know the exact rectangle onscreen that the button encompasses. At the end of the constructor, you calculate this rectangle by taking the location onscreen and adding the size of the source rectangle. You'll find out why you need this work in a few moments. Third (and finally), because it is a button, you want an event to be fired when someone clicks the button.

The Draw method is simple. Depending on whether or not the button is on, the appropriate sprite is rendered at the correct location. The only real differences between the two calls are the texture that is passed in and the source rectangle. The last thing you need is a way to actually click the button and have its state change based on the location of the mouse. Add the code in Listing 5.10 to your UiButton class.

LISTING 5.10 Handling the Mouse

```
/// <summary>
/// Update the button if the mouse is over it
/// </summary>
public void OnMouseMove(int x, int y)
{
    // Determine if the button is on or not
    isButtonOn = buttonRect.Contains(x, y);
}
/// <summary>
/// See if the user clicked the button
/// </summary>
public void OnMouseClick(int x, int y)
{
    // Determine if the button is pressed
    if(buttonRect.Contains(x, y))
    {
        if (Click != null)
            Click(this, EventArgs.Empty);
    }
}
```

These methods should be called as the mouse moves around the screen and when
the button is clicked. As the mouse moves around, the button state changes
depending on whether the current mouse coordinates are within the rectangle
onscreen where the button is rendered. This is the reason that you needed to calculate the exact screen rectangle where the button would be rendered. If the
mouse button is clicked, you once again check whether the mouse is in the button's rectangle, and if it is, you fire the Click event so that whatever created this
button will know about it.

The UiButton class was small and simple. Combining the UI screen classes with
the buttons, you can create simple UIs for your game.

Summary

During this chapter, you finished the rest of the "supporting" code. You added
your high-resolution timer, a more robust rendering method, and a frame rate
display. You also learned how to create a basic UI that fits in with the rest of your
application.

In the next chapter, you will begin to write the game logic.

CHAPTER 6

Implementing the User Interface

You've spent some time reading through the book now, and I would bet that you're probably anxious to have me stop rambling on about support code and timers. Good news, though, because now you are ready to delve into the actual process of writing your game. You've got your plan, you've got the supporting code, but where to start? It's probably common that you would want to start with the main game first, but doing so would only cause you pain later. Once you had the game engine working, you would need to "retro-fit" the user interface (UI) into the game to start playing. To avoid this potentially costly work, you should first start with the UI of the game. It's relatively simple, and then you can continue the rest of the game unabated.

For this game, you need just three UI screens. The first is the main menu screen, where you can start a new game or exit the application. After making this choice, you see a "character selection" screen, which will really just be a select-your-color screen. Finally, you need a quit-confirmation interface for when the player wants to quit while playing a level. You will do the quit screen in a later chapter because it won't be of any use until you can actually play the game.

In this chapter, you'll learn

- ▶ How to design and display the main menu
- ▶ How to design and display the selection screen

Designing the Main Menu

During the end of the last chapter, you wrote the base class for the UI screens you will be creating in this chapter. The first user screen to create is the main menu. Everything in your game spawns from this screen.

Add a new code file to your project called UiScreens.cs, and add the code in Listing 6.1 to the file.

LISTING 6.1 The MainUiScreen **Class**

```
/// <summary>
/// The main selection screen for the game
/// </summary>
public class MainUiScreen : UiScreen, IDisposable
{
    private Texture buttonTextures = null;
    private Texture messageTexture = null;

    private UiButton newButton = null;
    private UiButton exitButton = null;

    // Events
    public event EventHandler NewGame;
    public event EventHandler Quit;

    #region IDisposable Members
    /// <summary>
    /// Clean up in case dispose isn't called
    /// </summary>
    ~MainUiScreen()
    {
        Dispose();
    }
    /// <summary>
    /// Clean up any resources
    /// </summary>
    public override void Dispose()
    {
        GC.SuppressFinalize(this);
        if (messageTexture != null)
        {
            messageTexture.Dispose();
        }
        if (buttonTextures != null)
        {
            buttonTextures.Dispose();
        }
        buttonTextures = null;
        messageTexture = null;
        base.Dispose();
    }

    #endregion
}
```

The two textures you are using in this class are for the background and the buttons. Although this menu has two buttons, each of the images for these buttons is stored in a single texture (called MainButtons.png in the media folder). This texture contains four different images, the on and off states of the New Game and Quit buttons. The other texture is the background of the screen, which the buttons will sit on top of.

Notice that you've also declared two instances of the actual button classes you designed during the last chapter. These classes handle the actual rendering of the button but are a "child" of this UI screen. You also have declared two events, which correspond to the user clicking on each of the two buttons.

Finally, you have declared the cleanup code for this UI screen. Because you will be creating each of the two textures in the constructor for this object, you need to ensure that you clean up both of them in this object. Also notice that the base class's Dispose method is also called to ensure that the Sprite object is cleaned up as well.

You might be surprised to find that trying to compile this code will fail; I know I was! There is currently no constructor defined for the MainUiScreen object; the default one that is provided has no parameters. However, derived classes must also call the constructor for the base class, and the base class for this object has no parameter-less constructor. Because the compiler does not know what default parameters to pass on to this method, it simply fails. Add the constructor in Listing 6.2 to your class to fix this compilation error.

LISTING 6.2   Creating the MainUiScreen Class

```
public MainUiScreen(Device device, int width, int height)
   : base(device, width, height)
{
    // Create the texture for the background
    messageTexture = TextureLoader.FromFile(device, GameEngine.MediaPath
                   + "MainMenu.png");

    // Mark the background texture as stretched
    StoreTexture(messageTexture, width, height, false);

    // Create the textures for the buttons
    buttonTextures = TextureLoader.FromFile(device, GameEngine.MediaPath
        + "MainButtons.png");

    // Create the main menu buttons now

    // Create the new game button
    newButton = new UiButton(renderSprite, buttonTextures, buttonTextures,
        new Rectangle(0,LargeButtonHeight * 1,
        LargeButtonWidth, LargeButtonHeight),
        new Rectangle(0,0,
        LargeButtonWidth, LargeButtonHeight),
        new Point((width - LargeButtonWidth) / 2,
        (height - (LargeButtonHeight * 4)) / 2));
```

LISTING 6.2   Continued

```
newButton.Click += new EventHandler(OnNewButton);

// Create the new game button
exitButton = new UiButton(renderSprite, buttonTextures,
    buttonTextures, new Rectangle(0,LargeButtonHeight * 3,
    LargeButtonWidth, LargeButtonHeight),
    new Rectangle(0,LargeButtonHeight * 2,
    LargeButtonWidth, LargeButtonHeight),
    new Point((width - LargeButtonWidth) / 2,
    (height - (LargeButtonHeight * 2)) / 2));

exitButton.Click += new EventHandler(OnExitButton);
}
```

The first thing you should notice is the call to base immediately after the constructor's prototype. I just described this part, informing the compiler about the default parameters to the base class's constructor, which allows this code to be compiled. After that, the textures are loaded, using the media path variable you declared in the main game engine. Notice that the StoreTexture method is called after the background texture is created, and notice that false is passed in as the last parameter to ensure the image is stretched onscreen rather than centered.

After the textures are created, the code creates the two buttons for this screen and hooks the Click event for each. As you see, the protected variable renderSprite is passed in to the constructor for the button, so they share the same sprite object as the UI screen. Quite a bit of fancy math formulas determine where the button will be located onscreen and where the button's texture is located in the main texture. Each button is one of the "large" buttons that you defined in your UI class yesterday, so these constants are used to determine where the buttons should be rendered in the texture. The constants are also used to determine the middle of the screen (width - LargeButtonWidth) so they can be centered when they are rendered onscreen.

The image that contains the two buttons (and the two states of each) is a single 256x256 texture. Each button is 256 pixels wide by 64 pixels high. Modern graphics cards work well with textures that are square and that have heights and widths which are a power of 2 (which this texture is) and sometimes will not work at all without these restrictions. Knowing this, it is more efficient to combine the buttons into the single texture that meets the requirements, as you've done here. Common texture sizes range from 128x128 to 1024x1024 and can go even higher for highly detailed models if you want.

You might have noticed that the event handlers you used to hook the button click events used methods that you haven't defined in your class yet. You also need a way to render your UI, so add the code in Listing 6.3 to your class to take care of each of these issues.

LISTING 6.3   Rendering and Handling Events

```
/// <summary>
/// Render the main ui screen
/// </summary>
public override void Draw()
{
    // Start rendering sprites
    base.BeginSprite();
    // Draw the background
    base.Draw();

    // Now the buttons
    newButton.Draw();
    exitButton.Draw();

    // You're done rendering sprites
    base.EndSprite();
}
/// <summary>
/// Fired when the new button is clicked
/// </summary>
private void OnNewButton(object sender, EventArgs e)
{
    if (NewGame != null)
        NewGame(this, e);
}

/// <summary>
/// Fired when the exit button is clicked
/// </summary>
private void OnExitButton(object sender, EventArgs e)
{
    if (Quit != null)
        Quit(this, e);
}
```

The Draw method encompasses all the rendering that is required for the UI screen. Before any drawing is actually done, the BeginSprite method from the base class is called. In this case, simply calling the Begin method on the renderSprite object itself would have given us the same behavior, but encapsulating the call allows us to easily change the behavior later and let all subsequent derived classes get this new, improved behavior.

The base class was designed to handle rendering the background, so to render that, the Draw method is called on the base class. After that, it is a simple matter to call the Draw method on each of the buttons and mark the sprite as finished rendering.

The actual event-handler methods are amazingly simple. Depending on which button is clicked, you fire the appropriate event. However, if you remember from Chapter 5, "Finishing Up the Support Code," when you were designing the button, the only way to get the button to fire its click event was to call the OnMouseClick method on the button. On top of that, you needed to call the OnMouseMove method for the button to highlight correctly when the mouse moved over it. You also want the user to be able to control the UI without using the mouse. To handle these cases, add the three methods in Listing 6.4 to your class.

LISTING 6.4   Handling User Input on Screens

```
/// <summary>
/// Update the buttons if the mouse is over it
/// </summary>
public void OnMouseMove(int x, int y)
{
    newButton.OnMouseMove(x, y);
    exitButton.OnMouseMove(x, y);
}
/// <summary>
/// See if the user clicked the buttons
/// </summary>
public void OnMouseClick(int x, int y)
{
    newButton.OnMouseClick(x, y);
    exitButton.OnMouseClick(x, y);
}
/// <summary>
/// Called when a key is pressed
/// </summary>
public void OnKeyPress(System.Windows.Forms.Keys key){
    switch(key)
    {
        case Keys.Escape:
            // Escape is the same as pressing quit
            OnExitButton(this, EventArgs.Empty);
            break;
        case Keys.Enter:
            // Enter is the same as starting a new game
            OnNewButton(this, EventArgs.Empty);
            break;
    }
}
```

Nothing overly complicated here: you simply add new public methods to your UI screen that mirror the methods the buttons have. When they are called, you simply pass the data on to the buttons and allow them to do the work they need to do. The keyboard keys are a different matter, though. In this case, when the user presses a key, the code checks whether it is Esc, which is the same as pressing the Quit button, or Enter, which is the same as pressing the New Game button. This code allows the user to navigate the game without ever needing the mouse.

Plugging into the Game Engine

That's all there is to the main menu screen for your new game. Now all you'll need to do is plug it in to your game engine, and you'll be well on your way to having a fully functional game. Go back to your game engine class, and add the following two variables to your class:

```
// Is the main menu currently being shown
private bool isMainMenuShowing = true;
// The main UI screen
private MainUiScreen mainScreen = null;
```

These control the main menu UI screen, as well as determine whether this screen is currently being shown. Because the first thing you see when you start the game is the main menu, obviously you want this Boolean variable to default to true, as it does here. Now you actually create an instance of the main menu UI screen, which you do in the OnCreateDevice method. Add the following code to the end of that method:

```
// Create the main UI Screen
mainScreen = new MainUiScreen(device, desc.Width, desc.Height);
mainScreen.NewGame += new EventHandler(OnNewGame);
mainScreen.Quit += new EventHandler(OnMainQuit);
```

You won't be able to compile yet because the event-handler methods haven't been declared yet. For now, you can skip them because you will handle them in a few moments. First, because you've created your main menu screen, you want to ensure that it gets cleaned up when the application shuts down. In the OnDestroyDevice method for your game engine, add the following to the end of the method:

```
if (mainScreen != null)
{
    mainScreen.Dispose();
}
```

This code ensures that the textures and sprite used for rendering this UI screen are cleaned up properly. Speaking of rendering, you probably want to ensure that your screen will get rendered as well. For now, go ahead and remove the code that you used to render the sky box from your OnFrameRender method (don't worry, you'll replace it later) because you don't want the sky box to be rendered while the main menu is being displayed. Replace your OnFrameRender method with the one in Listing 6.5.

LISTING 6.5 Rendering Your Main Menu

```
public void OnFrameRender(Device device, double appTime, float elapsedTime)
{
    bool beginSceneCalled = false;

    // Clear the render target and the zbuffer
    device.Clear(ClearFlags.ZBuffer | ClearFlags.Target, 0, 1.0f, 0);
    try
    {
        device.BeginScene();
        beginSceneCalled = true;

        // Decide what to render here
        if (isMainMenuShowing)
        {
            mainScreen.Draw();
        }
        #if (DEBUG)
        // Show debug stats (in debug mode)
        debugFont.DrawText(null, sampleFramework.FrameStats,
            new System.Drawing.Rectangle(2,0,0,0),
            DrawTextFormat.NoClip, unchecked((int)0xffffff00));
        debugFont.DrawText(null, sampleFramework.DeviceStats,
            new System.Drawing.Rectangle(2,15,0,0),
            DrawTextFormat.NoClip, unchecked((int)0xffffff00));
        #endif
    }
    finally
    {
        if (beginSceneCalled)
            device.EndScene();
    }
}
```

Obviously, your rendering method got a lot less complex with that. Because the UI screen is encapsulated so well, it's only a single method call to ensure that everything gets rendered correctly. You're not entirely finished yet, though. Remember, for the buttons to work correctly, you need to call into the mouse and keyboard methods of the UI screen. You have hooked the mouse and keyboard user input callbacks from the sample framework. Go ahead and add the code from Listing 6.6 to them now to call into the appropriate UI screen.

LISTING 6.6 Handling User Input

```
private void OnMouseEvent(bool leftDown, bool rightDown, bool middleDown,
    bool side1Down, bool side2Down, int wheel, int x, int y)
{
    if (!leftDown)
    {
        if (isMainMenuShowing)
```

LISTING 6.6   Continued

```
            {
                mainScreen.OnMouseMove(x, y);
            }
        }
        else if (leftDown)
        {
            if (isMainMenuShowing)
            {
                mainScreen.OnMouseClick(x, y);
            }
        }
    }
}
/// <summary>Handle keyboard strokes</summary>
private void OnKeyEvent(System.Windows.Forms.Keys key,
 bool keyDown, bool altDown)
{
    // Only do this when it's down
    if (keyDown)
    {
        if (isMainMenuShowing)
        {
            mainScreen.OnKeyPress(key);
        }
    }
}
```

These methods are automatically called by the sample framework whenever the appropriate event occurs. For example, as you move the mouse cursor across the screen, the OnMouseEvent method is called; similarly, the OnKeyEvent method is called if you press a keyboard button. You've now implemented the main menu screen, except for the two event handlers you need to handle the button clicks on the screen. Go ahead and add those now:

```
private void OnNewGame(object sender, EventArgs e)
{
}
private void OnMainQuit(object sender, EventArgs e)
{
    sampleFramework.CloseWindow();
}
```

You can see an example of what the rendered screen would look like in Figure 6.1. Naturally, when you click the Quit button, you want the application to quit. However, what do you want to do when a user clicks on the New Game button? The next step in the process is to show the character select screen; however, you haven't implemented it yet, which is why the OnNewGame handler is still blank. Before you can implement the code there, create this new UI screen.

FIGURE 6.1
The main menu
user screen.

Selecting Your Character (Loopy)

After creating the main menu screen, you are probably an expert at this. The
code is simple, and encapsulated, and it should be easy to create a new UI screen.
This screen will be at least slightly different than the last one, mainly because not
only do you render the UI, but you also need to render the character model.
Before you get to that, however, you should add the class in Listing 6.7 to your
UiScreen.cs code file.

LISTING 6.7 The Character Selection Screen

```
/// <summary>
/// The screen to select the Loopy character
/// </summary>
public class SelectLoopyScreen : UiScreen, IDisposable
{
    private Texture buttonTextures = null;
    private Texture messageTexture = null;
    private UiButton okButton = null;
    private UiButton leftButton = null;
    private UiButton rightButton = null;

    // Events
    public event EventHandler Selected;
    /// <summary>
    /// Clean up in case dispose isn't called
    /// </summary>
    ~SelectLoopyScreen()
    {
```

LISTING 6.7   Continued

```
        Dispose();
    }
    /// <summary>
    /// Clean up any resources
    /// </summary>
    public override void Dispose()
    {
        GC.SuppressFinalize(this);
        if (messageTexture != null)
        {
            messageTexture.Dispose();
        }
        messageTexture = null;
        base.Dispose();
    }
}
```

Obviously, this code looks relatively familiar, so there is no need to go through it again. The only major differences between this and your previous UI screen are the number of buttons (four instead of two) and the fact that the buttons' texture isn't cleaned up in the Dispose implementation. The buttons' texture isn't cleaned up here because the Yes button is shared between this screen and the quit screen. Rather than create two instances of the same texture, which wouldn't be efficient, you create only one, in the game engine. Because the game engine creates the texture, the game engine is responsible for ensuring that it's cleaned up properly.

Before you write the constructor for this class, you should add some more variables, mainly to hold the character mesh. Add these now:

```
private Mesh loopyMesh = null;
private Texture loopyTexture = null;
private Material loopyMaterial;
private Device storedDevice = null;
private PlayerColor loopyColor = PlayerColor.Min;
```

The character's representation consists of the mesh (which holds all the geometry data), the texture (which determines the character's color), and the material. You've seen each of these before when you were loading and rendering your sky box, but this part is loaded slightly differently. Because switching to a different version of Loopy will in reality simply update the texture the model is currently using, you need a reference to the rendering device, which is why you need to store one. The last type you haven't even created yet, but it is essentially going to be an enumeration that contains the possible colors of Loopy. Add a new code file to your project called player.cs now, and add the code in Listing 6.8 to this new code file to declare this enumeration.

LISTING 6.8   The Player Colors

```
/// <summary>
/// The color of the player model
/// </summary>
public enum PlayerColor
{
    Blue,
    Green,
    Purple,
    Red,
    Gray,
    Yellow,
    Min = Blue,
    Max = Yellow,
}
```

Aside from the colors that Loopy can be, you'll also notice Min and Max items in the enumeration. These values are used to determine when you've made it to one "edge" of the enumeration to enable wrapping. For example, if you're currently on Blue and you scroll left, you want to go to Yellow, and scrolling right from there gets you back to Blue. Back in your SelectLoopyScreen class, add the constructor in Listing 6.9.

LISTING 6.9   Creating the Select Loopy Screen

```
public SelectLoopyScreen(Device device, Texture buttons, int width, int height)
    : base(device, width, height)
{
    // Store the device for texture creation
    storedDevice = device;

    // Store the textures for the buttons
    buttonTextures = buttons;

    // Create the loopy mesh
    loopyMesh = Mesh.FromFile(GameEngine.MediaPath + "Loopy.x",
    MeshFlags.Managed, device);

    // Create the loop texture
    CreateTexture(device);

    // Create a material
    loopyMaterial = new Material();
    loopyMaterial.Diffuse = loopyMaterial.Ambient = Color.White;

    // Create the texture for the background
    messageTexture = TextureLoader.FromFile(device, GameEngine.MediaPath +
    "Select.png");
    StoreTexture(messageTexture, width, height / 2, true);

    // Create the ok button
    okButton = new UiButton(renderSprite, buttonTextures, buttonTextures,
```

LISTING 6.9   Continued

```
        new Rectangle(SmallButtonWidth,SmallButtonHeight * 3,
        SmallButtonWidth,SmallButtonHeight),
        new Rectangle(0,SmallButtonHeight * 3,
        SmallButtonWidth,SmallButtonHeight),
        new Point((width - SmallButtonWidth) / 2,
        height - (SmallButtonHeight * 2)));

    okButton.Click += new EventHandler(OnSelectButton);

    // Create the yes/no buttons
    leftButton = new UiButton(renderSprite, buttonTextures, buttonTextures,
        new Rectangle(SmallButtonWidth,0,SmallButtonWidth,SmallButtonHeight),
        new Rectangle(0,0,SmallButtonWidth,SmallButtonHeight),
        new Point(SmallButtonWidth / 2,
        height - (SmallButtonHeight * 2)));

    leftButton.Click += new EventHandler(OnLeftButton);

    rightButton = new UiButton(renderSprite, buttonTextures, buttonTextures,
        new Rectangle(SmallButtonWidth,SmallButtonHeight * 1,
        SmallButtonWidth,SmallButtonHeight),
        new Rectangle(0,SmallButtonHeight * 1,
        SmallButtonWidth,SmallButtonHeight),
        new Point(width - (SmallButtonWidth + (SmallButtonWidth / 2)),
        height - (SmallButtonHeight * 2)));

    rightButton.Click += new EventHandler(OnRightButton);
}
```

First, you take the rendering device and the texture for the buttons and store them for later use. Once that's done, you can create the mesh for Loopy. Notice that when you call the method this time, you're not using the overload that returns the materials. Although it is possible to use this method here as well, because you switch the character's texture at will and define your own material, it's really not necessary, so you might as well just skip it.

After you create the model for Loopy, you create a texture that defines his overall color; however, you also use this method for the Next and Previous buttons. You define the CreateTexture method to handle that in a few moments. You also want to ensure that you have a material for Loopy because you need to add lights to this scene before you're done. Materials define how the lights interact with the object. Because you want Loopy to have the light affect him "normally," you set the material to a simple white material.

The background texture for this user screen is slightly different as well. After it is created, notice that the StoreTexture method is called just as before, but there is one major difference in the call. You don't want the background image to interfere with the selection of Loopy, so you scale down the height of the window when you pass it to this method to only the top half of the screen. The majority of the screen "real estate" displays Loopy when the user selects the one he or she wants.

The button creation is similar to the ones you did in the main screen earlier; you just change the source of the buttons and the locations onscreen and use the small button constants instead. Notice that the left button is in the bottom left of the screen and the right button is in the bottom right of the screen. The Yes button appears directly between them in the center of the screen.

Before you can compile this code, you need to add the `CreateTexture` method from Listing 6.10.

LISTING 6.10   Creating the Loopy Texture

```
private void CreateTexture(Device device)
{
    if (loopyTexture != null)
    {
        // Destroy and re-create a new texture
        loopyTexture.Dispose();
    }
    loopyTexture = TextureLoader.FromFile(device,
        GetTextureFileFromColor(loopyColor));
}
private static string GetTextureFileFromColor(PlayerColor color)
{
    switch(color)
    {
        case PlayerColor.Blue:
            return GameEngine.MediaPath + "LoopyBlue.bmp";
        case PlayerColor.Green:
            return GameEngine.MediaPath + "LoopyGreen.bmp";
        case PlayerColor.Purple:
            return GameEngine.MediaPath + "LoopyPurple.bmp";
        case PlayerColor.Red:
            return GameEngine.MediaPath + "LoopyRed.bmp";
        case PlayerColor.Yellow:
            return GameEngine.MediaPath + "LoopyYellow.bmp";
        case PlayerColor.Gray:
            return GameEngine.MediaPath + "LoopyGray.bmp";
        default:
            throw new ArgumentException("color",
                "An invalid color was passed in.");
    }
}
```

Because this method will potentially be called numerous times, you want to ensure that any loaded texture is destroyed before you create a new one. Then you can create the texture, but the enumeration alone doesn't tell you which texture file you need to use. Another helper method translates the color from the enumeration to a string representation of the filename the texture resides in.

Next, add the rendering code for this screen. You'll find the implementation in Listing 6.11.

LISTING 6.11 Rendering the Selection Screen

```
/// <summary>
/// Render the buttons
/// </summary>
public void Draw(float totalTime)
{
    // Render Loopy Should be "Set the world transform"
    storedDevice.Transform.View = Matrix.LookAtLH(
        CameraPos, CameraTarget, CameraUp);

    storedDevice.Transform.World = Matrix.RotationY(totalTime * 2);

    storedDevice.SetTexture(0, loopyTexture);
    storedDevice.Material = loopyMaterial;
    loopyMesh.DrawSubset(0);

    // Start rendering sprites
    base.BeginSprite();
    // Draw the background
    base.Draw();
    // Now the buttons
    leftButton.Draw();
    rightButton.Draw();
    okButton.Draw();

    // You're done rendering sprites
    base.EndSprite();
}
```

The first thing you'll probably notice is that you aren't overriding the Draw method from the base class but are instead defining your own. You want to make sure that Loopy spins around as the selection screen appears, and you need to know the time from the timer. Remember from an earlier chapter, the View transform defines where the camera is located, where it is looking, and what direction "up" is. In this case, you are using constants that you haven't defined yet, so add these to this class now:

```
private static readonly Vector3 CameraPos = new Vector3(0, 20.0f, -85.0f);
private static readonly Vector3 CameraTarget = new Vector3(0,20,0);
private static readonly Vector3 CameraUp = new Vector3(0, 1.0f, 0);
```

After you set up the camera, you update the World transform to do the rotation of Loopy. Notice that you simply rotate Loopy on the Y axis based on the current time of the application. Multiplying the value by two increases the rotation speed. Next, you can render Loopy just as you rendered the sky box earlier. Simply set the correct texture on the device and the material and call the DrawSubset method on your mesh. Because there is only one subset in the Loopy mesh, there is no need to do this in a loop; you can simply pass in 0 for the attribute ID.

The rest of the rendering method is pretty much the same as the last user screen you did, so there's no need to go through that once more. You do still need to add the event handlers for the buttons you declared earlier, so use Listing 6.12 to add them to your class now.

LISTING 6.12   Handling Button Click Events

```
/// <summary>
/// Fired when the left button is clicked
/// </summary>
private void OnLeftButton(object sender, EventArgs e)
{
    loopyColor--;
    if (loopyColor < PlayerColor.Min)
        loopyColor = PlayerColor.Max;
    // Create the loop texture
    CreateTexture(storedDevice);
}
/// <summary>
/// Fired when the right button is clicked
/// </summary>
private void OnRightButton(object sender, EventArgs e)
{
    loopyColor++;
    if (loopyColor > PlayerColor.Max)
        loopyColor = PlayerColor.Min;
    // Create the loop texture
    CreateTexture(storedDevice);
}
/// <summary>
/// Fired when the ok button is clicked
/// </summary>
private void OnSelectButton(object sender, EventArgs e)
{
    if (Selected != null)
        Selected(this, e);
}
```

The code here is relatively straightforward. Pressing the left button decrements the current color, and pressing the right increments it. Each of these operations handles the wrapping if you've gone past the bounds set for that button and then calls the CreateTexture method to ensure that the updated texture is loaded. When you click the Yes button, it means you've selected which version of Loopy you want to use, and the Selected event is fired. Obviously, you need to add the handlers for the mouse and keyboard events for this screen as well, so you find them in Listing 6.13.

LISTING 6.13 Handling User Input

```
public void OnMouseMove(int x, int y)
{
    leftButton.OnMouseMove(x, y);
    rightButton.OnMouseMove(x, y);
    okButton.OnMouseMove(x, y);
}
public void OnMouseClick(int x, int y)
{
    leftButton.OnMouseClick(x, y);
    rightButton.OnMouseClick(x, y);
    okButton.OnMouseClick(x, y);
}
public void OnKeyPress(System.Windows.Forms.Keys key)
{
    switch(key)
    {
        case Keys.Enter:
            // Enter is the same as selecting loopy
            OnSelectButton(this, EventArgs.Empty);
            break;
        case Keys.Left:
            // Same as pressing the left arrow
            OnLeftButton(this, EventArgs.Empty);
            break;
        case Keys.Right:
            // Same as pressing the left arrow
            OnRightButton(this, EventArgs.Empty);
            break;
    }
}
```

The mouse events behave exactly the same as they did last time, but the keystrokes are slightly different. You still use Enter to go to the next step (in this case, actually playing the game), but there are two new keys as well. Clicking the left and right arrows is the same as pressing the left or right user button.

Updating the Game Engine with This New Screen

Now you're ready to update the main game engine to use this new screen. As before, you want a Boolean variable to determine whether this screen is being shown, as well as an instance of the screen declared with your game engine variables:

```
// The Selection screen for choosing loopy
private SelectLoopyScreen selectScreen = null;
// Is the selection screen currently being shown
private bool isSelectScreenShowing = false;
// Textures that will be shared throughout UI screens
private Texture buttonTexture = null;
```

Naturally, you need to create this object as well. Notice that you've also declared the texture that contains the shared texture for the buttons. Find the spot where you created the main screen in the OnCreateDevice method earlier and add this code directly after that:

```
// Create the textures for the UI screens
buttonTexture = TextureLoader.FromFile(device, GameEngine.MediaPath
    + "buttons.png");

// Create the screen for selecting loopy
selectScreen = new SelectLoopyScreen(device, buttonTexture,
                                  screenWidth, screenHeight);
selectScreen.Selected +=new EventHandler(OnLoopySelected);
```

After you create the shared texture, you use that to create the new UI screen. Because you've now created two new resources, you must not forget to clean them up, so add this code to your game engine's OnDestroyDevice method directly after the cleanup of the first user screen:

```
if (selectScreen != null)
{
    selectScreen.Dispose();
}
// Clean up the textures used for the UI Screens
if (buttonTexture != null)
{
    buttonTexture.Dispose();
}
```

As with the main menu screen, you need to update the render method to ensure that this screen gets rendered as well. Because you already have an if statement for the first screen in that method, you can add this code to the else statement:

```
else if (isSelectScreenShowing)
{
    selectScreen.Draw(timer.TotalTime);
}
```

You must do a similar thing for the OnMouseEvent method when the left button is not down:

```
else if (isSelectScreenShowing)
{
    selectScreen.OnMouseMove(x, y);
}

As well as the when it is:
else if (isSelectScreenShowing)
{
    selectScreen.OnMouseClick(x, y);
}
```

And naturally the OnKeyEvent method as well:

```
else if (isSelectScreenShowing)
{
    selectScreen.OnKeyDown(key);
}
```

Before you add the event handler for the Selected event, remember from earlier that you had to set up a material for Loopy because he is going to be lit during the scene. To this point, you haven't added any lights to your scene yet, so you want to do this now. You use what is called a **directional** light. Think of a directional light as something like the sun in the sky. It is a never-ending light source that shines in a certain direction. Although most modern cards support directional lights, and at least eight in hardware, it's entirely possible that your device might not. The IsDeviceAcceptable method is checked for at least a single directional light so you can be sure that any device created has this support. Lights are lost when a device is reset, so the best place to actually define the lights is in the OnResetDevice method you've already declared. Add the code in Listing 6.14 to this method now.

LISTING 6.14   Setting Up Lights

```
// Set up the light

    // Light 0 will be the level light
    localDevice.Lights[0].DiffuseColor = new ColorValue(1.0f, 1.0f, 1.0f, 1.0f);
    localDevice.Lights[0].Direction = LevelLight;
    localDevice.Lights[0].Type = LightType.Directional;
    // Light 1 will be the select loopy light
    localDevice.Lights[1].DiffuseColor = new ColorValue(1.0f, 1.0f, 1.0f, 1.0f);
    localDevice.Lights[1].Direction = SelectLoopyLight;
    localDevice.Lights[1].Type = LightType.Directional;

EnableLights();
```

As you see here, if directional lights are available, you actually set two different lights, one with a direction of LevelLight, the other with the direction SelectLoopyLight. You haven't declared these constants yet but can do so now:

```
// Light constants
private static readonly Vector3 SelectLoopyLight = new Vector3(0, 0.0f, 1.0f);
private static readonly Vector3 LevelLight = new Vector3(0, -0.6f, 0.4f);
```

You actually have two separate lights for the game, one that is shown when the selection screen is showing and the other during the course of the main game. You might not have the game being rendered yet, but because you're setting up the lights anyway, you might as well do both. As you see, each light has a color of pure white, much like the sprite's color, with only the direction changing between the two. The selection light points directly at Loopy on the z axis. The "main" light points at an angle down. If directional lights aren't available, the ambient color is set to white. Ambient light ensures that everything is the correct "color," but there will be no shading of the objects. Everything is rendered the same color. Ambient color is by far the most unrealistic-looking type of light.

Notice that after the lights are set up, you make a call to EnableLights. Only one of the lights needs to be in use at any given time, so any time the lights are updated, you use this method to turn on the correct light. See Listing 6.15 for the code.

LISTING 6.15   Enabling the Correct Light

```
private void EnableLights()
{
    // Turn on the correct light, turn off the other light
    if (isSelectScreenShowing)
    {
        device.Lights[1].Enabled = true;
        device.Lights[0].Enabled = false;
    }
    else
    {
        device.Lights[0].Enabled = true;
        device.Lights[1].Enabled = false;
    }
}
```

If there isn't any support for directional lights, there is naturally nothing more you can do for this method, so you can just return. Otherwise, you turn on the light at index 1 if the select screen is showing and turn off the light at index 0. If the select screen is showing, you simply reverse which light is currently on. Pretty simple stuff.

You can now fix your initial event handler for creating a new game. Replace the blank method with this one:

```
private void OnNewGame(object sender, EventArgs e)
{
    // Show the select screen
    isMainMenuShowing = false;
    isSelectScreenShowing = true;

    // Fix the lights
    EnableLights();
}
```

After you click the New button, it turns off the main menu by switching to the selection screen and calls the EnableLights method to ensure that the correct light is turned on. You can go ahead and add a blank event handler for the Loopy selection now. You won't actually respond to the event until a later chapter, but you will want to compile your application and see your new screen:

```
private void OnLoopySelected(object sender, EventArgs e)
{
}
```

You can run the application now and select the New Game button to see the Select Loopy screen, as shown in Figure 6.2.

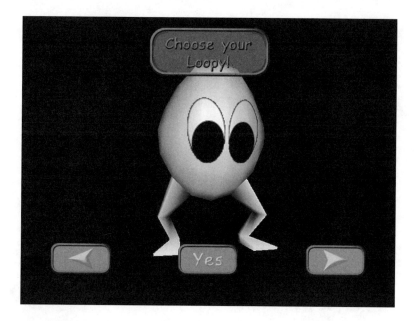

FIGURE 6.2
The select character screen.

Summary

During this chapter, you designed and implemented the major UI screens for the application. With a consistent look and feel throughout the application, and using none of the "ugly" standard Windows dialogs, your game can run in full-screen mode and be fully controllable by the user. Too often, this step is skipped or delayed until the last minute, even though the problem's solution is not something trivial to "add in" later.

In the next chapter, you will write the implementations for the player and the blocks that compose the levels.

CHAPTER 7

Implementing the Player and Blocks

With the user interface screens implemented, you now have a way to get an actual game started from within your game. As you are probably aware, you currently have nothing to play. The implementation of the game logic hasn't happened yet, and you have no code written to maintain any of the game state, outside of the user interface screens.

You need an object that will hold the implementation for both your player and the blocks that compose the level. Obviously, the player class is pretty important because you need something to control to play the game. The blocks are equally important because they are what you use to render the actual level. During this chapter, you will design and implement these features.

In this chapter, you'll learn

- ▶ How to design and implement the player class
- ▶ How to design and implement the block class

Writing the Player Object

One of the more important aspects of the player is to render it onscreen. You probably already realize that you've got the mesh loaded and already rendering in the select-your-character screen, so it wouldn't make sense to go through the entire loading process again. Instead, you use the objects you've already loaded during that screen. To do so, you need to add a few properties to your SelectLoopyScreen class:

```
/// <summary>
/// Return the mesh that represents loopy
/// </summary>
public Mesh LoopyMesh
{
```

```
        get { return loopyMesh; }
    }
    /// <summary>
    /// Return the texture that represents loopy's
    /// color
    /// </summary>
    public Texture LoopyTexture
    {
        get { return loopyTexture; }
    }
    /// <summary>
    /// Return loopy's material
    /// </summary>
    public Material LoopyMaterial
    {
        get { return loopyMaterial; }
    }
```

These properties allow you to take the already loaded mesh, texture, and material for the character and use them in the player's class after you create it. Speaking of which, now is a great time to do that! You've already created a code file for your player object, where you stored the player color enumeration. You can add your player class to that file now. Listing 7.1 contains the initial player class implementation.

LISTING 7.1   The Player Class

```
public class Player : IDisposable
{
    private Mesh playerMesh = null; // Mesh for the player
    private Material playerMaterial; // Material
    private Texture playerTexture = null; // Texture for the mesh
    /// <summary>
    /// Create a new player object
    /// </summary>
    public Player(Mesh loopyMesh, Texture loopyTex,
        Material mat)
    {
        // Store the mesh
        playerMesh = loopyMesh;

        // Store the appropriate texture
        playerTexture = loopyTex;

        // Store the player's material
        playerMaterial = mat;
    }
    #region IDisposable Members
    /// <summary>
    /// Clean up any resources in case you forgot to dispose this object
    /// </summary>
    ~Player()
    {
```

LISTING 7.1   Continued

```
        Dispose();
    }
    public void Dispose()
    {
        // Suppress finalization
        GC.SuppressFinalize(this);

        // Dispose of the texture
        if (playerTexture != null)
        {
            playerTexture.Dispose();
        }

        if (playerMesh != null)
        {
            playerMesh.Dispose();
        }

        playerTexture = null;
        playerMesh = null;
    }
    #endregion
}
```

After declaring the items, you need to render your mesh; you simply store them in the constructor so you do not need to re-create them once more. It's interesting to note that the Dispose method cleans up these items, even though the actual creation didn't occur in this class. You might have even noticed that you never cleaned up these objects from the select-character screen earlier. If you did, bravo; if you didn't, keep this thought in mind. To maintain the best performance, you want to always clean up the objects when you are finished with them.

Because the player's mesh and texture are cleaned up when the player object is disposed, this step takes care of the normal case, but what about the case when you quit the game before the game has actually been loaded and no player object is ever created? You want to ensure that the objects are still cleaned up properly. Because the SelectLoopyScreen class has the references to the objects, you can add a new method there to do this cleanup if the player object hasn't been created yet. Add the method from Listing 7.2 to your SelectLoopyScreen class.

LISTING 7.2   Cleaning Up the Player Mesh

```
/// <summary>
/// Clean up the loopy mesh objects
/// </summary>
public void CleanupLoopyMesh()
{
```

LISTING 7.2   Continued

```
    if (loopyMesh != null)
    {
        loopyMesh.Dispose();
    }
    if (loopyTexture != null)
    {
        loopyTexture.Dispose();
    }
}
```

After the player object is added to the main game engine, you add calls to the appropriate cleanup mechanism. Before you do this, however, you finish up the player object. One of the first methods to implement is the rendering method. The player needs some representation onscreen, so this is a pretty important method. Add the method in Listing 7.3 to your `Player` class to allow the player to be rendered.

LISTING 7.3   Rendering the Player

```
public void Draw(Device device, float appTime)
{
    // Set the world transform
    device.Transform.World = rotation * ScalingMatrix *
        Matrix.Translation(pos.X, playerHeight, pos.Z);

    // Set the texture for our model
    device.SetTexture(0, playerTexture);
    // Set the model's material
    device.Material = playerMaterial;

    // Render our model
    playerMesh.DrawSubset(0);
}
```

There are a few variables and constants in this method that you haven't actually declared yet. Before you go through this method, you should add these to your `Player` class:

```
private const float ScaleConstant = 0.1f;
private static readonly Matrix RotationMatrixFacingDown = Matrix.RotationY(
    (float)Math.PI * 3.0f / 2.0f);
private static readonly Matrix RotationMatrixFacingUp = Matrix.RotationY(
    (float)Math.PI / 2.0f);
private static readonly Matrix RotationMatrixFacingLeft = Matrix.RotationY(
    (float)Math.PI * 2);
private static readonly Matrix RotationMatrixFacingRight = Matrix.RotationY(
    (float)Math.PI);
private static readonly Matrix ScalingMatrix = Matrix.Scaling(
    ScaleConstant, ScaleConstant, ScaleConstant);
```

```
private Vector3 pos; // The player's real position
private float playerHeight = 0.0f;
private Matrix rotation = RotationMatrixFacingDown;
```

Obviously, the player will be able to move around the level, so you need to store the player's current position, which is stored in the `Vector` variable. When you are about to render the player, you translate the player model into the correct location. Notice that you actually use only the X and Z members of this vector: the height of the player (Y) is calculated later to provide a small "bounce" to the player. In addition, the default player model is a bit too large, and it's rotated the wrong way, so you want to both scale and rotate the model at this time as well. You should notice that constants are defined for these transformations so they don't need to be calculated every frame. Also notice that there are four different ways the player can be rotated depending on which direction the player is currently facing.

One of the interesting aspects of these transformations is that the order of the operations is important. In "normal" math, 3x4 is the same as 4x3; however, when creating transformation matrices, this isn't the case. Rotation * Translation is not the same as Translation * Rotation. In the first case, the rotation is performed before the translation, and the effect you want is most likely what you'll get. In the second case, the object is moved (translated) before the rotation is provided, but the center point remains the same, most likely applying the wrong effect.

Aside from that point, the rendering of the player is no different from the other rendering of meshes that you have done earlier. You set the texture to the correct one for the player, you set the material, and finally you call the `DrawSubset` method. This part is virtually identical to the code that renders the character in the selection screen; the only difference is scaling the character to a smaller size.

Moving the Player

There will be a time, normally when the level first loads, when you need to set the location of the player initially. Because the location is a private variable, you include a property accessor for the position, such as this:

```
public Vector3 Position
{
    get { return pos; }
    set { pos = moveToPos = value;}
}
```

What is this moveToPos variable here for? You certainly haven't declared it yet, but you can go ahead and add in the movement variables now:

```
private Vector3 moveToPos; // Where the player is moving to
private bool isMoving = false;
```

Aside from the current physical position of the player, you also want to store the location the player is moving to, which can be different from the place the player currently is. To maintain both of these positions, you obviously need a second variable, as you've declared here. Setting the Position property of the player implies that you will also move there, thus setting both variables in that property. You also want a method to update the moveTo variable as well, so include the method in Listing 7.4 to your Player class.

LISTING 7.4   Updating the Player Movement

```
public bool MoveTo(Vector3 newPosition)
{
    if (!isMoving)
    {
        isMoving = true;
        // Just store the new position, it will be used during update
        moveToPos = newPosition;
        return true;
    }
    else
    {
        return false;
    }
}
```

Here you want to check first whether you are already moving. If you are, there isn't any good reason to try moving again. Assuming you can move, you simply store the position you want to move to (it will be updated in a different method) and return true, which states the move was successful. Otherwise, you return false, which signifies that there was already a movement in progress and the movement wasn't successful.

You also want to rotate and face the direction that the player is currently moving as well. Earlier, the rotation transform constants that you declared had four different values, depending on the direction the player would be facing. Once again, you can store these values in an enumeration, such as the one in Listing 7.5.

LISTING 7.5   Player Direction Enumeration

```
/// <summary>
/// The direction the player model is facing
/// </summary>
public enum PlayerDirection
{
    Down,
    Up,
    Left,
    Right
}
```

You also add a new method to the Player class that will accept this enumeration as a parameter and use it to update the current rotation of the player. Use the method in Listing 7.6.

LISTING 7.6   Updating Player Direction

```
public void SetDirection(PlayerDirection dir)
{
    switch(dir)
    {
        case PlayerDirection.Down:
            rotation = RotationMatrixFacingDown;
            break;
        case PlayerDirection.Up:
            rotation = RotationMatrixFacingUp;
            break;
        case PlayerDirection.Left:
            rotation = RotationMatrixFacingLeft;
            break;
        case PlayerDirection.Right:
            rotation = RotationMatrixFacingRight;
            break;
    }
}
```

As you see here, you are simply taking the enumeration and applying the correct transformation matrix to the stored variable. The methodology to accomplish this task is quite readable but could be done slightly more efficiently at the cost of readability. For example, you could eliminate the case statement completely by using an array of matrix constants in place of the four named directional constants, such as the following:

```
private static readonly Matrix[] RotationMatrices = new Matrix[] {
    Matrix.RotationY((float)Math.PI * 3.0f / 2.0f),
    Matrix.RotationY((float)Math.PI / 2.0f),
    Matrix.RotationY((float)Math.PI * 2),
    Matrix.RotationY((float)Math.PI) };
```

This code would allow you to update the SetDirection method into a single line:

```
public void SetDirection(PlayerDirection dir)
{
    rotation = RotationMatrices[(byte)dir];
}
```

Although it is syntactically identical to the previous "version" of the code, this section is much less readable and only marginally better performing. Sometimes you need to get every bit of performance out of a method, but other times you want it to be more "maintainable." Determining which is the most appropriate quality for a particular scenario is really the crux of good development.

Anyway, movement appears at least partially covered because the current position of the player and the position the player is moving to have been separated, but currently there isn't anywhere that you update the physical position of the player and move it closer to where it's going. Remember, the main game engine has a method called every frame where the game state is updated, and the player's position seems like a great bit of game state that needs updating. Rather than do the work in the game engine class, though, you should add a method to the Player class that will do the work. You find this method in Listing 7.7.

LISTING 7.7   Updating the Player

```
/// <summary>
/// Update the player's position based on time
/// </summary>
/// <param name="elapsed">elapsed time since last frame</param>
/// <param name="total">total time</param>
public void Update(float elapsed, float total)
{
    // Calculate the new player position if needed
    playerHeight = (float)(Math.Abs(Math.Sin(total * BounceSpeed))) *
    MaxBounceHeight;

    if (pos != moveToPos)
    {
        Vector3 diff = moveToPos - pos;
        // Are we close enough to just move there?
        if (diff.LengthSq() > (MaxMovement * elapsed))
        {
            // No we're not, move slowly there
            diff.Normalize();
            diff.Scale(MaxMovement * elapsed);
            pos += diff;
        }
        else
        {
            isMoving = false;
            // Indeed we are, just move there
```

LISTING 7.7   Continued

```
            pos = moveToPos;
        }
    }
    else
    {
        isMoving = false;
    }
}
```

This method uses three constants to govern player movement that you will need to add to your class's declarations:

```
// Maximum speed the player will move per second
private const float MaxMovement = 30.0f;
// Maximum 'bounce' speed
private const float BounceSpeed = 10.0f;
private const float MaxBounceHeight = 0.4f;
```

These constants control the maximum speed the player can move per second (30 units is the default), the speed at which the player bounces, and the maximum height of the bounce. The playerHeight variable, which is used during the translation for rendering, is calculated first. Taking the absolute value of the sine of the total time the application has been running gives us a consistently updating range of numbers between 0 and 1. Multiplying them by the BounceSpeed constant can artificially increase the range (in this case, from 0 through 10). Increasing this constant causes the bouncing to become quicker, and decreasing it has the opposite effect.

After the player's height is established, you need to check whether you're in the position you're trying to move to. If you are, you set the isMoving variable to false because there isn't anything else to do and you are no longer moving. If you are not, however, there are some things you need to do. First, find the difference vector between where you are and where you want to be. The length of this vector tells you how far you need to go to get to where you want to be.

You'll notice that there is a Length property on the Vector, yet this code uses the LengthSq property instead, which is the Length property squared. Actually, the length of a vector is calculated by taking the square root of $x^2 + y^2 + z^2$. Obviously, taking the square root is an "expensive" operation, so eliminating that calculation can only help. You take the squared length variable and see whether that is greater than the maximum distance you could move this frame; if so, simply move there.

If you cannot simply move there, you need to normalize the difference vector. **Normalization** is the act of taking the vector and making it have a unit length (or a length of 1.0f). The "ratio" of the components stays the same; the length is simply scaled to unit size. You can then scale the now normalized difference vector by the maximum movement you can make this frame (based on the elapsed time since the last frame). Adding the newly scaled difference vector to your position moves you toward the position you are trying to get to.

Designing the Blocks

With the code for the player now implemented, you are probably anxious to get it into the game engine and make your player move around the level and play the game. Don't get too far ahead of yourself yet, though: you haven't even designed the level object or the requirements for the level object, namely the blocks that compose the levels. You should design these blocks now. First, add a new code file to your project called block.cs and then add the initial class implementation in Listing 7.8.

LISTING 7.8   The Initial Block Implementation

```
public class Block
{
    private const float BoxSize = 3.0f; // World size of box
    // List of colors available for boxes
    private static readonly Color[] BoxColors = {Color.Red , Color.Blue,
            Color.Green, Color.Yellow, Color.SandyBrown, Color.WhiteSmoke,
            Color.DarkGoldenrod, Color.CornflowerBlue, Color.Pink};

    // List of each possible material object for the box
    private static Material[] boxMaterials;
    // The static mesh of the box
    private static Mesh boxMesh = null;

    private Vector3 pos; // Current position of the box in the level
    private Material material; // Current material color of the box

    // Possible colors of the blocks
    private BlockColor[] colors;
    private int colorIndex;
    private bool canWrap;

    /// <summary>
    /// Create a new instance of the block class
    /// </summary>
    /// <param name="dev">D3D Device to use as the render object</param>
    public Block(Device dev, BlockColor[] list, int index, bool wrap)
    {
        if ((list == null) || (list.Length == 0))
```

LISTING 7.8   Continued

```
            throw new ArgumentNullException("list",
                "You must pass in a valid list");

        // Initialize the static data if needed
        if (boxMesh == null)
        {
            InitializeStaticData(dev);
        }

        // Set the default position
        pos = new Vector3(0,-1.0f, 0);

        // Store the information
        colors = list;
        colorIndex = index;
        canWrap = wrap;

        // Set the default material
        SetBlockColor(colors[colorIndex]);
    }
    /// <summary>
    /// Initialize the static data
    /// </summary>
    /// <param name="dev">D3D Device to use as the render object</param>
    private static void InitializeStaticData(Device dev)
    {
        // Create the mesh for each box that will be drawn
        boxMesh = Mesh.Box(dev, BoxSize, BoxSize, BoxSize);
        // Create the material list based on the colors of the boxes
        boxMaterials = new Material[BoxColors.Length];
        for (int i = 0; i < boxMaterials.Length; i++)
        {
            boxMaterials[i].Diffuse = boxMaterials[i].Ambient = BoxColors[i];
        }
    }
    /// <summary>
    /// Clean up any resources used for rendering the blocks
    /// </summary>
    public static void Cleanup()
    {
        if (boxMesh != null)
        {
            boxMesh.Dispose();
        }
        boxMesh = null;
        boxMaterials = null;
    }
}
```

One of the first things you'll notice is that the various block colors are all stored in a static read-only array. It is entirely possible for you to change these colors and add or remove others. Note that later when you create the level maker, doing so requires changes in there as well, but you haven't gotten there yet. One of the more interesting aspects of block mesh is that you'll notice that it's marked static. Regardless of how many blocks you have displayed onscreen, you only need a single mesh loaded. There's no reason to store many copies of the same data.

Because the blocks are all colored, the colors are controlled through the material that is applied to the rendering device before the block is rendered. Given that the light in the scene is white, if the material is say, blue, only the blue portion of the white light reflects on the block, making it appear blue. There is one material created for each of the block colors, and this array is static much like the colors array because you need only a single instance of this array. Finally, you declare the actual mesh, and again, it is static because you need only one for all blocks.

The actual instance variables for this class are similar to other classes you've already written. Obviously, because there will be many blocks in different places, you want to store the position of this block. You also store the current material of the block so it is colored correctly while rendering.

The last set of variables declared here control how the block reacts in the level. Each level has a minimum of two different block colors that any block can be at any time. You want to store the possible block colors in the order they will be used in this array. You also want to know the index of the color this block currently is. For the more difficult levels, these colors actually "wrap" back to the first index after they make it to the last color. To avoid passing the actual color structure around to specify the colors, you create an enumeration where each color is the index into the color array:

```
public enum BlockColor : byte
{
    Red = 0,
    Blue = 1,
    Green = 2,
    Yellow = 3,
    SandyBrown = 4,
    WhiteSmoke = 5,
    DarkGoldenRod = 6,
    CornflowerBlue = 7,
    Pink = 8
}
```

The constructor for the block takes the list of colors for this level (which is simply stored), the color index for this block (which is also stored), whether or not the colors will "wrap" (again, stored), and finally the rendering device. Assuming the static boxMesh variable hasn't been allocated yet, all the static data is initialized now. Because the boxMesh variable is set in that method, it is called only once.

The InitializeStaticData method uses the Mesh.Box method to create a cube with the width, height, and depth sizes, all using the constant declared earlier. You then set up the possible materials using the array of colors declared earlier. With all the static data now created, you're free to continue creating your individual blocks. You store a default position for the blocks and set the current block color to the correct color based on the list of colors passed in and the index of the color. You haven't actually implemented this method yet, but you can find it in here:

```
private void SetBlockColor(BlockColor color)
{
    material = boxMaterials[(byte)color];
}
```

As you see, it does nothing more than set the material of the block to the correct material based on the current block color. Because the BlockColor enumeration is just an index into the material and colors array, this method is easy to implement. Finally, you need a way to clean up the mesh the blocks use. Because it is a static method, you don't want to implement IDisposable on the Block class, which would cause the block's mesh to be disposed too soon and too often. You need to call the static method once before the application is closed. As a matter of fact, you should go ahead and add the call to your Dispose implementation in the game engine class now, just so you don't forget later. Directly before the device dispose call, add the cleanup for the blocks:

```
// Make sure to clean up the blocks
Block.Cleanup();
```

Because you need to update the position of the blocks, you want to ensure that you have a property to access it, so add this to the Block class:

```
/// <summary>
/// Current Box Position
/// </summary>
public Vector3 Position
{
    get { return pos; }
    set { pos = value; }
}
```

There are still a few methods to add to the Block class, which you will find in Listing 7.9.

LISTING 7.9   Controlling Blocks

```
/// <summary>
/// Retrieve the block color
/// </summary>
public BlockColor BlockColor
{
    get { return colors[colorIndex]; }
}
/// <summary>
/// Sets whether or not the block should pulse
/// </summary>
public void SetBlockPulse(bool pulse)
{
    shouldPulse = pulse;
}
/// <summary>
/// Sets the current total time on a block
/// </summary>
public void SetBlockTime(float totalTime)
{
    time = totalTime;
}
/// <summary>
/// Sets the block velocity after game over
/// </summary>
public void SetBlockVelocity(Vector3 vel)
{
    velocity = vel;
}
public void UpdateBlock(float elapsed)
{
    // Update the block position based on velocity
    Vector3 velocityFrame = velocity;
    velocityFrame.Normalize();
    velocityFrame.Scale(velocity.Length() * elapsed);

    // Move the block
    pos += velocityFrame;
}
```

You obviously need a way to get the color of any given block (which is used to check whether the level was completed), and you also want a way to set whether the block should "pulse." The blocks that are the incorrect color pulse slightly to give the player a visual cue about what blocks still need to be switched. You use the time variable to control the effect of the pulse.

When the game is over, you want all the blocks to "explode" away, to really let the user know he or she failed. You create this explosion by assigning a random velocity to the block. The UpdateBlock method uses a similar method to what you used when you moved the player around. The velocity is normalized and then scaled to the correct velocity based on the elapsed time. The position of the block is then updated with this new velocity. This method is called only after the game is over and only when the level was lost.

These methods all use some variables that haven't been declared yet, so declare them now:

```
private float time = 0.0f;
private bool shouldPulse = false;
private Vector3 velocity;
```

With all of this done, you still need a way to render the blocks. You will find the render method in Listing 7.10.

LISTING 7.10   Rendering Blocks

```
/// <summary>
/// Render the current box using instance settings
/// </summary>
public void Draw(Device dev)
{
    // Set the device's material to the color of this box
    dev.Material = material;
    // Move the box into position
    if (shouldPulse)
    {
        float scaling = (float)Math.Abs(Math.Sin(time * MaxBoxScaleSpeed));
        scaling *= MaxBoxScale;
        float scaleFactor = 1.0f + scaling;
        dev.Transform.World = Matrix.Translation(pos) * Matrix.Scaling(
            scaleFactor, 1.0f, scaleFactor);
    }
    else
    {
        // Move the box into position
        dev.Transform.World = Matrix.Translation(pos);
    }
    // Turn off any texture
    dev.SetTexture(0, null);
    // Draw the box
    boxMesh.DrawSubset(0);
}
```

The rendering of the block is pretty easy to see. To ensure that the block is the correct color, you first set the material. Then you determine whether the block should pulse; if it shouldn't—it's easy—you simply translate the box into position. If the block is pulsing, though, there is a slight difference because you also scale the box. You achieve the pulse effect by quickly scaling the box between normal size and slightly larger using a standard sine wave. After the transformation is complete, you simply use the DrawSubset call to render the box.

The Block class is almost done; you have only one more thing left to do. You need a way to make the block move to the next color when it is stepped on. Include the method from Listing 7.11 in your class.

LISTING 7.11   Selecting Next Block Color

```
public void SelectNextColor()
{
    // Are we at the end, and can wrap?  If so, reset the color index
    if ((colorIndex == (colors.Length - 1)) && (canWrap))
    {
        // Reset color index
        colorIndex = 0;
    }
    // Otherwise, if we're not at the end, increment the color index
    else if (colorIndex != (colors.Length - 1))
    {
        // Increment color index since we haven't gotten to the last one yet
        colorIndex++;
    }

    // Update material
    SetBlockColor(colors[colorIndex]);
}
```

Here you need to first check whether the color can wrap. If it can, and your index is already on the last color in your list, simply reset the index back to the first. Otherwise, if you haven't made it to the last color in your list, simply increment your index to select the next color. If you are on the last color in your list and you can't wrap, you won't do anything. Next, call the SetBlockColor method to update the material for your block.

Summary

In this chapter, you designed and implemented the player and block classes. Although you didn't see the code actually get any use yet, the implementation is complete, and you're ready to work on the level object, which starts bringing everything together.

In the next chapter, you will write the logic to maintain the level.

CHAPTER 8

Implementing the Level Object

The last thing you need to implement before you can update the main game engine to actually play the game is the level object. The level object is probably the most important object in the game because you use it to control virtually everything in the game. The player can't do much without the level, the blocks are all but useless without the level, and there's no way to win (or lose) before the level is there.

You need an object that will hold the implementation for the level. During this chapter, you will design and implement this feature.

In this chapter, you'll learn

- ▶ How to design and implement the level class
- ▶ How to control player movement
- ▶ How to update the level

Implementing the Level

Before you can start implementing the level, you need to add a new code file to your project to hold the level's code. You can call this file `level.cs` and add it to your project now. The initial implementation of your level class appears in Listing 8.1.

LISTING 8.1   The Level Class

```
public class Level
{
    private const float Spacing = 3.35f;
    private const int SquareSize = 13;
    private const float StartingLocation = (Spacing * SquareSize) / 2.0f;

    // The list of blocks that comprise the level
    private Block[] blocks = null;
    // The final color to win
    private BlockColor finalColor;
    // Store the player
    private Player currentPlayer = null;
    // Block index of the player
    private int playerIndex;
    // Total number of moves made so far
    private int totalMoves = 0;
    // Maximum moves allowed
    private int maxMoves = 0;
    // Maximum time allowed
    private float maxTime = 0.0f;
    // The amount of time that has currently elapsed
    private float elapsedTime = 0.0f;
    // Amount of time remaining
    private TimeSpan timeLeft;
    // Is the game over for any reason?
    private bool isGameOver = false;
    // Did you win the game once it was over?
    private bool isGameWon = false;
    // Is this the first game over?
    private bool isFirstGameOver = true;

    // Number of blocks (total)
    private int numberBlocks = 0;
    // Number of blocks that are currently correct
    private int numberCorrectBlocks = 0;
}
```

The game uses the constants here when determining the location of the blocks within the level. Each level contains a maximum of 13 rows of blocks and a maximum of 13 columns in each row. Not every block in this square needs to be filled, but this number is used as the maximum size of the game board. Also, the blocks are evenly spaced, 3.35 units apart. Considering that the cubes themselves are 3.0 units in size, this spacing makes sense because the blocks do not touch. The starting location constant marks where the beginning block is in world space (that is, blocks in row or column zero).

This list contains all the class variables you need for the entire level class. You will not need to add any more later in the chapter. Obviously, you need an array of blocks (which was originally going to be a class of itself before) and the "final" color each block must be turned to to win the level. You also need to know the player object for the game and the index of the block the player is currently standing on.

Because you need to know the total number of moves the player has made, as well as the maximum number of moves allowed on this level, you need to store them as well. Along with the moves, each level also has a strict time limit, which you also need to store, just as you do the amount of time left.

Because you want the blocks to explode when the game is over, and you want to notify the player about the game status, you need to know whether the level is over—and if it is over, whether the level was won or lost. If the game was lost, the first time you want to assign velocities to the blocks to allow them to explode. Finally, you need to store the number of blocks in the level and the number of those that are correct so you can inform the player.

As mentioned in an earlier chapter, the levels themselves are loaded from a file (or the resources of the executable—either is acceptable). Add the constructor in Listing 8.2 to your level class now.

LISTING 8.2   Creating an Instance of the Level Class

```
public unsafe Level(int level, Device device, Player player)
{
    // Check the params
    if (player == null)
    {
        throw new ArgumentNullException("player");
    }

    // Store the current player object
    currentPlayer = player;

    // First we need to read in the level file. Opening the file will throw an
    // exception if the file doesn't exist.
    using(FileStream levelFile = File.OpenRead(GameEngine.MediaPath +
            string.Format("Level{0}.lvl", level)))
    {

        // With the file open, read in the level data. First, the maximum
        // amount of time you will have to complete the level
        byte[] maxTimeData = new byte[sizeof(float)];
        levelFile.Read(maxTimeData, 0, maxTimeData.Length);
        maxTime = BitConverter.ToSingle(maxTimeData, 0);

        // Now read in the maximum moves item
        byte[] maxMoveData = new byte[sizeof(int)];
        levelFile.Read(maxMoveData, 0, maxMoveData.Length);
        maxMoves = BitConverter.ToInt32(maxMoveData, 0);
```

LISTING 8.2   Continued

```
        // Determine how many colors will be used.
        byte[] numColorsData = new byte[sizeof(int)];
        levelFile.Read(numColorsData, 0, numColorsData.Length);
        int numColors = BitConverter.ToInt32(numColorsData, 0);

        // Create the block of colors now
        BlockColor[] colors = new BlockColor[numColors];
        for (int i = 0; i < colors.Length; i++)
        {
            colors[i] = (BlockColor)levelFile.ReadByte();
        }s

        // Get the final color now
        finalColor = (BlockColor)levelFile.ReadByte();

        // Determine if the colors will rotate.
        byte[] rotateColorData = new byte[sizeof(bool)];
        levelFile.Read(rotateColorData, 0, rotateColorData.Length);
        bool rotateColor = BitConverter.ToBoolean(rotateColorData, 0);

        // Create the array of blocks now to form the level
        blocks = new Block[SquareSize * SquareSize];

        int blockIndex = 0;

        for (int j = 0; j < SquareSize; j++)
        {
            for (int i = 0; i < SquareSize; i++)
            {
                byte tempBlockColor = (byte)levelFile.ReadByte();

                if (tempBlockColor != 0xff)
                {
                    Block b = new Block(device, colors, tempBlockColor,
                                        rotateColor);
                    b.Position = new Vector3(-StartingLocation +
                        (Spacing * i), -1.5f,
                        -StartingLocation + (Spacing * j));

                    blocks[blockIndex++] = b;
                }
                else
                {
                    blockIndex++;
                }
            }
        }

        // Get the default player starting position
        byte[] playerIndexData = new byte[sizeof(int)];
        levelFile.Read(playerIndexData, 0, playerIndexData.Length);
        playerIndex = BitConverter.ToInt32(playerIndexData, 0);
    }
    UpdatePlayerAndBlock(true, playerIndex);

}s
```

One of the first things you should notice is the use of the unsafe keyword in the definition of the constructor. This keyword allows you to use things deemed unsafe in C#, such as the sizeof keyword. Soon you will see why this keyword is necessary. After a quick parameter check, and storing the current player object, you actually open a file that will hold the level data, based on the level number. The using keyword here automatically closes the file when you're done with it so you don't need to worry about doing that on your own.

What you're probably thinking now is "What files?" Aside from the fact that numerous levels are included on the accompanying CD, I haven't yet mentioned how these files would be constructed. In Appendix A, "Developing a Level Creator," you will see an application that will act as the level creator for this game. Obviously, level creation is an important aspect of creating a top-notch game, but it isn't central to the 3D game development aspect this book covers, so it resides in the appendix. You might also notice that you never actually check whether the file exists. Add this public method to your class so the game engine can detect whether a given level exists before it tries to load it:

```
public static bool DoesLevelExist(int level)
{
    return File.Exists(GameEngine.MediaPath +
        string.Format("Level{0}.lvl", level));
}
```

The file format itself is a relatively simple binary file. The first four bytes of the file are the maximum time (in seconds) you have to complete the level. It is stored in a float variable, and the constructor creates a new byte array of the size of a float variable. This is the code that required the use of the unsafe keyword. After that byte array is filled, the BitConverter class is used to take that array and convert it back to the float value it is intended to be.

Although multiple parameters are read from the file, each is read in the same way described in the last paragraph. Next, the maximum number of moves to complete the level is read in as an integer, followed by how many colors are used for the level. It should always be at least two and a maximum of four. Recall that the BlockColor enumeration from the last chapter was derived from the byte data type, so after creating an array of the appropriate number of colors, you can read in each color individually, a single byte at a time. You do the same with the final color, which is the next piece of data read in.

Next you need to determine whether the colors will wrap or not and read that in as a Boolean value. The block array size is always the same size, and the next 169 bytes of the file tell you everything you need to know about the blocks themselves. Each byte is either the index into the color array you just created or 0xff, signifying that there is no block at this location. First, create your array of blocks of the appropriate size, and then for each block you find that is a real block, create a new Block class, passing in the array of colors, the color index of the current block, and whether the block colors should rotate. You then assign it a position based on a simple formula using the starting location, the spacing constant, and the row or column index.

After each of the blocks is created, you need to store the index of the block the player is currently sitting on. Because the player is actually on a block now, you want to update the block's color to the next available color. The UpdatePlayerAndBlock method moves the player to the correct position as well as updates the block's state. You find the implementation of this method in Listing 8.3.

LISTING 8.3   Updating Player and Blocks

```
private bool UpdatePlayerAndBlock(bool force, int newPlayerIndex)
{
    // Get the block the current player is over
    Block b = blocks[newPlayerIndex] as Block;

    if (force)
    {
        // Move the player to that position
        currentPlayer.Position = new Vector3(b.Position.X, 0, b.Position.Z);
    }
    else
    {
        // Move the player to that position
        if (!currentPlayer.MoveTo(new Vector3(b.Position.X, 0, b.Position.Z)))
        {
            // The player can't move here yet, he's still moving,
            // just exit this method
            return false;
        }
    }

    // Update the color of this block
    b.SelectNextColor();
    return true;
}
```

This code assumes that the player index is only on a currently valid block. Later, outside of the call to this method in the constructor, you will be checking for valid moves anyway, so the only time it's possible for this index to be invalid is in the constructor. Considering it comes from the file that describes the level (and the level creator does not allow the starting position to be an invalid block), this shouldn't be a problem. The force parameter is only used during the constructor, and it signifies that you want to move the player instantly to the position if true. Otherwise, the MoveTo method on the player is called, and if it is not successful, it returns that "failure" to the caller of this method. At the end of the method, the selected block is moved to the next available color. If the move was invalid, the method will have already returned and will never get to this code. The constructor ignores the return value because there is no way for the method to return any value other than true if the force parameter is true.

Controlling Player Movement

Speaking of having the player move, you should implement this code as well. Considering that sometimes the player cannot move in a specific direction, you want to first check whether the move the player wants to make is valid and then do the move if necessary. Add the methods in Listing 8.4 to your Level class to handle these cases.

LISTING 8.4   **Controlling Player Movement**

```
/// <summary>
/// Can the player move horizontally
/// </summary>
/// <param name="right">Is the player moving right</param>
/// <returns>true if the move can be made; false otherwise</returns>
private bool CanPlayerMoveHorizontal(bool right)
{
    if ( ((playerIndex % SquareSize) == 0) && (!right))
    {
        return false;
    }
    else if ( ((playerIndex % SquareSize) == (SquareSize - 1)) && (right))
    {
        return false;
    }
    // Check to see if there is a piece in the new position
    return (blocks[playerIndex + ((right) ? 1 : -1)] != null);
}
/// <summary>
/// Can the player move vertically
/// </summary>
/// <param name="pos">Is the player moving in the positive z direction</param>
/// <returns>true if the move can be made; false otherwise</returns>
private bool CanPlayerMoveVertical(bool pos)
{
    if ( ((playerIndex / SquareSize) == 0) && (pos))
    {
        return false;
    }
    else if ( ((playerIndex / SquareSize) == (SquareSize - 1)) && (!pos))
    {
```

LISTING 8.4   Continued

```
            return false;
    }
    return (blocks[playerIndex + ((pos) ? -SquareSize : SquareSize)] != null);
}
/// <summary>
/// Update the player's position vertically
/// </summary>
/// <param name="pos">Is the player moving in the positive z direction</param>
/// <returns>true if the move was made; false otherwise</returns>
public bool MovePlayerZ(bool pos)
{
    if (isGameOver)
        return false; // Nothing to do if the game is over
    currentPlayer.SetDirection(pos ? PlayerDirection.Down : PlayerDirection.Up);
    if (CanPlayerMoveVertical(pos))
    {
        // Update the block here
        if (UpdatePlayerAndBlock(false, playerIndex + ((pos) ?
                              -SquareSize : SquareSize)))
        {
            // Update the player index
            playerIndex += (pos) ? -SquareSize : SquareSize;
            // Update the number of moves
            totalMoves++;
            return true;
        }
    }
    return false;
}
/// <summary>
/// Update the player's position horizontally
/// </summary>
/// <param name="right">Is the player moving right</param>
/// <returns>true if the move was made; false otherwise</returns>
public bool MovePlayerX(bool right)
{
    if (isGameOver)
        return false; // Nothing to do if the game is over
    currentPlayer.SetDirection(right ? PlayerDirection.Right :
                             PlayerDirection.Left);
    if (CanPlayerMoveHorizontal(right))
    {
        // Update the block here
        if (UpdatePlayerAndBlock(false, playerIndex + ((right) ? 1 : -1)))
        {
            // Update the player index
            playerIndex += (right) ? 1 : -1;
            // Update the number of moves
            totalMoves++;
            return true;
        }
    }

    return false;
}
```

Two methods check whether a move is valid, one for horizontal moves (moves along the X axis) and the other for vertical moves (moves along the Z axis). Each of these methods takes a single Boolean parameter that essentially determines whether the player is attempting to move along the positive or negative direction of the appropriate axis. Depending on which axis the move is along, the code first detects whether the player is on the bounding edge and whether the player is attempting to "jump off" the edge of the board. If he is, the method returns `false`, signifying that the move is invalid. If the player is moving to a valid location in the square of blocks, then the move is considered valid.

The two moving methods are similar, and they take the same parameters. Obviously if the game is over, there is nothing more to do, so you can simply exit from the method. The movement methods also return Boolean values so the caller can detect whether the move was actually made. (Although the code in this book does not detect the return value, it could be used to enhance the game on your own.) Notice that before the check to see whether the move is valid, the `SetDirection` call is made on the player. Even if the move isn't valid, the player should still turn toward the last direction a movement was attempted. Finally, the move is actually checked for validity. Assuming it is valid, the `UpdatePlayerAndBlock` method from earlier is called. If this move was successful, the player index is updated, the number of total moves is incremented, and the method returns `true`, signifying that the move was made. Any other scenario results in the method returning `false`.

How exactly does the player move, though? Obviously, there needs to be some type of user interaction to make this happen. You have two options that will jump out at you, namely the mouse and keyboard. Although using the mouse is technically feasible, clicking on the correct block to move to could be a bit tricky. Using the keyboard makes the most sense for this situation, so that's what you do here. Just like the user interface screens, the `Level` class needs a method to accept keyboard events. You will find this method in Listing 8.5.

LISTING 8.5 Reacting to User Input

```
public void OnKeyPress(System.Windows.Forms.Keys key)
{
    // Is the player trying to move?
    switch(key)
    {
        case System.Windows.Forms.Keys.Right:
            MovePlayerX(true);
            break;
        case System.Windows.Forms.Keys.Left:
            MovePlayerX(false);
```

LISTING 8.5   Continued

```
            break;
        case System.Windows.Forms.Keys.Up:
            MovePlayerZ(false);
            break;
        case System.Windows.Forms.Keys.Down:
            MovePlayerZ(true);
            break;
    }
}
```

The only keys this method cares about are the arrow keys. If the player presses one of them, the appropriate movement method is called, with the return value ignored.

Handling Level Updates

What about the level itself? Currently there is no way to render the level, so you should add that now. Add the code from Listing 8.6.

LISTING 8.6   Rendering the Level

```
public void Draw(Device device)
{
    // Render every block
    for each(Block b in blocks)
    {
        // It's possible the block may be null
        if (b != null)
        {
            b.Draw(device);
        }
    }
}
```

Wow, that's probably the easiest render method yet. You simply loop through every block in the level and, assuming it isn't null, call the Draw method on it. Because the work for rendering the blocks is encapsulated in the Block class, it makes the rendering of the entire level extremely simple. You're still currently missing one important method that the other classes had, namely a way to update the level state every frame. Add the Update method in Listing 8.7 to your class.

LISTING 8.7 Updating Level Each Frame

```
public void Update(float time)
{
    // Update the currently running time
    elapsedTime += time;

    // Calculate the time remaining
    if (maxTime > elapsedTime)
    {
        timeLeft = new TimeSpan(0,0, (int)(maxTime - elapsedTime));
    }

    // Has the player won the game?
    if (GameWon(elapsedTime))
    {
        // Set the variables and return
        isGameOver = true;
        isGameWon = true;
    }
    else if ((elapsedTime >= maxTime) || (totalMoves > maxMoves))
    {
        // Set the variables and quit
        isGameOver = true;
        isGameWon = false;
    }

    // Update the blocks if the game is over
    if ((isGameOver) && (!isGameWon))
    {
        // If this is the first time the game is over,
        // randomly assign a velocity to each block
        if (isFirstGameOver)
        {
            isFirstGameOver = false;
            Random r = new Random();
            int index = 0;
            foreach(Block b in blocks)
            {
                if ((b != null) && (playerIndex != index))
                {
                    // Assign a random velocity
                    float x, y, z = 0.0f;
                    x = (float)r.NextDouble() * Block.MaximumVelocity;
                    y = (float)r.NextDouble() * (Block.MaximumVelocity * 2);
                    z = (float)r.NextDouble() * Block.MaximumVelocity;
                    if (r.Next(50) > 25) { x *= -1; }
                    if (r.Next(50) > 25) { y *= -1; }
                    if (r.Next(50) > 25) { z *= -1; }
                    b.SetBlockVelocity(new Vector3(x, y, z));
                }
                index++;
            }
        }
        foreach(Block b in blocks)
        {
```

LISTING 8.7   Continued

```
            if (b != null)
            {
                b.UpdateBlock(time);
            }
        }
    }

}
```

The `time` parameter passed into this method is the time that has passed since the last frame was rendered or, more specifically, the time that has elapsed since the last call to this method. The current total elapsed time is incremented by this time, and the time remaining to solve the level is calculated (assuming you haven't already run out of time). Obviously, you should check whether the game is won before you check whether the player has lost. (You always want to give the player the benefit of the doubt.) The implementation of this method will be coming in just a few moments.

If the player hasn't won the game yet, you should check whether she's lost the game. The game is lost if the elapsed time exceeds the maximum time for the level or if the total number of moves exceeds the maximum number for the level. The next portion of code causes the blocks to explode off the screen in a nifty effect if the level is lost. First, you need to see whether this is the first time you've made it into this loop, and if it is, you randomly assign a velocity to each block with the exception of the one the player is currently on. After you set the velocity on the blocks, each subsequent call simply calls the `UpdateBlock` method to move the blocks based on the current velocity.

You still need to implement the `GameWon` method, so use the code in Listing 8.8 for this method.

LISTING 8.8   Checking Whether the Game Is Won

```
private bool GameWon(float totalTime)
{
    bool won = true;
    numberBlocks = 0;
    numberCorrectBlocks = 0;
    // Just scroll through each block and see if it is the correct color
    for each(Block b in blocks)
    {
        // Is there a block here?
        if (b != null)
        {
            numberBlocks++;
            b.SetBlockTime(totalTime);
            // Is it the right color?
```

LISTING 8.8   Continued

```
                    if (b.BlockColor != finalColor)
                    {
                        // Nope, you haven't won yet.
                        b.SetBlockPulse(true);
                        won = false;
                    }
                    else
                    {
                        b.SetBlockPulse(false);
                        numberCorrectBlocks++;
                    }
                }
            }

        return won;
}
```

The time is passed into this method because while this code scans through the blocks, the time is updated to allow the pulsating code to work correctly. Each time this method is called (which is every frame), the number of blocks and the number of correct blocks are both reset to zero, the method assumes the game is won, and then each block in the level is examined. If there is a block in any given position, the number of blocks is incremented and the time set. If the color of the block is correct (meaning it is equal to the final color), the pulse of the block is turned off, and the number of correct blocks is incremented. If the block isn't the correct color, the pulse is turned on, and the won variable is set to false to signify that the level hasn't been won yet. After each block is examined, the method returns either true if the level has been won or false otherwise and leaves the number of blocks and the number of correct blocks' variables set correctly.

The last thing that you need to add to your Level class is public accessibility for the members which the game engine will need to use. Add the properties in Listing 8.9 to the class to facilitate this.

LISTING 8.9   Public Properties

```
/// <summary>
/// Total number of blocks
/// </summary>
public int NumberBlocks
{
    get { return numberBlocks; }
}
/// <summary>
/// Total number of correct blocks
/// </summary>
public int NumberCorrectBlocks
```

LISTING 8.9   Continued

```
{
    get { return numberCorrectBlocks; }
}
/// <summary>
/// Get the time remaining in the level
/// </summary>
public string TimeRemaining
{
    get { return timeLeft.ToString(); }
}
/// <summary>
/// The total number of moves taken
/// </summary>
public int TotalMoves
{
    get { return totalMoves; }
}
/// <summary>
/// The total number of moves allowed
/// </summary>
public int MaximumMoves
{
    get { return maxMoves; }
}
/// <summary>
/// Determines if the game is over for any reason
/// </summary>
public bool IsGameOver
{
    get { return isGameOver; }
}
/// <summary>
/// Determines if the game has been won
/// </summary>
public bool IsGameWon
{
    get { return isGameWon; }
}
```

These standard properties really need no further explanation.

Summary

During this chapter, you designed and implemented the level class. The level controls much of the actual game-play logic. All you have left to do for this game is hook everything together. In my opinion, that's always the best part. You finally get to see your hard work in a complete game.

In the next chapter, you will hook the game objects into the game engine to make the actual game work.

CHAPTER 9

Putting the Pieces Together

With all the pieces of the game essentially done now, the last thing you need to do is combine them into the final game. Much of the game engine was designed in earlier chapters, but until you put everything into the game engine, it really isn't doing anything. You also need to design and implement the final user interface screen to allow you to quit the game once you've started. Get excited: finishing a game is always the most exhilarating part.

In this chapter, you'll learn

▶ How to add a player to the game engine

▶ How to add a level to the game engine

▶ How to design and implement a quit screen

Including the Player

Before you create the player object, do you remember back a few chapters ago when you were first rendering the sky box for the level? Well, the code is probably still there in the OnCreateDevice method of the game engine, but that probably isn't where it should be. You don't need to create the sky box, or the player, or the level until the user selects the character he will be using in the game. You left the event handler for this user interface screen "empty" before, so you should fill it now, using the method in Listing 9.1.

LISTING 9.1   Selecting Your Character Event Handler

```
private void OnLoopySelected(object sender, EventArgs e)
{
    SelectLoopyScreen screen = sender as SelectLoopyScreen;

    System.Diagnostics.Debug.Assert(screen != null, GameName,
        "The selection screen should never be null.");

    // Create the graphics items
    CreateGraphicObjects(screen);

    // And not showing the select screen
    isSelectScreenShowing = false;

    // Fix the lights
    EnableLights();
}
```

First, you want to get the `SelectLoopyScreen` object that fired this event, which you can do from the `sender` variable. Considering this event should only be fired from this object, it should never return `null` (thus the `Assert` here).

You might be wondering what an assert is or why you would ever want to use such a thing. An **assert** is essentially an evaluation of a condition that should never be true, and if that condition *is* true, there is a big problem. What the `Assert` method does is, in debug builds, check whether that condition is `true`. If it isn't, execution proceeds normally; however, if it is `true`, execution halts and a dialog appears with the message you've included.

Using this functionality can help uncover many common coding mistakes.

The "graphics" items are created next (you will implement this method presently), the select screen should no longer be showing, and the lights should now be enabled for the level. If you remember from earlier, this method keys off the `isSelectScreenShowing` variable, so with it `false`, it enables the light for the level.

Now, you should remove the code that creates the sky-box mesh from the `InitializeGraphics` method and add the method you are missing into your game engine code. You will find this method in Listing 9.2.

LISTING 9.2   Creating Graphics Objects

```
private void CreateGraphicObjects(SelectLoopyScreen screen)
{
    // No need to create the level mesh
    if (levelMesh == null)
    {
        // Create the mesh for the level
```

LISTING 9.2   Continued

```
            ExtendedMaterial[] mtrls;
            levelMesh = Mesh.FromFile(MediaPath + "level.x", MeshFlags.Managed,
                                device, out mtrls);

            // Store the materials for later use, and create the textures
            if ((mtrls != null) && (mtrls.Length > 0))
            {
                levelTextures = new Texture[mtrls.Length];
                for (int i = 0; i < mtrls.Length; i++)
                {
                    // Create the texture
                    levelTextures[i] = TextureLoader.FromFile(device, MediaPath +
                        mtrls[i].TextureFilename);
                }
            }
        }

    // Create our player object
    player = new Player(screen.LoopyMesh, screen.LoopyTexture,
                        screen.LoopyMaterial);
}
```

The code to create the sky-box mesh is the same as it was before, but now it is created only once. Because the mesh is never destroyed until the end of the application, creating it more than once is just a waste of time. When the levelMesh member is null, you can assume that the mesh hasn't been created yet and you can create it the first time. After that, the player object is created using the information from the Select Loopy screen to get the graphical content.

Do you remember earlier when the CleanupLoopy method was created in the Select Loopy screen? You did so when the player object wasn't created yet, and you were told that you would add a call to this method when the player object was added to the game engine. Well, now it's time to oblige. In your OnDestroyDevice overload, add the code from Listing 9.3 directly after your user screen cleanup methods.

LISTING 9.3   Cleaning Up Players

```
// If the player is null, and you are on the select screen, clean up
// those meshes as well
if ((player == null) && (selectScreen != null))
{
    selectScreen.CleanupLoopyMesh();
}
// Clean up the player
if (player != null)
{
    player.Dispose();
}
```

You've been working on the player for a while now, and you're probably thinking to yourself, "Self, what else do I need to do with the player?" Well, you need to declare it sometime, so how about now?

```
// The player's object
private Player player = null;
```

The only things left are drawing the player and updating the player. The update is simple because you already have a method in the game engine that will be called every frame. Add this section of code to your OnFrameMove method:

```
if ((isQuitMenuShowing) || (isMainMenuShowing) || (isSelectScreenShowing))
{
    return; // Nothing to do
}

// Update the player
player.Update(elapsedTime, timer.TotalTime);
```

Obviously, if one of the user interface screens is showing, you don't need to update the player. If they are not showing, though, you simply call the player's update method. You probably noticed that you haven't declared the isQuitMenuShowing member variable yet, so go ahead and do that now:

```
// Is the quit menu showing?
private bool isQuitMenuShowing = false;
```

You won't actually use this variable until later when you design the user interface screen for quitting, but this code allows you to compile for now. The last thing you need to do with the player is render it onscreen at the appropriate time. You also want to add the code back for rendering the sky box. Go back to the OnFrameRender method in your game engine, and notice that each of the "rendering" methods is encapsulated into a single call depending on the game state; the correct object is rendered depending on which state the game is currently in. Because no single object is used to render the game scene, you want a separate method to render the game scene so that you don't clutter your render method. Add this final else clause to your render method:

```
else
{
    RenderGameScene();
}
```

You then need to add the implementation of this method, which you will find in Listing 9.4.

LISTING 9.4   Rendering Your Game

```
private void RenderGameScene(Device device, double appTime)
{
    // First render the level mesh, but before that is done, you need
    // to turn off the zbuffer. This isn't needed for this drawing
    device.RenderState.ZBufferEnable = false;
    device.RenderState.ZBufferWriteEnable = false;

    device.Transform.World = Matrix.Scaling(15,15,15) *
                             Matrix.Translation(0,22,0);
    device.RenderState.Lighting = false;
    for(int i = 0; i < levelTextures.Length; i++)
    {
        device.SetTexture(0, levelTextures[i]);
        levelMesh.DrawSubset(i);
    }

    // Turn the zbuffer back on
    device.RenderState.ZBufferEnable = true;
    device.RenderState.ZBufferWriteEnable = true;

    // Now, turn back on our light
    device.RenderState.Lighting = true;

    // Render the player
    player.Draw(device, (float)appTime);

}
```

The first part of this method is naturally the replacement code for rendering the sky box that you removed earlier this chapter. The only new code here is the addition of the render call to the player.

Hooking Up the Level

The rest of the interaction with the player has already been implemented inside the code for the Level object, so for now you are done with this object. However, you do need to add the level into the game engine. Go ahead and declare some variables for it:

```
// The current level
private Level currentLevel = null;
// What level are we currently playing
private int levelNumber = 1;
// Is the level currently being loaded
private bool isLoadingLevel = false;
// Current camera position
private Vector3 currentCameraPosition;
// The amount of time the 'winning' screen is displayed
private float winningLevelTime = 0.0f;
```

The first two variables are pretty obvious: you need to know which level number you're currently playing as well as the level object itself. You also want to do a quick "flyby" of the level before you actually allow the player to start playing, which is controlled by the Boolean variable and the current camera position. Finally, after a level is finished, you want a message notifying the player to show onscreen for some period of time.

You should create the initial level at the same time you create the player object, directly after the character selection screen. So at the end of the `CreateGraphicsObjects` method, add a call to the method that will control the creation of the level:

```
// Load the current level
LoadCurrentLevel();
```

You can find the implementation of this method in Listing 9.5.

LISTING 9.5   Loading the Current Level

```
private void LoadCurrentLevel()
{
    // Load our level
    currentLevel = new Level(levelNumber, device, player);

    // Create a random camera location
    CreateRandomCamera();

    // Now we're loading the level
    isLoadingLevel = true;
    winningLevelTime = 0.0f;
}
```

As the name implies, the `CreateRandomCamera` method creates a random starting location of the camera, which then "flies" into position. You set the loading level variable to `true`, so later you'll know if the user can play the level yet. Because you obviously don't win the level when it is first loaded, you can reset the time here as well. You'll find the implementation for the camera method in Listing 9.6.

LISTING 9.6   Creating a Random Camera Location

```
private void CreateRandomCamera()
{
    Random r = new Random();

    currentCameraPosition = new Vector3(
        (float)r.NextDouble() * 5.0f + 15.0f,
        (float)r.NextDouble() * 10.0f + 120.0f,
        (float)r.NextDouble() * 5.0f + 15.0f
        );
```

LISTING 9.6   Continued

```
    // Randomly switch
    if (r.Next(100) > 49)
    {
        currentCameraPosition.X *= -1;
    }
    // Randomly switch
    if (r.Next(100) > 49)
    {
        currentCameraPosition.Z *= -1;
    }
}
```

There's nothing unusual going on in this method. You use the random number generator to generate a random location, always very high above the level. Because the random number generator only returns positive numbers, the X and Z axes are also randomly changed to negative.

As with the player, you also need to ensure that the level and now the camera are updated every frame. You can finish up the OnFrameMove method by including the code in Listing 9.7 at the end of the method.

LISTING 9.7   Updating the Level and Camera

```
// Make sure the level isn't started until the camera moves to position
UpdateCamera(elapsedTime);

// See if we need to keep showing the 'you win' screen
if ((currentLevel.IsGameWon) && (winningLevelTime > ShowWinningTime))
{
    // Make sure the new level exists
    if (Level.DoesLevelExist(levelNumber + 1))
    {
        // Reset the variables
        levelNumber++;
        LoadCurrentLevel();
    }
}

// If the level is won, then increment our timing for showing the screen
if (currentLevel.IsGameWon)
{
    winningLevelTime += elapsedTime;
}

// Update the current level
if (!isLoadingLevel)
{
    currentLevel.Update(elapsedTime);
}
```

The UpdateCamera method is used to fly the camera into position (if it isn't already there), and you need to implement this method. Skipping that for a moment, what else happens here? For one, you can detect whether the level has been won and, if it has, whether the winning message has been shown for long enough. You need to declare the constant used here as well:

```
private const float ShowWinningTime = 2.5f;
```

This value shows the winning message for two and a half seconds; feel free to adjust it to suit your needs. Assuming the level has been won for more than two and a half seconds, you can then check whether the next level exists and, if it does, increment the level counter and load the new level. This part resets all the game states and the winning time.

Otherwise, the only thing you want to do is update the winning time variable if the level has been won and call the Update method on your level object, which updates all the states in the level. You still need to implement the camera method, however, and you find that in Listing 9.8.

LISTING 9.8 Implementing a Camera Flyby

```
private void UpdateCamera(float elapsedTime)
{
    if (currentCameraPosition != CameraDefaultLocation)
    {
        Vector3 diff = CameraDefaultLocation - currentCameraPosition;
        // Are we close enough to just move there?
        if (diff.Length() > (MaximumSpeed * elapsedTime))
        {
            // No we're not, move slowly there
            diff.Normalize();
            diff.Scale(MaximumSpeed * elapsedTime);
            currentCameraPosition += diff;
        }
        else
        {
            // Indeed we are, just move there
            currentCameraPosition = CameraDefaultLocation;
        }

        // Set the view transform now
        device.Transform.View = Matrix.LookAtLH(currentCameraPosition,
            CameraDefaultLookAtLocation, CameraUp);
    }
    else
    {
        isLoadingLevel = false;
    }
}
```

First, you notice a few constants that haven't been declared yet, so you want to do that now:

```
// Camera constants
private const float MaximumSpeed = 30.0f;
private static readonly Vector3 CameraDefaultLocation = new Vector3(
    -2.5f, 25.0f, -55.0f);
private static readonly Vector3 CameraDefaultLookAtLocation = new Vector3(
    -2.5f, 0.0f, 0.0f);
private static readonly Vector3 CameraUp = new Vector3(0,1,0);
```

These constants define where the camera's final destination should be, as well as where the camera will be looking, and the up direction of the camera. (The latter two won't change.) The movement code is similar to what was used to move the player into the correct position. If the camera is not already in the correct position, it is moved directly into position (if is close enough to move there this frame). If it isn't close enough to move there directly, the camera is moved toward the final location at a rate of 30 units per second. After the camera is in place, the isLoadingLevel variable is set to false, and the game play can begin.

Notice that if the camera's position changes, the View transform on the device is updated as well. You originally set this transform in the OnResetDevice method with some default values. Because the camera can be moving when the device is reset, you want to update the camera back to the correct position, not the default values you have there now. Replace the setting of the View transform in the OnResetDevice method with the following:

```
// Set the view transform now
device.Transform.View = Matrix.LookAtLH(currentCameraPosition,
    CameraDefaultLookAtLocation, CameraUp);
```

As you see, this is the same transform you set in the UpdateCamera method; it's now used when the device is reset as well. You've almost got everything implemented, but before you finish the rest of the game engine, there's one important thing to take care of.

Implementing the Quit Screen

You've already designed two user interface screens in earlier chapters, so this part will be a cakewalk to you, but you must implement this last screen. While the game is being played, you want the user to be asked whether she is sure that she wants to quit if she presses the Escape key. If the user accidentally presses the key, you won't lose all the hard work on the level. Go back to your UiScreen.cs code file and add the class in Listing 9.9.

LISTING 9.9   The Quit User Screen

```
public class QuitScreen : UiScreen, IDisposable
{
    private Texture buttonTextures = null;
    private Texture messageTexture = null;
    private UiButton yesButton = null;
    private UiButton noButton = null;
    // Events
    public event EventHandler QuitGame;
    public event EventHandler Cancel;

    /// <summary>
    /// Create the quit screen
    /// </summary>
    public QuitScreen(Device device, Texture buttons, int width, int height)
        : base(device, width, height)
    {
        // Create the textures for the buttons
        buttonTextures = buttons;

        // Create the texture for the background
        messageTexture = TextureLoader.FromFile(device, GameEngine.MediaPath
                                            + "QuitConfirm.png");
        StoreTexture(messageTexture, width, height, true);

        // Calculate the spacing for the buttons
        float horizSpacing = (float)(width - (SmallButtonWidth * 3))
            / 2.0f;

        // Create the yes/no buttons
        yesButton = new UiButton(renderSprite, buttonTextures, buttonTextures,
            new Rectangle(SmallButtonWidth,SmallButtonHeight * 3,
            SmallButtonWidth,SmallButtonHeight),
            new Rectangle(0,SmallButtonHeight * 3,
            SmallButtonWidth,SmallButtonHeight),
            new Point((int)horizSpacing,
            (int)(centerUpper.Y + backgroundSource.Height)
            - (SmallButtonHeight * 2)));

        yesButton.Click += new EventHandler(OnYesButton);

        noButton = new UiButton(renderSprite, buttonTextures, buttonTextures,
            new Rectangle(SmallButtonWidth,SmallButtonHeight * 2,
            SmallButtonWidth,SmallButtonHeight),
            new Rectangle(0,SmallButtonHeight * 2,
            SmallButtonWidth,SmallButtonHeight),
            new Point(width - ((int)horizSpacing + SmallButtonWidth),
            (int)(centerUpper.Y + backgroundSource.Height)
            - (SmallButtonHeight * 2)));

        noButton.Click += new EventHandler(OnNoButton);
    }
}
```

The variables needed here are similar to what you used in the Select Loopy screen, with one button less. You also have events for each of the buttons that can be clicked. In the constructor, the texture for the buttons is stored, and a new texture for the background is created and stored. You create the buttons and calculate the position to center the buttons inside the background texture. The event handlers used to handle the button clicks simply fire the associated event for this class:

```
private void OnYesButton(object sender, EventArgs e)
{
    if (QuitGame != null)
        QuitGame(this, EventArgs.Empty);
}
private void OnNoButton(object sender, EventArgs e)
{
    if (Cancel != null)
        Cancel(this, EventArgs.Empty);
}
```

Obviously, you still need to add the cleanup code for the quit screen, which appears in Listing 9.10.

LISTING 9.10   Cleaning Up the Quit User Screen

```
/// <summary>
/// Clean up in case dispose isn't called
/// </summary>
~QuitScreen()
{
    Dispose();
}
/// <summary>
/// Clean up any resources
/// </summary>
public override void Dispose()
{
    GC.SuppressFinalize(this);
    if (messageTexture != null)
    {
        messageTexture.Dispose();
    }
    messageTexture = null;
    buttonTextures = null;
    base.Dispose();
}
```

This code is the same as that for the Select Loopy screen. The last thing you need for your quit screen is the rendering method and the user input handlers. You find these methods in Listing 9.11.

LISTING 9.11 Finishing Up the Quit User Screen

```
public override void Draw()
{
    // Start rendering sprites
    base.BeginSprite();
    // Draw the background
    base.Draw();
    // Now the buttons
    yesButton.Draw();
    noButton.Draw();

    // You're done rendering sprites
    base.EndSprite();
}
public void OnMouseMove(int x, int y)
{
    yesButton.OnMouseMove(x, y);
    noButton.OnMouseMove(x, y);
}
public void OnMouseClick(int x, int y)
{
    yesButton.OnMouseClick(x, y);
    noButton.OnMouseClick(x, y);
}
public void OnKeyPress(System.Windows.Forms.Keys key)
{
    switch(key)
    {
        case Keys.Escape:
        case Keys.N:
            // Escape will dismiss the dialog
            OnNoButton(this, EventArgs.Empty);
            break;
        case Keys.Enter:
        case Keys.Y:
            // Same as pressing the Yes Button
            OnYesButton(this, EventArgs.Empty);
            break;
    }
}
```

Rendering is accomplished as it was in the other user screens: the sprite is begun (with alpha blending because the background of the dialog is transparent), the background is drawn, the buttons are drawn, and the sprite is ended. The mouse input is simply passed directly to the buttons, and the keyboard input is mapped into the appropriate button.

You can see the quit screen in action in Figure 9.1.

FIGURE 9.1
Do you really want to quit?

Finishing Up

Figure 9.1 has some text being rendered that you haven't added yet. Obviously, you want the user to know the current state of the game and how close he is to winning (or losing)! You need to declare a new font variable to render this text, as well as one for the quit screen you just created:

```
// The main game font
private Direct3D.Font gameFont = null;
// The UI Screen for quitting
private QuitScreen quitScreen = null;
```

Naturally, you must also create these objects. In your `OnCreateDevice` method directly before the `OnResetDevice` call, add the following code to create these objects:

```
gameFont = new Direct3D.Font(device, new System.Drawing.Font(this.Font.Name,
                                                               28.0f));
// Create the screen for the UI Screen
quitScreen = new QuitScreen(device, buttonTexture, screenWidth, screenHeight);
quitScreen.Cancel += new EventHandler(OnQuitScreenCancel);
quitScreen.QuitGame += new EventHandler(OnQuitScreenQuit);
```

The quit screen object hooks the two events and uses these event handlers:

```
private void OnQuitScreenCancel(object sender, EventArgs e)
{
    // The game is paused, they clicked no, unpause
    sampleFramework.Pause(false, false);
    isQuitMenuShowing = false;
}
private void OnQuitScreenQuit(object sender, EventArgs e)
{
    // The game is paused, they want to quit, quit to main screen
    isMainMenuShowing = true;
    isQuitMenuShowing = false;
    sampleFramework.Pause(false, false);
    // Reset the level back to the first
    levelNumber = 1;
}
```

When the quit screen is showing, you obviously don't want the user to be punished, so you pause the timer during this time. If she clicks the No button and does not want to quit, all you need to do is restart the timer and reset the variable. However, if she clicks the Yes button and does want to quit, not only do you do these things, but you also reset the level back to one and return to the main menu screen. This move allows the player to restart a new game.

You need to ensure that these objects are cleaned up correctly, so add the cleanup code to your OnDestroyDevice method:

```
if (quitScreen != null)
{
    quitScreen.Dispose();
}
// Clean up the game font
if (gameFont != null)
{
    // Clean up the game font
    gameFont.Dispose();
    gameFont = null;
}
```

You might think that you're done creating these objects, but the font still needs a bit more work. Just like the debug font you created in an earlier chapter, the font needs to respond to a device being lost or reset. Add this call to the end of OnResetDevice:

```
// Reset the game font
gameFont.OnResetDevice();
```

Add this code to the end of `OnLostDevice`:

```
if (gameFont != null)
{
    // Make sure the game font cleans up resources
    gameFont.OnLostDevice();
}
```

Now you have all the objects created, but you haven't updated the rendering yet.
Add the code in Listing 9.12 to the end of your `RenderGameScene` to handle showing both the quit menu and the user statistics.

LISTING 9.12   Rendering Stats and Quit User Screen

```
if (isQuitMenuShowing)
{
    quitScreen.Draw();
}
if (isLoadingLevel)
{
    string loadingText = string.Format(
        "Try Level {0}\r\nAre you ready?", levelNumber);
    if (!isQuitMenuShowing)
    {
        gameFont.DrawText(null, loadingText, this.ClientRectangle,
            DrawTextFormat.Center | DrawTextFormat.VerticalCenter |
            DrawTextFormat.NoClip, Color.WhiteSmoke);
    }
}
else
{
    // if there is a level happening, update some stats
    if (currentLevel != null)
    {
        // Draw current state
        string blockInfo = string.Format("Blocks Remaining {0} - Correct {1}",
            currentLevel.NumberBlocks - currentLevel.NumberCorrectBlocks,
            currentLevel.NumberCorrectBlocks);

        Color statColor = Color.White;
        // Change the color once you've gotten more than halfway complete
        if ((currentLevel.NumberBlocks - currentLevel.NumberCorrectBlocks)
            > currentLevel.NumberCorrectBlocks)
        {
            statColor = Color.Turquoise;
        }

        gameFont.DrawText(null, blockInfo, new Rectangle(0, screenHeight - 60,
            ClientRectangle.Width, ClientRectangle.Height),
            DrawTextFormat.Center | DrawTextFormat.NoClip,
            statColor);
```

LISTING 9.12   Continued

```
    if (!currentLevel.IsGameOver)
    {
        string gameState = string.Format("Moves: {0} (Max: {1})\r\nTime
                                  Remaining: {2}",
            currentLevel.TotalMoves, currentLevel.MaximumMoves,
            currentLevel.TimeRemaining);

        gameFont.DrawText(null, gameState, new Rectangle(0, 30,
            ClientRectangle.Width, ClientRectangle.Height),
            DrawTextFormat.Center | DrawTextFormat.NoClip,
            Color.Yellow);
    }
    else
    {
        string gameState;
        Color c;
        if (currentLevel.IsGameWon)
        {
            gameState = string.Format("Congratulations! You win this level!");
            c = Color.White;
        }
        else
        {
            gameState = string.Format("Game Over!!");
            c = Color.Red;
        }
        gameFont.DrawText(null, gameState, new Rectangle(0, 30,
            ClientRectangle.Width, ClientRectangle.Height),
            DrawTextFormat.Center | DrawTextFormat.NoClip,
            c);
    }
  }
}
```

As you see here, if the quit menu is showing, you draw that. After that, you really just need to update the player statistics. Before the level is loaded, you don't want to show any level-specific stats, so instead you simply draw some text notifying the player to get ready and center it in the client area.

If someone is actually playing a level, player statistics should be rendered instead. You always render the number of blocks that are correct and the number of blocks remaining in the level, at the bottom of the screen. Notice that when less than half of the blocks are correct, the text changes to turquoise, rather than the default white. If the game isn't over, the only statistics needed are the amount of time currently passed and the time remaining, which are rendered at the top of the screen. If the game is over, you simply render the appropriate message to the screen. If the player won the level, and there are more levels remaining, it is automatically loaded in the OnFrameMove method. If the player lost the level or is on the last level, he is required to quit.

Can you feel the anticipation? You have only one thing left to do: handle the user input in your game engine. For each of these methods, you already have code handling the main menu screen and the Select Loopy screen; you simply add the final `else` statement. In the `OnMouseEvent` method, make sure the quit screen is handled when the left button is not down:

```
else if (isQuitMenuShowing)
{
    quitScreen.OnMouseMove(x, y);
}
```

Also handle it when it is:

```
else if (isQuitMenuShowing)
{
    quitScreen.OnMouseClick(x, y);
}
```

It all ends with the keyboard input and the `OnKeyEvent` method:

```
else if (isQuitMenuShowing)
{
    quitScreen.OnKeyPress(key);
}
else
{
    // Allow you to quit at any time
    if (key == System.Windows.Forms.Keys.Escape)
    {
        ShowQuitMenu();
    }

    // Ignore any keystrokes while the fly through is displayed
    if (!isLoadingLevel)
    {
        // Otherwise, let the level handle the keystrokes
        currentLevel.OnKeyPress(key);
    }
}
```

As you see, this one is a little different because not only do you want the quit screen to handle the keyboard input, but you want the level to as well. If the quit screen isn't showing, and the key is escape, you should show the quit menu. Otherwise, if you are playing the level, pass the keystroke on. This part is the last thing that actually allows your player to move around the screen and win the levels. You can find the implementation for the `ShowQuitMenu` method here:

```
private void ShowQuitMenu()
{
    isQuitMenuShowing = !isQuitMenuShowing;
    if (isQuitMenuShowing)
    {
        // The game is now paused, the 'quit' message will be shown
```

```
        // Pause the timer as well
        sampleFramework.Pause(true, false);
    }
    else
    {
        // Restart the timer
        sampleFramework.Pause(false, false);
    }
}
```

It simply flips the Boolean value for determining whether the quit menu is show-ing and either pauses or restarts the timer, depending on the new value. Can you believe it? You're done!

You can see the finished product in Figure 9.2.

FIGURE 9.2
Blockers—The
Game.

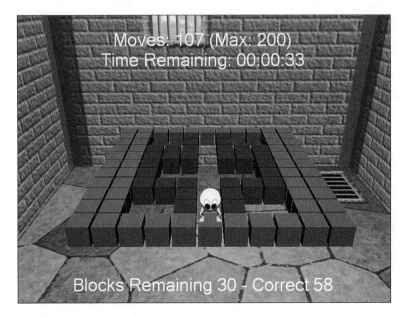

Summary

Congratulations! You've written your first fully 3D puzzle game. You went through all the steps to create a high-quality game, including a design and plan-ning phase, the implementation of a custom user interface, and the implementa-tion of the game objects. Finally seeing the fruits of the labor turn into a fully functional game is by far the most rewarding experience you can have as a game developer.

In the next chapter, we can start with a little background in math to help you for the later chapters and games.

PART III

Basic Math Principles

CHAPTER 10

A Quick 3D-Math Primer

Depending on the skill level you had when you started reading this book, the math for the Blockers game might have been overly simplistic or way out of the realm of things you've done thus far. Because the formulas in the latter two games of this book get even more in-depth, now is a good time to take a step back and look at some basic math concepts that are used for manipulating the objects in a 3D world.

This chapter is in no way designed to be the ultimate 3D math graphics chapter, but it should get you started by giving you the information you need to do the calculations that are used throughout this book. I highly recommend that you spend some time on this chapter: rather than simply *read* everything here, you should try to *do* the things as well. As the old saying goes, you'd rather be a doer than a reader. Well, maybe that isn't an old saying, but it should be!

If you really want to write rich 3D games, you need to master the mathematics of the 3D worlds. If this area interests you, I highly recommend finding out more information about the specifics of the mathematics that this chapter covers.

In this chapter, you'll learn

- ▶ Basic math concepts
- ▶ Simple vector concepts
- ▶ Basic matrix math

2D? 3D? What Are You Talking About?

Before you can dive into the wonderful world of 3D math, you need at least a basic understanding of the differences between a 2D world and a 3D world. Grab a piece of paper and a pencil. Draw something on the piece of paper, and look at it. It is an example of a basic 2D world. The image you drew has two different dimensions, width and height. Now, look at this book you're holding. You'll notice that it too has width and height, but it also has an "added" dimension, namely depth. Each page of the book is essentially flat, but the book itself has depth.

In the 2D world, any point in space can be defined by a coordinate that represents the width and height of that point. You have an x axis (which is the width axis) that runs horizontally and the y axis (height), which runs perpendicular to the x axis or, in this case, vertically. Starting at the origin (0,0—the center), the positive x axis coordinates run to the right, and the positive y axis coordinates run up. You can see an example in Figure 10.1.

FIGURE 10.1
A basic 2D
Cartesian system.

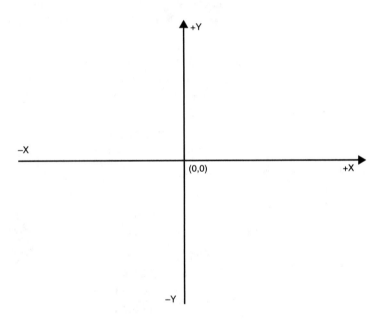

Remember that piece of paper and the pencil you had? Take that pencil and push a hole through the center of the piece of paper so that half of the pencil is on either side of the paper. To make your 2D world 3D, you simply need to add a new axis to your coordinate system, for depth. This axis is the z axis and can be represented by the pencil you have sticking in the paper. Look at Figure 10.2 for a better idea of what the z axis is.

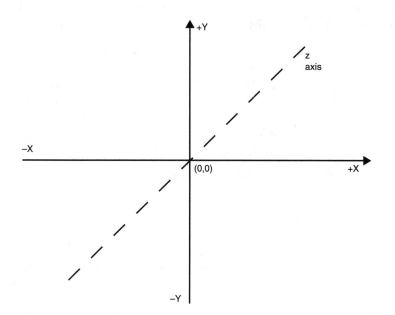

FIGURE 10.2
A basic 3D
Cartesian system.

Left-handed? Right-handed?

Did you notice that I didn't mention which direction the positive z axis faces? I did so intentionally because (much like your computer screen's y axis going down) "it depends." The direction of the positive z axis is relative to which coordinate system you are using, either **left-handed** or **right-handed**.

I can just see the puzzled look you have right now. Left-handed? Right-handed? What is that supposed to mean? It's just a fancy way of informing the user of which way the positive z axis faces. Assuming you are looking directly at your sheet of paper with the pencil through it (so you see either eraser point of the pencil), positive z can be either away from you (toward the writing point of the pencil) or toward you (back toward the eraser side). To see where these names came from, take your left hand with the palm facing the sky (or ceiling if you happen to be inside). Rotate your hand so that your fingers point toward the positive x axis (to your right). Now, do the same thing with your right hand, palm up, fingers pointing toward the positive x axis. Look at the thumb on each hand. Assuming you've got a normal human body, the thumb on your left hand is pointing away from you, but the thumb on your right hand is pointing toward you. Whichever way your thumb is pointing is the direction of the positive z axis, hence the name of the coordinate system. See Figure 10.3 for a graphical representation.

FIGURE 10.3
Left- or right-
handed coordinate
system?

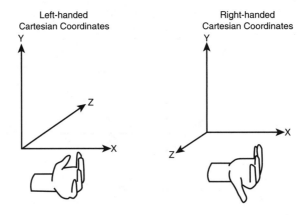

Direct3D (which is the Application Programming Interface [API] this book covers) uses a left-handed coordinate system. So throughout this book, you can assume that we are using this system.

With that out of the way, you should be able to plot simple points in a 3D graph. For example, you know the origin has a point of (0,0,0), but what about a point that is located at say (-3,4,17)? This point is located 3 units to the left of origin, 4 units above origin, and 17 units away from you (assuming you're at the origin and this is a left-handed coordinate system). Plotting these points is what is actually used to create your rich worlds.

Using These 3D Points

Whether you realized it or not, the models you were loading in the Blockers game had many of these points built into the .x files you were loading. Each point in 3D space can be called a **vertex**, and if you group three of these vertices together, you can create a triangle. As mentioned earlier, the triangle is the building block for all 3D render-able objects. Triangles are used as the primitive type for all 3D objects because they are the simplest polygons possible that are guaranteed to be coplanar (or all on the same plane). Using these objects as the primitives allows the math to be more efficient than worrying about noncoplanar points. For this chapter (and book), it isn't important to understand this point in depth, so let's continue.

Now that you understand that all 3D objects consist of triangles, it's important to visualize it. You remember seeing the character Loopy bounce around the screen in the Blockers game, but did you realize that he is nothing more than a series of triangles stitched together to appear as a solid object? See Figure 10.4 for a view of Loopy as he really is.

As you can see, the character is nothing but a series of triangles. Any time you see some complex 3D world and wonder how it's all generated, for the most part, there's your answer. Any object, no matter how complex, can be approximated using enough triangles.

FIGURE 10.4
The real Loopy.

Manipulating 3D Objects

You probably remember earlier when I briefly described transformations, or moving from one coordinate system to another, and how I would discuss it more in depth later. Well, it is later now, so it seems like the perfect time to get into it. There are three basic transformations you want to accomplish:

▶ *Translation*—You can think of translation as actually moving the object. It's essentially adding a new point in 3D space to every vertex in your model to move it to a new location. For example, if you had a single vertex at point (1,2,3) and translated it (-2,3,1), you would calculate the new vertex position by simply adding each of the axis coordinates. In this case, the new vertex would be located at (-1,5,4) after the translation. Doing this for every vertex in your object has the effect of moving the entire object

▶ *Scaling*—You use scaling to change the actual size of the object, by multiplying each coordinate of a vertex by a fixed amount. Assume that the size of the Loopy model earlier was (3,8,3) or 3 units wide, 8 units high, and 3 units deep. You have two options when scaling, either **uniformly** or nonuniformly: uniform scaling uses the same scaling factor for each axis, but nonuniform scaling uses differing scaling factors. Using our Loopy model, scaling uniformly by 5 (5,5,5) makes the new size (15,40,15); Loopy still looks the same, just much larger. However, scaling nonuniformly by something such as (3,0.5,3) causes Loopy to look squished, being "compressed" into a new size of (9,4,9).

▶ *Rotation*—You can rotate an object around any of the three axes you have defined in your coordinate system. Actually, by combining these different rotations on each of the axes, you can simulate rotating around any arbitrary axis in a 3D world. Think of rotating an object around an axis with the sheet of paper you stuck the pencil through. Holding on to the pencil, spin the paper around the pencil, and you are rotating it around the z axis. See Figure 10.5 for an illustration.

FIGURE 10.5
Rotating around the z axis.

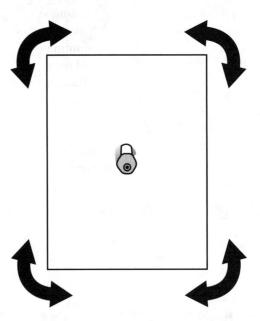

What kind of math chapter would this be if there weren't any nifty formulas for you to look at? Obviously, everything I just described could be written as a formula, so now you should look at the formulas for each of these items.

Translating (Moving) Objects

The formula here is quite simple based on the description I gave earlier (where T is the distance you want to move your object):

Scaling

The scaling formula is also simple based on the description (where S is the scaling factor you want to move your object):

$$X_{new} = X_{original} * S_x$$
$$Y_{new} = Y_{original} * S_y$$
$$Z_{new} = Z_{original} * S_z$$

Rotation

I didn't really mention a formula for this concept earlier because rotation is more complex than the two preceding sets of formulas. Rotations always rotate around an axis, and the amount of rotation is specified as an angle. It's also interesting to note that the coordinate on the axis you are rotating with will never move; unlike earlier, when all three axis coordinates had the potential to change, during rotation, only two ever change, and the two that change depend on the axis of rotation (or theta, θ). Look at the formulas for each axis:

▶ X axis

$$Y_{new} = Y_{original} * \cos(\theta) - Z_{original} * \cos(\theta)$$
$$Z_{new} = Y_{original} * \sin(\theta) + Z_{original} * \sin(\theta)$$

▶ Y axis

$$X_{new} = X_{original} * \cos(\theta) - Z_{original} * \sin(\theta)$$
$$Z_{new} = X_{original} * \sin(\theta) + Z_{original} * \cos(\theta)$$

▶ Z axis

$$X_{new} = X_{original} * \cos(\theta) - Y_{original} * \sin(\theta)$$
$$Y_{new} = X_{original} * \sin(\theta) + Y_{original} * \cos(\theta)$$

Exactly why these formulas work is a matter for another book or a trigonometry class. (Writing up a proof would take a lot more than this chapter.) It is important that you understand what the formulas are, however, and I highly recommend that you do a few calculations rotating around various axes and determining the new coordinates after rotation so you can see how the objects are rotated.

Coordinate Systems

As mentioned earlier, the idea of transformation is to move between one coordinate system and another, but what exactly does that mean? The rotation formulas only work when the object is centered at the origin. For example, let's take Loopy: rather than center him at the origin, let's say his center is (30,20,10). Now, you want to rotate him on the z axis 90°, and I bet you're expecting him to rotate in place, but you will be vastly surprised. Let's simply use the earlier formula on the center point (which, if he were rotating in place, wouldn't change):

$$X_{new} = 30 * \cos(90) - 20 * \sin(90)$$
$$Y_{new} = 30 * \sin(90) + 20 * \cos(90)$$

Finishing up the equation, you see the following:

$$X_{new} = 30 * 0 - 20 * 1 = -20$$
$$Y_{new} = 30 * 1 + 20 * 0 = 30$$

That gives us a new coordinate of (-20,30,10), which I imagine you found completely surprising (I know I did the first time I tried it). To combat this, 3D graphics worlds normally have a multitude of coordinate systems, such as local and world. The **local** coordinate system is what you use for your models, such as Loopy. Look back at Figure 10.4, and imagine where the center point of that Loopy model appears. In the local coordinates, the head of Loopy would be slightly above the center, and the feet would be slightly below and to the left or right of the center. See Figure 10.6 for an example of how the local coordinates for Loopy might be envisioned.

FIGURE 10.6
A local coordinate system.

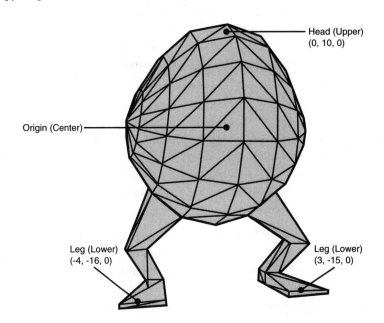

Head (Upper)
(0, 10, 0)

Origin (Center)

Leg (Lower)
(-4, -16, 0)

Leg (Lower)
(3, -15, 0)

This point is important because now no matter what you do with Loopy in the local coordinate system, it behaves how you expect. It doesn't matter if his center in the world is over at (30,20,10) because when you do the rotations, you do so in the local coordinate system, which is centered on his body and never changes.

Math Structures

You've covered a lot so far during this chapter, but now you get to see how (and why) some of these math formulas work and see some of the routines you use for later games during this book. I hope that your head isn't spinning (in a local coordinate system, of course) because now things start to get interesting.

Vectors

You've seen vectors already within this book, and it's possible you think that they are simply a representation of a point in space, such as a vertex. Although it's true that the vector can store this information, it does so in the DirectX API mainly for a convenience. The mathematical definition of a **vector** is an object that denotes both direction and velocity (or magnitude). For example, if you fire a bullet out of a tank (for which you will write code in the next game), that bullet has both a direction and a velocity. They are stored in one vector, which incidentally has the same members as a vertex, namely x, y, and z components. You're probably thinking, wait, how can you specify these two things with a single set of three coordinates? Look at Figure 10.7 for an example.

You'll notice that in this figure, each of the two vectors has similar directions, but the velocity is different. In practice, you can have these vectors measure both direction and velocity because most times a vector is defined as a free vector, which is when the root of the vector is at the origin. Thus, the single set of coordinates are where the arrow of your vector is, and you now know the direction and velocity of that vector by taking those two points. Vectors do not *have* to be rooted at the origin, but it certainly makes things easier for most calculations, as you saw during the rotation example earlier this chapter.

How do you calculate the velocity of a vector knowing its arrow coordinates? The formula is derived from the Pythagorean Theorem ($a^2 + b^2 = c^2$). You can find out more information about this formula in many different places, but it goes beyond the scope of what you're trying to learn here, which is the length of a vector. This formula can be defined as the following:

$$\text{Length} = \sqrt{x^2 + y^2 + z^2}$$

FIGURE 10.7
Two different
vectors.

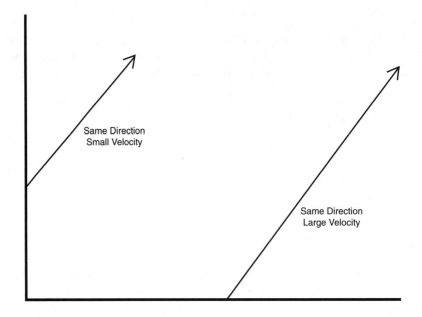

When dealing with the vector classes while you're developing, you'll notice that the vector has a `length` method that you can use to calculate this for you, but it's important to see the formula to understand that calculating the length can be expensive. Squaring each of the components and adding them together isn't that bad, but taking the square root of that result can be an expensive operation. You'll notice that the vector classes also have a `LengthSq` method that you can use to return the squared length of the vector to avoid this expensive step. Many times, it is "less expensive" to square the length you're comparing against than for you to take the square root of the length of this vector. This point is something you'll want to remember.

It isn't all that exciting, though: what about adding even more knowledge to your repertoire and doing some addition, subtraction, or multiplication of some vectors? Addition is basic because it is much like translation from earlier; you simply add each new component to the existing component to form the new vector. Subtracting is the same as adding; you just negate the new component before the addition. See Figure 10.8 for a visual representation of these concepts.

Multiplication with a vector is exceedingly simple as well; you simply multiply each component of the vector with a single constant value.

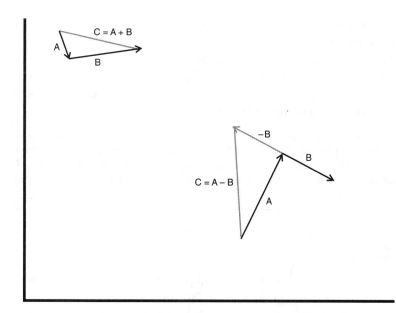

FIGURE 10.8
Adding and sub-
tracting vectors,
oh my!

One of the important aspects of vectors that you will use numerous times throughout this book is something called a **normalized vector** or unit vector. It is just a fancy way of saying a vector with a length of 1. This vector is extremely important because it can store direction without regard to velocity, which allows you to change direction without changing velocity by first calculating the length of your vector, normalizing it, modifying the direction, and then multiplying it by the calculated length. These calculations cause you to have a new vector pointing in a new direction with the same velocity.

Calculating the normalized version of a vector is really pretty simple: you simply take each component of the vector and divide it by the length of the vector. Imagine you had a free vector with coordinates (23,18,7). The length of this vector is approximately 30.0333 (based on the earlier formula), so dividing each component by this number gives a vector with coordinates of (0.7658,0.5993,0.233). The length of this vector is 0.99994956372809118, which is awfully close to the 1.0 you should have expected. The reason it's not exact is because I didn't use the full precision value when calculating the original length (to save on some math time). When dealing with values with decimal points (especially with computers), close is often as good as exact.

All the functionality you've learned about vectors so far already exists in the classes in the Managed DirectX runtime, but it's important to understand the how and why in some cases rather than just see the black box and not necessarily understand where these weird formulas come from. There are plenty of methods that I did not cover here (such as the dot product, which you can use to calculate the angle between two vectors, or the cross product, which you can use to calculate a vector perpendicular to two other vectors), but read up on them as well so you can understand the math behind these methods.

Construction Cue

> It's also interesting to note that in this book, you deal only with 3D vectors. The built-in classes actually have a representative for 2D, 3D, and even 4D vectors. The basic functionality and logic is the same regardless of how many dimensions you are working on.

Matrices

Ah, the matrix, by far the most esoteric and potentially "frightening" aspect of 3D programmers to the beginners who are just starting out. Things just appear so complicated when you jump in without a firm grasp of what's going on, but in reality, matrix math can be simple after you get used to it.

By definition, a **matrix** is a rectangular array where each entry contains a number, such as the following:

$$\begin{vmatrix} 3 & 2 & 4 & 5 \\ 1 & 9 & 5 & 3 \\ 3 & 4 & 1 & 3 \\ 2 & 9 & 8 & 3 \end{vmatrix} \qquad \begin{vmatrix} 3 & 3 & 3 \\ 2 & 2 & 2 \\ 1 & 1 & 1 \end{vmatrix}$$

In this example, the first matrix is a 4x4 matrix and the second, a 3x3 matrix. (The numbers are completely arbitrary and have no bearing on the matrix itself.) Matrices are not required to be square; you could just as easily have a 4x1 matrix or a 1x18 matrix. The majority of work in 3D graphics and matrices uses a 4x4 matrix, and the Matrix class that is included in the Managed DirectX runtime is this type as well.

Why would you actually want to use matrices? Take this (extremely common) scenario. You have a model with say 50,000 vertices that you want to have rendered. However, before they are rendered, you want them rotated 90° on the x axis, rotated 180° around the y axis, scaled to twice the size they are now, and then moved 300 units to the left. As you can see, that is 2 rotations, 1 scale, and

1 translation, or a minimum of 12 math computations. For every single vertex in the model! You've come up with a whopping 600,000 math operations to transform your vertices the way you want.

What if you found out that with a single matrix, you could combine each of those four transformations and then use that one matrix to transform each of the coordinates? I'm sure you could understand why doing just over 50,000 math calculations is more desirable than doing 600,000. Even with the speed of modern processors, needlessly wasting time isn't anything you ever want to do.

Another benefit of using matrices is that every one of the transformation formulas you learned early can be expressed by a single matrix operation. This makes your code more readable as well as easier to understand because you don't have all these crazy algebra equations cluttering the code.

By far the most common operation you can perform on a matrix is multiplication. Although it's true that you can use built-in methods to perform this multiplication for you, it's important that you understand how the multiplication happens. For the basic 4x4 matrices that our 3D graphics programs use, what is the formula for the matrix multiplication? Don't be afraid of this function you're about to see:

$$C_{ij} = \sum A_{ik} B_{kj} \text{ (for } i = 1..4 \text{ and } j_{k=1}^{n} = 1..4)$$

What you're probably saying right now is "What in the heck is that?" Aside from looking bad, all it is really saying is that for each component in the new matrix C, you go through each row/column in the original matrices (A and B) and add them. Take two simple 2x2 matrices, such as these:

$$\begin{vmatrix} 2 & 4 \\ 3 & 6 \end{vmatrix} \times \begin{vmatrix} 3 & 7 \\ 4 & 5 \end{vmatrix}$$

To multiply them together, you simply plug the values in the formula. For the first row/column of the new matrix, you use this formula:

$$C_{1,1} = \sum_{k=1}^{2} A_{1k} B_{k1}$$

The Σ (sigma) symbol is a fancy math character for a `for` loop, so the preceding formula breaks down like this:

$$C_{1,1} = (A_{1,1} * B_{1,1}) + (A_{1,2} * B_{2,1})$$

Using the two entry matrices, plug in the actual values and you see the following:

$$C_{1,1} = (2 * 3) + (4 * 4)$$
$$C_{1,1} = (6) + (16)$$
$$C_{1,1} = 22$$

Notice the order of the columns and vectors, particularly the A(1,2) and B(2,1). Did you expect the A(1,2) member to be 3 and the B(2,1) member to be 7? It is a common mistake that many people run into. Just to drive the point home, you should finish this matrix multiply:

$$C_{2,1} = (A_{2,1} * B_{1,1}) + (A_{2,2} * B_{2,1})$$
$$C_{2,1} = (3 * 3) + (6 * 4)$$
$$C_{2,1} = (9) + (24)$$
$$C_{2,1} = 33$$

What about C(1,2)?

$$C_{1,2} = (A_{1,1} * B_{1,2}) + (A_{1,2} * B_{2,2})$$
$$C_{1,2} = (2 * 7) + (4 * 5)$$
$$C_{1,2} = (14) + (20)$$
$$C_{1,2} = 34$$

Then, what about C(2,2)?

$$C_{2,2} = (A_{2,1} * B_{2,2}) + (A_{2,2} * B_{2,2})$$
$$C_{2,2} = (3 * 5) + (6 * 5)$$
$$C_{2,2} = (15) + (30)$$
$$C_{2,2} = 45$$

It gives you the resulting matrix C:

$$\begin{vmatrix} 22 & 34 \\ 33 & 45 \end{vmatrix}$$

The same basic principle applies no matter how big your matrix is. Notice that the rules are slightly different if you're multiplying matrices of different sizes, but because that never happens in this book, I leave it as an exercise for you to figure out if you want. It's well beyond the scope of what this primer is intended for. To show that the basic principles are the same, here is the formula for calculating the first member of a 4x4 matrix multiplication:

$$C_{1,1} = (A_{1,1} * B_{1,1}) + (A_{1,2} * B_{2,1}) + (A_{1,3} * B_{3,1}) + (A_{1,4} * B_{4,1})$$

Notice that it's the same formula you used for the 2x2 matrix; it's just that the sigma has been expanded to a larger for loop of four members rather than two.

> If you follow the algorithm through a few permutations (which I highly recommend), you'll notice that matrix multiplication is not commutative; that is, A*B does not equal B*A. For example, in the 2x2 matrix multiplication example, if the matrices were reversed, the resulting member of C(1,1) would have been 27, not 22. It's important to remember this point.

Construction Cue

You might have noticed that you can think of the rows and columns of a matrix as somewhat like a vector. In fact, this is why you can use matrices to perform all your rotations. For example, when you have a matrix that has been translated (moved), you'll notice that the first three columns of row 4 will have the newly translated positions for the x, y, and z coordinates, respectively. Add in a new translation (through another matrix multiply), and you'll notice it's as if you did a vector add on those three components.

Consequently, scaling transformations are stored as C(1,1) – x, C(2,2) – y, and C(3,3) – z in the matrix. Rotations are stored somewhat differently, depending on the axis of rotation, but the end result is that the first three members of column 0 end up facing the up direction (when normalized); the first three members of column 1 end up facing the right direction (when normalized); and the first three members of column 2 are the actual direction the object is facing (when normalized).

You'll notice many methods on the Matrix object that perform these operations for you. For example, to make a single matrix that rotates twice, scales, and translates (as described earlier,) you could write something like the following C# code:

```
Matrix transformMatrix = Matrix.RotationY(1.0f) * Matrix.RotationZ(0.3f)
  * Matrix.Scaling(15.0f) * Matrix.Translation(30.0f, 0.0f, 0.0f);
```

Isn't that so much easier than reading the formulas that you learned just a few minutes ago?

Summary

Whew, that was a lot of information in a short amount of time. I hope that you didn't get too much of a headache reading it. The reality is that even though we're only spending a chapter on the topic now, this is probably one of the most important principles you can learn in your quest to become a game developer. No amount of beautiful art can make up for the shortcomings of not understanding the math behind the world you are creating.

During this chapter, you covered all the basics of 3D math and how they are used. I covered the ideas of vectors, matrices, and the formulas required to get the most out of these objects. If there's one chapter during this learning process that you need to read once more, this is the one.

With that out of the way, in the next chapter you can start the design of the next game, which is more graphically challenging, and even include a multiplayer option.

PART IV

Intermediate Graphics, Peer-to-Peer Networking, Game 2

CHAPTER 11

Now Let's Really Get Started

Now that you've finished writing a complete 3D game, you might think you're ready to tackle something a little more complicated. Well, luckily, you are! Not only do you want to design something with richer graphics, but you also want to make sure that you include some things that weren't in the last game, namely sound and multiplayer and more robust user input. Of course, you need to come up with a plan for the game as well, which is what you do during this chapter.

In this chapter, you'll learn

- ▶ How to come up with a new game idea
- ▶ How to design specifications
- ▶ How you get the framework started
- ▶ How to create an object pool

Tankers—The Next Game Idea

The puzzle game you created in earlier chapters was pretty fun to write. Many of the basic concepts you needed to write a great game were included in the application, even though it was decidedly simple, both in implementation and game play. Now, with those concepts still freshly ingrained into your brain, it's the perfect time to begin expanding on them and coming up with an even more challenging game.

This new game will not only include the concepts that were addressed in the last chapter, but will also add more challenges to the development. Nowadays, virtually all the games on the market have at least some aspect of multiplayer support. Many times, the game can't be considered "complete" without this support, so naturally you want to include the ability to play this new game over the Internet. You also want to include sound in the game, which was lacking in the last one.

So what type of game should you write now? You still haven't dug all the way into the concepts you need to understand for an overly complex game, so this one should be more difficult than the last one but not so overly difficult that it becomes frustrating. For this section, you should concentrate on writing a multi-player tank-battle game.

In this game, the players will be in some field of combat, or arena. With two players in the arena, the objective of the game is to disable the other player's tank before that player can disable yours. Rather than a large open arena, the battlefield will have obstacles that will help shield your player from the opponent's. So as you did with the last game, you should get a list of all the features to implement in this game.

Detailing the Proposal

With the basic idea I just outlined, you can create the list of features you want this game to support:

- ▶ This arcade-type battle game is called Tankers.
- ▶ Multiple players will play via the Internet.
- ▶ The environment will be fully 3D.
- ▶ The object is disabling the opponent's tank.
- ▶ The game will contain multiple battlefields.
- ▶ Each battlefield will contain obstacles that provide cover.
- ▶ Player movement will be controlled with either keyboard, mouse, or joystick.
- ▶ Hitting an opponent's tank three times will disable it.
- ▶ After disabling the opponent's tank, the player will respawn at its original location.
- ▶ Disabling the opponent's tank three times will win the game.
- ▶ Each player's tank gun turret and barrel can be moved independently of the tank.

Once again, this list shouldn't be considered exhaustive because, obviously, it won't be. If you remember the classic game Combat for the Atari 2600, you have a rough idea of the inspiration for this game. This list is a nice road map to start with, though. Once more, you want to design a rough object model for this game, which you can see in Figure 11.1.

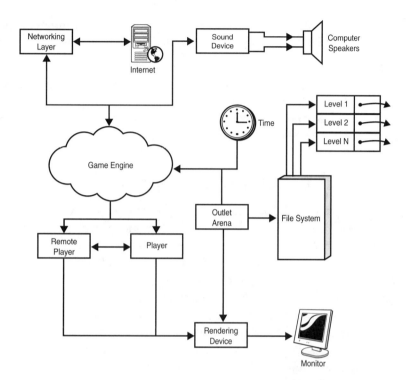

FIGURE 11.1
A high-level object diagram for the game.

As you can see here, the magic cloud that is the game engine once again makes its appearance. The game engine will be the central repository for virtually everything that happens in the game. It will interact with a few new items as well. You have a new sound device, which will output the audio data to the speakers, as well as a networking layer, which will communicate with the Internet. Actually, it will just communicate with a secondary machine via Transmission Control Protocol/Internet Protocol (TCP/IP), but close enough.

Obviously, you also need a player object to represent both your tank and the opponent's tank, which will be accessed from the game engine. The battlefield is also a separate object, and each of the arenas will be stored locally on the file system. The other objects are still around from your first game, namely the high-precision timer and the rendering device, which will output the data to the screen.

The overall diagram still has items missing, such as the user interface screens, which will drive the player interaction before the game actually starts. The goal of this exercise is not to provide an exhaustive look at the scope of the project, but to get you thinking about the items you need to implement in a broad sense.

Remember from the last game, the final product didn't match the initial diagram exactly, but it did have the rough guidelines in place.

You might realize pretty quickly that many of the items used in the Blockers game can be brought over wholesale for this new game. Without wasting any time, you should get right into writing code, and I explain things as we move along. It's been my experience that you learn more from doing than hearing (or in this case, reading), so now is the time to get started.

Creating the Tankers Project

Load the Visual Studio .NET 2003 environment and create a new C# Windows application project. Call this Tankers if you are planning on matching it with the code included on the CD. The first thing you want to do is use the sample framework as you did in Blockers because you do not need to modify this code at all to work with your new Tankers game. You can either copy the code into your new project or "link" the files from your old project. Personally, I recommend linking because then you have only the one set of source files that are "shared" between multiple projects. The benefit is that any fixes made to one are automatically picked up by all others. The Visual Studio .NET integrated development environment (IDE) way of linking a new source file into your project isn't intuitive, in my opinion. If you didn't realize it was there, you might not even see it. See Figure 11.2 for an example of linking a file to your project.

FIGURE 11.2
Linking a file.

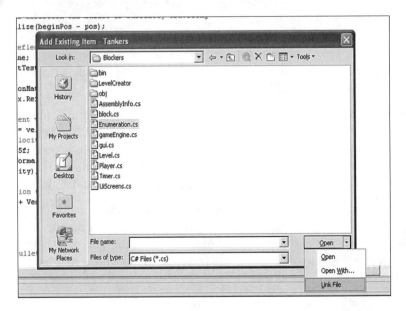

You could also try copying the gameengine.cs file from Blockers (not linking) because some of the code will be similar, but it's probably easier to start from scratch rather than get yourself in a bind by forgetting to erase the right code or deleting too much. Go ahead and rename the form1.cs file that was automatically generated to gameengine.cs. You want to ensure that you have the references you need, namely Microsoft.DirectX.dll, Microsoft.DirectX.Direct3d.dll, and Microsoft.directx.direct3dx.dll (at least for now). Then, replace the automatically generated code in your game engine with the code in Listing 11.1 (which should look somewhat familiar).

LISTING 11.1 The Game Engine Framework

```
using System;
using System.Configuration;
using System.Drawing;
using System.Windows.Forms;
using Microsoft.DirectX;
using Microsoft.DirectX.Direct3D;
using Direct3D = Microsoft.DirectX.Direct3D;

namespace Tankers
{
    /// <summary>
    /// Main Game Engine
    /// </summary>
    public class GameEngine : IFrameworkCallback, IDeviceCreation
    {
        public const string GameName = "Tankers";
        public static readonly string MediaPath =
            ConfigurationSettings.AppSettings.Get("MediaPath");
        public static Material WhiteMaterial;
        public static readonly Vector3 UpDirection = new Vector3(
                                            0.0f, 1.0f, 0.0f);

        private Framework sampleFramework = null; // Framework for samples
        #if (DEBUG)
        private Font debugFont = null;
        public int numberVerts = 0;
        public int numberFaces = 0;
        #endif
        public bool IsDeviceAcceptable(Caps caps, Format adapterFormat,
            Format backBufferFormat, bool windowed)
        {
            // Skip back buffer formats that don't support alpha blending
            if (!Manager.CheckDeviceFormat(caps.AdapterOrdinal, caps.DeviceType,
                adapterFormat, Usage.QueryPostPixelShaderBlending,
                ResourceType.Textures, backBufferFormat))
                return false;

            // Skip any device that doesn't support at least a single light
            if (caps.MaxActiveLights == 0)
                return false;
```

LISTING 11.1   Continued

```
            return true;
        }

        public void ModifyDeviceSettings(DeviceSettings settings, Caps caps)
        {
            // This application is designed to work on a pure device by not
            // using any get methods, so create a pure device if supported
            // and using HWVP.
            if ( (caps.DeviceCaps.SupportsPureDevice) &&
                ((settings.BehaviorFlags & CreateFlags.HardwareVertexProcessing)
                  != 0 ) )
                settings.BehaviorFlags |= CreateFlags.PureDevice;
        }

        private void OnCreateDevice(object sender, DeviceEventArgs e)
        {
            SurfaceDescription desc = e.BackBufferDescription;
            #if (DEBUG)
            // In debug mode, use this font to render stats
            debugFont = new Font(e.Device, new System.Drawing.Font("Arial", 12));
            #endif
        }

        private void OnResetDevice(object sender, DeviceEventArgs e)
        {
            SurfaceDescription desc = e.BackBufferDescription;
#if (DEBUG)
            // Make sure the debug font resets correctly
            debugFont.OnResetDevice();
#endif
        }

        private void OnLostDevice(object sender, EventArgs e)
        {
#if (DEBUG)
            if ( (debugFont != null) && (!debugFont.Disposed) )
            {
                // Make sure the debug font gets rid of any resources
                debugFont.OnLostDevice();
            }
#endif
        }
        private void OnDestroyDevice(object sender, EventArgs e)
        {
            // Clean up our objects
            try
            {
    #if (DEBUG)
                // Cleanup the font
                debugFont.Dispose();
    #endif
            }
            catch
            {
```

LISTING 11.1   Continued

```
            System.Diagnostics.Debugger.Log(0, GameEngine.GameName,
                                   "Error during cleanup.");
        }
      }
    }
}
```

Obviously, this code isn't ready to be compiled, but here is the basic stuff you need to get started, most of which you've seen before from Blockers. The big difference is the material that is marked static, and the debug information includes counts for the number of vertices and faces. The new material is used for rendering; because most everything in the game requires a white material, it makes sense to have one that is shared everywhere. Also, this time, you actually implement a camera class that will perform basic culling (which means it does not render objects it cannot see). To verify it is working, you need to know how many vertices and faces you are drawing.

You'll notice that the white material object hasn't actually been created yet. Because it is static, you only want it to be created once, and there is a mechanism in .NET to handle this for you. Add the creation code you find in Listing 11.2 to your game engine class now.

LISTING 11.2   The Game Engine Creation Code

```
/// <summary>Create a new instance of the class</summary>
public GameEngine(Framework f)
{
    // Store framework
    sampleFramework = f;
}
/// <summary>Static constructor used to initialize materials</summary>
static GameEngine()
{
    WhiteMaterial = new Material();
    WhiteMaterial.DiffuseColor = new ColorValue(1.0f, 1.0f, 1.0f, 1.0f);
    WhiteMaterial.AmbientColor = new ColorValue(1.0f, 1.0f, 1.0f, 1.0f);
}
```

The "normal" constructor here is basically the same as the one from Blockers. When the object is created, the sample framework is simply stored. The next constructor is new, however, and it is called a static constructor. This constructor is called before any other piece of code for this class (whether it is an instance method or static data). Because the white material object still needs creation, this is the perfect place to add the creation code for that object.

The rest of the initialization for the graphics device is similar to the code you wrote for Blockers, and going through it here isn't necessary. Now, you need to add the main method to your application, which appears in Listing 11.3.

LISTING 11.3 The Executable Entry Point

```
/// <summary>
/// Entry point to the program. Initializes everything and goes into
/// a message processing loop. Idle time is used to render the scene.
/// </summary>
static int Main()
{
    using(Framework sampleFramework = new Framework())
    {
        GameEngine tankersEngine = new GameEngine(sampleFramework);
        // Set the callback functions. These functions allow the sample
        // framework to notify the application about device changes, user
        // input, and windows messages. The callbacks are optional so you
        // need only set callbacks for events you're interested in. However,
        // if you don't handle the device reset/lost callbacks, then the sample
        // framework won't be able to reset your device since the application
        // must first release all device resources before resetting. Likewise,
        // if you don't handle the device created/destroyed callbacks then
        // the sample framework won't be able to re-create your device resources.
        sampleFramework.Disposing += new EventHandler(
                                    tankersEngine.OnDestroyDevice);
        sampleFramework.DeviceLost += new EventHandler(
                                    tankersEngine.OnLostDevice);
        sampleFramework.DeviceCreated += new DeviceEventHandler(
                                    tankersEngine.OnCreateDevice);
        sampleFramework.DeviceReset += new DeviceEventHandler(
                                    tankersEngine.OnResetDevice);

        sampleFramework.SetKeyboardCallback(new KeyboardCallback(
                                    tankersEngine.OnKeyEvent));
        // Catch mouse move events
        sampleFramework.IsNotifiedOnMouseMove = true;
        sampleFramework.SetMouseCallback(new MouseCallback(
                                    tankersEngine.OnMouseEvent));

        sampleFramework.SetCallbackInterface(tankersEngine);
        try
        {
#if (!DEBUG)
            // In retail mode, force the app to fullscreen mode
            sampleFramework.IsOverridingFullScreen = true;
#endif
            // Show the cursor and clip it when in full screen
            sampleFramework.SetCursorSettings(true, true);

            // Initialize the sample framework and create the desired window
            // and Direct3D device for the application. Calling each of these
            // functions is optional, but they allow you to set several options
```

LISTING 11.3 Continued

```
                // which control the behavior of the sampleFramework.
                sampleFramework.Initialize( false, false, true );
                // Parse the command line, handle the default hotkeys,
                // and show msgboxes
                sampleFramework.CreateWindow("Tankers - The Game");
                sampleFramework.CreateDevice( 0, true, Framework.DefaultSizeWidth,
                    Framework.DefaultSizeHeight, tankersEngine);

                // Pass control to the sample framework for handling the message
                // pump and dispatching render calls. The sample framework will
                // call your FrameMove and FrameRender callback when there is idle
                // time between handling window messages.
                sampleFramework.MainLoop();

        }
#if(DEBUG)
        catch (Exception e)
        {
                // In debug mode show this error (maybe - depending on settings)
                sampleFramework.DisplayErrorMessage(e);
#else
    catch
    {
        // In release mode fail silently
#endif
                // Ignore any exceptions here, they would have been handled
                // by other areas
                return (sampleFramework.ExitCode == 0) ? 1 :
                        sampleFramework.ExitCode; // Return an error code here
        }

        // Perform any application-level cleanup here. Direct3D device
        // resources are released within the appropriate callback functions
        // and therefore don't require any cleanup code here.
        return sampleFramework.ExitCode;
    }
}
```

The idea here is pretty basic: create the game engine, initialize the graphics, and run. It's just what the Blockers game did, actually. If you see any errors, notify the user and bail out of the game. If you planned to release this game on the retail shelves, you would want much more verbose and deductive error handling and probably logging. That would just add clutter to the code here, though, and would do more harm than good for this scenario because your goal is to teach yourself game programming, not error handling. You need to add the OnKeyEvent and OnMouseEvent methods to your class because you can't even compile without them there. (See Listing 11.4.)

LISTING 11.4   Handling User Input

```
/// <summary>
/// Handle keyboard strokes
/// </summary>
private void OnKeyEvent(System.Windows.Forms.Keys key, bool keyDown,
                        bool altDown)
{
}

/// <summary>
/// Hook the mouse events
/// </summary>
private void OnMouseEvent(bool leftDown, bool rightDown, bool middleDown,
    bool side1Down, bool side2Down, int wheel, int x, int y)
{
}
```

This code should appear familiar because you did essentially the same thing in Blockers. Now with the boilerplate code in place, you can get started.

Getting the Project Rendering

I know you want to get to the fancy 3D graphics being rendered. Doesn't everyone? Even in the wonderful world of game development, you need to learn to walk before you can run (as they say). If you recall from earlier, you declared some variables to keep track of the amount of vertices and faces rendered. This part needs to be reset each frame, so add the code from Listing 11.5 to your OnFrameMove method.

LISTING 11.5   The Heart of the "Game Loop"

```
#if (DEBUG)
// Reset the rendering variables in debug mode
numberVerts = 0;
numberFaces = 0;
#endif

if (FrameworkTimer.IsStopped)
    return; // Nothing to do
```

Notice that the first thing to do is reset your counters for the number of vertices and frames you've rendered. You haven't actually started rendering anything yet, so it isn't that big of a deal right now, but better to remember it now than forget it later. You also bail out of the call completely if the timer isn't running because there wouldn't be anything to do.

You haven't quite arrived at the point where you are ready to do much (or render much), but you will at the very least need to add code to clear out the render target. Add the code in Listing 11.6 to your `OnFrameRender` method.

LISTING 11.6   Basic Rendering

```
bool beginSceneCalled = false;

// Clear the render target and the zbuffer
device.Clear(ClearFlags.ZBuffer | ClearFlags.Target, 0, 1.0f, 0);
try
{
    device.BeginScene();
    beginSceneCalled = true;

    #if (DEBUG)
    // Show debug stats (in debug mode)
    debugFont.DrawText(null, sampleFramework.FrameStats,
        new System.Drawing.Rectangle(2,0,0,0),
        DrawTextFormat.NoClip, unchecked((int)0xffffff00));
    debugFont.DrawText(null, sampleFramework.DeviceStats,
        new System.Drawing.Rectangle(2,15,0,0),
        DrawTextFormat.NoClip, unchecked((int)0xffffff00));

    // Draw the number of vertices and face information
    debugFont.DrawText(null, string.Format
        ("\r\nNumber Of Vertices Rendered: {0}\r\nNumber of Faces Rendered: {1}"
        ,numberVerts, numberFaces), new System.Drawing.Rectangle(2,30,0,0),
        DrawTextFormat.NoClip, unchecked((int)0xffffffff));
    #endif
}
finally
{
    if (beginSceneCalled)
        device.EndScene();
}
```

Aside from the updated code to handle drawing the number of frames rendered, this code does the same as the game code for Blockers. Running your basic game framework now will show you a black screen with a frame rate informing you that you're currently rendering zero vertices and zero faces.

Building an Object Pool for Textures

Next, you should think about a problem that wasn't all that important when you were writing the Blockers game but could present itself as a problem now. What if you had three or four different objects that all used the same texture? In the Blockers game, you simply would have loaded the same texture three or four times, which does indeed work; however, I'm sure you can realize that the extra "wasted" space can't be a good thing. Instead of having a system like that, wouldn't it be so much nicer if you had a "cache" of textures so that whenever you created one, you would never re-create it again? That's what you should do now.

Building this object pool is actually pretty easy because you can use one of the existing classes in the .NET Framework to do the majority of the work for you, and that object is the HashTable. This class essentially maintains a "dictionary" (a key and pair value) using the hash code of the key (which theoretically is unique). You should use the filename of the texture you are trying to load as the key (because that will be unique), and naturally, the texture will be the value. Add a new code file to your application called ObjectPool.cs and add the code in Listing 11.7 to this new code file.

LISTING 11.7   The Texture Pool Class

```
using System;
using System.IO;
using System.Collections;
using Microsoft.DirectX;
using Microsoft.DirectX.Direct3D;

namespace Tankers
{
    /// <summary>
    /// The texture pool class
    /// </summary>
    class TexturePool
    {
        // Constant texture path
        private const string TexturePath = "Textures\\";
        // The hash table of valid textures
        private static Hashtable textureTable = new Hashtable();
        /// <summary>
        /// Create a new texture, or return one from the pool
        /// </summary>
        /// <param name="file">Texture file to create</param>
        /// <returns>A texture</returns>
        public static Texture CreateTexture(Device renderDevice, string file)
        {
            // Make sure a texture was passed in
            if ((file == null) || (file.Length == 0))
            {
                // No texture
                return null;
            }
            // Before we create a texture, return one from the
```

LISTING 11.7 Continued

```
            // pool if it exists
            string lowerCaseFile = file.ToLower();
            if (textureTable.ContainsKey(lowerCaseFile))
            {
                return textureTable[lowerCaseFile] as Texture;
            }
            // We've made it here, this is a new texture,
            // Create the texture and add it to the pool
            Texture t = TextureLoader.FromFile(renderDevice,
                    GameEngine.MediaPath + TexturePath + file);

            System.Diagnostics.Debug.Assert(t != null, "Created Texture is null",
                "Textures being loaded by the pool should never be null");

            // Add it to the pool
            textureTable.Add(lowerCaseFile, t);

            return t;
        }
    }
}
```

That's an exceedingly simple method actually. You have a single static member variable, which is the hash table you're using to maintain the pool. If you've installed the code and media from the CD already, you'll notice that all the textures are stored within a Textures folder within the media folder. A constant defines that folder name from within this class. The class then defines a single public function, which takes in the name of the texture you're trying to create and returns the texture object.

Notice that (after a basic check to make sure you really are asking for a file) the code checks the hash table to see whether it contains the key already (the filename in all lowercase letters). If it does, it simply returns that texture to the caller, and it isn't created again. However, if that texture does not exist, it is created and then added to the hash table. The next time this method is called for the same file, the texture is returned from the cache rather than re-created.

The last thing you want to do is add some cleanup code. Because the hash table and textures are stored in a static variable, they don't really have a "lifetime" outside of the application's lifetime. It's logical to assume that you want to release all the textures simultaneously and only when the application is about to quit. You can add a single method (from Listing 11.8) to this class to perform this operation for you.

LISTING 11.8   Releasing Textures from the Pool

```
public static void ReleaseAllTextures()
{
    foreach(string s in textureTable.Keys)
    {
        // Simply dispose of each texture in the list
        (textureTable[s] as Texture).Dispose();
    }

    // Clear the texture list
    textureTable.Clear();
}
```

Pretty basic stuff here: it simply goes through each "key" in the hash table, gets the texture from that, disposes it, and then clears the hash table. You should ensure that this code always gets called by adding this line to your OnDestroyDevice override back in the main game engine class. (It doesn't matter that you don't create any textures yet; when you do, they'll "automagically" get cleaned up.)

```
// Clean up all textures
TexturePool.ReleaseAllTextures();
```

Summary

You've got the basic idea and the framework of the new game done now, and you're ready to start adding new and exciting functionality to it. You've already added a new feature that you can use to store a "pool" of textures, so you're only creating a single instance of each of the textures you need.

In the next chapter, you can start on the user interface, which is more complicated this time around.

CHAPTER 12

Developing a More Advanced User Interface

The user interface you built for Blockers wasn't too bad, but it was overly simplistic; it required too many calls, and it wasn't self-contained. Plus, you didn't implement many features because you didn't need to. For example, everything in that game was done with "buttons"; however, in this game, you want it to be multiplayer aware, so you need to allow the player to enter a server to play on.

This requirement adds complexity to the user screens.

In this chapter, you'll learn

- ▶ How to update the Blockers GUI classes
- ▶ How to add a dialog class
- ▶ How to add a text-box class

Using Blockers Base Classes

Just because you plan to replace the user interface you wrote for Blockers doesn't mean you need to write the entire thing from scratch again. Instead, you should take the code you already wrote for the base classes in Blockers and use it in this project. As in the last chapter, when you used the sample framework code files for the project, you want to add an existing file and add gui.cs from Blockers as well; only this time, you don't want to *link* the file, but instead, you just click Open and add it normally. This move has the effect of copying the code into your new project, so modifying it does not break your existing Blockers implementation.

You use fonts in this class this time (for rendering the text-box text later), because since you will have references to both `System.Drawing.Font` and `Microsoft.DirectX.Direct3D.Font`, you add the following using clause to this file:

```
using Direct3D = Microsoft.DirectX.Direct3D;
```

With that out of the way, you can get right to modifying the class to include the features you need and want for Tankers. You don't want the button sizes defined as part of the base class because they might change depending on the game (and size of your user interface items), so go ahead and remove those four protected constants from the `UiScreen` class now.

One of the things you might have noticed with the `UiScreen` class from Blockers is that the "background" image was required to be the full texture that was passed in. This requirement was fine with Blockers, but what if you have more than one screen stored per texture? What you need is a way to the rectangle source of the texture that will be used for the screen. The screen width and height member variables are stored in the `StoreTexture` method, which worked fine during the last game. However, because you'll be adding a second overload to `StoreTexture`, you don't want that code duplicated, so remove it from that method and put it into the `UiScreen` class constructor:

```
// Store the width/height
screenWidth = width;
screenHeight = height;
```

Now, you can replace the single `StoreTexture` method with the two different overloads in Listing 12.1.

LISTING 12.1   Storing Textures for User Screens

```
/// <summary>
/// Store the texture for the background
/// </summary>
protected void StoreTexture(Texture background, int width, int height,
    bool centerTexture)
{
    Rectangle computedSource = Rectangle.Empty;
    if (background != null)
    {
        // Get the background texture
        using (Surface s = background.GetSurfaceLevel(0))
        {
            SurfaceDescription desc = s.Description;
            computedSource = new Rectangle(0, 0,
                desc.Width, desc.Height);
        }
    }
```

LISTING 12.1   Continued

```
        StoreTexture(background, computedSource, width, height, centerTexture);
}

/// <summary>
/// Store the texture for the background
/// </summary>
protected void StoreTexture(Texture background, Rectangle source, int width,
    int height, bool centerTexture)
{
    // Store the background texture
    backgroundTexture = background;
    backgroundSource = source;

    // Store the centered texture
    isCentered = centerTexture;

    if (isCentered)
    {
        centerUpper = new Vector3((float)(width - backgroundSource.Width) / 2.0f,
            (float)(height - backgroundSource.Height) / 2.0f, 0.0f);
    }
}
```

As you can see, the first overload is the same as the one that was originally written for the last game; however, in this case, only the first step is performed, getting the full size of the texture. After that texture rectangle is calculated, the code calls the additional overload, which simply stores that texture and the appropriate size and calculates its position if the screen should be centered. Essentially, it's the same code as what you used the last time; it's just now broken into two separate methods to get the deriving classes more flexibility and freedom.

That's the only changes you need to make to the UiScreen class; now you can tackle that button class. Remember from the last game, you had to manually call the user input methods for keyboard and mouse on the button classes, which ended up with "spaghetti code"—where your game engine user input code called your derived screen classes' user input code, which finally called the actual user input code for the buttons. If you want to talk about too many levels of indirection, that right there is the poster child. It would be significantly more maintainable if the button simply took care of this data itself, and luckily, you can make it do just that.

First, you add three new member variables to the UiButton class:

```
private System.Windows.Forms.Keys shortcut;
private GameEngine parentOwner = null;
private bool enabled = true; // Should we handle user input?
```

The first variable will be the "shortcut" key to this button. For example, the quit button's shortcut key could be Esc or some other variation. The second variable is the "owner" of the game engine whose events the button will want to hook. The last is whether the button is actually enabled. You wouldn't want a disabled button to be handling user input, would you?

Now you need some good way to get the events hooked. Add the method in Listing 12.2 to your UiButton class to handle hooking and unhooking the events.

LISTING 12.2   Hooking User Input Events

```
private void HookEvents()
{
    if (enabled)
    {
        // Hook the parents events
        parentOwner.MouseClick += new MouseEventHandler(OnMouseClick);
        parentOwner.MouseMove += new MouseEventHandler(OnMouseMove);
        parentOwner.KeyDown += new KeyEventHandler(OnKeyDown);
    }
    else
    {
        // Unhook the parents events
        parentOwner.MouseClick -= new MouseEventHandler(OnMouseClick);
        parentOwner.MouseMove -= new MouseEventHandler(OnMouseMove);
        parentOwner.KeyDown -= new KeyEventHandler(OnKeyDown);
    }
}
```

Here the game owner is used to hook the events we care about (the mouse moving over the button, the mouse clicking on the button, or a keyboard click) when the button is enabled. If the button is disabled, we unhook the event.

Construction Cue

You may be wondering why you unhook the event when the button is disabled.

In .NET, when you hook an event such as the MouseUp event, each time an object hooks that event, the delegate used for the event handler is stored in a list. Each time that event is fired, each delegate in that list is called in the order it was created. So let's say you had two buttons, each of them hooking the MouseUp event. The button that hooks the event first is "enabled," whereas the button hooking the event second is "disabled." The user clicks that first button, which inside that delegate enables the second button. Now that the first button is finished executing its code, the next event in the queue is fired—in this case, the second button's click handler. You've just clicked both buttons mistakenly because of the order in which the events were processed. It's much easier (and less error-prone) to simply unhook the events when you're not supposed to be listening to them.

You might have noticed that the events you just hooked don't actually exist anywhere in the game engine code. Add the following event declarations to your game engine code file:

```
public event System.Windows.Forms.KeyEventHandler KeyDown;
public event System.Windows.Forms.KeyEventHandler KeyUp;
public event System.Windows.Forms.KeyPressEventHandler KeyPress;
public event System.Windows.Forms.MouseEventHandler MouseMove;
public event System.Windows.Forms.MouseEventHandler MouseClick;
```

You also need some code that fires these events at the appropriate time. You already have the methods to handle the mouse and keyboard events, so that is the place to add this code. First, add this code to the OnMouseEvent method:

```
if (MouseMove != null)
    MouseMove(this, new System.Windows.Forms.MouseEventArgs(0, 0, x, y, wheel));

if (leftDown)
    if (MouseClick != null)
        MouseClick(this, new System.Windows.Forms.MouseEventArgs(0, 0, x, y,
wheel));
                                                      wheel));
```

And then, add the OnKeyEvent method:

```
if (keyDown)
{
    if (KeyDown != null)
        KeyDown(this, new System.Windows.Forms.KeyEventArgs(key));

}
else
{
    if (KeyUp != null)
        KeyUp(this, new System.Windows.Forms.KeyEventArgs(key));

    if (KeyPress != null)
        KeyPress(this, new System.Windows.Forms.KeyPressEventArgs((char)key));
}
```

Back in the gui.cs code file, you need something in the button code that actually calls this method. There are two good places to do so; the first is when the object is created. You need to modify the constructor parameters to accept an extra one, namely a GameEngine named parent, and then add these two lines to the end of the constructor's code:

```
parentOwner = parent;
HookEvents();
```

The other area where you want to ensure that this code gets called is when the user changes the state of the button. You need a property to get the state of the button along with the keyboard shortcut anyway, so add the two properties in Listing 12.3 to the class now.

LISTING 12.3   Button Properties

```
public System.Windows.Forms.Keys ShortcutKey
{
    get { return shortcut; }
    set { shortcut = value; }
}
public bool IsEnabled
{
    get { return enabled; }
    set { enabled = value; HookEvents(); }
}
```

The keyboard shortcut is a "normal" property with simple get/set items, but the enabled property is unique in that it calls the HookEvents method on set. This step ensures that no matter whether you enable or disable the button, the appropriate action takes place. You might also notice that the method declarations you had for the mouse before no longer compile because the signature of the method changed now that you're using the event handlers. Replace the mouse code with the code in Listing 12.4 (which also includes the keyboard code as well).

LISTING 12.4   Handling User Input for Buttons

```
private void OnMouseMove(object sender, MouseEventArgs e)
{
    if (enabled)
    {
        // Determine if the button is on or not
        isButtonOn = buttonRect.Contains(e.X, e.Y);
    }
}
private void OnMouseClick(object sender, MouseEventArgs e)
{
    if (enabled)
    {
        // Determine if the button is pressed
        if(buttonRect.Contains(e.X, e.Y))
        {
            if (Click != null)
                Click(this, EventArgs.Empty);
        }
    }
}
private void OnKeyDown(object sender, KeyEventArgs e)
{
```

LISTING 12.4　Continued

```
    if (enabled)
    {
        // See if the shortcut key was pressed
        if (e.KeyCode == shortcut)
        {
            // It was, raise the event
            if (Click != null)
                Click(this, EventArgs.Empty);
        }
    }
}
```

The check for enabled here *probably* isn't necessary, given that the events are unhooked when the object is disabled, but as I mentioned earlier, it's possible for a disabled button that was recently enabled to be clicked because of the order of the event messages. It's also possible for a recently disabled button to be clicked as well. This code handles that case. The mouse handlers are pretty much unchanged outside of the arguments passed in, and the keyboard method is self-explanatory. If the user presses the magic shortcut key, the click event is fired just as if he or she clicked the button.

Adding New Base Classes

That's all the changes you need to make to the existing classes you got from the Blockers game, but now you should add a new control, something that you haven't done before but that is common—the text box. This object is actually pretty simple, so go ahead and add the class in Listing 12.5 to your gui.cs code file (might as well keep all the base classes together).

LISTING 12.5　The Text Box

```
public class UiTextBox
{
    private Texture textureSource = null;
    private Rectangle textureRect;
    private Rectangle textRectangle;
    private Point renderLocation;
    private Direct3D.Font textFont = null;
    private string currentText = string.Empty;
    private bool enabled = false;

    /// <summary>
    /// Create a new text box
    /// </summary>
    public UiTextBox(Device device, Texture background, Rectangle source,
```

LISTING 12.5   Continued

```
    Point loc, GameEngine parent)
{
    // Store the information
    textureSource = background;
    textureRect = source;
    renderLocation = loc;
    textRectangle = new Rectangle(loc.X + 20, loc.Y + 15,
        source.Width-40, source.Height - 30);
    // Create the font
    textFont = new Direct3D.Font(device, new System.Drawing.Font(
        parent.Font.Name, 20.0f));
    // Hook the device events to handle fonts
    device.DeviceLost += new EventHandler(OnDeviceLost);
    device.DeviceReset += new EventHandler(OnDeviceRest);
    // Hook the keyboard
    parent.KeyPress += new KeyPressEventHandler(OnKeyPress);
    }
}
```

Here, the "background" of the text box is stored as a texture, much like the background of the user screens and buttons. Because the texture might contain more than just the text-box background, you need to store the source rectangle. You also want a separate rectangle to do clipping on the text that you will be drawing. (It will be slightly smaller than the rectangle for the texture.) You also need to know exactly where on the screen you should be drawing this text box. The renderLocation variable is the upper-left corner of this position. You need something to actually render the text currently being held (and the text itself), and as with the buttons, you want to make sure that you know when you're enabled.

The constructor mainly stores the information being passed in for later rendering; however; it does do a few new things. First, it calculates the rectangle to be used for rendering the text by "shrinking" the rectangle size of the source texture. It creates a new font that is pretty much a duplicate of the main font the window is using, just with a larger size. Remember from earlier chapters, you need to ensure that the font is handled during a device lost and reset event, so those events are hooked now. Because this is a text box, hooking the KeyPress event is probably a good idea as well. You can find the event handlers in Listing 12.6.

LISTING 12.6   Text Box Event Handlers

```
private void OnDeviceLost(object sender, EventArgs e)
{
    System.Diagnostics.Debug.Assert(textFont != null, "Font cannot be null.");
    textFont.OnLostDevice();
}
private void OnDeviceRest(object sender, EventArgs e)
{
```

LISTING 12.6   Continued

```
        System.Diagnostics.Debug.Assert(textFont != null, "Font cannot be null.");
        textFont.OnResetDevice();
}
private void OnKeyPress(object sender, KeyPressEventArgs e)
{
    if (!enabled)
    {
        // Nothing to do
        return;
    }
    if (e.KeyChar == (char)8)
    {
        if (currentText.Length > 0)
        {
            // Remove a char
            currentText = currentText.Substring(0, currentText.Length - 1);
        }
    }
    else
    {
        currentText += e.KeyChar;
    }
}v
```

The two device events are short because they only need to call the appropriate method on the font. The key-press event handler is a little more complex because it has a couple of things to do. First, if the text box isn't enabled, just exit the handler because there's nothing for it to do. You're probably wondering where the check against (char)8 comes from. This key character is the magic code for a backspace, so when that key is pressed, the current text string is shortened by one character (assuming it has any characters in it). Otherwise, the new character is simply appended to the string you're storing.

You haven't yet added any properties to access the text that has been entered or a way to enable or disable the text box, so you should add these two properties to your class now:

```
public bool IsEnabled
{
    get { return enabled; }
    set { enabled = value; }
}
public string Text
{
    get { return currentText; }
}
```

The only thing you have left to do before you're finished is actually render the text box. Add the method in Listing 12.7 to your class to handle this.

LISTING 12.7   Rendering a Text Box

```
public virtual void Draw(Sprite renderSprite, int color)
{
    // Render the element if it exists
    if (textureSource != null)
    {
        // Render to the screen centered
        renderSprite.Draw(textureSource, textureRect,
            UiScreen.ObjectCenter, new Vector3(renderLocation.X,
            renderLocation.Y, 1.0f), UiScreen.SpriteColor);

        // Render text
        textFont.DrawText(renderSprite, currentText, textRectangle,
            DrawTextFormat.None, color);
    }
}
```

Nothing complex: you simply use the passed-in sprite and render the background of the text box on it. Then, you call DrawText with the font you created earlier and draw that text directly on the sprite that was passed in. Did you notice that the DrawTextFormat.None flag is passed in? This causes the font object to automatically clip the text so it doesn't go beyond the rectangle you have defined. You also draw the text in any color you want (based on what the user passes in).

Implementing the Main Screen

What you want now is the ability to start your game via the user interface you're about to create. See Figure 12.1 for an example of what the main screen will look like.

FIGURE 12.1
The main starting
screen for Tankers.

How can you use the classes you've already created to make this screen a reality? For this case, it's pretty simple. The majority of the screen consists of a single background (which is the user screen) with two simple buttons on it. If you look at the texture for the buttons, you see that it has quite a few buttons on it, as shown in Figure 12.2.

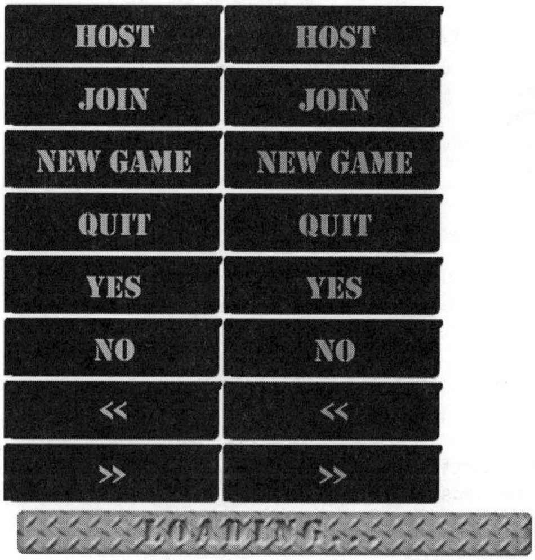

FIGURE 12.2
The button texture.

Each button has an off state (the grayish color) and an on state. Notice the extra use of the bottom spot to show a loading image. You'll see this image in use later in the game, but for now, just consider the texture as a good use of texture space. Rather than have all this data stored in multiple small texture files (which is inefficient), you store one larger texture file with all the information instead. How do you actually implement this, though?

First, add a new code file called UiScreens.cs to your project, much as you did for Blockers. This code encompasses the user screens you'll be using (and uses the base classes you already defined in the project). Use the code in Listing 12.8 as your starting point.

LISTING 12.8   The Main Screen Class

```
using System;
using System.Drawing;
using Microsoft.DirectX;
using Microsoft.DirectX.Direct3D;
using Microsoft.Samples.DirectX.UtilityToolkit;

namespace Tankers
{
```

LISTING 12.8   Continued

```
/// <summary>
/// The main selection screen for the game
/// </summary>
public class MainUiScreen : UiScreen, IDisposable
{
    /// <summary>
    /// Current state of the user screen
    /// </summary>
    private enum ScreenState
    {
        Main,
        Connection,
        SelectTank,
        SelectHost,
        Loading,
    }
    // Button sizes
    private const int ButtonWidth = 208;
    private const int ButtonHeight = 58;

    // Texture names
    private const string MainScreenTitleTexture = "title.png";
    private const string ButtonTexture = "Buttons.png";

    private Texture buttonTextures = null;
    private Texture messageTexture = null;

    // Buttons
    private UiButton newButton = null;
    private UiButton exitButton = null;

    // Default to the main screen
    private ScreenState currentScreen = ScreenState.Main;
    /// <summary>
    /// Create the main menu screen
    /// </summary>
    public MainUiScreen(Device device, int width, int height, Control parent)
        : base(device, width, height)
    {
        // Create the texture for the background
        messageTexture = TexturePool.CreateTexture(device,
                                    MainScreenTitleTexture);

        // Mark the background texture as centered
        StoreTexture(messageTexture, width, height, true);

        // Create the textures for the buttons
        buttonTextures = TexturePool.CreateTexture(device, ButtonTexture);
    }
    #region IDisposable Members
    /// <summary>
    /// Clean up any resources
    /// </summary>
    public override void Dispose()
    {
```

LISTING 12.8   Continued

```
            base.Dispose();
        }
        #endregion
    }
}
```

Rather than have a bunch of different user screens as Blockers did, this time you can take a different approach and have a single user screen handle all your user input needs. You can then determine which one meets your needs the best and suits your style most. Notice first that because the screens are all encompassed in the same class, an enumeration is created for you to track what screen you're on. As you can see here, the possible screens are the main screen (Figure 12.1); the connection screen (where you choose whether you want to host a game or join an existing game); the tank selection screen; and if you've chosen to join an existing game, the screen where you enter the server name. There's also a loading screen between the time the user interface ends and the real game begins.

After the constant and variable declarations, the constructor is pretty basic. It uses the texture pool object you created in the last chapter to load the textures needed for the user interface and, in the case of the title texture, to store that in the user screen. Notice, though, that two buttons are in your list of variables, but you don't actually create them yet. I arranged this part intentionally because you eventually have quite a few more buttons in the user interface, and you want a centralized place to create them all. Add the method in Listing 12.9 to your project, and add a call to this method at the end of the constructor.

LISTING 12.9   Creating Buttons

```
private void CreateDialogs(Device device, int width, int height, Control parent)
{
    // Create the new game button
    newButton = new UiButton(renderSprite, buttonTextures, buttonTextures,
        new Rectangle(ButtonWidth,ButtonHeight * 2,
        ButtonWidth, ButtonHeight),
        new Rectangle(0, ButtonHeight * 2,
        ButtonWidth, ButtonHeight),
        new Point((width - ButtonWidth) / 2,
        ((height - ButtonHeight) / 2) + (ButtonHeight * 2)),
        parent);

    newButton.Click += new EventHandler(OnNewButton);
    newButton.ShortcutKey = System.Windows.Forms.Keys.Enter;

    // Create the quit game button
    exitButton = new UiButton(renderSprite, buttonTextures, buttonTextures,
        new Rectangle(ButtonWidth,ButtonHeight * 3,
```

LISTING 12.9   Continued

```
        ButtonWidth, ButtonHeight),
        new Rectangle(0, ButtonHeight * 3,
        ButtonWidth, ButtonHeight),
        new Point((width - ButtonWidth) / 2,
        ((height - ButtonHeight) / 2) + (ButtonHeight * 3)),
        parent);

    exitButton.Click += new EventHandler(OnExitButton);
    exitButton.ShortcutKey = System.Windows.Forms.Keys.Escape;

    // Set up first button states
    SetButtonStates(true, false, false, false);
}
```

The button creation code is pretty much the same type of code you used in Blockers. You can see the code on the included CD for a detailed list of how the first user interface screen is implemented, but rather than regurgitate this stuff you already know, you should look at some of the things you haven't covered yet. What you want is to implement the screen in Figure 12.3.

FIGURE 12.3
Selecting your host.

Now that's something you haven't done before. Sure, you implemented the text box code earlier this chapter, but now you need to make this work. This code actually requires a new base class to be implemented because the screen consists of more than one background screen. See the texture used in Figure 12.4.

The top half of this texture makes the background of the dialogs, but the next three lines of text in the texture are various messages that can be drawn on top of that background. The bottom of the texture is what forms the text box that you're writing on. So the single screen you see in Figure 12.3 is actually rendered through a combination of three different pieces of data in this texture (the background, the "Enter Host Name" text, and the text box itself). To handle this part, you want to add a new dialog class to your gui.cs code file. This class essentially allows you to render any section of a texture anywhere onscreen that you want. See Listing 12.10.

FIGURE 12.4
The texture used
for dialogs.

LISTING 12.10 The Dialog Class

```
public class DialogElement
{
    private Texture textureSource = null;
    private Rectangle textureRect;
    private Point renderLocation;

    /// <summary>
    /// Create a new dialog element
    /// </summary>
    public DialogElement(Texture background, Rectangle source, Point loc)
    {
        // Store the information
        textureSource = background;
        textureRect = source;
        renderLocation = loc;
    }
    /// <summary>
    /// Render the button in the correct state
    /// </summary>
    public virtual void Draw(Sprite renderSprite)
    {
        // Render the element if it exists
        if (textureSource != null)
        {
            // Render to the screen centered
            renderSprite.Draw(textureSource, textureRect,
                UiScreen.ObjectCenter, new Vector3(renderLocation.X,
                renderLocation.Y, 1.0f), UiScreen.SpriteColor);
        }
    }
}
```

210   Chapter 12

It doesn't get much simpler than that right there. You simply store the texture of the sprite you want to render, the source rectangle of the actual data you plan to render, and the location of the upper-left corner of the position you want to render this sprite to. Then, when you are ready to render, you simply render to that location. The only reason this part is even implemented is for more readable code. It doesn't necessarily help (nor hurt) the actual execution of the game. Add the following variable declarations to handle rendering this screen:

```
// Yes button (will be used in more than one spot)
private UiButton yesButton = null;
private DialogElement dialogBackground = null;
private DialogElement enterHostName = null;
private UiTextBox hostnameBox = null;
```

You want to make sure that you actually create these things sometime, so in your `CreateDialogs` method you implemented earlier, go ahead and use the code from Listing 12.11 and add it to the end to make sure these objects get created for use.

LISTING 12.11   Creating the Enter Host Screen Items

```
// Create the yes button
yesButton = new UiButton(renderSprite, buttonTextures, buttonTextures,
    new Rectangle(ButtonWidth,ButtonHeight * 4,
    ButtonWidth, ButtonHeight),
    new Rectangle(0, ButtonHeight * 4,
    ButtonWidth, ButtonHeight),
    new Point((width - ButtonWidth) / 2,
    (height - ButtonHeight) - (height / 4 - 20)), parent);
yesButton.Click += new EventHandler(OnYesButton);
yesButton.ShortcutKey = Keys.Enter;

dialogBackground = new DialogElement(dialogTexture, new Rectangle(0,0, 512, 256),
    new Point((width - 512) / 2, (height - 256) - 50));
enterHostName = new DialogElement(dialogTexture, new Rectangle(0,384, 512, 64),
    new Point((width - 512) / 2, (height-64)/2 + 25));
hostnameBox = new UiTextBox(device, dialogTexture, new Rectangle(0,448, 512, 64),
    new Point((width - 512) / 2, (height-64)/2 + 75), parent);
```

Here you can see that the actual creation code is equally as simple, and rendering is just as simple. (The code in Listing 12.12 is an excerpt from the rendering method you will find on the included CD.)

LISTING 12.12   Rendering the Select Host Screen

```
else if (currentScreen == ScreenState.SelectHost)
{
    dialogBackground.Draw(renderSprite);
    enterHostName.Draw(renderSprite);
    hostnameBox.Draw(renderSprite, unchecked((int)0xff00AB08));
    yesButton.Draw();
}
```

As I said, it doesn't get much simpler. I know you're excited to get into the game development, so I try not to bore you with this user interface stuff you've already done in Blockers. (Besides, isn't that what the included CD is for?) However, before you're done with this chapter, I want to point out one more thing: how to combine the user interface with a new class that will be used to render the tank you play as. This part is the Select Your Tank screen, naturally, and you can see an example in Figure 12.5.

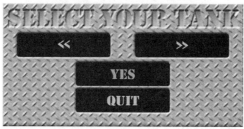

FIGURE 12.5
Picking your tank.

Rendering Your 3D Model with Your User Interface

You've already loaded 3D meshes in your games up to this point, and in Blockers, you actually did something similar to what you'll do here, but there you had the mesh a part of the user interface screen itself, rather than its own separate object. Add a new code file called tank.cs to your project, and add the code from Listing 12.13 to that file.

LISTING 12.13 The Tank Selection Model

```
using System;
using System.Drawing;
using System.Windows.Forms;
using Microsoft.DirectX;
using Microsoft.DirectX.Direct3D;
using Microsoft.Samples.DirectX.UtilityToolkit;

namespace Tankers
{
```

LISTING 12.13   Continued

```
/// <summary>
/// Will hold the possible tank colors
/// </summary>
public enum TankColors : byte
{
    Gray,
    Black,
    Green,
    Sand,
    FirstColor = Gray,
    LastColor = Sand,
}
/// <summary>
/// Will hold the model information for selecting the tank
/// </summary>
public class TankSelectionModel : IDisposable
{
    private Mesh tankMesh = null;
    private Texture tankTexture = null;
    private int numberSubsets = 0;
    // Stored rendering device
    private Device device = null;

    // Current Tank Color
    private TankColors currentColor = TankColors.Sand;

    /// <summary>
    /// Create a new tank object
    /// </summary>
    public TankSelectionModel(Device renderingDevice)
    {
        // Store the device
        device = renderingDevice;

        // First create our 'flat' hierarchy mesh
        ExtendedMaterial[] mtrl = null;
        tankMesh = Mesh.FromFile(GameEngine.MediaPath + Tank.TankMeshFile,
            MeshFlags.Managed, renderingDevice, out mtrl);

        // Store the number of subsets
        if ((mtrl != null) && (mtrl.Length > 0) )
        {
            numberSubsets = mtrl.Length;
        }
        tankTexture = GetTankTexture(device, currentColor);
    }
    public void Dispose()
    {
        if (tankMesh != null)
        {
            tankMesh.Dispose();
        }
    }
}
```

Check out the enumeration used to define the tank colors. There are a few things to notice about the enumeration. First, realize that it derives from byte. The major reason is for network traffic. If you want to send over the color of the tank, using a single byte is more efficient than any other single piece of data you could pass. Besides, do you really need more than 255 differently colored tanks? The other things to notice are the first and last color members. They are used to indicate when you've gone beyond the scope of the tank colors, which you'll see in a moment.

The creation of the mesh itself is standard, but notice that there is a change from how you did things before. You're not storing the materials or textures that came from the mesh. You record the number of subsets and then call the GetTankTexture method (see Listing 12.14) to retrieve the texture. You can do this because the texture uses only a single texture, and each material is simply pure white anyway (which you defined in the game engine). There is no good reason to store multiple versions of the same data, so you don't.

LISTING 12.14   Getting the Tank Texture

```
public static Texture GetTankTexture(Device device, TankColors color)
{
    switch(color)
    {
        case TankColors.Black:
            return TexturePool.CreateTexture(device, "LowResBlack.png");
        case TankColors.Gray:
            return TexturePool.CreateTexture(device, "LowResGray.png");
        case TankColors.Green:
            return TexturePool.CreateTexture(device, "LowResGreen.png");
        case TankColors.Sand:
            return TexturePool.CreateTexture(device, "LowResSand.png");
        default:
            throw new ArgumentException("Not a valid color.", "color");
    }
}
```

This method simply returns a texture from the pool based on which color you've passed in. For each of the tank colors defined, there is a corresponding texture. This method is marked public because more than one class will be using it later. You'll notice in Figure 12.5 that there are left and right buttons to select the next and previous tanks, which update the color of the tank (and thus its texture). This part is where those two "extra" enumeration values come into play. See Listing 12.15 for more information.

LISTING 12.15   Selecting a New Tank Color

```
public void SelectNextColor()
{
    // Update the color
    currentColor++;
    if (currentColor > TankColors.LastColor)
    {
        currentColor = TankColors.FirstColor;
    }

    // Update the textures
    tankTexture = GetTankTexture(device, currentColor);
}
public void SelectPreviousColor()
{
    // Update the color
    currentColor--;
    if ((byte)currentColor == 0xff)
    {
        currentColor = TankColors.LastColor;
    }

    // Update the textures
    tankTexture = GetTankTexture(device, currentColor);
}
```

When you select the next color, you increment the current color counter, and if it's gone past the last color, you simply set it back to the first color. This move allows the colors to wrap as you go through them. Selecting the previous color does the same thing, with one minor caveat. If you're on the first color (the value is 0), and you move back one (via the decrement operator), you go back to 0xff in your byte. So you simply catch that and move to the last color. Drawing the tank is similar to what you've done before, but do you remember the count of vertices and faces rendered in the main game engine? Here is the first time you get to see it happen. See Listing 12.16 for the code that updates these member variables and renders the tank.

LISTING 12.16   Rendering the Selected Tank

```
public void Draw(GameEngine engine)
{
    // Set the device's texture that will be used for rendering
    // the tank in either scenario
    engine.RenderingDevice.SetTexture(0, tankTexture);

#if (DEBUG)
    engine.numberFaces += tankMesh.NumberFaces;
    engine.numberVerts += tankMesh.NumberVertices;
```

LISTING 12.16 Continued

```
#endif
    for (int i = 0; i < numberSubsets; i++)
    {
        tankMesh.DrawSubset(i);
    }
}
```

Summary

This chapter could go on for quite a few more pages explaining the interactions of the various user interface screens, but you've already gone through this exercise before, and you wouldn't get as much benefit out of going through it again. With only 24 chapters for learning these things, you are probably interested in focusing more on the actual 3D graphics than the simple 2D user interfaces. Study the code on the CD for more information on finishing the user interface.

Now that you've got your new user interface working like a charm and players can navigate through the user interface to select the tanks they'll be using, they are almost ready to play the game.

In the next chapter, you can start on that game, and work on the "real" tank.

CHAPTER 13

Rendering a Realistic Tank

At the end of the last chapter, you got to render a tank. It spun around as you were waiting for the user to pick its color, but was it realistic? Could you move the gun turret around, raise or lower the barrel, or move the tank? Did you even see any options on the mesh class that implies this is possible?

The normal mesh class doesn't allow any of these things. It can do two main things, load a mesh and render it. However, many meshes have a "hierarchy" of data that you can use to manipulate certain parts of the final visual model.

In this chapter, you'll learn

- ▶ All about mesh hierarchy
- ▶ How to load a mesh with a hierarchy
- ▶ How to render the mesh hierarchy
- ▶ Why you create a camera class

Understanding a Mesh Hierarchy

The problem (if you want to call it one) with the standard mesh class is that it treats the object it is going to render as a single solid object. In the real world, though, that's almost always not the case. Take your body, for example: sure it is a single "solid" object, but the various parts of your body can move independently. How about an example?

Take your arm and hold it straight out in front of you. Now move your arm up and down. Do you notice how only your arm is moving? If you were being rendered as a single mesh, your entire body would be moving up and down, which is definitely not what you want to do (even if levitating sounds exciting).

Now, you can break it down even further. With your arm still sticking straight out in front of you, bend it at the elbow. Notice that you can move only the small section after your elbow without moving any other part of your body. One last visual to get before you're done: with your arm straight out in front of you once more, stand up and then rotate your upper body by turning at your waist. Notice how your arm moves with you and rotates when you do? The arm can be considered a "child" of the upper body. Look at Figure 13.1.

FIGURE 13.1
A tank hierarchy.

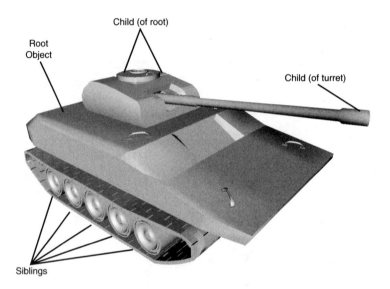

Here you can see the tank, and you can tell that the tank shouldn't be a single solid object. The gun turret should be able to rotate, the gun barrel should be able to move up and down, and the wheels should be able to spin. During your work in this chapter, that's what you will be implementing.

Luckily, a mechanism built in to the API makes this work relatively simple. When a mesh is created by an artist, that mesh can have a *hierarchy*, meaning that the entire mesh can consist of numerous other child meshes. Using the analogy with your body, your single body mesh actually contains a few different parts. You have your torso, your legs, your feet, your arms, your head, and so on. In a hierarchy, these various parts can be children to another part (such as your hands are children of your arms), and other parts would be siblings (such as your two legs would be siblings of each other).

Meshes are the same way. In the tank, you have a central parent section, which is basically the hull of the tank. The wheels are children of the hull but siblings to each other. The gun turret is also a child of the hull, and it too has a child in the gun barrel. Allowing these pieces to move individually will give you a realistic-looking tank.

Now I'm sure that you're anxious to start writing some code. (Aren't you always?) As they say, there's no time like the present, so let's get going! You should add a new class to your `tank.cs` code file. (Feel free to add it to a new file if you want, but I just prefer to keep the tank-related stuff together.) See Listing 13.1 for the base framework of this class.

LISTING 13.1   The Basic Tank Class

```
public class Tank : IDisposable
{
    public const string TankMeshFile = "LowResTank.X";
    private const string GunBarrelFrame = "GunBarrel";
    private const string GunCasingFrame = "GunCasing";
    private const string GunTurretFrame = "GunTurret";
    private static readonly string[] WheelFrames = new string[] { "LeftWheel15",
        "LeftWheel13", "LeftWheel16" ,"RightWheels04", "RightWheels03",
        "LeftWheel17", "RightWheels02", "RightWheels01", "RightWheels",
        "RightWheels05", "RightWheels07", "RightWheels08", "RightWheels09",
        "RightWheels10" };

    private const float MaxTurretAngle = 1;
    private const float MinTurretAngle = -1;
    private const float MaxBarrelAngle = 0;
    private const float MinBarrelAngle = -0.5f;
    public const float GunBarrelLength = 280.0f;

    private Texture tankTexture = null;
    // Used for the full hierarchy mesh
    private TankFrame rootFrame = null;
    // Stored rendering device
    private Device device = null;
    // Stored direction
    private Vector3 facingDirection;
    // Stored rotation matrix
    private Matrix rotationMatrix;
    // Gun Barrel information
    private Vector3 gunDirection;
    private Vector3 gunPosition;
    // State values
    private float wheelAngle = 0.0f; // The current rotation angle of the wheels
    private float barrelAngle = 0.0f; // The current angle of the gun barrel
    private float turretAngle = 0.0f; // The current angle of the gun turret
    private float rotationAngle = 0.0f; // The current rotation angle
                                        // of the tank itself
    private Vector3 tankPosition; // The current position of the tank
    private float tankRadius = 0.0f; // The radius of the bounding sphere
                                     // the tank encompasses
    private Vector3 tankCenter; // The center of the tank
    // Current Tank Color
    private TankColors currentColor = TankColors.Sand;
}
```

All you've really done is define the constants and variables that will be used for rendering the tank in the game. The string constants at the top of the file are actually the names of some of the objects within the mesh hierarchy. You use them later when you're learning how to manipulate each section individually. The other constants are bounds for the tank's gun turret and barrel. Although I'm sure it would have been awesome to make a turret pitch 360° and shoot itself, the real world just doesn't work that way. We want the tank to behave somewhat realistically.

Construction Cue

> If you look at the code on the included CD, you'll notice that you can use a compiler directive called USE_HIGH_RES. The game will by default use a lower-resolution mesh for playing, but it ships with a high-resolution model to be used during the game as well. The code is remarkably similar regardless of which model you use, so if you want to use the high-resolution model in the game, simply include USE_HIGH_RES define. See the code for more information on the differences.

For the instance variables, the tank has a texture (which you'll just get from the texture pool) that is picked by the user before the game starts. The rest of the variables are used for controlling the tank itself, but you can learn about them once you get to the methods they manipulate. Let's look at the constructor for this object, which you'll find in Listing 13.2.

LISTING 13.2   Creating the Tank Object

```
public Tank(Device renderingDevice)
{
    // Store the device
    device = renderingDevice;

    // Set up the matrices
    TankRotation = 0.0f;

    // Now create our allocate hierarchy object
    AnimationRootFrame ar = Mesh.LoadHierarchyFromFile(GameEngine.MediaPath +
        TankMeshFile, MeshFlags.Managed, renderingDevice
        , new TankAllocHierarchy(), null);
    rootFrame = ar.FrameHierarchy as TankFrame;

    tankRadius = Frame.CalculateBoundingSphere(rootFrame, out tankCenter);
}
```

Loading a Tank Hierarchy

That seems pretty simple, doesn't it? Unfortunately, nothing is ever as simple as it seems because outside of storing the device variable and setting a property, you haven't covered any of the other methods before. The animation root frame object is completely new. In the Direct3D API, the mesh hierarchies are commonly used to facilitate animation (and technically, that's what you're doing as well). The primary function of the mesh hierarchy is skeletal animation, but your tank doesn't have any bones. The only thing you care about is the frame hierarchy, which maintains the child/sibling relationship for the data in the frame. After that frame is loaded, you can use a method on the frame class to get the bounding sphere of the tank.

> You might be asking yourself, why do I care about the bounding sphere of the tank? What could it possibly mean? Well, right now, you don't need it, but soon when you want to see whether a player has been shot, or whether the tank is trying to leave a level, it will be important. It's easy to calculate whether an object is within a sphere, so when you are testing to see if any objects collide with your tank, you will use this value to do so.

Construction Cue

Loading the hierarchy from a file takes many of the same parameters that loading a mesh normally takes, but an entire new class is instantiated during the process, and you haven't even defined that class yet. You want to do that now, so add a new code file into your project. You can call it `hierarchy.cs` because that's what its job will be. You will find the implementation for this class in Listing 13.3.

LISTING 13.3   The Allocate Hierarchy Class

```
public class TankAllocHierarchy : AllocateHierarchy
{
    /// <summary>
    /// Create a new hierarchy frame
    /// </summary>
    public override Frame CreateFrame(string name)
    {
        // Create the new derived tank frame
        TankFrame frame = new TankFrame();
        // Store the variables
        frame.Name = name;
        frame.TransformationMatrix = Matrix.Identity;
        frame.CombinedTransformationMatrix = Matrix.Identity;

        return frame;
    }
    /// <summary>
    /// Create a new mesh container for the tank hierarchy
    /// </summary>
    public override MeshContainer CreateMeshContainer(string name,
        MeshData meshData, ExtendedMaterial[] materials,
        EffectInstance[] effectInstances,
        GraphicsStream adjacency, SkinInformation skinInfo)
    {
```

LISTING 13.3   Continued

```
        TankMeshContainer mesh = new TankMeshContainer();

        // Store the variables we care about
        mesh.Name = name;
        mesh.MeshData = meshData;

        return mesh;
    }
}
```

As you see here, the `TankAllocHierarchy` class derives from the `AllocateHierarchy` abstract class, which requires you to implement a `CreateFrame` and `CreateMeshContainer` method. The frames hold the actual hierarchy data, but the mesh containers hold the vertex and adjacency data for each section of the hierarchy. In each of these methods, the objects are simply created, the name is set, and then they are returned. The name corresponds to the string constants you declared earlier this chapter (although you didn't cover all the names the tank files have). You might also notice in the frame creation sets some matrices as well.

The matrices are needed because of the relationship between the full object (for example, the whole tank) and the partial object (for example, the gun barrel). The stored transformation matrix is the matrix that will transform a particular frame into the correct position and orientation relative to its parent. The combined transformation matrix is simply the combination of the frame matrix with those of its parents. It might benefit you to see the implementations of these two classes, which appear in Listing 13.4.

LISTING 13.4   The Frame and Mesh Container Classes

```
public class TankFrame : Frame
{
    // Store the combined transformation matrix
    private Matrix combined = Matrix.Identity;
    public Matrix CombinedTransformationMatrix
    {
        get { return combined; } set { combined = value; }
    }
}
public class TankMeshContainer : MeshContainer
{
    // We need no extra data here
}
```

You'll notice that you don't define the normal transformation matrix in the frame because that is stored in the base class. The mesh container class doesn't need any extra data, but because the mesh container base class is marked abstract, you must take the time to derive a new class from it. That's it for loading a frame hierarchy. Are you surprised how simple it was?

Back in the tank's object constructor, when the LoadHierarchyFromFile method is called, the CreateMeshContainer and CreateFrame methods are called quite a few times while each submesh is loaded into the hierarchy. Next, you simply store the root frame, and you're now off and ready to start rendering a tank. You can see the draw method in Listing 13.5.

LISTING 13.5   Drawing a Tank

```
public void Draw(GameEngine engine)
{
    // Set the device's texture that will be used for rendering
    // the tank in either scenario
    engine.RenderingDevice.SetTexture(0, tankTexture);

    // Draw the mesh hierarchy
    DrawFrame(engine, engine.RenderingDevice, rootFrame);
}
```

Rendering a Mesh Hierarchy

You're probably thinking to yourself right now, "Wow! That was pretty easy!" You wouldn't be wrong, but it is a little more complicated than the two lines shown here make it out to be. After setting the texture (all the mesh subsets in the hierarchy use the same texture), you draw the root frame. Sounds simple enough, but drawing the root frame takes a few different steps. You can see its implementation in Listing 13.6.

LISTING 13.6   Drawing a Frame

```
private void DrawFrame(GameEngine engine, Device renderDevice, TankFrame frame)
{
    TankMeshContainer mesh = frame.MeshContainer as TankMeshContainer;
    while(mesh != null)
    {
        DrawMeshContainer(engine, renderDevice, mesh, frame);

        mesh = mesh.NextContainer as TankMeshContainer;
    }
```

LISTING 13.6   Continued

```
    if (frame.FrameSibling != null)
    {
        DrawFrame(engine, renderDevice, frame.FrameSibling as TankFrame);
    }

    if (frame.FrameFirstChild != null)
    {
        DrawFrame(engine, renderDevice, frame.FrameFirstChild as TankFrame);
    }
}
```

The structure of this method is used in a few places because this is how you "walk the hierarchy." Starting at the root (the initial call), you want to see whether this frame has any meshes that could be rendered. If it does, you call the DrawMeshContainer method to do the actual mesh rendering. (You see that method in Listing 13.7 in just a moment.) It continues looking for more meshes to render in the current frame until there are no more left, and then it calls back into itself recursively for any siblings or children of the current frame. It's important to realize that any one frame can have a maximum of one sibling and one child. In the case of the wheels in Figure 13.1 earlier, the first wheel has one sibling, and the second wheel, in turn, has one sibling (the third wheel). Children are the same way. You'll see this structure in a method again soon.

LISTING 13.7   Drawing a Mesh Container

```
private void DrawMeshContainer(GameEngine engine, Device renderDevice,
        TankMeshContainer mesh, TankFrame frame)
{
#if (DEBUG)
    engine.numberFaces += mesh.MeshData.Mesh.NumberFaces;
    engine.numberVerts += mesh.MeshData.Mesh.NumberVertices;
#endif
    // Each mesh in the hierarchy will have a single subset
    engine.SetWorldTransform(frame.CombinedTransformationMatrix);
    mesh.MeshData.Mesh.DrawSubset(0);
}
```

This code should look familiar because it is similar to how you always render a mesh. One of the new items here is the SetWorldTransform method from the game engine, which you haven't implemented yet. Back in your game engine code class, add this method so you can call it:

```
public void SetWorldTransform(Matrix worldTransform)
{
    device.Transform.World = worldTransform * sceneCamera.ViewMatrix;
}
```

The camera class hasn't been defined yet, but that happens in the near future. In the meantime, you should understand why the world transform is being set this way. In Direct3D when you set the View transform (as you did for the Blockers game), you must store or recalculate a multitude of internal states, which can cause slowdowns if done many times per frame. However, this isn't the case with the world matrix (because it is designed to be set plenty of times). Because everything in the "world" will be transformed by the coordinates, you can get by without ever setting the view transformation by simply combining the world matrix with the current view matrix. This can be a significant performance boost, which is why it's done here.

Manipulating the Tanks

Remember earlier when you were looking at the new frame class? Two sets of matrices were being stored, the transformation matrix and the combined matrix. However, they were never actually set to anything, so how are they supposed to work? Well, the transformation matrices are actually set by the runtime, after the model is loaded. It knows, for example, that the tank's gun turret should sit just above the tank's body, and it sets the transformation matrix to make this happen. The combined transformation matrix, however, is something you've added that the runtime knows nothing about. Look at the Update method in Listing 13.8 and add it to your tank class.

LISTING 13.8 Updating the Tank

```
/// <summary>
/// Update the tank
/// </summary>
public void Update(float time)
{
    // Update the matrices for this tank based on where the tank
    // currently is in the world
    UpdateFrameMatrices(rootFrame, Matrix.Translation(tankPosition),
                        rotationMatrix);
    // Now get the wheel frames and update them
    for(int i = 0; i < WheelFrames.Length; i++)
    {
        TankFrame wheelFrame = Frame.Find(rootFrame, WheelFrames[i]) as TankFrame;
        wheelFrame.CombinedTransformationMatrix = Matrix.RotationY(wheelAngle)
            * wheelFrame.CombinedTransformationMatrix;
    }
}
```

The goal of this method is to assign the combined matrix transformation for every frame in the hierarchy, and the UpdateFrameMatrices method that is called first is the major part of this. When you look at the implementation (Listing 13.9), you'll see it's structured similarly to the DrawFrame method you implemented earlier because it will walk the hierarchy to set the data.

LISTING 13.9 Updating Frame Matrices

```
private void UpdateFrameMatrices(TankFrame frame, Matrix parentMatrix,
                                 Matrix rotationMatrix)
{
    // Check which frames we are updating
    switch(frame.Name)
    {
        case GunBarrelFrame:
        case GunCasingFrame:
            Matrix barrelRotation = Matrix.RotationX(barrelAngle);
            Matrix turretRotation = Matrix.RotationY(turretAngle);

            Matrix combinedRotation = (barrelRotation * turretRotation)
                * rotationMatrix * parentMatrix;

            frame.CombinedTransformationMatrix = frame.TransformationMatrix
                * combinedRotation  ;

            // Calculate the direction the barrel is facing
            if (frame.Name == GunBarrelFrame)
            {
                gunDirection = new Vector3(combinedRotation.M31,
                    combinedRotation.M32, combinedRotation.M33);
                gunDirection.Normalize();
                gunPosition = new Vector3(frame.CombinedTransformationMatrix.M41,
                    frame.CombinedTransformationMatrix.M42 + 23.0f,
                    frame.CombinedTransformationMatrix.M43);
            }
            break;
        case GunTurretFrame:
            Matrix gunTurretRotation = Matrix.RotationY(turretAngle);
            frame.CombinedTransformationMatrix = frame.TransformationMatrix
                * gunTurretRotation * rotationMatrix * parentMatrix;
            break;
        default:
            // by default, just multiply the transformation matrix
            // by the parent matrix
            frame.CombinedTransformationMatrix = frame.TransformationMatrix
                * rotationMatrix * parentMatrix;
            break;
    }

    if (frame.FrameSibling != null)
    {
        UpdateFrameMatrices(frame.FrameSibling as TankFrame, parentMatrix,
                            rotationMatrix);
    }

    if (frame.FrameFirstChild != null)
    {
        // No need to include the rotation in any children frames,
```

LISTING 13.9   Continued

```
        // just use identity
        UpdateFrameMatrices(frame.FrameFirstChild as TankFrame,
            frame.CombinedTransformationMatrix, Matrix.Identity);
    }
}
```

Now there's a scary-looking method! First impressions are always deceiving, though, because when you break it down, it's pretty simple. First, you need to check which frame you are using, and if it's one you happen to care about, do some fancy math calculations. What are these calculations actually intending to accomplish? You want to look at the gun's barrel and casing. (The casing is what connects the barrel to the turret.) Because the barrel and casing sit on top of the turret, you want to combine these matrices. Notice that first you get a rotation matrix for the turret and the barrel, the turret rotates along the Y axis, and the barrel rotates along the X axis.

Remember from Chapter 10, "A Quick 3D-Math Primer," combining matrices has to happen in the correct order. The combined rotation matrix that we have for the barrel and casing is calculated by multiplying first the child matrix (barrel) by the parent matrix (turret). Then, that result is multiplied against the global rotation matrix (which is passed in to the function), and finally, that result is multiplied against the parent matrix (which is also passed in to the method).

Once that is calculated, you have a single matrix that represents the rotation of the gun barrel and the gun casing. To calculate the combined transformation matrix, you take the automatically generated transformation matrix and the combined rotation matrix and multiply them together (ensuring that the automatically generated one is used first). You'll notice the gun turret frame does an almost identical thing, except it doesn't calculate the parent matrix first. You'll also notice that the default case is simply multiplying the automatically generated transformation matrix by the rotation matrix and the parent matrix (which is the simplest case).

Did you notice the extra checks for the gun barrel's direction and position? Later, during the game development, you need to know where the gun barrel is so you know where to fire your weapon. One of the nice things about the matrices being used is you can use the members to calculate your rotation and your position quite easily. As you can see from the code, the first three items of the third column relate to the direction the object is facing. The first three items of the fourth row is the position of the object in world space. The direction vector is normalized to make calculations easier. These two variables are very important later.

After the combined transformation matrix is calculated for this frame, you need to finish walking the frame hierarchy to ensure that each frame gets updated. For siblings, you simply pass on the same two matrices as you received from the method (because the siblings should each have the same parent). However, for the child frames, you actually pass in the combined matrix of this frame as the parent matrix and the identity matrix as the rotation matrix. You don't want to pass in the global rotation matrix again, but it's already been transformed by the parent matrix—and if you do include it again, you get your objects being rotated twice as quickly as they should be.

FIGURE 13.2
The tank with a rotated turret.

With that, depending on the position and orientation of your tank, and the values of the angle variables for the turret and gun barrel, when you render the tank now, you will see it being rendered with each object able to move independently (see Figure 13.2).

Tank Properties

If you remember earlier when you first defined the tank class, plenty of variables declared were private and you didn't have any public way to access them. Naturally, you need to rectify this situation because the game engine (and player objects you will be creating) need to manipulate the tanks. Add the properties in Listing 13.10 to your tank class to round out its implementation.

LISTING 13.10 Tank Properties

```
public Vector3 Position
{
    get { return tankPosition; }
    set { tankPosition = value; }
}
public float GunTurretAngle
{
    get { return turretAngle; }
    set
    {
        if (value > MaxTurretAngle)
            turretAngle = (float)MaxTurretAngle;
        else if (value < MinTurretAngle)
            turretAngle = (float)MinTurretAngle;
        else
            turretAngle = value;
    }
```

LISTING 13.10   Continued

```
}
public float GunBarrelAngle
{
    get { return barrelAngle; }
    set
    {
        if (value > MaxBarrelAngle)
            barrelAngle = (float)MaxBarrelAngle;
        else if (value < MinBarrelAngle)
            barrelAngle = (float)MinBarrelAngle;
        else
            barrelAngle = value;
    }
}
public float WheelRotation
{
    get { return wheelAngle; }
    set { wheelAngle = value; }
}
public float TankRotation
{
    get { return rotationAngle; }
    set
    {
        // Set the new rotation angle
        rotationAngle = value;
        // Update the rotation matrix
        rotationMatrix = Matrix.RotationY(rotationAngle);
        // Calculate the direction you're facing
        facingDirection = new Vector3(rotationMatrix.M31, rotationMatrix.M32
            , rotationMatrix.M33);
        facingDirection.Normalize();
    }
}

public Matrix TankRotationMatrix
{
    get { return rotationMatrix; }
}
public Vector3 TankDirection
{
    get { return facingDirection; }
}
public float Radius
{
    get { return tankRadius; }
}
public Vector3 Center
{
    get { return tankCenter; }
}
public Vector3 BarrelDirection
{
    get { return gunDirection; }
}
```

LISTING 13.10 Continued

```
public Vector3 BarrelPosition
{
    get { return gunPosition; }
}
public TankColors Color
{
    get { return currentColor; }
    set
    {
        // Set the color
        currentColor = value;
        // Update the textures
        tankTexture = TankSelectionModel.GetTankTexture(device, currentColor);
    }
}
```

You'll notice that the majority of the properties are simple public accessors (either read-only or normal), but a few actually do a little extra, normally when the value is set. For example, setting the color updates the texture using the method you wrote in the last chapter. Modifying the gun angles enforces the maximum and minimum limits on them. Finally, updating the tank rotation builds the rotation matrix and stores the direction the tank is currently facing. Just like the gun turret, the entire tank is rotated on the Y axis.

Creating the Camera Class

Before you finish this chapter, you implement the camera class. During the Blockers game, you handled all the camera movements (mainly the view transform) on your own. Although it is a completely viable option, it can be a little annoying. Having an abstracted camera class is more natural. Create a new code file (call it camera.cs) in your project, and use the code from Listing 13.11 for the initial implementation.

LISTING 13.11 Initial Camera Class

```
using System;
using Microsoft.DirectX;
using Microsoft.DirectX.Direct3D;

namespace Tankers
{
    public class Camera
    {
        // Attributes for view matrix
        private Vector3 eyeVector;
        private Vector3 lookAtVector;
```

LISTING 13.11   Continued

```
            private Vector3 upVector;
            // Matrix for the view transform
            private Matrix  viewMatrixTransform;
            // Attributes for projection matrix
            private float fieldView;
            private float aspectRatio;
            private float nearPlane;
            private float farPlane;
            // Matrix for the projection transform
            private Matrix  projectionMatrixTransform;
    }
}
```

You probably recognize many of these variables from Blockers when you were setting up the camera for that game. These values map directly to the associated
items in the projection and view matrices that you can create. You provide read-
only properties for these as well, but there's no need for that information to
appear in this book because you can see the code on the included CD for the
implementation. Plus, defining read-only properties has been done numerous
times, even in this chapter. You only have the properties as read-only so you cannot set them, which makes it pretty difficult to have the camera update any of
these variables. Instead, you add two methods (Listing 13.12) to the class to set
each of the required variables at the same time.

LISTING 13.12   Setting Camera Properties

```
public void SetViewParameters( Vector3 vEyePt, Vector3 vLookatPt,
                               Vector3 vUpVec )
{
    // Set attributes for the view matrix
    eyeVector    = vEyePt;
    lookAtVector = vLookatPt;
    upVector     = vUpVec;

    viewMatrixTransform = Matrix.LookAtLH( eyeVector, lookAtVector, upVector );
    UpdateViewFrustum();
}
public void SetProjParameters( float fFOV, float fAspect, float fNearPlane,
                               float fFarPlane )
{
    // Set attributes for the projection matrix
    fieldView       = fFOV;
    aspectRatio     = fAspect;
    nearPlane   = fNearPlane;
    farPlane    = fFarPlane;

    projectionMatrixTransform = Matrix.PerspectiveFovLH( fFOV, fAspect,
                                                fNearPlane, fFarPlane );
}
```

For the most part, these methods don't do much more than store the variables passed in and then update the associated matrix, but in reality, they don't need to do anything more. When the view matrix is updated, a method you haven't defined yet is called to update the view frustum.

I discussed the view frustum a few chapters ago, and if you remember, it's essentially the trapezoid area where the camera can see. The idea here is that you don't want to waste time by drawing things the camera obviously cannot see. You create an internal view frustum that in reality is a series of planes that define the boundaries of the frustum, and then you check whether an object is inside that frustum before rendering it. This practice is a quick and efficient way of rendering only objects the camera can see. The implementation of the method appears in Listing 13.13.

LISTING 13.13   Creating the Frustum Planes

```
public void UpdateViewFrustum()
{
    // First get the inverse viewproj matrix
    Matrix mat = viewMatrixTransform * projectionMatrixTransform;
    mat.Invert();

    // Get the 8 corners of the view frustum
    frustumPoints[0] = new Vector3(-1.0f, -1.0f,  0.0f); // xyz
    frustumPoints[1] = new Vector3( 1.0f, -1.0f,  0.0f); // Xyz
    frustumPoints[2] = new Vector3(-1.0f,  1.0f,  0.0f); // xYz
    frustumPoints[3] = new Vector3( 1.0f,  1.0f,  0.0f); // XYz
    frustumPoints[4] = new Vector3(-1.0f, -1.0f,  1.0f); // xyZ
    frustumPoints[5] = new Vector3( 1.0f, -1.0f,  1.0f); // XyZ
    frustumPoints[6] = new Vector3(-1.0f,  1.0f,  1.0f); // xYZ
    frustumPoints[7] = new Vector3( 1.0f,  1.0f,  1.0f); // XYZ

    for( int i = 0; i < frustumPoints.Length; i++ )
        frustumPoints[i] = Vector3.TransformCoordinate(frustumPoints[i], mat);

    // Now calculate the planes
    frustumPlanes[0] = Plane.FromPoints(frustumPoints[0], frustumPoints[1],
                        frustumPoints[2] ); // Near
    frustumPlanes[1] = Plane.FromPoints(frustumPoints[6], frustumPoints[7],
                        frustumPoints[5] ); // Far
    frustumPlanes[2] = Plane.FromPoints(frustumPoints[2], frustumPoints[6],
                        frustumPoints[4] ); // Left
    frustumPlanes[3] = Plane.FromPoints(frustumPoints[7], frustumPoints[3],
                        frustumPoints[5]); // Right
    frustumPlanes[4] = Plane.FromPoints(frustumPoints[2], frustumPoints[3],
                        frustumPoints[6] ); // Top
    frustumPlanes[5] = Plane.FromPoints(frustumPoints[1], frustumPoints[0],
                        frustumPoints[4]); // Bottom
}
```

To calculate the trapezoid where the frustum will reside, you first get the view and projection matrices and invert them. You then manually set the frustum points as if they were a cube with a length of 1 on each side. You do this because right after, you transform each of the coordinates by the inverted view and projection matrix, which "transforms" them into the trapezoid shape that is the view frustum. You then create the six planes that make up each side of the frustum. You've probably noticed that you never defined the points' and planes' variables being used here, so you want to do that as well:

```
// View frustum data
private Vector3[] frustumPoints = new Vector3[8];
private Plane[] frustumPlanes = new Plane[6];
```

With your set of planes defined now, how do you actually know whether an object lies within the frustum and should be rendered? There's a simple mathematical formula you can use to see whether a point is outside of a plane. (See Listing 13.14.)

LISTING 13.14   Checking Whether an Object Is in Frustum

```
public bool ObjectInFrustum(IMoveableObject obj)
{
    // Check to see if this point is in the plane
    foreach(Plane p in frustumPlanes)
    {
        if (p.A * obj.Position.X + p.B * obj.Position.Y + p.C *
            obj.Position.Z + p.D <= (-obj.Radius))
        {
            // The object is not in the view frustum, do not draw it
            return false;
        }
    }
    // By default, the object is in the frustum
    return true;
}
```

Here you see that by default, the object is assumed to be within the frustum (and thus drawn); however, if it can be guaranteed that it is not, it is skipped. Did you notice the type of object passed into this method? This interface isn't defined anywhere but will be used for objects you want to render, particularly those that can be culled. You'll find the definition of this interface in Listing 13.15, and starting next chapter, you'll be using it. The code on the included CD has this interface defined in the game engine source file, but you may put it wherever you find it convenient.

Construction Cue

> *Culling* is the act of not drawing an object that is in the scene because it would not have been seen anyway.

LISTING 13.15 The `IMoveableObject`

```
public interface IMoveableObject
{
    float Radius { get; } // The radius of the moveable object
    Vector3 Position { get; } // The current position of the moveable object
    Vector3 Direction { get; } // The direction the moveable object
                               // is facing or moving
    void Update(float elapsedTime, Level currentLevel);
    // Update the moveable object
    void Draw(GameEngine engine, Camera c); // Render the moveable object
}
```

Unfortunately, you can't compile this code because you haven't defined the level class yet. That's coming up right about now.

Summary

This was a busy chapter! You learned about mesh hierarchies and how to load and render them, and you are ready to start implementing a little bit of the game play features. You encapsulated the camera in its own object to make things easier for you, and you created an interface to help define particular properties of your objects.

In the next chapter, you will start working on the level and player class, which will be the root controlling object of your tanks.

CHAPTER 14

The Sky? A Level? The Player!

You've got a lot of things implemented now, but there's still quite a bit more left to do. Currently, there isn't anything rendering and there's definitely not much game play going on. In this chapter, you start working on this area by building first the world where the game will be played, and then the player who will, well, play the game.

In this chapter, you'll learn

- ▶ How to implement a sky box
- ▶ How to implement a level world
- ▶ How to implement the player

A World Without a Sky Would Be Black

You implemented a sky box early in this book for Blockers; it was the inside of a dungeon room, and it was a way to encompass the level. Sky boxes are always implemented because without one, you would have an empty area where the objects of your world weren't rendered. A plain black sky isn't realistic unless, of course, your game resides inside a vacuum in space (or maybe a black hole). I don't think the tanks here would work too well in a black hole.

I hope you've been noticing a consistent theme in the implementation of Tankers. The code has been rearranged to form more logical units, and that practice continues for the sky box. Rather than make this code reside within the game engine, you create a new class. Go ahead and add a new code file to your project, call it skybox.cs or whatever you want, and look at the implementation from Listing 14.1.

LISTING 14.1   The World Class (Sky Box)

```
using System;
using System.Drawing;
using System.Windows.Forms;
using Microsoft.DirectX;
using Microsoft.DirectX.Direct3D;

namespace Tankers
{
    public class Skybox : IDisposable
    {
        private const float ScaleSize = 1950.0f;
        private const float Height = ScaleSize * 2.0f;
        private static readonly Matrix ScaleMatrix = Matrix.Scaling(ScaleSize,
            ScaleSize, ScaleSize) * Matrix.Translation(0,Height,0);
        private const string SkyboxMeshName = "skybox.x";

        private Mesh skyboxMesh = null;
        private Texture[] skyboxTextures = null;
        public Skybox(Device device)
        {
            // First create the mesh
            ExtendedMaterial[] mtrls = null;
            skyboxMesh = Mesh.FromFile(GameEngine.MediaPath + SkyboxMeshName,
                    MeshFlags.Managed, device,  out mtrls);

            // With the mesh created, create each of the textures
            // used for the sky box
            if ((mtrls != null) && (mtrls.Length > 0))
            {
                skyboxTextures = new Texture[mtrls.Length];
                for(int i = 0; i < mtrls.Length; i++)
                {
                    skyboxTextures[i] = TexturePool.CreateTexture(device,
                                        mtrls[i].TextureFilename);
                }
            }
        }

        /// <summary>
        /// Render the sky box
        /// </summary>
        public void Draw(GameEngine engine, Device device)
        {
#if (DEBUG)
            engine.numberFaces += skyboxMesh.NumberFaces;
            engine.numberVerts += skyboxMesh.NumberVertices;
#endif
            // When rendering the sky box you will want to turn off the zbuffer
            device.RenderState.ZBufferEnable = false;
            device.RenderState.ZBufferWriteEnable = false;

            // Scale the world transform and turn off lighting
            engine.SetWorldTransform(ScaleMatrix);
            device.RenderState.Lighting = false;

            // Render each subset of the mesh
```

LISTING 14.1   Continued

```
        for(int i = 0; i < skyboxTextures.Length; i++)
        {
            device.SetTexture(0, skyboxTextures[i]);
            skyboxMesh.DrawSubset(i);
        }

        // Turn the zbuffer back on
        device.RenderState.ZBufferEnable = true;
        device.RenderState.ZBufferWriteEnable = true;
        // Turn lighting back on
        device.RenderState.Lighting = true;
    }
    /// <summary>
    /// Will be used to clean up objects
    /// </summary>
    public void Dispose()
    {
        if (skyboxMesh != null)
        {
            skyboxMesh.Dispose();
            skyboxMesh = null;
        }
    }
}
}
```

The constants are used to manipulate the transformation of the sky box (and define the name of the model that you will be using). The transformation matrix is defined by scaling the model to a much larger size, and it is translated up along the Y axis twice the scale size. This move forces the sky box to be large enough to encompass the entire world. (The tank model is large, and rather than scale that model down, you scale the sky up.)

The instance variables should be instantly recognizable by now, the mesh that is being used to render the sky box and the series of six textures that compose the sky that the sky box gets its name from. During the creation of the object, the mesh is loaded and each texture is loaded from the pool; then, you're ready to render the world. I hope you noticed that the materials weren't stored for the object now as they were during Blockers.

> You'll notice that even these textures are loaded from the texture pool you created a few chapters ago. You might be wondering why you need to use that even here, when it's obvious you won't be reusing these textures later. The fact is you *could* skip the texture pool and simply create it for use only here, but you should be consistent throughout the application. Besides, just because these textures aren't reused currently doesn't mean they won't be reused at any time in the future.

Construction Cue

The rendering here includes the debug code for counting the number of vertices and faces being rendered. Because it is just a textured cube, the number of vertices and faces is small, but because you have the information, you might as well use it. After that, you turn off the depth buffer because there is no way that anything can be rendered behind the sky box; the extra calculation is unnecessary. You also turn off lighting because you want to use the texture color as the only source of color for the sky. Finally, before the actual rendering takes place, the world transform is set from the game engine. (Do you remember why we have a method for this?)

After the sky is rendered, you reset the render states that you were using to handle the rendering of the sky box; namely, you turn the depth buffer and lighting back on. The Dispose method shouldn't need any explanation by now.

Did you notice that you've stopped implementing a "finalizer" (destructor) to the objects on which you've implemented IDisposable? If you were designing a library that other users would use, this step would not be a good idea because you wouldn't be able to guarantee that the caller of your object would call Dispose(). Because the only caller of these objects is you, you can ensure that you are calling Dispose on these objects.

You're probably asking yourself, "Well, why do I care? Wouldn't I rather be safe than sorry and just leave them implemented? If they don't get used, well, that's great." Although that is an option, it wouldn't be a good idea, and it has everything to do with the garbage collector. Let's look at a scenario.

You've just created an object that has both a Dispose method and a finalizer. Your code only uses the object for a brief moment and then no longer needs the object, but it never calls the Dispose method. The garbage collector sees an unused short-lived object and decides, "I should probably get rid of that because it's obviously not needed anymore," and a generation 0 collection starts. As the collection notices that this object is no longer needed, it sees that the object also has a finalizer. An object cannot be collected until after the finalizer runs, and the garbage collector can't sit around and wait for the object to be finalized. So the object is marked that it's ready to be finalized and promoted to generation 1. In a few chapters, when you get to the performance chapter and I discuss the garbage collector in detail, you'll get a better understanding of why this is a bad thing.

Construction Cue

| A good rule of thumb is to *never* have a finalizer unless you are sure you need it. For now, you do not. |

You Have a Sky, but the Tank Can't Drive There

In Blockers, you loaded the levels from a file, and the data that was required to be rendered was generated dynamically based on the contents of that file. For this game, the entire level is loaded from a mesh file. The actual vertex data defining the mesh will also be used to determine the physics of the world and the interaction between the world and the inhabitants it shares (for example, the tank). You once again want this code to be encapsulated in its own file, so create a new code file called level.cs and use the code from Listing 14.2 as the base implementation.

LISTING 14.2   The Level Class

```
using System;
using System.Drawing;
using System.Windows.Forms;
using Microsoft.DirectX;
using Microsoft.DirectX.Direct3D;

namespace Tankers
{
    public class Level : IDisposable
    {
        private const float Height = 0.0f;
        private static readonly Matrix LevelMatrix = Matrix.Translation(
                                          0,Height,0);
        private const string LevelMeshName = "Level1.x";
        private const float LevelSize = 3000.0f;

        private Mesh levelMesh = null;
        private Texture[] levelTextures = null;

        /// <summary>
        /// Create a new instance of the level class
        /// </summary>
        public Level(Device device)
        {
            // First create the mesh
            ExtendedMaterial[] mtrls = null;
            levelMesh = Mesh.FromFile(GameEngine.MediaPath + LevelMeshName,
                MeshFlags.Managed, device, out mtrls);

            // With the mesh created, create each of the textures
            // used for the level
            if ((mtrls != null) && (mtrls.Length > 0))
            {
                levelTextures = new Texture[mtrls.Length];
                for(int i = 0; i < mtrls.Length; i++)
                {
```

LISTING 14.2   Continued

```
                    levelTextures[i] = TexturePool.CreateTexture(device,
                                    mtrls[i].TextureFilename);
                }
            }
        }
        /// <summary>
        /// Render the level
        /// </summary>
        public void Draw(GameEngine engine, Device device)
        {
#if (DEBUG)
            engine.numberFaces += levelMesh.NumberFaces;
            engine.numberVerts += levelMesh.NumberVertices;
#endif
            // Set the world transform
            engine.SetWorldTransform(LevelMatrix);

            device.RenderState.Lighting = false;
            // Render each subset of the mesh
            for(int i = 0; i < levelTextures.Length; i++)
            {
                device.SetTexture(0, levelTextures[i]);
                levelMesh.DrawSubset(i);
            }
            device.RenderState.Lighting = true;
        }
        /// <summary>
        /// Will be used to clean up objects
        /// </summary>
        public void Dispose()
        {
            if (levelMesh != null)
            {
                levelMesh.Dispose();
                levelMesh = null;
            }
        }
    }
}
```

The initial code here looks similar to the code for the sky box. You have some constants defined, and a constant transformation matrix is built. The code on the included CD includes two different level mesh files (aptly named level1.x and level2.x), either of which would work fine with this code. Pick which one you like best and use that as the constant. The levels themselves are square with each side having a length of 3,000 units, which is where the last constant comes from.

Creation is exactly the same as creating the sky box, and the first portion of the rendering is as well. Notice that before you render the level mesh, however, you do *not* turn off the depth buffer. It will be possible to have objects rendered "behind" the level (or at least behind walls in the level), so you want the depth buffer on for this rendering. Lighting is off. You can see the textures used for the models, so you're not driving your tank down some dark hallway of a level where you can barely see anything. After the mesh is rendered, you turn the lighting render state back on.

Have you noticed that you've stopped setting the material object on the device? Remember from the beginning of the implementation of this game, you created a static "white" material. Because all the objects in the game (so far) require a single white material, it is set in the rendering method in the game engine and doesn't need to be set in these individual rendering methods.

Construction Cue

Someone Has to Control the Tanks

Now that you have an actual world as well as a tank to reside in that world, you need some way to allow your players to interact with the tank (and as a side effect, the world). The player object you're about to take will be the first object you create that implements the IMoveableObject interface you defined in the last chapter. You will be able to detect whether any object that implements the interface is within the view frustum and should be rendered at all. Before you get there, though, you probably want to implement the class itself. Add a new code file player.cs, and see Listing 14.3 for an initial implementation.

LISTING 14.3   The Player Class

```
using System;
using System.Windows.Forms;
using Microsoft.DirectX;
using Microsoft.DirectX.Direct3D;
using Input=Microsoft.DirectX.DirectInput;

namespace Tankers
{
    /// <summary>
    /// This class will maintain a player in the game
    /// </summary>
    public class Player : IDisposable, IMoveableObject
    {
        private const float MaximumMovementSpeed = 600.0f;
        private const float MaximumMovementSpeedWheels = MaximumMovementSpeed /
                                                         100.0f;
        private const float MaximumRotationSpeed = 1.15f;
        private const float MaximumGunSpeed = 0.003f;
        private const float GunCoolDown = 2.5f;

        private Tank gameTank = null;
        private bool isMovingForward = false;
        private bool isMovingBackward = false;
```

LISTING 14.3   Continued

```
            private bool isRotatingLeft = false;
            private bool isRotatingRight = false;
            private bool isPlayerLocal = true;
            private bool isPlayerActive = false; // Only for remote players

            // Default the mouse stats to -1 so we know they haven't been used yet.
            private int mouseX = -1;
            private int mouseY = -1;

            // The device for DirectInput will only be used for the local player
            private Input.Device joystickDevice = null;
            private bool hasHat = false; // Will be used to determine if the
                                         //        joystick has a hat for control
            private bool isMovingForwardJoy = false;
            private bool isMovingBackwardJoy = false;
            private bool isRotatingLeftJoy = false;
            private bool isRotatingRightJoy = false;

            // Tank firing items
            public event EventHandler Fired;
            private float lastFiredTime = -GunCoolDown; // So you can fire right away
            private float totalTime = 0.0f;

            // Store the player's name and allow it to be rendered
            private string playerName = string.Empty;
            private Font playerFont = null;
            private Sprite playerFontSprite = null;
        }
    }
```

One of the first things you might have noticed in that code was a reference to
`DirectInput`. You can't use it yet because you haven't added a reference to this
component. Do you remember how to get it added? See Figure 3.1 in Chapter 3,
"Understanding the Sample Framework," for a refresher, and add a reference to
the latest version of `Microsoft.DirectX.DirectInput`. You use this Application
Programming Interface (API) to control the tank with your joystick or game pad.
Don't worry, you'll still be able to use the mouse and keyboard just as easily.

The constants defined here for the player are all designed to control the tank,
including the maximum speed the tank can move (and its wheels!). To give you
an idea of how these constants work, notice that the maximum moving speed is
600 units. These measurements are calculated in seconds, so knowing that the
level is 3,000 units in length, you could extrapolate that driving your tank from
one side of the level to the other would take about 5 seconds (sec).

Notice also that the rotation speed and gun speed are defined here, as well as the
"cool down" period for the gun. You don't want the player to be able to fire too
fast, and you can modify this constant to allow the players to fire faster (or

slower). The default is allowing them to fire every 2.5 sec, which seems adequate to me. You might want to adjust this rate to suit your needs.

Virtually all the variables here are designed to control or manipulate the tank in some way, so the first variable is the tank itself. Every player has his own tank object. Because you want to control movement based on time, you don't want to simply move the tank when the player presses the correct key or button, but instead you want the movement to be fluid. You implement this part later, but for now, all you need to know is at any given time whether you're moving or rotating in a particular direction. The variables determining whether a player is active and local are both there for networking purposes, which you'll get to in a few short chapters.

> It's important to understand why two sets of variables control movement and rotation, one for the joystick (or game pad) and the other for the keyboard. When a player uses both the joystick and the keyboard to try to gain an advantage (by moving twice as fast, for example), you want the ability to stop that maneuver, and using two sets of variables affords you this opportunity.

Construction Cue

The player also has an event to let anyone who cares (the game engine) know when this player has fired a round. You'll also see that the last time the player fired is stored so you can detect whether he is firing too fast. You keep the total time in the game for this reason as well. The last section of variables is used to render the player's name over his tank, so even in multiplayer modes, you'll be able to see your opponent's name, which is always fun.

How do you create a player object? It seems logical that you want to load up the tank and do any setup work you need to get the player ready, and that's exactly what you'll be doing. See the constructor in Listing 14.4 for an implementation.

LISTING 14.4   Creating the Player

```
public Player(Device device, GameEngine parent, IntPtr parentHandle,
    string name, bool isLocal)
{
    // Create a new tank
    gameTank = new Tank(device);

    // Store the info here
    isPlayerLocal = isLocal;

    // Hook the events if the player is local
    if (isPlayerLocal)
    {
        //Hook windows events for user input
        parent.KeyDown += new KeyEventHandler(OnKeyDown);
```

LISTING 14.4   Continued

```
        parent.KeyUp += new KeyEventHandler(OnKeyUp);
        // Hook mouse events too
        parent.MouseMove += new MouseEventHandler(OnMouseMove);
        parent.MouseClick += new MouseEventHandler(OnMouseClick);

        InitializeJoystick(parentHandle);
    }

    // Store the player's name
    playerName = name;
    float fontSize = isPlayerLocal ? 12.0f : 36.0f;

    // Create the font for the player
    playerFont = new Font(device, new System.Drawing.Font(
        ""Arial", fontSize, System.Drawing.FontStyle.Bold |
        System.Drawing.FontStyle.Italic));
    playerFontSprite = new Sprite(device);

    // Hook the font's events
    device.DeviceLost += new EventHandler(OnDeviceLost);
    device.DeviceReset += new EventHandler(OnDeviceReset);
}
```

As you guessed, the tank object is created first. Without it, there isn't much use to have the player do anything. When the player is created, the code defines whether or not it's a local player; if it is, the keyboard and mouse events are hooked (Listing 14.5) to allow the player to be manipulated by those items, and a new InitializeJoystick method is called (Listing 14.6) to allow use of the joystick or game pad (if it exists on the system).

Regardless of whether the player is local, you need to create the objects to render the player name. Because this text will be rendered in the world somewhere (and probably rotated and transformed to get above the tanks), you need to create a sprite as well as the font to do the rendering. You also need to hook the OnDeviceLost and OnDeviceReset events (Listing 14.7) to ensure that these objects behave correctly when you lose exclusive mode to the screen.

LISTING 14.5   Handling Mouse and Keyboard Input

```
private void OnKeyDown(object sender, KeyEventArgs e)
{
    if (e.KeyCode == Keys.W)
    {
        isMovingForward = true;
    }
    else if (e.KeyCode == Keys.S)
    {
        isMovingBackward = true;
    }
```

LISTING 14.5   Continued

```csharp
        else if (e.KeyCode == Keys.A)
        {
            isRotatingLeft = true;
        }
        else if (e.KeyCode == Keys.D)
        {
            isRotatingRight = true;
        }
}
private void OnKeyUp(object sender, KeyEventArgs e)
{
    // Depending on which key was let up, reset the variables
    if (e.KeyCode == Keys.W)
    {
        isMovingForward = false;
    }
    else if (e.KeyCode == Keys.S)
    {
        isMovingBackward = false;
    }
    else if (e.KeyCode == Keys.A)
    {
        isRotatingLeft = false;
    }
    else if (e.KeyCode == Keys.D)
    {
        isRotatingRight = false;
    }
}
private void OnMouseMove(object sender, MouseEventArgs e)
{
    if ((mouseX == -1) || (mouseY == -1))
    {
        // Set the first mouse coordinates
        mouseX = e.X;
        mouseY = e.Y;
        // Nothing else to do now
        return;
    }

    if (gameTank != null)
    {
        gameTank.GunTurretAngle += ((e.X - mouseX) * MaximumGunSpeed);
        gameTank.GunBarrelAngle += ((e.Y - mouseY) * MaximumGunSpeed);
    }

    // Save the mouse coordinates
    mouseX = e.X;
    mouseY = e.Y;
}
private void OnMouseClick(object sender, MouseEventArgs e)
{
    // If they clicked the left mouse button, fire
    RaiseFireEvent();
}
```

Pretty self-explanatory code here. If the right keys are pressed, the associated movement variables are enabled; when they are released, the variables are disabled. The mouse controls the gun turret and barrel, and clicking the mouse button calls the RaiseFireEvent method (Listing 14.8), which handles cooling down the gun and actually firing the gun.

LISTING 14.6   Initializing the Joystick Device

```
private void InitializeJoystick(IntPtr parent)
{
    // See if there is a joystick attached to the system
    // Enumerate joysticks in the system
    foreach (Input.DeviceInstance instance in Input.Manager.GetDevices(
        Input.DeviceClass.GameControl, Input.EnumDevicesFlags.AttachedOnly))
    {
        // Create the device. Just pick the first one
        joystickDevice = new Input.Device(instance.InstanceGuid);
        break;
    }

    bool hasButton = false;
    bool hasXAxis = false;
    bool hasYAxis = false;

    // If no joystick was found, simply exit this method after a quick message
    if (joystickDevice == null)
    {
        System.Diagnostics.Debugger.Log(0, GameEngine.GameName + ": Warning"
            , "No joystick found, will use mouse and keyboard");
    }
    else
    {
        // There is a joystick attached, update some state for the joystick

        // Set the data format to the predefined format.
        joystickDevice.SetDataFormat(Input.DeviceDataFormat.Joystick);
        // Set the cooperative level for the device.
        joystickDevice.SetCooperativeLevel(parent,
                Input.CooperativeLevelFlags.NonExclusive
            | Input.CooperativeLevelFlags.Background);

        // Enumerate all the objects on the device
        foreach (Input.DeviceObjectInstance d in joystickDevice.Objects)
        {
            if ((d.ObjectId & (int)Input.DeviceObjectTypeFlags.Axis) != 0)
            {
                // This is an axis, set its range
                joystickDevice.Properties.SetRange(
                    Input.ParameterHow.ById, d.ObjectId,
                    new Input.InputRange(-5000, +5000));

                // Set the dampening zone of this as well
                joystickDevice.Properties.SetDeadZone(
                    Input.ParameterHow.ById, d.ObjectId,
                    500);
            }
```

LISTING 14.6   Continued

```
        // See if we have a hat that will be used for gun turret movement
        if (d.ObjectType == Input.ObjectTypeGuid.PointOfView)
        {
            hasHat = true;
        }

        // Make sure we have at least one button and an x/y axis
        if (d.ObjectType == Input.ObjectTypeGuid.Button)
        {
            hasButton = true;
        }
        if (d.ObjectType == Input.ObjectTypeGuid.XAxis)
        {
            hasXAxis = true;
        }
        if (d.ObjectType == Input.ObjectTypeGuid.YAxis)
        {
            hasYAxis = true;
        }
    }
    // Now if there isn't an x/y axis and button, reset the
    // joystick to null since it can't be used
    if ( (!hasButton) || (!hasXAxis) || (!hasYAxis) )
    {
        System.Diagnostics.Debugger.Log(0, GameEngine.GameName + ": Warning"
            , "Joystick found but without necessary features,
                will use mouse and keyboard");

        joystickDevice.Dispose();
        joystickDevice = null;
    }
  }
}
```

This code is pretty much all brand new because you've never seen any
`DirectInput` code. The first thing you do is enumerate all the joysticks on the system, which is what you're specifying with the `Input.DeviceClass.GameControl`
flag. You also don't care about any joysticks that aren't connected to the system
currently so you pass in the `Input.EnumDevicesFlags.AttachedOnly` flag to enumerate only attached devices. For the first device that you find, create it and stop
the enumeration. No sense in continuing once you have a device.

If you've ever seen more than one joystick for the PC, you probably already know
that there are quite a few, and each has different options. You might have a
super-simple joystick that has a button and that's it or something so complex you
need a degree in rocket science just to look at it. Right now, you don't know
enough about the joystick device that was created (assuming one was created) to
even detect whether it's capable of being used by the game. Figuring that out is
what you do now.

Before you do that work, however, let `DirectInput` know about the joystick data, which is what the `SetDataFormat` method does. Because more than one object can have access to the devices at a time, you want to specify what kind of access you need, in this case, nonexclusive access in the background. Any other foreground applications could take access of the device, but otherwise, you want access to it.

With that out of the way, you can detect all the objects on the device now. For every object attached to the device, you check what type it is. If the object is an axis, you set the range of the axis to some reasonably high level (10,000 "units"). You should note that if it is a digital axis, it simply moves to the highest level instantly; if it is an analog axis, the data is returned based on how far the axis has been moved. In case you're wondering, an **axis** is the portion of a joystick that allows movement. For example, a flight stick allows you to move both horizontally (the x axis) and vertically (the y axis). Most joysticks have at least an x and y axis and some number of buttons. The dead zone is the zone in which the axis is considered "centered." In this case, you have a dead zone of 5%, which means you need to move the axis more than 5% away from center before it's marked as "moving."

Depending on the other features the joystick has (for example, buttons, hats), you simply store that information. After each object is detected, you detect whether this device is capable of playing the game (does it have an x axis, a y axis, and a button?), and if it does not, you dispose of the joystick and use the keyboard and mouse. Later, when you implement the updating player method, you'll see how to read data from the joystick.

LISTING 14.7   Handling Sprites and Fonts During Reset

```
private void OnDeviceLost(object sender, EventArgs e)
{
    if ( (playerFont != null) && (!playerFont.Disposed) )
    {
        playerFont.OnLostDevice();
        playerFontSprite.OnLostDevice();
    }
}
private void OnDeviceReset(object sender, EventArgs e)
{
    if (playerFont != null)
    {
        playerFont.OnResetDevice();
        playerFontSprite.OnResetDevice();
    }
}
```

Recognizing these event handlers should be second nature to you by now. If one of the objects was created, it's probably a safe bet that they both were—so in each event, you simply check one and then perform the appropriate operation on each.

LISTING 14.8   Ready, Aim, Fire!

```
public bool RaiseFireEvent()
{
    // Can the gun be fired again?
    if ((totalTime - lastFiredTime ) > GunCoolDown)
    {
        // Yes it can, do so now
        if (Fired != null)
        {
            Fired(this, EventArgs.Empty);
        }
        // Store the last time the gun was fired
        lastFiredTime = totalTime;

        // The gun was fired
        return true;
    }
    return false;
}
```

This method is simply a small wrapper around the firing logic to ensure that you can't fire until the gun has cooled down enough. A simple check indicates whether enough time has passed since the last time you fired the gun; if it has, the Fired event is, well, fired, and the last fired time is stored again. This method returns a Boolean value so the caller can detect whether the gun was really fired.

IMoveableObject **Indeed**

Have you noticed that you haven't implemented the IMoveableObject members yet? If you've tried to compile, you have because you can't compile the class until you do. Listing 14.9 contains the implementation of these members.

LISTING 14.9   IMoveableObject **Implementation**

```
/// <summary>
/// Draw the player (the tank) in the world
/// </summary>
/// <param name="device">Device used to render tank</param>
public void Draw(GameEngine engine, Camera c)
{
```

LISTING 14.9 Continued

```
    if (gameTank != null)
    {
        // Only draw the tank if it lies in the view frustum
        if (c.ObjectInFrustum(this))
        {
            gameTank.Draw(engine);
        }
    }
}
/// <summary>
/// The tank's current position
/// </summary>
public Vector3 Position
{
    get { return gameTank.Position; }
    set { gameTank.Position = value; }
}
/// <summary>
/// The direction the player is currently facing
/// </summary>
public Vector3 Direction
{
    get { return gameTank.TankDirection; }
}

/// <summary>
/// The current rotation of the tank
/// </summary>
public float Rotation
{
    get { return gameTank.TankRotation; }
    set { gameTank.TankRotation = value; }
}
/// <summary>
/// Radius of the player model
/// </summary>
public float Radius
{
    get { return gameTank.Radius; }
}
```

There is still one method left to implement in the interface (the Update method), but that method is quite large and I discuss it separately. The rest of the implementation is straightforward. When rendering, you check whether the player is within the view frustum, and if he is, you call the draw method on the tank. The properties simply return the associated tank property you've already defined. Now it's time to look at the big one, which is in Listing 14.10.

LISTING 14.10   Updating the Player

```
public void Update(float elapsedTime, Level currentLevel)
{
    System.Diagnostics.Debug.Assert(gameTank != null, "Tank object cannot
                                                be null.");

    // Keep track of the total time
    totalTime += elapsedTime;

    // Update movement if the player is local
    if (isPlayerLocal)
    {
        // If the joystick can be used, try to use it
        if (joystickDevice != null)
        {
            UpdateJoystick(joystickDevice);
        }

        // Is the player moving?
        if ((isMovingForward) ¦¦ (isMovingBackward) ¦¦ (isMovingForwardJoy)
            ¦¦ (isMovingBackwardJoy))
        {
            // Movement is happening, first get the direction the tank is facing
            Vector3 dir = gameTank.TankDirection;

            // Now scale it to move, first check keyboard
            if ((isMovingForward) ¦¦ (isMovingBackward))
            {
                dir.Scale((isMovingForward) ? (elapsedTime *
                MaximumMovementSpeed) : (elapsedTime * -MaximumMovementSpeed));
            }
            else // Must be joystick
            {
                dir.Scale((isMovingForwardJoy) ? (elapsedTime *
                MaximumMovementSpeed) : (elapsedTime * -MaximumMovementSpeed));
            }

            // Now append that to the current position
            gameTank.Position += dir;

            Plane reflectionPlane;
            if (currentLevel.HitTest(this, out reflectionPlane))
            {
                // Well, you're hitting a wall. Back up
                gameTank.Position -= dir;
                // Now stop moving
                isMovingBackward = false;
                isMovingForward = false;
            }
            // Now update the wheel rotation animation
            gameTank.WheelRotation += (isMovingForward) ? (elapsedTime *
                -MaximumMovementSpeedWheels) :
                (elapsedTime * MaximumMovementSpeedWheels);
        }
```

LISTING 14.10 Continued

```
        // Is the player rotating?
        if ((isRotatingLeft) || (isRotatingRight) || (isRotatingLeftJoy)
            || (isRotatingRightJoy))
        {
            // First check keyboard
            if ((isRotatingLeft) || (isRotatingRight))
            {
                gameTank.TankRotation += (isRotatingRight) ? (
                    MaximumRotationSpeed * elapsedTime) :
                    (-MaximumRotationSpeed * elapsedTime);
            }
            else // Must be joystick
            {
                gameTank.TankRotation += (isRotatingRightJoy) ? (
                    MaximumRotationSpeed * elapsedTime) :
                    (-MaximumRotationSpeed * elapsedTime);
            }
        }
    }
    // Finally update the tank
    gameTank.Update(elapsedTime);
}
```

Because you need to know the total time when determining whether it's "safe" to fire, you constantly increment the total time based on the elapsed time since the last update. Next, you need to check whether the player you're updating is a local player, and if he is, you need to find out whether you need to move the player. Assuming the player is local and a joystick is attached, first you check the joystick data (see Listing 14.11).

Next, you detect whether you should be moving either forward or back (by either the joystick or the keyboard). If you are moving, the direction you are facing is stored first and then scaled by the movement speed of the tank (or a fraction of that because you're basing it on the elapsed time since the last frame). Notice that the scaling only happens once, regardless of whether you're using both the joystick and the keyboard, and that the scaling is "negated" (reversed) if you are moving backwards. You then update the position of the tank by adding the newly scaled direction to the current position.

The next call is to a `HitTest` method on the level object, which you certainly didn't implement yet. You do that shortly (see Listing 14.12), but the goal of the method is to see whether the object (in this case, the tank) has hit an obstacle in the level. If you hit an obstacle, you return to your original position and stop moving because you shouldn't be allowed to move through the obstacle. Rotating is much like the movement, but there is no check for hitting an obstacle. Finally, you call the `Update` method on the tank itself; it correctly sets up the frame matrices and the orientation of the tank based on the rotation.

LISTING 14.11 Updating the Player

```
private void UpdateJoystick(Input.Device joystick)
{
    try
    {
        // See if we can get the joystick data
        joystick.Poll();
    }
    catch(Input.InputException e)
    {
        if ((e is Input.NotAcquiredException) || (e is Input.InputLostException))
        {
            // If the joystick wasn't acquired, or was lost,
            // try to acquire it now
            try
            {
                // Acquire the device
                joystick.Acquire();
            }
            catch(Input.InputException)
            {
                // Failed to acquire the device, nothing we can do, exit
                return;
            }
        }
    }

    // Get the state of the device.
    Input.JoystickState state = joystick.CurrentJoystickState;

    // Now update the player
    if (state.X > 0) { isRotatingRightJoy = true; isRotatingLeftJoy = false; }
    else if (state.X < 0) { isRotatingLeftJoy = true;
                            isRotatingRightJoy = false;}
    else { isRotatingLeftJoy = false; isRotatingRightJoy = false;}
    if (state.Y < 0) { isMovingForwardJoy = true;
                       isMovingBackwardJoy = false; }
    else if (state.Y > 0) { isMovingBackwardJoy = true;
                            isMovingForwardJoy = false;}
    else {isMovingBackwardJoy = false; isMovingForwardJoy = false; }

    // See if the first button has been fired
    byte[] buttons = state.GetButtons();
    if ((buttons[0] & 0x80) != 0)
    {
        // Fire!
        RaiseFireEvent();
    }

    // Check the hat
    if (hasHat)
    {
        // Update the gun barrel based on POV
        int[] pov = state.GetPointOfView();
        switch(pov[0])
        {
```

LISTING 14.11   Continued

```
            case 0:
                // Move barrel up
                gameTank.GunBarrelAngle -= (MaximumGunSpeed);
                break;
            case 4500:
                // Move barrel up, and turret over
                gameTank.GunBarrelAngle -= (MaximumGunSpeed);
                gameTank.GunTurretAngle += (MaximumGunSpeed);
                break;
            case 9000:
                // Move turret over
                gameTank.GunTurretAngle += (MaximumGunSpeed);
                break;
            case 13500:
                // Move barrel down, and turret over
                gameTank.GunBarrelAngle += (MaximumGunSpeed);
                gameTank.GunTurretAngle += (MaximumGunSpeed);
                break;
            case 18000:
                // Move barrel down
                gameTank.GunBarrelAngle += (MaximumGunSpeed);
                break;
            case 22500:
                // Move barrel down, and turret over
                gameTank.GunBarrelAngle += (MaximumGunSpeed);
                gameTank.GunTurretAngle -= (MaximumGunSpeed);
                break;
            case 27000:
                // Move turret over
                gameTank.GunTurretAngle -= (MaximumGunSpeed);
                break;
            case 31500:
                // Move barrel up, and turret over
                gameTank.GunBarrelAngle -= (MaximumGunSpeed);
                gameTank.GunTurretAngle -= (MaximumGunSpeed);
                break;
        }
    }
}
```

This method looks longer and more difficult than it really is. The first call is intended to poll the device (your joystick) for the latest data. However, if you've lost the device for some reason (such as another application taking exclusive access), the call will fail. If it fails because the device isn't acquired or it has been lost, try to acquire it, and if that fails, well, there's nothing else you can do, so simply leave the method. It will be tried again next frame.

If the device was polled successfully, though, you get the current joystick state because it will have the current data in it. You can then check the x axis, see whether it's moving right or left, and set the appropriate variable (or set them both to `false` if you aren't moving on the x axis). You do the same thing for the y axis. If the first joystick button is pressed, you call the `RaiseFireEvent` method, just as you do when the user clicks the mouse button that handles the firing and gun cool-down.

Finally, you check the device is checked for a hat, and if it has one, you use its state to determine which way to move the gun turret and barrel. Notice the pattern here: the position of the hat would be equivalent to the angle of the hat (in degrees) multiplied 100, so the possible values go from 0 to 36,000. A value of -1 means the hat is in its default position.

A Basic Collision Detection

One of the basic things that virtually all games have is a collision detection method. In this case, all you need to determine is whether a particular moveable object is colliding with the level. (See Listing 14.12.)

LISTING 14.12 Collision Detection Algorithm

```
public bool HitTest(IMoveableObject obj, out Plane hitPlane)
{
    // Default to an empty plane
    hitPlane = Plane.Empty;

    // This object hasn't left the level, has it hit a wall?
    IntersectInformation closestHit = new IntersectInformation();
    if (levelMesh.Intersect(obj.Position, obj.Direction, out closestHit))
    {
        // This will always return true since you will always be hitting the
        // outside of the level. Now you need to check to see if you're
        // close enough to really be hitting the closest point
        hitPlane = facePositions[closestHit.FaceIndex].GetFacePlane();
        return (closestHit.Dist < obj.Radius);
    }
    return false;
}
```

This method should go into the level class, in case you didn't gather that already. It returns a Boolean value to determine whether you've hit and also a plane (as an out parameter) that will be the object that you've actually hit. For the player, this plane is irrelevant, but the bullets that are fired require it. First, the code calls the `Intersect` method on the mesh, which tells you based on an object's position and direction whether or not they will collide. Because the tank will always be inside the level that is walled in, this method will always return `true`. After it returns true, you check the distance between the object and the obstacle (which is returned in the IntersectInformation structure) and return true only if the distance is less than the radius of the object you're checking.

What about setting the plane variable? It calls a method on an object you've never created. Declare the variable in the class now:

```
private SingleFace[] facePositions = null;
```

I'm sure you've just realized that you haven't declared the SingleFace object yet either. See Listing 14.13 for the implementation of this object.

LISTING 14.13 The Single Face Object

```
private struct SingleFace
{
    public Vector3[] positions;
    public Vector3 singleVertex;
    public Vector3 singleNormal;

    /// <summary>
    /// Return the plane that this face creates
    /// </summary>
    /// <returns></returns>
    public Plane GetFacePlane()
    {
        return Plane.FromPoints(positions[0], positions[1], positions[2]);
    }
    public Plane GetFacePlaneNormal()
    {
        return Plane.FromPointNormal(singleVertex, singleNormal);
    }
}
```

There are two ways to create a plane. One is to use three points (which happen to make a triangle, which is the primitive that Direct3D uses to render its data), and another is to use a single point and its normal. Because the normal is perpendicular from the plane, it's relatively easy to calculate the plane from those two points as well. You'll notice that the single face class will store both and return the plane by using either the points or the normal. How do you create the array of these faces? Add the code in Listing 14.14 to your constructor for the level (at the end of the method, naturally).

LISTING 14.14 Creating the Face Objects Array

```
// Allocate the correct number of faces
facePositions = new SingleFace[levelMesh.NumberFaces];
using (IndexBuffer ib = levelMesh.IndexBuffer)
{
```

LISTING 14.14   Continued

```
    // Find each face, first by locking the data
    short[] faces = ib.Lock(0, typeof(short), LockFlags.None,
        levelMesh.NumberFaces * 3) as short[];

    using (VertexBuffer vb = levelMesh.VertexBuffer)
    {
        // Get a list of triangles that make the walls and floors
        CustomVertex.PositionNormalTextured[] verts = vb.Lock(
            0, typeof(CustomVertex.PositionNormalTextured),
            LockFlags.None, levelMesh.NumberVertices) as
            CustomVertex.PositionNormalTextured[];

        // Now, find each face vertex position
        int faceIndex = -1;
        for(int i = 0; i < faces.Length; i++)
        {
            if ( (i % 3) == 0)
            {
                // Allocate the position array
                facePositions[++faceIndex].positions = new Vector3[3];
            }
            facePositions[faceIndex].positions[i % 3] = verts[faces[i]].Position;
            facePositions[faceIndex].singleVertex = verts[faces[i]].Position;
            facePositions[faceIndex].singleNormal = verts[faces[i]].Normal;
        }
        // Make sure to unlock the buffer
        vb.Unlock();
    }

    // Make sure you unlock the index buffer
    ib.Unlock();
}
```

What you do is actually walk all the data in the mesh and store every triangle that will be rendered. The levels aren't very big, and this step will give you exact planes that are hit, which makes calculations easier later. So first, you allocate the array of faces using the number of faces in the mesh as a count because that's what you'll be storing. Next you want to look through the index buffer of the mesh by locking it and getting the list of indices back. Once you have the list of indices, you can lock the vertex buffer as well because as you walk through the list of indices, you need to find the associated vertex information from the vertex buffer. The level mesh vertex data includes position, normal, and texture information, so you use this type when locking the buffer and getting the array back.

With all the data loaded, you can scan through the list of faces. Each triangle consists of three indices, so for every three indices you've seen, you increase your face counter and create a new array of three "positions" in your single face array.

You then store the position of the vertex referenced by that index (and the normal) into your array. After you go through each of the indices, you can unlock both the index and vertex buffers because you no longer need them.

Construction Cue

> An index buffer is used to store indices into a vertex buffer, which allows you to render the same vertex multiple times without needing to declare duplicate vertices. Vertex buffers are used to store vertices efficiently.
>
> See the DirectX documentation for more information on index and vertex buffers.

Summary

With that, you have a pretty robust collision-detection algorithm implemented. In the next chapter, you actually use it!

In this chapter, you accomplished quite a bit. You have the logic for your world and your levels now, and you implemented a lot of the player. You even implemented a collision-detection routine that you use more later. It's almost looking like a game now.

CHAPTER 15

Ready. Aim. Fire!

If you want some tanks to battle in a level, it only makes sense that you are going to need some way for the tanks to battle each other. In this case, you allow the tanks to move and rotate the gun turrets (and barrels) and then fire at the enemy. You finished the implementation of the tank moving and controlling the turret and barrel; now you can start adding some of the game play elements and allowing that player to fire.

In this chapter, you'll learn

- ▶ How to implement bullets
- ▶ How to finish up the player
- ▶ How to add sounds

Implementing the Ammunition Class

Although tanks firing huge missiles with a lot of explosions everywhere is probably what you're used to seeing in a game (or movie), you can make this implementation simpler. Your bullets can be small bouncing pellets because, after all, I'm sure you don't want to promote violence! What you need now is an implementation.

Continuing with the theme in Tankers, you create a new code file for the "bullet" class. The included CD calls the file bullet.cs, and the initial implementation appears in Listing 15.1.

LISTING 15.1   The Bullet Class

```
using System;
using System.Collections;
using Microsoft.DirectX;
using Microsoft.DirectX.Direct3D;
using Microsoft.Samples.DirectX.UtilityToolkit;

namespace Tankers
{
    /// <summary>
```

LISTING 15.1 Continued

```
/// This class will maintain the bullets used by the game
/// </summary>
public class Bullet : IMoveableObject
{
    public const float BulletMass = 8.0f; // The size of the bullets
    private const float GravityForce = -9.8f * BulletMass * 5;
    // The force of gravity
    private const int SlicesStacks = 4; // How complex the bullet's mesh is
    private const float LifeTime = 20.0f;
    // Amount of time the bullet will stay alive
    public const float BulletStrength = 1800.0f;
    // Strength of the bullets being fired
    private static Mesh bulletMesh = null;
    private Vector3 pos; // Current position of the bullet
    private Vector3 vel; // Velocity of the bullet
    private Vector3 dir; // Current direction of the bullet
    private float aliveTime = 0.0f;
    // Amount of time the bullet has been alive
    private Player owner = null; // The tank that fired this bullet
    private Material alphaMaterial; // Current material of the bullet
}
}
```

As you can see, the Bullet class is also implementing the IMoveableObject interface, which means you need to implement the properties and methods from that
interface soon, but first, look at the constants and variables that are currently
defined. The "mass" of the bullet is used during creation to define its size. The
force of gravity on the bullet is defined (with some added gravity to make the bullets fall faster). The bullet's mesh is defined by a sphere, and the complexity of
the vertices in the sphere is defined by the SlicesStacks member. Lower numbers
make less complex spheres, but higher numbers make spheres that look more
realistic. In this case, you don't want a very realistic sphere, so it is easy to decide
to use the lower polygon version.

The lifetime of the bullet is defined in seconds, in this case 20. From the moment
the bullet is fired, it is in play for another 20 seconds after that. The strength of
the bullet is the initial velocity at which the bullet is fired. This velocity changes
over time due to gravity, but the starting velocity should have decent enough
power to behave realistically.

You might notice that the mesh variable is listed as static, rather than just
another instance variable to be used for the class. The reason is the same reason
that the cube meshes in Blockers were static. There isn't any good reason to keep
separate meshes for the bullets because each and every bullet is rendered with the
same mesh.

Rounding out the variables is the information to track the actual bullet. You need to know the current position of the bullet and its velocity (which, as you learned back in Chapter 10, "A Quick 3D-Math Primer," includes both the direction and magnitude of that velocity). You're storing the direction here separately for ease of use. You also need to ensure that you know how long the bullet has been alive so you can decide whether that bullet is still in play.

The last two variables are used to control certain design features that you might or might not want in your version of the game. You use the owner variable so that during checks it is impossible for the player to hit himself with his own bullet. You use the new material object to slowly fade the bullets (make them render transparently) as they get closer and closer to death (when alive time has exceeded the maximum allowed). These features have no real effect on game play; they are more of a matter of choice.

You should look at the constructor for the Bullet class now, in Listing 15.2.

LISTING 15.2   Creating a Bullet

```
public Bullet(Device device, Vector3 initialPos, Vector3 initialVel,
              Player parent)
{
    // First create the mesh if it doesn't exist yet
    if (bulletMesh == null)
    {
        bulletMesh = Mesh.Sphere(device, BulletMass, SlicesStacks, SlicesStacks);
    }

    // Create the material for the bullets
    alphaMaterial = new Material();
    alphaMaterial.AmbientColor = new ColorValue(1.0f, 1.0f, 1.0f, 1.0f);
    alphaMaterial.DiffuseColor = new ColorValue(1.0f, 1.0f, 1.0f, 1.0f -
                                            (aliveTime /LifeTime) );

    // Store the position and velocity of the bullet
    pos = initialPos;
    vel = initialVel;

    // Store the parent
    owner = parent;
}
```

Aside from storing the data (which you do at the end of the constructor), you need to accomplish only two things here. First you need to see whether the mesh used to render the bullets is created yet, and if it isn't, well, then create it. The bullets here are represented by low-resolution spheres that can bounce around the levels. The material that is created by default is a fully white material, as was defined by the static material class used by the game engine. I break it down here to show you the formula that is used for marking the items as transparent. (I discuss that in just a few moments during the Update method.)

> You might be asking yourself, "Why did we have a static constructor for the game engine to initialize its static data, but for the Bullet class, we initialize its static data in a normal constructor?" If so, good job in noticing. The reasoning here is that the static constructor does not (and cannot) take parameters. When creating the mesh for the Bullet class, you *need* the rendering device already created and ready for use, which cannot be guaranteed in the static constructor.

Did you notice that the Bullet class didn't derive from IDisposable? Because the only disposable data it has is the mesh (which is static), it didn't make sense to have each bullet implement this interface. You do still need a way to clean up the data, though, so instead, you should add a static Cleanup method to the class to handle it

```
public static void Cleanup()
{
    if (bulletMesh != null)
    {
        bulletMesh.Dispose();
        bulletMesh = null;
    }
}
```

What about the interface you did implement? You definitely need to get the implementations for the IMoveableObject interface done before you can compile, so see Listing 15.3 for those (except for Update, which I discuss separately).

LISTING 15.3   IMoveableObject **Implementation of Bullets**

```
/// <summary>
/// The bullet's radius
/// </summary>
public float Radius
{
    get { return BulletMass; }
}
/// <summary>
/// The bullet's position
/// </summary>
public Vector3 Position
{
    get { return pos; }
}
/// <summary>
/// The direction the bullet is currently traveling
```

LISTING 15.3   Continued

```
/// </summary>
public Vector3 Direction
{
    get { return dir; }
}
/// <summary>
/// Render the bullet
/// </summary>
public void Draw(GameEngine engine, Camera c)
{
    // Set the world transform
    engine.SetWorldTransform(Matrix.Translation(pos));

    // Render the bullet mesh if it's viewable
    if (c.ObjectInFrustum(this))
    {
#if (DEBUG)
        engine.numberFaces += bulletMesh.NumberFaces;
        engine.numberVerts += bulletMesh.NumberVertices;
#endif
        engine.RenderingDevice.SetTexture(0, null);
        engine.RenderingDevice.Material = alphaMaterial;
        bulletMesh.DrawSubset(0);
    }
}
```

The radius of the sphere mesh that was created was also the mass of the bullet from the constant you defined earlier this chapter. Rather than actually calculate the radius of each bullet, you can simply use this constant. For the remaining two read-only properties, you simply return the stored values back to the caller. The drawing method sets the world transform to the current bullet's position, checks whether the bullet is within the camera's view frustum, and draws it. Did you notice in debug mode that the number of vertices and faces are stored for each bullet as well? Also notice that for the first time, you are setting a material to the device, namely the alpha material you defined earlier.

You might be wondering what *alpha* is. In short, it's the component of a color that determines how opaque or transparent an item is. For example, if you look over at the wall closest to you, unless you're Superman and you have x-ray vision, odds are that you cannot see through this wall. It has an alpha value of 1.0f, or fully opaque. A newly cleaned window could have an alpha value of 0.0f, or completely transparent. There can be varying degrees of alpha in between, such as sheer stockings, which are only partially transparent.

Because of the extra calculations required to render something using alpha transparency, this feature is disabled by default in Direct3D. You want a way to turn it

on while you are rendering the bullets but then off again when you finish.
Because you should avoid setting render state values more often than necessary
for performance reasons, the best solution is to have two static functions, one that
turns on the blending and one that turns it off. (See Listing 15.4.)

LISTING 15.4   Rendering Objects with Alpha

```
/// <summary>
/// Sets the device up for rendering the bullets
/// </summary>
public static void SetBulletRenderStates(GameEngine engine)
{
    // Turn on alpha blending
    engine.RenderingDevice.RenderState.AlphaBlendEnable = true;
    engine.RenderingDevice.RenderState.SourceBlend = Blend.SourceAlpha;
    engine.RenderingDevice.RenderState.DestinationBlend = Blend.InvSourceAlpha;
}
/// <summary>
/// Resets the device back to defaults
/// </summary>
public static void EndBulletRenderStates(GameEngine engine)
{
    // Turn off alpha blending
    engine.RenderingDevice.RenderState.AlphaBlendEnable = false;
}
```

The main component you are setting here is the `AlphaBlendEnable` render state.
You do set the source blend and destination blend options as well, but they don't
have any effect unless the alpha state is turned on (which is why they are not
turned off when the alpha is). Before you can render any bullets, you want to call
the `SetBulletRenderStates` method, and when you're done rendering the bullets,
you then call the `EndBulletRenderStates` method.

The `Update` method is the largest method in this class because it has the most to
do. See Listing 15.5 for the implementation of this method.

LISTING 15.5   Updating a Bullet

```
/// <summary>
/// Update the bullet based on the time since the last frame
/// </summary>
public void Update(float elapsedTime, Level currentLevel)
{
    // Update the bullet's lifetime
    aliveTime += elapsedTime;
    // And alpha mode
    alphaMaterial.DiffuseColor = new ColorValue(1.0f, 1.0f, 1.0f, 1.0f -
                                                (aliveTime /LifeTime) );
```

LISTING 15.5   Continued

```
Vector3 beginPos = pos;
// Velocity needs to scale by gravity first, gravity only affects the y axis
vel.Y += GravityForce * elapsedTime;

// Update the bullet's position
pos += Vector3.Scale(vel, elapsedTime);

// Now calculate the direction the bullet is currently traveling
dir = Vector3.Normalize(beginPos - pos);

// We may need to reflect our direction if there's a collision,
// store the points
Plane reflectionPlane;
if (currentLevel.HitTest(this, out reflectionPlane))
{
    Matrix reflectionMatrix = Matrix.Identity;
    reflectionMatrix.Reflect(reflectionPlane);

    // Get the current velocity
    float velocity = vel.Length();
    Vector3 newPos = Vector3.TransformCoordinate(beginPos, reflectionMatrix);
    vel = Vector3.Normalize(pos - newPos);
    vel.Scale(velocity);
    pos = newPos;
}
}
```

First, you update the amount of time the bullet has been alive so you know when they are no longer alive. Then, you calculate the alpha color. As discussed earlier, a value of 1.0f is fully opaque, and 0.0f is fully transparent. In this formula, when the alive time is 0, you see that the alpha value is 1.0f (fully opaque). When the alive time gets to the halfway point of the maximum life time, the value is 0.5f, partially transparent.

Next, you store the initial position of the bullet (because it will be modified in a moment) and update the velocity to be affected by gravity. Notice that only the y axis is modified for the gravity because gravity only pulls downward (at least on Earth). Next, you modify the position by adding the velocity to the current position (with the velocity scaled down by the elapsed time, of course). The direction is calculated by taking the difference vector from the start position and the ending position and normalizing it.

Here's where you actually use the reflection plane that you calculated in the hit testing on the level. If the bullet hits an obstacle, you want it to bounce off that obstacle in a realistic fashion, so what you do is grab the plane that the bullet has hit and build a "reflection matrix" based on that plane. The reflection matrix is used to transform the starting coordinate to a new, reflected coordinate. You then calculate the updated velocity by subtracting the reflected position from the position that was updated earlier in this method and then scaling it back to its original magnitude.

One more thing you need to add to the bullet class is another hit detection method, this time for when the bullet is going to hit an opposing tank. This task is slightly less complicated than the level detection because you only check whether the bounding spheres of the objects collide. Add the code from Listing 15.6 to your class.

LISTING 15.6 Bullets Collision Detection

```
/// <summary>
/// Does a hit test on the object
/// </summary>
public bool HitTest(IMoveableObject obj)
{
    // Don't do hit testing if you fired the bullet
    if (obj == owner)
    {
        return false;
    }
    // The hit testing for this will be simpler, simply compare the distance
    Vector3 diff = this.Position - obj.Position;
    return diff.Length() < (this.Radius + obj.Radius);
}
```

As you see, you check the owner first. If the owner is the object (tank) that fired the bullet, simply skip the test and return `false`. (They didn't collide.) This allows a player to fire a bullet and not hit herself. If this tank isn't the owner, though, find the difference in the two objects' positions. If the length of this vector is greater than the combined radius of the two bounding spheres, the objects must have hit.

A Bullets Collection

For the bullets, there's really nothing else left to do; however, you will probably store numerous bullets to render and update throughout the game play. It is probably useful to have a collection class to store the bullets in. Go ahead and add the `Bullets` class (in Listing 15.7) to this same code file.

LISTING 15.7 The Bullets Collection

```
/// <summary>
/// A collection of bullets
/// </summary>
public class Bullets : IEnumerable
{
    private ArrayList bulletList = new ArrayList();
    /// <summary>
    /// Indexer for bullets
    /// </summary>
    public Bullet this[int index]
    {
        get { return bulletList[index] as Bullet; }
        set { bulletList[index] = value; }
    }
    /// <summary>
    /// Add a new bullet to the list
    /// </summary>
    public void Add(Bullet b)
    {
        bulletList.Add(b);
    }
    /// <summary>
    /// Remove a bullet from the list
    /// </summary>
    public void Remove(Bullet b)
    {
        bulletList.Remove(b);
    }
    /// <summary>
    /// Remove all bullets from the list
    /// </summary>
    public void Clear()
    {
        bulletList.Clear();
    }
    /// <summary>
    /// The number of items in the list
    /// </summary>
    public int Count
    {
        get { return bulletList.Count; }
    }
    /// <summary>
    /// Returns the enumerator for the bullet list
    /// </summary>
    public IEnumerator GetEnumerator()
    {
        return bulletList.GetEnumerator();
    }
}
```

As you can see, this is a simple wrapper around an array list that makes it typesafe for a Bullet class instead. Only the items that you actually care about are implemented (instead of the entire thing). There isn't anything overly complex here.

Finishing Up the Player

You need to finish up just a few things in the player class before you're ready to begin using it. One of those things is to add the code that fires the bullets! You couldn't do it up to this point because the classes weren't defined, but now that you've implemented the bullet classes, this is the perfect time. What you want to do first is add a method to fire the round (Listing 15.8) to the player class.

LISTING 15.8   Firing a Round

```
/// <summary>
/// Will add a new bullet to the list
/// </summary>
public void FireRound(Device device, Bullets list)
{
    // Get the bullet start and velocity
    Vector3 bulletStart;
    Vector3 bulletVel;
    GetBulletStartLocation(out bulletStart, out bulletVel);

    // Finally add the new bullet
    list.Add(new Bullet(device, bulletStart, bulletVel, this));
}
```

This method doesn't do much other than add a bullet to the list after it calculates where the starting location of the bullet and the velocity should be. That method is defined in Listing 15.9.

LISTING 15.9   Calculating Initial Position and Velocity

```
/// <summary>
/// Get the starting bullet location and velocity
/// </summary>
public void GetBulletStartLocation(out Vector3 bulletStart,
                                   out Vector3 bulletVelocity)
{
    // First, get the bullet start
    bulletStart = gameTank.BarrelPosition;

    // Scale the bullet in the correct direction to the end of the barrel
    bulletStart.Add(Vector3.Scale(gameTank.BarrelDirection,
                                  Tank.GunBarrelLength));
    bulletVelocity = Vector3.Scale(gameTank.BarrelDirection,
                                   Bullet.BulletStrength);
}
```

This method calculates the initial position of the bullet by first setting it to the position of the gun's barrel. However, the gun's barrel position is at the base of the gun barrel (at the turret). You don't want your bullet to fire from way down there: you want it to be coming out of the barrel's end. So take the position you have and add to it the length of the gun barrel, in the direction the barrel is facing. See Figure 15.1.

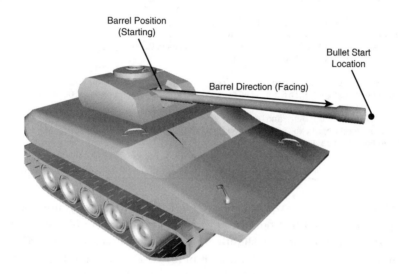

Barrel Position
(Starting)

Bullet Start
Location

Barrel Direction (Facing)

FIGURE 15.1
Calculating the bullet position.

After you have the starting position of the bullet, calculating the velocity is simple. Take the direction the barrel is facing (which is already normalized), and scale it by the speed you want the bullet to be initially traveling (which you defined as a constant earlier in this chapter).

You might wonder why you have two events used for firing a round, one that raises the event and the other that adds the newly fired bullet to the collection. The reason is encapsulation. The event firing method handles the gun cooldown logic and the firing of the event (so the game engine knows when a bullet has been fired). Because the game engine needs to maintain the list of bullets (not the player), the game engine responds to the event and calls the method on the player that actually causes the bullet to be created.

Construction Cue

One other thing you haven't done in the player class yet is add a method to draw the player's name above the tank. Remember, during the constructor, you stored the player's name and created a sprite and font to render it, but you haven't done anything with it yet. Add the following method (in Listing 15.10) to the player class to allow the name to be rendered.

LISTING 15.10 Rendering the Player Name

```
public void DrawPlayerName(GameEngine engine)
{
    // Calculate where to put the player's name
    Vector3 pos = Position;
    pos.Y += Radius / 1.75f;

    // Set the world transform to the correct location
    engine.SetWorldTransform(Matrix.RotationX((float)Math.PI) *
        gameTank.TankRotationMatrix * Matrix.Translation(pos)
        * Matrix.Translation(gameTank.Center));

    // Now draw the text onto the sprite
    playerFontSprite.Begin( SpriteFlags.AlphaBlend | SpriteFlags.ObjectSpace);
    playerFont.DrawText(playerFontSprite, playerName,
        System.Drawing.Rectangle.Empty,
        DrawTextFormat.NoClip, System.Drawing.Color.CornflowerBlue);
    playerFontSprite.End();

}
```

You first need to calculate where you'll be rendering the text, so you use the tank's position as a starting point. You want the text to appear above the tank, so you translate the y position up slightly. Then you need to set the world matrix by combining a few different transformation matrices. First, you rotate around the x axis so the text is facing the correct direction, then add in the rotation of the tank, then translate to the position of the text, and finally add one last translation to the center of the tank.

With the world matrix now set, you can draw the text. Notice that in the Begin method on the sprite class, you added a new flag, SpriteFlags.ObjectSpace. Without this flag, the sprite assumes it will be rendering 2D content in screen space and will ignore the world matrix you've just set. Finally, you draw the text on the sprite and call the End method.

Adding Sound

Driving a tank around, shooting these bullets off, and yet never hearing a sound would be somewhat strange, I believe you'd agree. Although you don't focus on any in-depth sound functionality for this game (you do some more for the next game), unlike in Blockers, having no sound at all would be terrible. Besides, it's the perfect opportunity to introduce the basic sound concepts now.

First, you add a reference to the sound libraries to your project. In the Add References dialog, add the reference to Microsoft.DirectX.DirectSound.dll now.

In keeping with the theme, create a new code file called soundengine.cs and add it to your project file as well. It will be the main source of sound for your game. Look at the basic implementation in Listing 15.11.

LISTING 15.11 The Sound Engine

```
using System;
using System.Drawing;
using System.Windows.Forms;
using Microsoft.DirectX;
using Microsoft.DirectX.DirectSound;

namespace Tankers
{
    /// <summary>
    /// This class will maintain the sound engine for this game
    /// </summary>
    public class SoundEngine : IDisposable
    {
        private const string FireFile = @"sounds\fire.wav";
        private const string ExplosionFile = @"sounds\hit.wav";

        private Device soundDevice = null;
        private SecondaryBuffer fireBuffer = null;
        private SecondaryBuffer hitBuffer = null;
        private bool canUseSounds = true;

        /// <summary>
        /// Done with this object, clean it up
        /// </summary>
        public void Dispose()
        {
            // Clean up all data here
            if (fireBuffer != null)
            {
                fireBuffer.Dispose();
            }
            if (hitBuffer != null)
            {
                hitBuffer.Dispose();
            }
            if (soundDevice != null)
            {
                soundDevice.Dispose();
            }
        }
    }
}
```

The constants define where the sound files are loaded from. These particular sound files come from the DirectX SDK, but you can simply get them from the included CD. Think of the Device object as your sound card. It is the base object that is required to play any sounds. The two buffers are the actual sound data that is loaded. Because it's possible for the computer you're using to not support sounds (for example, maybe it has no sound card), you want to know whether sounds should be played. Not having a sound card or being able to play sounds shouldn't require the game to be exited (it's a nonfatal error), so just store that information.

Naturally, you need to clean up your sound objects as well. Because the sound object is created globally, you can simply dispose the buffers and the device at the same time. Look at the constructor in Listing 15.12 and add it to this class now.

LISTING 15.12   Creating the Sound Engine

```
/// <summary>
/// Constructor where the device will be created.
/// </summary>
public SoundEngine(IntPtr parent)
{
    try
    {
        // Create a default sound object
        soundDevice = new Device();
        // Set the coop level
        soundDevice.SetCooperativeLevel(parent, CooperativeLevel.Normal);

        // Now create the two buffers
        fireBuffer = new SecondaryBuffer(GameEngine.MediaPath +
                                        FireFile, soundDevice);
        hitBuffer = new SecondaryBuffer(GameEngine.MediaPath +
                                        ExplosionFile, soundDevice);
    }
    catch
    {
        // We cannot use sounds for some reason
        canUseSounds = false;
    }
}
```

Here the default sound device is created first. Other overloads for creating a sound device take a Guid that uniquely identifies the device you're wanting to use, but for now, the default device should be good enough. (See the DirectX documentation for more information on creating devices.) Just as you had to do for your DirectInput device, you are required to call the SetCooperativeLevel on the device. In most cases, you want to use Normal, as you do here.

Creating the sound buffers is amazingly easy, as you can see. Simply pass in the device and the filename, and you're all set. You could use much more complicated options, but they aren't required for this example. In the next game, you'll have more in-depth sound features.

Luckily, playing sounds is just as easy. Add the two methods in Listing 15.13 to your class to control the playing of these sounds you've created.

LISTING 15.13   Playing Sounds

```
/// <summary>
/// Will play the fire weapon sound
/// </summary>
public void FireWeapon()
{
    if ((canUseSounds) && (fireBuffer != null))
    {
        fireBuffer.Play(0, BufferPlayFlags.Default);
    }
}
/// <summary>
/// Will play the explosion sound
/// </summary>
public void Explosion()
{
    if ((canUseSounds) && (hitBuffer != null))
    {
        hitBuffer.Play(0, BufferPlayFlags.Default);
    }
}
```

Simple, just as I promised! Assuming the sounds can be played, you just call `Play`, passing in 0 (start at the beginning), and play with the `Default` flags (play once and stop).

Summary

The game is really coming together now. You've added the bullets, updated the player to allow the player to fire the bullets, and got a basic sound engine working. In the next chapter, you'll begin hooking everything together and write the networking layer.

CHAPTER 16

Playing Alone Isn't Fun

It doesn't seem so long ago to me that all games were single player, or multiplayer on the same machine through various mechanisms such as a split screen. Although allowing people to play the games with each other was great, a majority of games didn't lend themselves well to this format. With some types of strategy games, it removed any tactical advantages you might have gained because your opponent knew what you were doing. In other game types (such as first-person shooters [FPSs]), you wanted (and needed) the screen real estate to view your enemies more readily.

Plus you had the problem of getting the people you were hoping to challenge together in the same room. Then you had the problem of the physical limitation to the number of players who could fit. Enter the Internet: Now you can play your favorite game with thousands of people across the world simultaneously. It's amazing what a few years can do for the quality of multiplayer gaming. Although you won't be designing any massively multiplayer online games in this book (it is only a beginner's guide, you realize), you will be allowing multiplayer access over the Internet.

In this chapter, you'll learn

- ► How to introduce DirectPlay
- ► How to host a networking session
- ► How to join a networking session
- ► How to send and receive data

Using DirectPlay

For the most part, the DirectX Application Programming Interfaces (APIs) have included components that cover just about every aspect of game development. Naturally, graphics is a big part of that, but as you've seen in earlier chapters, it includes other types of things, such as sound and user input. Networking is included as well.

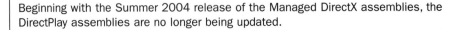

Construction Cue

Beginning with the Summer 2004 release of the Managed DirectX assemblies, the DirectPlay assemblies are no longer being updated.

In the world of networking, you can follow two major types of designs: peer-to-peer and client/server. You should take a moment to understand the differences between these two architectures.

In the *peer-to-peer* architecture, every member of the session is responsible for its own state and data, and it provides every other peer in the session with this information. In small games or games with a small number of players, this arrangement is sometimes adequate, but I'm sure you can imagine that as the number of players increases, the amount of data each player needs to send increases as well. See Figure 16.1 for a small peer-to-peer session.

FIGURE 16.1
A small peer-to-peer session.

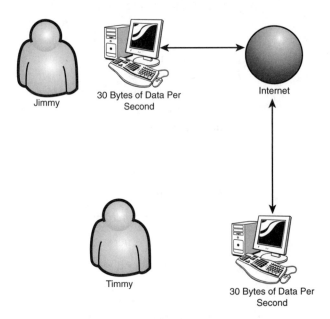

As you see here, two players talking to each other over the Internet doesn't require that much data. If they're both sending a mere 30 bytes per second of data to the peers in the session, they are each only sending 30 bytes of data. Imagine a large-scale game, with many peers, as in Figure 16.2.

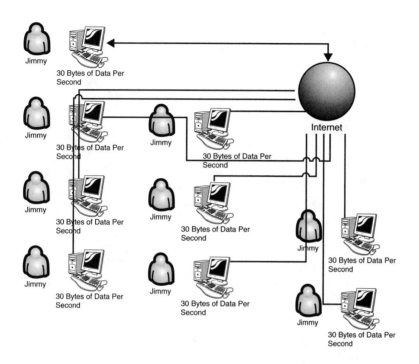

FIGURE 16.2
A large peer-to-peer
session.

As you saw in the first figure, a small networking session, each player was sending a total of 30 bytes per second. Multiply that by the number of players (2), and you have a grand total of 60 bytes per second of data being sent. Looking at the large-scale session here, what do you see? Each player is still sending 30 bytes of data; however, he is sending that data to *every* player in the session (9), so each player is sending out a total of 270 bytes of data per second. As a whole, the group is sending out 2,430 bytes of data per second. The amount of data being sent doesn't scale linearly.

In the *client/server* architecture, this problem is eliminated by making one of the members of the networking session the master, or the server. Each client in the session speaks only to the server, and the server in turn relays any necessary data to only the clients that require it. See Figure 16.3 for a visual representation.

You might be able to tell here that for the clients, the amount of data sent is much lower. Regardless of the number of session members that exist, the client only ever needs to send the 30 bytes of data to the server. However, the server's resource requirements are much higher than any of the clients', even those clients that exist in a large peer-to-peer session. The server is responsible not only for receiving the constant updates from the clients, but also for sending out any necessary data to all required constants, plus maintaining the entire game world state instead of just a small portion of it.

FIGURE 16.3
A typical client/server session.

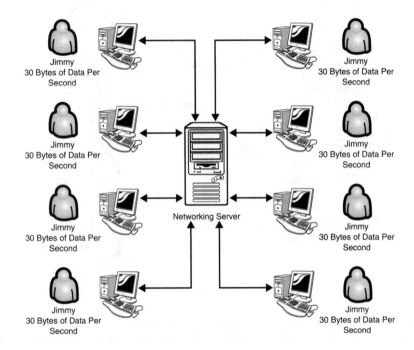

Because Tankers will only be a two-player game, it wouldn't make sense to add the overhead of requiring a client/server architecture, so it uses a peer-to-peer methodology instead. If you begin getting above say four peers in a session (or you have peers with a slow network connection, such as a modem), you might want to look into the client/server model. With a little groundwork out of the way, now you're ready to start writing some code. Before you can start, you need to make sure that you've added your reference to the networking API. In your project, add a reference to `Microsoft.DirectX.DirectPlay` and add a new code file called `network.cs`, which will hold all the code. You can find a initial implementation in Listing 16.1.

LISTING 16.1   The Networking Engine

```
using System;
using System.Drawing;
using System.Windows.Forms;
using Microsoft.DirectX;
using Microsoft.DirectX.DirectPlay;
```

LISTING 16.1   Continued

```
namespace Tankers
{
    /// <summary>
    /// Stores each possible network message (with a byte backend)
    /// </summary>
    public enum NetworkMessage : byte
    {
        UpdatePlayerLocation,
        UpdateTankTurret,
        UpdateTankTexture,
        PlayerFired,
    }

    /// <summary>
    /// This class will maintain the network engine for this game
    /// </summary>
    public class NetworkEngine : IDisposable
    {
        private unsafe static readonly int PacketSizePlayerLocation =
            sizeof(byte) + sizeof(Vector3) + sizeof(float);
        private unsafe static readonly int PacketSizePlayerTurret =
            sizeof(byte) + sizeof(float) + sizeof(float);
        private unsafe static readonly int PacketSizePlayerFire =
            sizeof(byte);
        private unsafe static readonly int PacketSizeColorChange =
            sizeof(byte) + sizeof(byte);

        private const string SessionName = "'s game.";
        private static readonly Guid gameGuid =
         new Guid("{4695EAA3-B9A6-4388-A2FC-D2A36BA9A235}");
        private const int GamePort = 9897;
        private const int MaximumMessagesInQueue = 5;

        private Peer networkDevice = null;
        // Will be used to maintain network state
        private Address deviceAddress = null;
        // Address for the device being used
        private bool isConnected = false; // Are you connected yet?
        private Player remotePlayer = null; // The remote player
        private int remotePlayerId = 0; // The remote player id

        public event PlayerCreatedEventHandler NewPlayer;
        public event PlayerDestroyedEventHandler DestroyedPlayer;
    }
}
```

First, you see an enumeration that holds the possible messages you will send to the other player in this game. The enumeration itself is derived from byte so you can minimize the amount of data passed over the network (which is always a good thing). The possible messages you want to send are the player's current location (and orientation), the turret (and barrel) orientation, the texture color the tank is using, and whether the player fired a round. Later in this chapter, you will see how these enumeration values are used to send the data to the other players.

In the actual class, though, did you remember to put your project back into the mode that allows unsafe code? Go back and look at Figure 8.1 for a refresher if you've forgotten. The static read-only members that are declared are used to determine the packet size for the particular messages that will be sent. The packet size is important so you send a minimal amount of data. Each "application" in the DirectPlay world must be uniquely identified, so the gameGuid member is this identifier for Tankers. The session name and port constants aren't anything the user would see but make things easier for us later.

The instance members are somewhat interesting as well. You have the Peer object that will represent a single player in the peer-to-peer session (in this case, yourself). You also need to maintain an "address" for the device you are using for the connection (which I explain shortly). You're also interested in whether the connection has been established, as well as information about the remote player. Last, you want to have two events that can be fired when a player either joins the session (NewPlayer) or leaves the session (DestroyedPlayer). These events use event handlers from DirectPlay that I discuss in just a moment.

The constructor for this object should get everything ready for you to either host your own session or join an existing one. See Listing 16.2 for the constructor's code.

LISTING 16.2   Initializing Networking Engine

```
/// <summary>
/// Constructor where the device will be created.
/// </summary>
public NetworkEngine()
{
    // Create the peer object
    #if (DEBUG)
    networkDevice = new Peer();
    #else
    networkDevice = new Peer(InitializeFlags.DisableParameterValidation);
    #endif

    // Check if the Internet provider is available
    if(!IsInternetAvailable())
    {
        throw new InvalidOperationException
            ("You must have a valid TCP/IP connection to play this game.");
    }
    // Hook the events that we will care about
    networkDevice.Receive += new ReceiveEventHandler(OnDataReceive);
    networkDevice.ConnectComplete += new
```

LISTING 16.2   Continued

```
        ConnectCompleteEventHandler(OnConnectComplete);
    networkDevice.PlayerCreated += new
      PlayerCreatedEventHandler(OnPlayerCreated);
    networkDevice.PlayerDestroyed += new
      PlayerDestroyedEventHandler(OnPlayerDestroyed);
    networkDevice.SessionTerminated += new
      SessionTerminatedEventHandler(OnSessionLost);
    networkDevice.FindHostResponse += new
      FindHostResponseEventHandler(OnFoundHost);

    // Create any addresses
    deviceAddress = new Address();
    // Use the TCP/IP provider on our port
    deviceAddress.ServiceProvider = Address.ServiceProviderTcpIp;
    deviceAddress.AddComponent(Address.KeyPort, GamePort);
}
```

When the peer object is created in release mode, the flags passed in turn off
parameter validation. It is more efficient to skip the validation of the parameters,
so during debugging, you should leave the option on, but in release mode, just
skip the parameter validation. If the parameters being passed in are so different
between debug and release that this choice causes problems, you have bigger
problems than the parameter validation code. After the peer object is created, you
can check whether the Internet service provider is available (see Listing 16.3).

LISTING 16.3   Checking for Internet

```
/// <summary>
/// Checks to see if the TCP/IP service provider is available
/// </summary>
/// <returns>true if available; false otherwise</returns>
private bool IsInternetAvailable()
{
    // Ask about the providers attached
    ServiceProviderInformation[] providers = networkDevice.GetServiceProviders(
        false);

    // See if we have TCP/IP
    foreach(ServiceProviderInformation info in providers)
    {
        if (info.Guid == Address.ServiceProviderTcpIp)
        {
            // we do, return true
            return true;
        }
    }

    // We've made it here, the Internet provider must not be available
    return false;
}
```

DirectPlay provides quite a few different ways of connecting to a session. You have the Internet, which I'm sure most people are familiar with, but other service providers can be accessed as well, such as Internetwork Packet Exchange (IPX) and a direct modem-modem dialup service. Although these items might be interesting, they go beyond what we want to do, which is to simply play the game over the Internet. This method checks the service providers that are installed by the system and looks at each one to determine whether a TCP/IP provider is found. Assuming one is, it returns true immediately. If you got to the end and haven't found one yet, the method throws an exception informing you of this failure.

After the check, a number of events are hooked from the networking device. DirectPlay uses these events to update the status on the peers in the session. DirectPlay can trigger quite a few events, but only a small portion of them are hooked here. When data is received is an obvious one because what point would there be to a networking layer if you couldn't receive data? Other interesting things include a connection being complete (either successful or failure), players being created and destroyed, the session being lost, and an event called FindHostResponse, which I discuss shortly.

Finally, after the events are hooked, you want to set up your address. If you've been on the Internet a while, you recognize that you have something called an IP address. In DirectPlay, an address is simply a way of uniquely identifying a piece of networking hardware, whether it is a network card, a modem, or the IPX protocol. With Tankers, you only use a TCP/IP address, so after the device is created, you set the ServiceProvider to it. Finally, the port that will be used for this game is added to the address. TCP/IP can use a range of ports. In most cases, ports under 1024 are reserved, but you can use any port above that. There's no symbolic reason to use 9897 (the value of the constant used here); it just sounded good at the time. As long as the value is not in the reserved range and it is unused, you should be good to go.

Hosting the Session

When you're trying to get started in a peer-to-peer session, a "first" connection must accept the incoming network data from the other peers. In normal terms, this player is considered the host, even though each peer in the session is in reality its own host, considering that it holds its own data and so on. The player who is the host of this session must call a special method, Host (fancy that), to get the session started, so add the code from Listing 16.4 to your class now.

LISTING 16.4   Hosting a Session

```
/// <summary>
/// Will host a session on your computer
/// </summary>
public void Host()
{
    // Update with your information
    PlayerInformation info = new PlayerInformation();
    info.Name = Environment.UserName;
    networkDevice.SetPeerInformation(info, SyncFlags.PeerInformation);

    // Create the application description
    ApplicationDescription desc = new ApplicationDescription();
    desc.SessionName = Environment.UserName + SessionName;
    // Should be a relatively unique name
    desc.MaxPlayers = 2; // 1 on 1 battles
    desc.GuidApplication = gameGuid; // Unique ID all games will use
    desc.Flags = SessionFlags.NoDpnServer; // We don't want to use the server

    // Now host the session
    networkDevice.Host(desc, deviceAddress, SessionName);
}
```

Before hosting the session, you set the username of your peer to the username you're currently logged in as (using the Environment class from the .NET runtime). Most calls in DirectPlay happen asynchronously on different threads, so when you actually call SetPeerInformation, you do so with the SyncFlags enumeration to ensure that it only happens on this thread, and the call doesn't complete until it has finished.

After you set your player name, you're ready to host the session. If you look at the Host method, you'll see that it requires an application description to be passed in. You create that structure and set the four properties you care about. First, you set the session name, which a player could see if you were allowing that. You also set the maximum number of players to two (for some intense one-on-one action). The application Guid is the unique identifier for Tankers that you specified earlier.

The last flag is somewhat special. In the default case, when a session is hosted in DirectPlay, a new process is spawned called DpnSvr. The purpose of this process is to listen for connections on a particular port and then forward them onto the correct applications. This process allows more than one application to be listening for connections on the same port, but a performance cost is incurred by doing so. (A whole other process is running.) Not allowing this process to spawn is the goal of this flag, and it could cause the application to fail when trying to host the session if another application is already using the port. If so, simply change the port you're using.

Next, you're ready to host the session. You pass in the application description and the device address you're using to host the session on, but why did you also pass in the session name? This parameter is the user context parameter, which allows you to provide an arbitrary identifier or a context-based instance relevant to the action taken in the event handler. In this case, you're providing an identifier (SessionName) to uniquely identify any events fired by the hosting peer. Because the player creation event is fired during the call to Host (after all, you are a player as well), you want a quick and easy way to detect whether the player being created is the local player. This parameter is the easiest way to do so. Later in this chapter when I discuss event handling, you will see this part in action.

Joining the Session

With the session up and being hosted by one of the peers, you need another player to join this session. See Listing 16.5 for the code to have the player join the session.

LISTING 16.5   Joining a Session

```
/// <summary>
/// Join an existing session with the following hostname
/// </summary>
public void Join(string hostName)
{
    // Create the application description
    ApplicationDescription desc = new ApplicationDescription();
    desc.GuidApplication = gameGuid; // Unique ID all games will use

    // Now try to find the host and connect to it
    using(Address localAddress = new Address())
    {
        // Set the local provider
        localAddress.ServiceProvider = Address.ServiceProviderTcpIp;
        // Set the host's address name
        deviceAddress.AddComponent(Address.KeyHostname, hostName);

        // Search for hosts.
        networkDevice.FindHosts(desc, deviceAddress, localAddress, null, 0, 0, 0,
            FindHostsFlags.None);
    }
}
```

As you see in this code, you still need to use the application description before you can connect. However, the only thing you know (or need to know) about the application is the Guid because that is what uniquely identifies the application. When you plan to join an existing session, you need two separate addresses: one to represent the address you're using to connect and a second representing the address you are connecting to. So before you attempt to call the `FindHosts` method, you need to create a new address and set the service provider to TCP/IP, like the one you've already created. Finally, you add the hostname you are trying to connect to and call the `FindHosts` method.

The Event Handlers

That's all fine and good, but where did you connect? Fact is, currently, you haven't. The `FindHosts` method searches the hostname you've specified for valid sessions of this game. If it finds any, the `FindHostResponse` event is fired (which is why you hooked that method earlier). See Listing 16.6 for the implementation of this method, which is where the connection will occur.

LISTING 16.6 Connecting to a Found Session

```
/// <summary>
/// Fired when a host has been found
/// </summary>
private void OnFoundHost(object sender, FindHostResponseEventArgs e)
{
    // If you've already connected, don't try again
    if (isConnected)
    {
        return;
    }

    // Try to connect now
    isConnected = true;
    Peer connection = sender as Peer;
    connection.Connect(e.Message.ApplicationDescription, e.Message.AddressSender,
        e.Message.AddressDevice, null, 0);
}
```

The find method actually searches a particular subnet of the network for hosts, depending on the hostname that you've entered. When more than one host is found, you only want to try to connect to one, so first you check whether you're already connected, and if so, you simply leave the method. If you are not connected, first mark yourself as connected, and then try to connect. You see that you can get the `Peer` object from the event-handler parameters, as well as all the parameters to the `Connect` method. What if the connection fails? Currently, you set the connected Boolean value to `true`, and it will never try to connect again. See Listing 16.7 for the implementation of the connection-complete event handler.

LISTING 16.7   Connection Is Complete

```
/// <summary>
/// Fired when the connection is completed
/// </summary>
private void OnConnectComplete(object sender, ConnectCompleteEventArgs e)
{
    // Was the connection completed successfully?
    if (e.Message.ResultCode == ResultCode.Success)
    {
        isConnected = true;
        if (remotePlayer != null)
        {
            SendNewColor(remotePlayer.Color);
        }
    }
    else
    {
        // Well that sucks, the connection wasn't made
        System.Diagnostics.Debugger.Log(9, GameEngine.GameName,
            string.Format("The connection failed.  Result was {0}.",
            e.Message.ResultCode));

        // Let the game engine know
        isConnected = false;
    }
}
```

This event will let you know whether the connection was successful. If it wasn't, you just spew some debug text and reset your variable. If the result was successful, and you have a remote player, you send the color of that remote player to the other peer in the session. I show you this method in a few moments. Before you get there, however, look through the other event handlers you need to implement (in Listing 16.8).

LISTING 16.8   The Event Handlers

```
/// <summary>
/// Fired when a new player was created, including yourself
/// </summary>
private void OnPlayerCreated(object sender, PlayerCreatedEventArgs e)
{
    // See if this player is the host
    if (e.Message.PlayerContext as string != SessionName)
    {
        // Store the player ID
        remotePlayerId = e.Message.PlayerID;
        // This player is not, notify the game engine
        if (NewPlayer != null)
        {
            NewPlayer(this, e);
        }
```

LISTING 16.8 Continued

```
            // Update the player name too
            PlayerInformation info = networkDevice.GetPeerInformation(
                e.Message.PlayerID);

            remotePlayer.Name = info.Name;
        }
    }
/// <summary>
/// Fired when a new player was destroyed, including yourself
/// </summary>
private void OnPlayerDestroyed(object sender, PlayerDestroyedEventArgs e)
{
    // See if this player is the host
    if (e.Message.PlayerContext as string != SessionName)
    {
        // Remove the player ID
        remotePlayerId = 0;
        // This player is not, notify the game engine
        if (DestroyedPlayer != null)
        {
            DestroyedPlayer(this, e);
        }
    }
}
/// <summary>
/// Fired when the networking session was lost
/// </summary>
private void OnSessionLost(object sender, SessionTerminatedEventArgs e)
{
    // No longer connected.
    isConnected = false;
}
```

You'll notice that the `Receive` event handler is not handled currently. I address this part in the next section because it's pretty tightly coupled with sending data. In the meantime, look at the three new handlers implemented here. When the session is lost (maybe the host has quit or the Internet went down), you simply mark yourself as no longer connected: nothing major. In the case of a player being created or destroyed, you first check the player's context variable. Notice here is where you're checking whether it is the local player by comparing this context value to the session name you passed in to the host call. If this player is *not* the local player, then you store (or clear out) the player ID number and fire the appropriate event to let the game engine know about the status. If it is a new player, you call `GetPeerInformation` to get the player name of the remote player to render it while playing.

Sending and Receiving Data

When it comes right down to it, a network session is a way for the various players within the session to transfer data to one another. That is the heart of a network game. So what you need to do first is figure out the way to send some data to another player. Look at the method in Listing 16.9 for the implementation of sending the player's location and orientation to the other peer member.

LISTING 16.9   Sending Position and Orientation

```
/// <summary>
/// Will send the player's position and orientation to the other peer
/// </summary>
public bool SendPlayerLocation(Vector3 position, float rotation)
{
    // Check to see if we can send this message
    if (CanSendData())
    {

        // Create a new network packet to send the player location
        NetworkPacket packet = new NetworkPacket(PacketSizePlayerLocation);
        // Write the message
        packet.Write((byte)NetworkMessage.UpdatePlayerLocation);
        packet.Write(position);
        packet.Write(rotation);
        // Now send the message
        networkDevice.SendTo(0, packet, 0, SendFlags.NoLoopback |
                            SendFlags.NonSequential);
        // Message sent
        return true;
    }
    // The data cannot be sent, too many messages in queue
    return false;
}.
```

The position and orientation of the player are sent quite often throughout the game's lifetime. Because they are, this message doesn't *have* to be delivered every time. First, you check whether the network is available to send data (which I discuss in just a moment), and if so, you create a network packet of the appropriate size. You then write the message you're sending, followed by the data (or in this case, two pieces of data). Finally, you send the piece of data out, passing in the `NoLoopback` flag as well as the `NonSequential` flag. Because you're the one sending the message, you won't need to receive the sent data back, and it doesn't really matter what order these pieces are received in. You then return `true` if the method was able to send the data and `false` otherwise.

What about the method to check whether you're able to send the data? The implementation is pretty simple, as you see in Listing 16.10.

LISTING 16.10   Checking Network Statistics

```
/// <summary>
/// Uses the send queue to determine if data can be sent
/// </summary>
/// <returns></returns>
private bool CanSendData()
{
    int numMessages = 0;
    int numBytes = 0;

    // Get the number of messages
    networkDevice.GetSendQueueInformation(remotePlayerId, out numMessages,
        out numBytes, GetSendQueueInformationFlags.PriorityNormal);

    // Don't send if the message queue has more than 5 members
    return (numMessages < MaximumMessagesInQueue);
}
```

DirectPlay is smart enough to queue up data if the computer you are sending the data to cannot process it fast enough. Although that's a great feature to have, it can also cause problems if you continue to send data at a rate too fast for the remote system to maintain. To prevent this problem, you'll build a "throttling" system that allows you to lower (or raise) the amount of data that you're sending. The point of this method is to detect the number of messages waiting to be sent in the queue; if there are more than the maximum you've allowed (five, in this case), you return false, signifying that you shouldn't send data. What about some messages that you want to be guaranteed, though, such as the firing of the weapon? See Listing 16.11 for an implementation of this type of method.

LISTING 16.11   Sending the Fire Message

```
/// <summary>
/// Will send the player's position and orientation to the other peer
/// </summary>
public bool SendFireMessage()
{
    // Create a new network packet to send the player location
    NetworkPacket packet = new NetworkPacket(PacketSizePlayerFire);
    // Write the message
    packet.Write((byte)NetworkMessage.PlayerFired);
    // Now send the message
    networkDevice.SendTo(0, packet, 0, SendFlags.NoLoopback |
                        SendFlags.Guaranteed);
    // Since this is guaranteed, we should always send it, but let the game
    // engine slow down data transfer
    return CanSendData();
}
```

Notice that the packet is created and sent no matter what, and when it is sent, the Guaranteed flag is included. You still want the game engine to realize whether network data is being sent too fast, so you still do the check and use that as the return value of the method. You want to send two other messages to the other player in this session; see Listing 16.12 for the implementations.

LISTING 16.12   Sending Data

```
/// <summary>
/// Will send the player's position and orientation to the other peer
/// </summary>
public bool SendTurretInfo(float turretRotation, float gunRotation)
{
    // Check to see if we can send this message
    if (CanSendData())
    {
        // Create a new network packet to send the player location
        NetworkPacket packet = new NetworkPacket(PacketSizePlayerTurret);
        // Write the message
        packet.Write((byte)NetworkMessage.UpdateTankTurret);
        packet.Write(turretRotation);
        packet.Write(gunRotation);
        // Now send the message
        networkDevice.SendTo(0, packet, 0, SendFlags.NoLoopback |
                            SendFlags.NonSequential);
        // Message sent
        return true;
    }
    // The data cannot be sent, too many messages in queue
    return false;
}
/// <summary>
/// Will send the player's position and orientation to the other peer
/// </summary>
public bool SendNewColor(TankColors newcolor)
{
    // Create a new network packet to send the player location
    NetworkPacket packet = new NetworkPacket(PacketSizeColorChange);
    // Write the message
    packet.Write((byte)NetworkMessage.UpdateTankTexture);
    packet.Write((byte)newcolor);
    // Now send the message
    networkDevice.SendTo(0, packet, 0, SendFlags.NoLoopback |
                        SendFlags.Guaranteed);
    // Since this is guaranteed, we should always send it, but let the
    // game engine slow down data transfer
    return CanSendData();
}
```

These implementations are just like the two previous ones; they just send different data. Now that you've got the data being sent, you need a way to handle receiving that data. See the event handler in Listing 16.13.

LISTING 16.13   Receiving Data

```
/// <summary>
/// Fired when data is received from the other peer in the session
/// </summary>
private void OnDataReceive(object sender, ReceiveEventArgs e)
{
    System.Diagnostics.Debug.Assert(remotePlayer != null,
                          "Remote player should not be null.");
    using(NetworkPacket data = e.Message.ReceiveData)
    {
        NetworkMessage msg = (NetworkMessage)data.Read(typeof(byte));
        switch(msg)
        {
            case NetworkMessage.UpdatePlayerLocation:
                remotePlayer.Position = (Vector3)data.Read(typeof(Vector3));
                remotePlayer.Rotation = (float)data.Read(typeof(float));
                break;
            case NetworkMessage.UpdateTankTurret:
                remotePlayer.UpdateTurret((float)data.Read(typeof(float)),
                    (float)data.Read(typeof(float)));
                break;
            case NetworkMessage.UpdateTankTexture:
                remotePlayer.Color = (TankColors)data.Read(typeof(byte));
                break;
            case NetworkMessage.PlayerFired:
                remotePlayer.RaiseFireEvent();
                break;
        }
    }
}
```

The first thing that happens is that the remote player is checked for null. It
should never be null, which is why the assert is there, just in case. Notice that the
event handler gives you a network packet just like the one you used to send the
data. First, you read a single byte from the packet to get the message type, and
then, you do your switch statement on the possible values. In each case, you
update the remote player with the appropriate action, by either updating a property or calling a method. One of these methods hasn't even been defined yet. Add
the method in Listing 16.14 to your player class now.

LISTING 16.14   Setting Player Properties

```
/// <summary>
/// Updates the gun turret and barrel
/// </summary>
public void UpdateTurret(float turret, float gun)
{
    gameTank.GunTurretAngle = turret;
    gameTank.GunBarrelAngle = gun;
}
```

You could have just as easily used two properties rather than a method, but because they're both updated simultaneously every time, a single method was "cleaner." You might have noticed that there is nowhere the remote player variable can be updated either. Add the following method to the networking class to allow it to be:

```
public void UpdatePlayer(Player p)
{
    remotePlayer = p;
}
```

Cleaning Up Resources

Last but not least, you probably noticed that the class implements IDisposable just as everything else does. You want to ensure that your networking session can be cleaned up easily, so add the Dispose implementation in Listing 16.15 to your networking class.

LISTING 16.15   Setting Player Properties

```
/// <summary>
/// Done with this object, clean it up
/// </summary>
public void Dispose()
{
    // Clean up all data here
    if (networkDevice != null)
    {
        networkDevice.Dispose();
    }
    if (deviceAddress != null)
    {
        deviceAddress.Dispose();
    }
}
```

Summary

The networking layer is complete. You learned about the differences between client/server applications and peer-to-peer networking sessions. You discovered how to host and join peer-to-peer sessions and how to send and receive data. It was a busy chapter that brought you almost to the end of this section.

The only thing left to do is hook everything together in the game engine and have your working game.

CHAPTER 17

Finally, Finishing Tankers

You've put so much work into Tankers that you could actually play the game, and I'd bet it feels great to realize that you are just about done. As I mentioned at the beginning of the book, writing games isn't easy, but when you're finally finished, well, it doesn't get much better than that.

So what's left for Tankers anyway? You've mostly written all the code to handle all the scenarios; the only thing you need to do now is hook everything together. It will be a little bit like a jigsaw puzzle!

In this chapter, you'll learn

- ▶ How to hook everything together
- ▶ How to finish the game

Plugging into the Game Engine

Before you start writing any code to hook things together, you need to make sure that you have the required variables and constants declared. Add the declarations from Listing 17.1 to your game engine class.

LISTING 17.1   Declarations

```
// Constants for starting locations and rotations within the levels
private static readonly Vector3 Player1StartLocation = new Vector3(-2600,0,-2600);
private static readonly Vector3 Player2StartLocation = new Vector3(2600,0,2600);
private const float Player1StartRotation = (float)Math.PI / 4.0f;
private const float Player2StartRotation = (float)Math.PI + (float)Math.PI / 4.0f;

// Store the sky box
private Skybox worldSky = null;
// Store the level
private Level worldLevel = null;

// The local player
private Player localPlayer = null;
// The remote player
private Player remotePlayer = null;

// The bullet collection
private Bullets allBullets = new Bullets();

// The sound engine
private SoundEngine sounds = null;

// The network engine
private NetworkEngine network = null;
private float networkTime = 0.0f;

// How often should we update the network data?
private float minNetworkTime = 0.1f;

// is the world loaded?
private bool isWorldLoaded = false;
```

The constants listed here are pretty self-explanatory. When the players start (either player one or two), they need to start in a particular location, and it would probably be beneficial to have them rotated a certain way. You wouldn't want to start the game looking at the wall! The rest of the variables are the classes you've written in the previous chapters, such as the sky box and the level classes. Notice that there are two player classes, one for your local player and the other for the remote player that can join your session. The collection of bullets is stored in the game engine as well.

You can see that the two "engines" are declared here as well. The sound engine is relatively small and self-explanatory, but the networking engine has a few different things that go along with it. First, you see the network time, which stores the last time a network packet was sent, and then a minimum network time, which is the minimum amount of time that must elapse before you can send any more network packets. This time is here so you can throttle the amount of data you're passing into the network. If too much data is being passed, this value increases, but it decreases if the network is too idle.

Now, you want to create the sound and network engines somewhere, so find the constructor for the game engine. Create these objects before you initialize the graphics engine. Add the code in Listing 17.2 to the end of your constructor to initialize the network object.

LISTING 17.2 Initializing Network Objects

```
// Try to create the network engine as well
network = new NetworkEngine();

// Hook the events
network.DestroyedPlayer += new
    Microsoft.DirectX.DirectPlay.PlayerDestroyedEventHandler(
    OnRemoveRemotePlayer);
network.NewPlayer += new
    Microsoft.DirectX.DirectPlay.PlayerCreatedEventHandler(
    OnCreateRemotePlayer);
```

Next, find the `Main` method in your game class and add this line before the call to the `MainLoop` method from the sample framework to initialize the sound engine:

```
// Try to create the sound engine
tankersEngine.sounds = new SoundEngine(sampleFramework.Window);
```

The sound engine will handle the code internally if it fails because sound isn't a "requirement" for the game. Remember from your implementation, the sound engine holds a variable designed to not play sounds if the initialization fails for some reason. The network code, however, is a requirement, and you'll notice that there are no checks here for any failures. That is handled by the caller of this method, in this case, the "main" method of the application. Notice also that the events for the new and destroyed players are hooked here. You need to include these implementations into the game engine as well (see Listing 17.3). Also remember to add a using clause for DirectPlay into your game engine file (using `Microsoft.DirectX.DirectPlay;`); otherwise, the preceding code won't compile.

LISTING 17.3 Handling Player Connections

```
private void OnRemoveRemotePlayer(object sender,
    Microsoft.DirectX.DirectPlay.PlayerDestroyedEventArgs e)
{
    lock(remotePlayer)
    {
        // The remote player was destroyed.
        remotePlayer.IsPlayerConnected = false;
    }
}
private void OnCreateRemotePlayer(object sender,
    Microsoft.DirectX.DirectPlay.PlayerCreatedEventArgs e)
{
```

LISTING 17.3   Continued

```
    lock(remotePlayer)
    {
        // Hey, the remote player was created
        remotePlayer.IsPlayerConnected = true;
        // Tell the remote player what color I am
        network.SendNewColor(localPlayer.Color);
    }
}
```

The events that get fired from DirectPlay happen on different threads, which means it's possible to have more than one of these events fire simultaneously (especially on a computer with more than one processor). To make this less of an issue, the remote player object is locked. What the lock keyword does is allow only a single thread access to the variable inside the lock block at any given time, which ensures that two threads won't be accessing the remote player simultaneously.

As you see here, the actual events simply call a new method that (depending on whether the player is joining or leaving) sets the IsPlayerConnected property to true or false, and if they are joining, it sends the local player's color over. So I know what you're thinking, "Wait a minute: I never defined a property like that." You're right, so do that now (in the player class, naturally):

```
public bool IsPlayerConnected
{
    get { return isPlayerActive; }
    set { isPlayerActive = value; }
}
```

This property is used throughout the game engine to determine whether the remote player has been created and connected yet. With the networking and sound engines out of the way for now, you need to make sure that the user interface gets created and called. In the OnCreateDevice method right after you create the debug font, add the following lines of code:

```
// Create the main UI Screen
mainScreen = new MainUiScreen(device, screenWidth, screenHeight, this);
mainScreen.HostGame += new EventHandler(OnHostGame);
mainScreen.JoinGame += new EventHandler(OnJoinGame);
mainScreen.Quit += new EventHandler(OnMainQuit);
```

The main user interface can inform the game engine that it is ready to play by either hosting a new session or joining an existing session or that the application should quit. You can see the implementations of these event handlers in Listing 17.4.

LISTING 17.4   Starting a Game

```
/// <summary>
/// The user is going to play now and be the host, load everything
/// </summary>
private void OnHostGame(object sender, EventArgs e)
{
    // Get the screen and draw it so the loading screen shows up
    MainUiScreen screen = sender as MainUiScreen;
    FullsceneRender();

    // Load the world
    LoadWorld(true, screen.TankColor);

    // Now host
    network.Host();

    // We're done with the main menu
    isMainMenuShowing = false;
}
/// <summary>
/// The user is ready to join a game now
/// </summary>
private void OnJoinGame(object sender, EventArgs e)
{
    // Get the screen and draw it so the loading screen shows up
    MainUiScreen screen = sender as MainUiScreen;
    FullsceneRender();

    // Load the world
    LoadWorld(false, screen.TankColor);

    // Now join
    network.Join(screen.HostName);

    // We're done with the main menu
    isMainMenuShowing = false;
}
/// <summary>
/// The user wants to quit, let them
/// </summary>
private void OnMainQuit(object sender, EventArgs e)
{
    // Allow the application to quit now
    sampleFramework.CloseWindow();
}
```

In the quit scenario, the only obvious solution here is to close the form, which is what you do. When the other options are selected (either hosting or joining a new session), the scene is rendered once more. The user interface is still showing for this render, but it is updated to show the loading screen, which allows the game engine to load the models in the background in the LoadWorld method (see Listing 17.5). After the world is loaded, the network either hosts a new session or joins an existing one, depending on the options chosen.

LISTING 17.5   Getting Engine Ready for Play

```
/// <summary>
/// Will load everything the world needs
/// </summary>
private void LoadWorld(bool isHost, TankColors color)
{
    // Create the players and hook the events
    localPlayer = new Player(device, this, Environment.UserName, true);
    localPlayer.Color = color;
    localPlayer.Fired += new EventHandler(OnPlayerFire);

    // Now create the remote player
    remotePlayer = new Player(device, this, string.Empty, false);
    remotePlayer.Fired += new EventHandler(OnPlayerFire);
    network.UpdatePlayer(remotePlayer);

    // Start at the default location
    if (isHost)
    {
        // Host starts as player 1, remote as player2
        localPlayer.Position = Player1StartLocation;
        localPlayer.Rotation = Player1StartRotation;
        remotePlayer.Position = Player2StartLocation;
        remotePlayer.Rotation = Player2StartRotation;
    }
    else
    {
        remotePlayer.Position = Player1StartLocation;
        remotePlayer.Rotation = Player1StartRotation;
        localPlayer.Position = Player2StartLocation;
        localPlayer.Rotation = Player2StartRotation;
    }

    // Create the world sky box
    worldSky = new Skybox(device);
    // Create the level
    worldLevel = new Level(device);

    // Now the world is loaded
    isWorldLoaded = true;
}
```

The object of this method is to load all the data that the world (game) requires while playing. This part can take a few seconds even on a faster computer, which is why the loading screen is displayed in the user interface. Notice that not only is the local player created now, but the remote player is created as well. When the remote player joins the game, you don't want to have to wait for his data to load, too, so you do it all at once, and then when that player joins, you simply mark him as connected (as you did in the NewPlayer event handler just a short while ago). Notice too that the fire event is hooked on each player. (The implementation is in Listing 17.6.)

Whether or not the local player is the host determines where the local and remote players are placed. Notice that the host is always placed in the Player 1 position, and the joining player is always placed at the Player 2 position. After the players are placed, the sky box and the level are loaded and the world is marked as being loaded (because it now is). Back in the event handlers, you'll notice that the main menu variable is marked as false because it is no longer showing the user interface and the game is ready to be played.

LISTING 17.6 Handling Player Firing

```
/// <summary>
/// The player fired its weapon
/// </summary>
private void OnPlayerFire(object sender, EventArgs e)
{
    // Play the fire sound
    sounds.FireWeapon();
    Player p = sender as Player;
    // Make sure only one thread has access to this collection
    lock(allBullets)
    {
        p.FireRound(device, allBullets);
    }
    if ((p.IsLocal) && (remotePlayer.IsPlayerConnected))
    {
        // Also send this over network
        network.SendFireMessage();
    }
}
```

I should point a few things out here. First, notice that the fire weapon sound is played when the gun is fired. Finally, you'll be able to hear some sound! Next, notice the FireRound method (which takes in the bullets' collection) is wrapped inside a Lock statement. Because this event can be fired from the networking engine (and thus can happen on a separate thread), you need to ensure that only one thread has access to the bullets' collection at a time. Assuming that the local player is the one firing the bullet, and the remote player has been connected, you also want to send the information over the network that you just fired the bullet. This step allows the remote player to see it as well.

You also need to make sure that the IsLocal property is defined in the player class:

```
public bool IsLocal
{
    get { return isPlayerLocal; }
}
```

Rendering the Game

Now you need to update the rendering code that you wrote a few chapters ago to handle rendering both the user interface screens and the game itself. Use the code from Listing 17.7 to replace the current rendering method you have defined.

LISTING 17.7   Rendering the Scene

```
public void OnFrameRender(Device device, double appTime, float elapsedTime)
{
    bool beginSceneCalled = false;

    // Clear the render target and the zbuffer
    device.Clear(ClearFlags.ZBuffer | ClearFlags.Target, 0, 1.0f, 0);
    try
    {
        device.BeginScene();
        beginSceneCalled = true;


        if (isMainMenuShowing)
        {
            mainScreen.Draw(this);
        }
        else
        {
            // Set the white material, it will be used for the
            // majority of the rendering
            device.Material = WhiteMaterial;

            // Render the game's scene
            RenderGameScene(device);
        }

        #if (DEBUG)
        // Show debug stats (in debug mode)
        debugFont.DrawText(null, sampleFramework.FrameStats,
            new System.Drawing.Rectangle(2,0,0,0),
            DrawTextFormat.NoClip, unchecked((int)0xffffff00));
        debugFont.DrawText(null, sampleFramework.DeviceStats,
            new System.Drawing.Rectangle(2,15,0,0),
            DrawTextFormat.NoClip, unchecked((int)0xffffff00));

        // Draw the number of vertices and face information
        debugFont.DrawText(null, string.Format
            ("\r\nNumber Of Vertices Rendered: {0}\r\nNumber of
              Faces Rendered: {1}"
            ,numberVerts, numberFaces), new System.Drawing.Rectangle(2,30,0,0),
            DrawTextFormat.NoClip, unchecked((int)0xffffffff));
        #endif
    }
    finally
    {
        if (beginSceneCalled)
```

LISTING 17.7 Continued

```
                device.EndScene();
        }
}
/// <summary>
/// Renders the game scene, including the level, the tanks, etc.
/// </summary>
private void RenderGameScene(Device device)
{
    // Render the sky box first
    worldSky.Draw(this, device);
    // Now, the level
    worldLevel.Draw(this, device);

    // Track the local player
    sceneCamera.Track(localPlayer);

    // Draw the player
    localPlayer.Draw(this, sceneCamera);
    // Is there a remote player to draw?
    if (remotePlayer.IsPlayerConnected)
    {
        remotePlayer.Draw(this, sceneCamera);
    }

    // Make sure only one thread has access to this collection
    lock(allBullets)
    {
        // Draw all of the bullets currently onscreen
        Bullet.SetBulletRenderStates(this);
        foreach(Bullet b in allBullets)
        {
            b.Draw(this, sceneCamera);
        }
        Bullet.EndBulletRenderStates(this);
    }

    // Now render the player names
    localPlayer.DrawPlayerName(this);
    // Is there a remote player to draw?
    if (remotePlayer.IsPlayerConnected)
    {
        remotePlayer.DrawPlayerName(this);
    }

    particleEffects.Draw(this);
}
```

The main rendering method is quite similar to the first one that you implemented earlier for this game, but it actually draws the user interface or the game, depending on what should be rendered currently.

See Figure 17.1 for a shot of the game, finally finished. Congratulations!

Summary

Just because the game is done now doesn't mean you can't expand it even more. For example, you might want to add a little explosion effect when you fire your bullets out of the tank. The next chapter will focus on this behavior. You can expand and update the game in any way that your mind desires!

PART V

Advanced Graphics, Client/Server Networking, Game 3

CHAPTER 18

Adding Special Effects

Although the majority of the great games rely on more than fancy graphics to sell well, the fact remains that having great graphics can only help. You don't want a game that's nothing but great graphics (you need some type of game play element that's fun), but just as the movies invest large sums of money into special effects, you should spend a little bit of time adding some special effects to your games.

One of the more common effects you see in computer games is something called a particle system. You'll be designing one in this chapter.

In this chapter, you'll learn

▶ How to implement a basic particle system

▶ How to render point sprites

▶ How to hook the system into the game

Implementing a Basic Particle System

You can think of a *particle system* as a system that generates small pieces of materials which are responding to some sort of environmental change. For example, a particle system could generate snowflakes, fog, sparks, or dust. In Tankers, you have a tank firing a projectile out of its barrel. Adding a small bit of spark particles to this firing should be easy to do.

Direct3D uses *point sprites* to render these particles. In the context of Direct3D, they are essentially generalizations of points in space that are rendered using textures. Adding them is also quite simple. In your project file, add a new file called specialeffects.cs and add the code from Listing 18.1 to the code file.

LISTING 18.1   Starting the Particle System

```
using System;
using System.Windows.Forms;
using Microsoft.DirectX;
using Microsoft.DirectX.Direct3D;
using Microsoft.Samples.DirectX.UtilityToolkit;

namespace Tankers
{
    /// <summary>
    /// Information about a particle
    /// </summary>
    public struct Particle
    {
        public Vector3 positionVector;      // Current position
        public Vector3 velocityVector;      // Current velocity
        public Vector3 initialPosition;     // Initial position
        public Vector3 initialVelocity;     // Initial velocity
        public float creationTime;     // Time of creation
        public ColorValue diffuseColor; // Initial diffuse color
        public ColorValue fadeColor;    // Faded diffuse color
        public float fadeProgression;      // Fade progression
    };
}
```

Before you actually add the particle system into the application, you need to know a few things about the particles you'll be designing for the game. This structure you've just declared will maintain all this information, and as you can see, it stores four different vectors. There is one each for the current position and velocity of the given particle, along with one each for the initial position and velocity for the particle.

You also want to know when this particular particle was created because in this scenario (sparks), the particles do not last forever; they fade away. Speaking of fading away, the next two items are the initial color of the spark and the color the spark should fade into. A fade progression member will determine how to interpolate between the two colors you have.

Construction Cue

> Reusing objects that have already been created is almost always a good performance win. It is rarely better performancewise to create a new object rather than simply use one over again. It's important to remember this point.

Now that you have the particle structure declared, you can start implementing the special effect class. In the same code file, take the code in Listing 18.2 and implement it in your code.

LISTING 18.2   The Special Effects Class

```
/// <summary>
/// Our special effects class will use a particle system
/// </summary>
public class SpecialEffects : IDisposable
{
    #region Constant Data
    private static readonly ColorValue WhiteSmoke = new ColorValue(
        (float)System.Drawing.Color.WhiteSmoke.R / 255.0f,
        (float)System.Drawing.Color.WhiteSmoke.G / 255.0f,
        (float)System.Drawing.Color.WhiteSmoke.B / 255.0f,
        1.0f);
    private static readonly ColorValue Black = new ColorValue(
        0.0f, 0.0f, 0.0f, 0.0f);
    private const int MaximumParticles = 1024;
    // This seems like a nice round number
    private static readonly int VertexBufferSize =
      CustomVertex.PositionColored.StrideSize * MaximumParticles;
    private static readonly int FlushSize = MaximumParticles / 4;
    private static readonly int FlushLockSize =
      CustomVertex.PositionColored.StrideSize * FlushSize;
    #endregion
}
```

The first two constants you've declared are the starting color and the faded color of the particle. You want the particle color to start like the white smoke color; notice how you've calculated the color into a ColorValue structure. In the System.Drawing.Color structure where WhiteSmoke is a member, there is a single integer (4 bytes), where each byte represents one of the basic colors, red (R), green (G), and blue (B), and an extra byte represents the alpha (A). Each of the color components range from 0 (no color of this component) to 255 (full color of this component), so to calculate the floating-point color value, you take the color component value and divide it by 255.0f. Because the fade color is black, this calculation isn't necessary. All components (other than alpha) are 0.

The next few constants determine the rendering behavior of the particle system. The first controls the maximum number of particles available in the system at any given time, and the next is the size of the vertex buffer that needs to be created to handle these particles.

Up until this point, all the rendering was done with meshes, and you haven't had to deal with a VertexBuffer outside of briefly calculating a bounding sphere or handle level collisions. A vertex buffer is essentially just a place on your Direct3D device where you can store vertices for later use (namely, rendering). In all actuality, the meshes that you've been using to render with so far are all using these vertex buffers in their private implementations anyway; you just might not have been aware of it at the time. The rest of the constants deal with when a vertex buffer is "flushed" (more on that when you get there) and the size of the lock when the flush happens.

Now, the first code you write for the particle system is the constructor in Listing 18.3.

LISTING 18.3 Creating the Special Effects Class

```
/// <summary>
/// Constructor for creating the special effects object
/// </summary>
public SpecialEffects(Device device)
{
    System.Diagnostics.Debug.Assert(device != null,
        "You must pass in a valid device to create this class.");

    // The texture needs to be created once
    particleTexture = TexturePool.CreateTexture(device, "particle.bmp");

    // Hook the device events since the vertex buffer will need to be destroyed
    // and re-created when the device is lost or reset
    device.DeviceLost += new EventHandler(OnDeviceLost);
    device.DeviceReset += new EventHandler(OnDeviceReset);

    // Fire the OnDeviceRest once
    OnDeviceReset(device, EventArgs.Empty);
}
```

You'll first notice that you create a texture that hasn't been declared yet. You'll declare the instance variables for the class in just a moment. This texture is the same texture used for every particle in the system, and if you look at it from the media folder, you notice it looks similar to a small round circle. This causes the particles to take this shape as well. Because you deal directly with device resources, you need to hook the lost and reset events yourself to handle those situations, and because you can't be sure when the device reset will occur, you call that method directly the first time.

Before you go on, you need to declare the following instance variables for this class:

```
// We will store one particle texture
private Texture particleTexture = null;
// A vertex buffer will be needed to render the particles
private VertexBuffer vertexBuffer = null;
private float time = 0.0f;
private int baseParticle = MaximumParticles;
private int particles = 0;
private System.Collections.ArrayList particlesList =
 new System.Collections.ArrayList();
```

```
private System.Collections.ArrayList freeParticles =
 new System.Collections.ArrayList();
private System.Random rand = new System.Random();
```

Naturally, the vertex buffer and texture are needed because I already discussed them. You also want to maintain the current application time, as well as the base particle you are currently working on. Aside from the total number of particles in the system, you need two collections of particles, one containing the particles currently being used and the other containing the currently free particles. Last, because you don't want each of the particles to be fired from the exact same location with the exact same trajectory, you supply a little randomness.

You still need to implement the IDisposable interface as well as the device event handlers you declared earlier, so add the code from Listing 18.4 to the class now.

LISTING 18.4   Event Handlers and Cleanup

```
/// <summary>
/// Clean up the vertex buffer used by the special effects
/// </summary>
public void Dispose()
{
    // The OnDeviceLost method does what we need, use it
    OnDeviceLost(null, EventArgs.Empty);
}
/// <summary>
/// Fired when the device is about to be lost
/// </summary>
private void OnDeviceLost(object sender, EventArgs e)
{
    // The vertex buffer simply needs to be destroyed here
    if (vertexBuffer != null)
    {
        vertexBuffer.Dispose();
    }
    vertexBuffer = null;
}
/// <summary>
/// Fired after the device has been reset
/// </summary>
private unsafe void OnDeviceReset(object sender, EventArgs e)
{
    Device device = sender as Device;

    System.Diagnostics.Debug.Assert(device != null,
        "For some reason the event handler has no device.");

    // Create a vertex buffer for the particle system. The size of this buffer
    // does not relate to the number of particles that exist. Rather, the
    // buffer is used as a communication channel with the device. We fill in
    // a bit, and tell the device to draw. While the device is drawing, we
    // fill in the next bit using NoOverwrite. We continue doing this until
```

LISTING 18.4 Continued

```
// we run out of vertex buffer space, and are forced to discard the buffer
// and start over at the beginning.

vertexBuffer = new VertexBuffer(device, VertexBufferSize,
    Usage.Dynamic ¦ Usage.WriteOnly ¦ Usage.Points,
    CustomVertex.PositionColored.Format, Pool.Default);
}
```

Because the cleanup is the same for either the device lost or the special effects object being disposed, you could have either method call the other. In this case, the Dispose method is calling the OnDeviceLost method. In that method, the only thing required is the cleanup of the vertex buffer. Because the texture is created as a part of the texture pool, it isn't required to be cleaned up by this object because it will be destroyed when the texture pool is.

When the device is reset, on the other hand, the vertex buffer needs to be re-created because the plan is to put the vertex buffer in the default memory pool (which is video memory). That's also the reason why the vertex buffer needs to be destroyed when a device is lost. All resources that live in the default memory pool must be destroyed before a device is allowed to be reset. Look at the constructor for the vertex buffer that is being used:

```
public VertexBuffer ( Microsoft.DirectX.Direct3D.Device device ,
    System.Int32 sizeOfBufferInBytes ,
    Microsoft.DirectX.Direct3D.Usage usage ,
    Microsoft.DirectX.Direct3D.VertexFormats vertexFormat ,
    Microsoft.DirectX.Direct3D.Pool pool )
```

The device is always needed for any resources that are created, so that's not a big surprise. The next parameter is the size of the vertex buffer in bytes, and as you can see, you've used the constant that was declared earlier for this value. The *usage* parameter tells Direct3D how you plan to use this resource; in this case, you plan to use it for point sprites, as a dynamic vertex buffer, and you never read from it. This set is the most efficient set of parameters you can pass to this method for this scenario.

Next, you need to tell Direct3D the format of the data you will be filling the vertex buffer with, and in your case, it contains the position of the vertex along with its color. (Texture coordinates are implied with point sprites.) Finally, you specify the memory pool that this resource should occupy, in this case, the default pool.

Now that you have the class created and the resources behaving correctly, you need a way to create the particles when the tank fires its projectile. Take the method in Listing 18.5 and add it to the class.

LISTING 18.5   Adding Sparks

```
/// <summary>
/// Add new 'firing' effect
/// </summary>
public void AddFiringEffect(int numberParticlesAdding, Vector3 currentPosition,
                          Vector3 vel)
{
    // Add some new firing particles
    int particlesEmit = particles + numberParticlesAdding;

    while((particles < MaximumParticles) && (particles < particlesEmit))
    {
        Particle particle;

        if (freeParticles.Count > 0)
        {
            particle = (Particle)freeParticles[0];
            freeParticles.RemoveAt(0);
        }
        else
        {
            particle = new Particle();
        }

        // Emit new particle
        particle.initialPosition = currentPosition;
        particle.initialVelocity = Vector3.Normalize(vel);

        particle.initialVelocity.X += ((float)rand.NextDouble() > 0.5f)
            ? ((float)rand.NextDouble() * 0.1f) :
            (((float)rand.NextDouble() * 0.1f) * -1);
        particle.initialVelocity.Y += ((float)rand.NextDouble() > 0.5f)
            ? ((float)rand.NextDouble() * 0.1f) :
            (((float)rand.NextDouble() * 0.1f) * -1);
        particle.initialVelocity.Z += ((float)rand.NextDouble() > 0.5f)
            ? ((float)rand.NextDouble() * 0.1f) :
            (((float)rand.NextDouble() * 0.1f) * -1);

        particle.initialVelocity.Normalize();
        particle.initialVelocity.Scale(vel.Length() * (float)rand.NextDouble());

        particle.positionVector = particle.initialPosition;
        particle.velocityVector = particle.initialVelocity;

        particle.diffuseColor = WhiteSmoke;
        particle.fadeColor = Black;
        particle.fadeProgression = (float)rand.NextDouble();
        particle.creationTime = time;

        particlesList.Add(particle);
        particles++;
    }
}
```

This method might appear a bit scary at first glance, but once you break it down, it really is quite simple. The goal of this method is to add a group of particles to the system any time it is called. As you can imagine, a single spark particle generated during firing wouldn't seem overly realistic (or exciting), so when this method is called, you pass in a number of particles to add. The two vectors that are passed in are the ones you calculated earlier for the bullet's position and velocity because that's where the sparks will be shooting from.

Now you need to calculate the number of particles that will be emitted once this method is complete, which is the sum of the current number of particles in the system and the number of particles you are trying to add now. You then begin adding particles in a loop until you've added the correct number or until the number of particles in the system has reached the maximum number you specified in the constant. You could simply increase the constant if you wanted to add more particles, but with the gun cool-down rate and the current constant value, you wouldn't be able to get to the maximum number anyway.

The first thing you do in the loop is determine whether any particles are in the free array list you have stored. If so, you retrieve that particle and remove it from the free list because you'll be adding it to the active list in a few moments. Next, you store the initial position and velocity using the parameters passed in, and then, you take that initial velocity and randomize it so that each particle does not take off in the exact same direction. After you calculate a new random velocity (based on the initial velocity), you store the current position and velocity based on the initial values (because this is the initial point in the particle). You set the diffuse and fade colors to the constants defined earlier, set the creation time to the current time, and add the particle to your list. Finally, you update the particle count and continue with the loop until all the particles are added.

You might have noticed that you were taking particles out of the free list during that last method, but you haven't defined any code where you're adding any dead particles to that list yet! You add any particles that have "died" into that list, so you need a way to determine when a particle has died and to update all the particles in the system. Add the method from Listing 18.6 to your class to do so.

LISTING 18.6   Updating the Particle System

```
/// <summary>
/// Updates the particles in the scene
/// </summary>
public void Update(float elapsedTime)
{
    time += elapsedTime;
    for (int ii = particlesList.Count-1; ii >= 0; ii--)
    {
```

LISTING 18.6 Continued

```
        Particle p = (Particle)particlesList[ii];
        // Calculate new position
        float fT = time - p.creationTime;
        float fGravity;

        fGravity = -290.8f;
        p.fadeProgression -= elapsedTime * 0.25f;

        p.positionVector    = p.initialVelocity * fT + p.initialPosition;
        p.positionVector.Y += (0.5f * fGravity) * (fT * fT);
        p.velocityVector.Y  = p.initialVelocity.Y + fGravity * fT;

        if (p.fadeProgression < 0.0f)
            p.fadeProgression = 0.0f;

        // Kill old particles
        if (p.fadeProgression <= 0.0f)
        {
            // Kill particle
            freeParticles.Add(p);
            particlesList.RemoveAt(ii);
            particles--;
        }
        else
            particlesList[ii] = p;
    }
}
```

This method is eventually called every frame, so everything that needs to happen
to update the particles should happen here. Notice first that the total time is constantly being updated by adding the elapsed time since the last frame. This step
ensures that any particles are allowed to die quickly enough. Once done, you
start looping through each particle starting at the last one and moving to the first
and perform a series of operations on each. First you calculate how long the particle has been alive, and then you update the fade progression. You update the
position of the particle based on the time it's been alive and then update the y
axis once more to account for gravity. Finally, you determine whether the particle
has died by checking the fade progression, and if it's now below zero, you add the
particle to the free list and remove it from the active list. Otherwise, you store it in
the active list.

Construction Cue

You start at the end of the array list and move to the beginning because you might
be removing members of the list. If you start at the beginning and remove a member, you just reorder the items you haven't had the chance to look at yet. By moving
in reverse, any removal reorders only the items you've already processed.

Rendering the Particle System

There is only one more method to implement in the special effects class before you can hook it into the game engine and see the results of your work. If you guessed the Draw method, you are absolutely correct. See Listing 18.7.

LISTING 18.7   Rendering the Particle System

```
/// <summary>
/// Renders the particles currently in use for the device
/// </summary>
public void Draw(GameEngine engine)
{
    // Set the render states for using point sprites
    engine.RenderingDevice.RenderState.ZBufferWriteEnable = false;
    engine.RenderingDevice.RenderState.AlphaBlendEnable = true;
    engine.RenderingDevice.RenderState.SourceBlend = Blend.One;
    engine.RenderingDevice.RenderState.DestinationBlend = Blend.One;
    engine.RenderingDevice.RenderState.Lighting = false;

    engine.SetWorldTransform(Matrix.Identity);
    engine.RenderingDevice.RenderState.PointSpriteEnable = true;
    engine.RenderingDevice.RenderState.PointScaleEnable = true;
    engine.RenderingDevice.RenderState.PointSize = Bullet.BulletMass / 2.0f;
    engine.RenderingDevice.RenderState.PointScaleA = 0.0f;
    engine.RenderingDevice.RenderState.PointScaleB = 1.0f;
    engine.RenderingDevice.RenderState.PointScaleC = 1.0f;

    // Set up the vertex buffer to be rendered
    engine.RenderingDevice.SetTexture(0, particleTexture);
    engine.RenderingDevice.SetStreamSource(0, vertexBuffer, 0,
                            CustomVertex.PositionColored.StrideSize);
    engine.RenderingDevice.VertexFormat = CustomVertex.PositionColored.Format;

    int numParticlesToRender = 0;
    // Lock the vertex buffer. We fill the vertex buffer in small
    // chunks, using LockFlags.NoOverwrite. When we are done filling
    // each chunk, we call DrawPrim, and lock the next chunk. When
    // we run out of space in the vertex buffer, we start over at
    // the beginning, using LockFlags.Discard.
    baseParticle += FlushSize;
    if (baseParticle >= MaximumParticles)
    {
        // We've gone too far, reset back to 0
        baseParticle = 0;
    }
    GraphicsStream vertexData = vertexBuffer.Lock(baseParticle *
        CustomVertex.PositionColored.StrideSize, FlushLockSize,
        (baseParticle != 0) ? LockFlags.NoOverwrite : LockFlags.Discard);

    foreach(Particle p in particlesList)
    {
        Vector3 vPos = p.positionVector;
        Vector3 velocityVector = p.velocityVector;
        float LengthSq = velocityVector.LengthSq();
        uint steps;
        if (LengthSq < 1.0f)         steps = 2;
        else if (LengthSq <  4.00f) steps = 3;
```

LISTING 18.7 Continued

```
        else if (LengthSq <  9.00f) steps = 4;
        else if (LengthSq < 12.25f) steps = 5;
        else if (LengthSq < 16.00f) steps = 6;
        else if (LengthSq < 20.25f) steps = 7;
        else                        steps = 8;
        velocityVector *= -0.01f / (float)steps;
        ColorValue diffuse = ColorOperator.Lerp(p.fadeColor, p.diffuseColor,
                                        p.fadeProgression);
        // Render each particle a bunch of times to get a blurring effect
        for (int i = 0; i < steps; i++)
        {
            // Write the position and color
            vertexData.Write(vPos);
            vertexData.Write(diffuse.ToArgb());
            if (++numParticlesToRender == FlushSize)
            {
                // Done filling this chunk of the vertex buffer. Let's unlock and
                // draw this portion so we can begin filling the next chunk.
                vertexBuffer.Unlock();
                engine.RenderingDevice.DrawPrimitives(PrimitiveType.PointList,
                    baseParticle, numParticlesToRender);
                // Lock the next chunk of the vertex buffer. If we are at the
                // end of the vertex buffer, LockFlags.Discard the vertex buffer
                // and start at the beginning. Otherwise, specify
                // LockFlags.NoOverWrite, so we can continue filling the VB
                // while the previous chunk is drawing.
                baseParticle += FlushSize;
                if (baseParticle >= MaximumParticles)
                {
                    baseParticle = 0;
                }
                vertexData = vertexBuffer.Lock(baseParticle *
                    CustomVertex.PositionColored.StrideSize, FlushLockSize,
                    (baseParticle != 0) ? LockFlags.NoOverwrite :
                     LockFlags.Discard);

                numParticlesToRender = 0;
            }
            vPos += velocityVector;
        }
    }

    // Unlock the vertex buffer
    vertexBuffer.Unlock();
    // Render any remaining particles
    if (numParticlesToRender > 0)
    {
        engine.RenderingDevice.DrawPrimitives(PrimitiveType.PointList,
            baseParticle, numParticlesToRender);
    }
    // Reset render states
    engine.RenderingDevice.RenderState.PointSpriteEnable = false;
    engine.RenderingDevice.RenderState.PointScaleEnable = false;
    engine.RenderingDevice.RenderState.Lighting = true;
    engine.RenderingDevice.RenderState.ZBufferWriteEnable = true;
    engine.RenderingDevice.RenderState.AlphaBlendEnable = false;
}
```

Unfortunately (as you can tell), this method is quite long, but it does have a lot to do. Before any particle rendering starts, the device must be set up for rendering the point sprites. You'll notice the z buffer and lighting are turned off (as when you render the sky box), alpha blending is turned on, and then a number of render states related to point sprites are set. You can see the DirectX documentation for more information on these render states.

You need to prepare the device for rendering your particles. First, you set the texture to the particle texture that was created earlier. Next, you set the stream source to the vertex buffer you've created earlier. This part is telling Direct3D when you eventually are ready to render some primitives to use the data stored in this vertex buffer to do the rendering. You then tell Direct3D the vertex format of the point sprites (which you also used when creating the vertex buffer).

Here you are about to render the particles, and you've yet to fill the vertex buffer with any data. Remember earlier when you created the vertex buffer, one of the usage parameters you passed in was Dynamic, which tells Direct3D to optimize the buffer for frequent small updates, and that's exactly what you do now.

Because you're going to be rendering the point sprites in chunks, you keep track of the number of particles left in the queue to render, and naturally because you're just starting, you initialize it to zero. You also update the baseParticle variable and ensure that it hasn't gone past the maximum number of particles. The next section of code is quite important because the entire vertex buffer and rendering logic is encapsulated here.

First, you call the Lock method on the vertex buffer, which is telling Direct3D you are ready to add data to the buffer now. This method returns a GraphicsStream, which you use to write data into the buffer. Now, you start a loop through each of the particles in the active particle list. You get the position and velocity of the particle and use the velocity to determine how many point sprites to render for each particle. The faster the particle is moving, the more point sprites you use to render it (up to a maximum of 8). This part gives the effect of "blurring."

After you have that information, you calculate the color of the particle by interpolating between the normal color (white smoke) and the faded color (black). You then use the Write method on the returned stream to update the vertex buffer data with this information, and if you've got enough particles to render now, you unlock the buffer, render the primitives, and then relock the buffer. A locked buffer cannot be used during rendering, so this step is required.

After each particle is processed, the vertex buffer is unlocked a final time, and if any particles are left to be rendered, that is done. Finally, the device's state is returned back to the original values it had before this call.

> You can save and restore the device settings more efficiently using a `StateBlock` object; however, that discussion goes beyond the scope of what was intended for this chapter.

Putting the Pieces Together

Now that you have the special effects class implemented, you can go back to the game engine code file and implement the code there to make the game engine use these newly created special effects. First, you need to declare the class as a variable to the game engine:

```
// The special effects class
private SpecialEffects particleEffects = null;
```

Then, you create the special effects class. You should do this part in the `LoadWorld` method, directly after loading the level:

```
// Create the special effects class
particleEffects = new SpecialEffects(sampleFramework.Device);
```

Next, you want to ensure that the particles are updated every frame, so find the `OnFrameMove` method and add this code directly before updating the local player:

```
// Update the special effects if they exist
if (particleEffects != null)
{
    particleEffects.Update(elapsedTime);
}
```

It goes without saying that you want to actually render the particles as well. Add this code to the end of the `RenderGameScene` method:

```
particleEffects.Draw(this);
```

Of course, the particle system is useless unless you add some particles into it at some point. Because this system is used to add a spark to the firing of the bullets, add this code to the end of the `OnPlayerFire` method:

```
// Fire effect
if (particleEffects != null)
{
```

```
    // Get the barrel position and bullet velocity
    Vector3 start, vel;
    p.GetBulletStartLocation(out start, out vel);
    // Now add a firing effect to that
    particleEffects.AddFiringEffect(50, start, vel);
}
```

Finally, all you need to do is ensure that the particle system is cleaned up at the appropriate time. Add the cleanup code to the OnDestroyDevice method:

```
// Clean up the special effects
if (particleEffects != null)
{
    particleEffects.Dispose();
}
```

With that, you now have the special effects implemented and hooked into the game. See Figure 18.1 for an example of the particle system in action. I'm sure you can think of even better effects to add.

FIGURE 18.1
Tankers—with special effects.

Summary

Just because the game is done now doesn't mean you can't expand it even more. For example, you might want to add a little explosion effect when you fire your bullets out of the tank. The next chapter will focus on this behavior. You can expand and update the game in any way your mind desires!

CHAPTER 19

Building Your Own Game

You've been focusing on building the games in the book, which as a learning experience can be quite rewarding. However, nothing beats actually getting to the point where you can write something yourself, and that's the point where you are now. For the remainder of this book, you will explore the building blocks for a Kart Racing game, but in the end, you will finish the game yourself.

For this chapter, you get started on the new project, and you learn about the custom user interface items the sample framework has to offer and how to use them instead of relying on writing your own.

In this chapter, you'll learn

- ▶ What's involved in defining a new idea
- ▶ How to create a new project
- ▶ How to render the sample framework user interface
- ▶ Why you'd want to modify the user interface

Formulating the Idea

This section is smaller for this game because you'll be finishing the work on your own. Although I discuss some of the features of the game here, I don't describe all of them because you'll be defining some. I highly suggest that you still go through this exercise as you determine which features you will add to your game.

The basic premise of this last game is a go-kart racing game. The code for the book focuses on the graphics programming of the game (after all, this is a graphics programming book) but leaves out all the nongraphics elements. It is your challenge to finish the game in a fun and exciting way, possibly even throwing in some new tricks.

What features does the game require that we will implement in the next few chapters? One of the first things you do (later in this chapter) is use the user interface classes that are provided by the sample framework which ships with the latest DirectX SDK. Although you could have used them on earlier projects, they are more involved and they handle many corner cases that might not be required in your game. Because there isn't time to describe the inner workings of each, it was easier to build small custom classes earlier to gain the benefits of learning.

Another major change for this game is that you design it to run on the programmable pipeline using High-Level Shader Language (HLSL). Don't worry: you'll learn more about that in the next chapter.

You should get together a list of features that the game will have for your own reference. The following small list includes the features implemented in this last section, as well as some potential ideas for other features you can implement on your own:

- A racing game using go-karts
- Using DirectX SDK Sample Framework user interface classes
- Graphics driven by the HLSL
- Real-time level of detail for meshes
- Rearview mirror
- And some ideas that you could implement on your own:
  - Multiplayer code for more than one player
  - Artificial intelligence for computer players
  - Special effects such as sparks or smoke
  - Sound support
  - Joystick and wheel support
  - Weapons and power-ups
  - Whatever your imagination desires

Given that the final product for this section comes not entirely from this book but from some of your own hard work, it isn't entirely feasible to include a Unified Modeling Language (UML) diagram for the code this game uses. Instead, I skip this step, but I recommend that you take the time to do the design yourself for a high-quality implementation.

Creating Your Project

I hope that you took the time to write down your design ideas and goals and imagine a good design layout. It's time to start writing some code and get this project started.

Remember back to the second chapter when you first started learning about the differences between 3D and 2D programming: you wrote a quick and simple application designed to show these differences. It created a 3D teapot rotating around your screen. You initially created the project by running the sample browser that ships as part of the DirectX software development kit (SDK). (You should be using the Summer 2004 update.) (Refer to Figure 2.2.) After that application was running, you clicked the Install Project link next to the managed Empty Project application. Do the same thing once more and call the project KartRacers.

Refer to Figure 2.2.

> Notice that there is no space in the new project name because you use this name throughout the code file, including for the name of the class. Characters that are invalid for classnames (such as spaces) are not allowed.

Construction Cue

As you can see in Figure 19.1, running the application as it is created results in a running application with a few user interface controls rendered off to the side. The upper section of these controls resides in all the samples, but the other controls are "sample-specific" (even though they don't actually have any purpose in this project).

To get ready for the game, you fix up this code to remove the unnecessary items. Plus, you want to make the game run in full-screen mode when you're not debugging, as with the previous games you've written. You also don't need all this text that's all over the sample.

First, you get rid of the current user interface. Find the following variable and constant declarations in the only code file in the project:

```
private Dialog hud = null; // dialog for standard controls
private Dialog sampleUi = null; // dialog for sample specific controls

// HUD Ui Control constants
private const int ToggleFullscreen = 1;
private const int ToggleReference = 3;
private const int ChangeDevice = 4;
```

FIGURE 19.1
The default empty
project running.

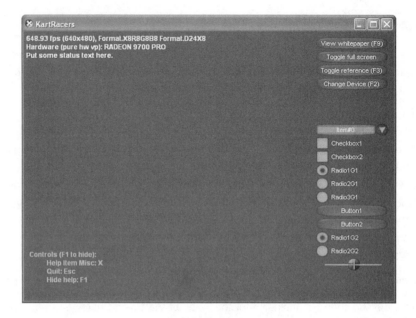

The two dialog parameters are for the two sets of user interfaces. The sample framework groups the user interface controls into dialogs much as Windows itself does. Each of the controls in a dialog should have a unique integer identifier, and these constants are used to create what the samples call the HUD. It is the set of user controls that all the samples use to toggle full-screen mode, change device settings, or toggle into a reference device. Because you won't be using any of these items, remove all the lines listed here.

Trying to compile the application now means that you see quite a few compilation errors, but considering that you just removed some variables, you should expect them. First, find the constructor of the KartRacers object and remove the two lines that create the dialogs:

```
// Create dialogs
hud = new Dialog(sampleFramework);
sampleUi = new Dialog(sampleFramework);
```

Next, find the OnResetDevice method and remove the four calls to the dialogs that you've already removed:

```
// Setup UI locations
hud.SetLocation(desc.Width-170, 0);
hud.SetSize(170,170);
sampleUi.SetLocation(desc.Width - 170, desc.Height - 350);
sampleUi.SetSize(170,300);
```

You also need to fix the OnFrameRender method so it doesn't try to render those user interface controls, so remove these calls from that method:

```
// Show UI
hud.OnRender(elapsedTime);
sampleUi.OnRender(elapsedTime);
```

Because the controls have any messages coming from windows processed in the OnMsgProc method, you remove the Dialog variables from that method as well:

```
// Give the dialog a chance to handle the message first
noFurtherProcessing = hud.MessageProc(hWnd, msg, wParam, lParam);
if (noFurtherProcessing)
    return IntPtr.Zero;

noFurtherProcessing = sampleUi.MessageProc(hWnd, msg, wParam, lParam);
if (noFurtherProcessing)
    return IntPtr.Zero;
```

Finally, you remove every line of code from the InitializeApplication method (but not the method itself). With that, you should be able to compile and run again, but the only difference is that the user controls are now missing. Although it's not required to remove the event handlers for the user interface buttons you've just removed, it is probably a good idea. Remove the following handlers from the code: OnChangeDeviceClicked, OnFullscreenClicked, and OnRefClicked. You need to add the new controls later in this chapter, but for now, you should get rid of the extra text that's cluttering the running application.

Find the RenderText method in the code because that is where all the text is being rendered. The frame rate text is something you want to keep while debugging, but the rest of that text is pretty much useless for this game. Replace the method with the one in Listing 19.1.

LISTING 19.1   Rendering Text

```
private void RenderText()
{

    #if (DEBUG)
    TextHelper txtHelper = new TextHelper(statsFont, textSprite, 15);

    // Output statistics
    txtHelper.Begin();
    txtHelper.SetInsertionPoint(5,5);
    txtHelper.SetForegroundColor(System.Drawing.Color.Yellow);
    txtHelper.DrawTextLine(sampleFramework.FrameStats);
    txtHelper.DrawTextLine(sampleFramework.DeviceStats);

    txtHelper.End();
    #endif
}
```

As you see here, the majority of the text rendering code was removed, and even the code that stayed is put into a #if clause that only renders the text if the game is running in debug mode. Notice that the text is rendered using the TextHelper object rather than direct calls to the DrawText method on the font class. This helper object is used to maintain the location of where the next section of text will be drawn, and it makes drawing a series of lines of text such as this much simpler.

Running the application now results in a completely blank screen if you're running in release mode or a blank screen with some frame statistics if you're running in debug mode. Now you need to ensure that the game runs in full-screen mode if you're not debugging, so find the Main method and add this code directly after the InitializeApplication call:

```
#if (!DEBUG)
sampleFramework.IsOverridingFullScreen = true;
#endif
```

You also want to change the call to the Initialize method on the sample framework object so it doesn't respond to the normal keyboard commands or parse the command line as the samples do:

```
sampleFramework.Initialize( false, false, true );
```

Before you start designing the new user interface by using the sample framework's controls, there are just a few things you should do first. You need some way to know what state the game is in. For now, you know that there are at least two different states that the game can be in (showing the user interface or playing the game), so add this enumeration to your code:

```
public enum GameState
{
    MainMenu,
    Gameplay
}
```

You also need to add a variable to the KartRacers class so that it knows which state the game is in, and you start in the main menu state because that's the way the game should begin:

```
private GameState currentState = GameState.MainMenu; // State of the game
```

The main menu screen should also have a background screen that will be rendered behind the user interface. Because this screen requires some media, you need a way to figure out the location of the media. As you did back in the first two games, click the Add New Item selection from the project menu, add an Application Configuration File to your project, and replace the automatically generated Extensible Markup Language (XML) with the XML in Listing 19.2.

LISTING 19.2 Configuration File for the Media

```
<?xml version="1.0"?>
<configuration>
        <appSettings>
                <add key="MediaPath" value="..\..\..\..\Media\KartRacers\"/>
        </appSettings>
        <startup>
        <supportedRuntime version="v1.1.4322"/>
        <requiredRuntime version="v1.1.4322" safemode="true"/></startup>
</configuration>
```

Obviously, you want the MediaPath value to match wherever you have copied the media on your hard drive. If you used the installation program, the value shown here will work for you. With the configuration file in your project now, you need to have a variable to actually access this key, so add this variable to your KartRacers class:

```
public static readonly string MediaPath =
 ConfigurationSettings.AppSettings.Get("MediaPath");
```

You probably notice that this code doesn't compile. The ConfigurationSettings class resides in the System.Configuration namespace, which currently hasn't been imported, so you need to either fully qualify the ConfigurationSettings classname or add the using clause to the application. I prefer the latter:

```
using System.Configuration;
```

You need a few things to get the background rendering correctly now. First, you declare two new variables in your KartRacers class:

```
// Background image variables
private Sprite backgroundSprite = null;
private Texture backgroundTexture = null;
```

You also instantiate these objects. Find the `OnCreateDevice` method, and add the following code to the end of that method to get these objects created:

```
backgroundSprite = new Sprite(e.Device);
backgroundTexture = ResourceCache.GetGlobalInstance().CreateTextureFromFile(
    e.Device, MediaPath + "splash.jpg");
```

The sprite is pretty straightforward because the only parameter it takes is the device (which is retrieved from the event arguments that this method receives). The texture, however, is created from the sample framework's resource cache, which is similar to the texture pool you created for Tankers but instead can store more than one type of object. A benefit of using this cache is that you no longer have to worry about cleaning up the objects stored there, unlike the sprite, which you do.

Construction Cue

You might notice that the texture image is not square (it is 800x600). This particular overload for the texture creation will automatically resize the texture to the next largest square texture size, where the size is a power of 2, in this case, 1024x1024. In most cases, this automatic resize of the texture would cause problems because the texture coordinates for a mesh would be messed up, but because this part is just used as a background, it will look fine.

Speaking of cleanup for the sprite, you need to do that now. You handle three scenarios for the sprite: when the device is lost, reset, and destroyed. Find the `OnLostDevice` method first and add this code to the end:

```
// Clean up sprite if required
if (backgroundSprite != null)
{
    backgroundSprite.OnLostDevice();
}
```

Similarly, find the `OnResetDevice` method and use this code at the end:

```
// Reset sprite if required
if (backgroundSprite != null)
{
    backgroundSprite.OnResetDevice();
}
```

Finally, destroy the sprite when the `OnDestroyDevice` method is called:

```
// Destroy sprite if required
if (backgroundSprite != null)
{
    backgroundSprite.Dispose();
    backgroundSprite = null;
}
```

With everything created and cleaned up properly now, you only need to add the rendering code. Find the `OnFrameRender` method, and add this code after the begin scene variable is set:

```
if (currentState == GameState.MainMenu)
{
    backgroundSprite.Begin(SpriteFlags.None);
    backgroundSprite.Draw2D(backgroundTexture, System.Drawing.Rectangle.Empty,
        sampleFramework.ClientRectangle, System.Drawing.Point.Empty,
        unchecked((int)0xffffffff));
    backgroundSprite.End();
}
```

Naturally, you only want this background image to display when the main menu is open, so you first make sure that the game state is the correct one, and then you call `Begin` on the sprite object.

You'll notice that the next call is to a new `Draw2D` method that didn't exist before this release of the Managed DirectX assemblies. As its name implies, its goal is to simplify drawing a 2D image onscreen. This particular overload takes the texture to render (in this case, your splash screen texture) and the rectangle portion of that texture that will be rendered. Because you want to use the entire texture as the splash screen, you pass `System.Drawing.Rectangle.Empty` here. The next rectangle parameter is the area where you want this texture to be rendered. Because you want the splash screen to cover the entire area of the window, you use the client rectangle of the sample framework. Next, you need to know where you want the upper-left corner of the texture to be rendered. In this case, the upper-left corner of the window happens to be (0, 0), or `Point.Empty`. The final parameter is the color you want to blend the texture with; in this case, you want the full texture to be shown as is, so you use the integer value for white.

Finally, you just call the `End` method on the sprite. You can see the result of this work in Figure 19.2.

FIGURE 19.2
Splash screen is done.

Designing the User Interface

Now you need to implement a basic user interface for the few features that you'll be adding to the game (and some that you will add yourself when you finish the game, I hope). Earlier in this chapter, you removed two Dialog variables that were used to make the user interface for the empty project sample. Now you add back a new Dialog variable to create your own user interface:

```
// User interface for the game
private Dialog gameUI = null;
```

Of course, you need to instantiate this object somewhere, so find the constructor of the KartRacers class and add the creation code there:

```
gameUI = new Dialog(sampleFramework);
```

Regardless of what controls you end up having within this dialog, you need to have it rendered at some point. Find the OnFrameRender method of the class and add this code after the call to End on the sprite object:

```
gameUI.OnRender(elapsedTime);
```

Make sure that call is within the if statement dealing with the current state of the game. You wouldn't want the interface being rendered while the game is being played. Now, you also need to ensure that the dialog has a way to react to

any changes going on, such as the mouse moving over them and so on. Find the
OnMsgProc method and add this code to the beginning of that method:

```
if (currentState == GameState.MainMenu)
{
    // Give the dialog a chance to handle the message first
    noFurtherProcessing = gameUI.MessageProc(hWnd, msg, wParam, lParam);
    if (noFurtherProcessing)
        return IntPtr.Zero;
}
```

Notice that this code also checks the current state of the game. There is no need
for the dialog to respond to user input if it isn't being shown. What you need now
is a place to add the user controls to this dialog. Remember from earlier, you
removed the code from the InitializeApplication method but not the method
itself. That is where you add the code to create your controls. Replace the method
with the one in Listing 19.3.

LISTING 19.3 Creating Controls

```
public void InitializeApplication()
{
    int y = 10;

    // Game title text
    gameUI.AddStatic(StaticControlNonChanging, "Kart Racers - The Game",
        30, y, 600, 30);

    // User name information
    gameUI.AddStatic(StaticControlNonChanging, "User Name:", 30, y += 34,
        80, 30);
    gameUI.AddEditBox(UserNameBoxControl, System.Environment.UserName,
        30, y += 34, 500, 30);

    // Buttons
    Button single = gameUI.AddButton(NewButtonControl, "New Game", 30,
        y += 34, 120, 24);
    Button multi = gameUI.AddButton(MultiButtonControl, "AI Game", 200,
        y, 120, 24);
    Button network = gameUI.AddButton(NetworkButtonControl, "Network Game", 370,
        y, 120, 24);

    // All the buttons should have the same handler for now
    single.Click += new EventHandler(OnNewGame);
    multi.Click += new EventHandler(OnNewGame);
    network.Click += new EventHandler(OnNewGame);

    // Slider for AI opponents (unused in this code)
    gameUI.AddStatic(ChangingStaticControl, "Number of AI Opponents: 1", 30,
        y += 34, 200, 20);
    Slider opponents = gameUI.AddSlider(AISliderControl, 30, y += 24,
        200, 20, 1, 7, 1, false);
    opponents.ValueChanged += new EventHandler(OnSliderChanged);
```

LISTING 19.3   Continued

```
// Combo box for picking correct kart
gameUI.AddStatic(StaticControlNonChanging, "Pick your kart style:",
    30, y += 24, 150, 20);
ComboBox kart = gameUI.AddComboBox(PickKartControl, 30, y += 24, 200, 24);
if (kart != null)
{
    kart.SetDropHeight(100);
    kart.AddItem("Kart #1", "KartAndDriver_YYYB.jpg");
    kart.AddItem("Kart #2", "KartAndDriver_BBRY.jpg");
    kart.AddItem("Kart #3", "KartAndDriver_RRBR.jpg");
    kart.AddItem("Kart #4", "KartAndDriver_RRYY.jpg");
}

// Combo box for picking the level
gameUI.AddStatic(StaticControlNonChanging, "Pick your level:",
    250, y -= 24, 100, 20);
ComboBox level = gameUI.AddComboBox(PickLevelControl, 250, y += 24, 200, 24);
if (level != null)
{
    level.SetDropHeight(100);
    level.AddItem("Level #1", "track.x");
}

// Exit Game
Button exitGame = gameUI.AddButton(ExitGameControl, "Exit Game", 50,
                                   y += 30, 120, 30);
exitGame.Click += new EventHandler(OnExitGame);
}
```

You add a few types of controls in this method. The Static control is basically just a control to render some text, much like the Label control in WinForms. The EditBox control, which works much like a TextBox in WinForms, is where you can input data directly. Button controls, as the name implies, are simple buttons. There is a Slider control, which works much like the Trackbar control from WinForms. Finally, the ComboBox controls work just like the WinForms controls of the same name.

You'll notice first that each control is created with an integer identifier; in the preceding code, constants are used to describe each of them, but they haven't been declared yet. Add these constants to your class:

```
// UI Control constants
private const int StaticControlNonChanging = 1;
private const int UserNameBoxControl = 2;
private const int NewButtonControl = 3;
private const int MultiButtonControl = 4;
private const int NetworkButtonControl = 5;
private const int ChangingStaticControl = 6;
private const int AISliderControl = 7;
private const int PickKartControl = 8;
private const int PickLevelControl = 9;
private const int ExitGameControl = 10;
```

As the controls are created and sized, some of the events that can be fired by these controls are hooked. (You can find the event handlers in Listing 19.4.) Most of the controls need a simple piece of text to describe them (such as the text on the button), but two of the controls (the combo boxes) require more information. Notice that the AddItem method takes two parameters. The first parameter is the data that will be rendered on the control (the description), and the second parameter is the actual data of the control. For example, in the kart picking combo box, the data represents the texture file that is loaded for that go-kart.

LISTING 19.4   Event Handlers for Controls

```
/// <summary>
/// Fired when the exit game button is clicked
/// </summary>
private void OnExitGame(object sender, EventArgs e)
{
    // We should exit the game
    sampleFramework.CloseWindow();
}

/// <summary>
/// Fired when one of the new game buttons is clicked
/// </summary>
private void OnNewGame(object sender, EventArgs e)
{
    currentState = GameState.Gameplay;
}

/// <summary>
/// Fired when the slider changes
/// </summary>
private void OnSliderChanged(object sender, EventArgs e)
{
    Slider slider = sender as Slider;
    gameUI.GetStaticText(ChangingStaticControl).SetText(
        string.Format("Number of AI Opponents: {0}", slider.Value));

}
```

The event handlers are basically self-explanatory. When the exit button is clicked, the form is closed. When one of the new game buttons is clicked, the game state is changed to GamePlay because you play the game after you click those buttons. (Currently, you just go back to a blue screen, but eventually, that's what you'll be doing.) You won't use the slider code for anything unless you decide to add artificial intelligence (AI) opponents.

One more thing you should do is make sure that the dialog is resized if the device is reset. Find the OnResetDevice method and add the following code to the end:

```
if (gameUI != null)
{
    int width = desc.Width - 10;
    int height = desc.Height - 30;

    gameUI.SetLocation(5,30);
    gameUI.SetSize(width, height);

    // Exit Game
    gameUI.GetButton(ExitGameControl).SetLocation((width - 120) / 2,
                                                    height - 50);
}
```

This code sets the location and size of the dialog and ensures that the exit button is always located at the center of the screen toward the bottom. See Figure 19.3 for the finished user interface screens.

FIGURE 19.3
Complete with user interface.

Summary

Now that you have a rough idea of the game you will be writing, and a robust user interface designed for this game, you're ready to move on to more challenging things. The next chapter will focus on using the HLSL and the programmable pipeline, both of which are new concepts.

CHAPTER 20

The Programmable Pipeline

Everything you've done until this point in this book has focused on using what is called the **fixed-function pipeline**. The name comes from the fact that the functionality in the pipeline is fixed and cannot be changed aside from some minor tweaks to certain variables. Back in the early days of 3D programming, it was perfectly adequate for the vast majority of applications; however, today it is not.

What you will focus on in this chapter is understanding the programmable pipeline and the High-Level Shader Language (HLSL).

In this chapter, you'll learn

▶ About the programmable pipeline

▶ How to use HLSL

▶ How to transform vertices

▶ How to use a pixel shader

Defining the Programmable Pipeline

Prior to the release of DirectX 8 a few years ago, the only way for you to render any 3D graphics using DirectX was by using the fixed-function pipeline. The fixed-function pipeline is essentially a set of rules and behaviors that govern how a particular type of data is rendered by the system. For example, a directional light is always calculated by taking the dot product of the normal and light direction. That is just the way it is designed, and there were no options to change it.

With more powerful graphics hardware coming out, it became apparent that something more robust would be required. The fixed-function pipeline was serving its purpose well, but it would be unrealistic to assume it could handle every possible case that a developer might want to use. What was needed was a way to allow the developer to execute some arbitrary code on the vertices or pixels that would be rendered, preferably inside the graphics hardware.

With DirectX 8, the first notion of this **programmable pipeline** was released to the public, and developers finally had the opportunity to expand beyond the realms of the fixed-function pipeline. Small programs called vertex shaders could be executed against the vertices that were going to be rendered. Other types of these programs, pixel shaders, were designed to be executed against every pixel in the scene.

One of the first problems developers noticed with this new technology was that it was pretty esoteric. The language used to write these shader programs closely resembled assembly language, making the code required to run them more elaborate than some developers wanted. Another issue was the limited amount of instruction slots on the hardware at the time. Given that these programs were going to be running on the graphics cards themselves, the card would allow only a small number of "instructions" to be executed for any one program. This setup was particularly bad for the pixel shader programs.

With the release of DirectX 9, many of these issues were addressed. It introduced a new language, HLSL, a simple C-like language that would be compiled directly into the real shader code. With more familiar syntax and a powerful compiler, HLSL made writing complex shaders much simpler than it had been with the DirectX 8 release.

Another big change was the addition of new **shader models**. In the DirectX 8 release, the vertex and pixel shader models were 1.x, where 1 was the major version and .x was the minor version. Vertex shaders had versions 1.0 and 1.1 in the DirectX 8 releases, and pixel shaders went from 1.0 through 1.4. With the DirectX 9 release, the shader models were increased to be supported all the way through versions 2.x and 3.x. Each new model increases the number of instructions that can be used and the intrinsic instructions in the shaders themselves.

Construction Cue

The 3.x shader models were available at the release of DirectX 9, but there was no hardware yet capable of running these shaders. The Radeon 9700 was the first card capable of running 2.0 shaders, and although all the top cards today support the 2.0 shader model, as of this writing, only one publicly announced card supports the 3.0 shader model.

Using HLSL

One of the nicest features of the DirectX 9 release was something called the **effects system**, which utilizes HLSL. You might have even noticed that the project you're working on now declares (and uses) a variable of type `Effect`. This is the major entry point to the effects system and the easiest way to use HLSL to write your programs.

The effects system is designed to integrate both the vertex and pixel shader programs along with the pipeline state to render your objects. Most times, you have a text file that you pass into the effects system, and that file is compiled into the correct shader code, either at runtime or at build time, depending on how you've set it up. The basic layout of one of these files is like this:

```
<Variable Declarations>

void SomeVertexFunction()
{
// Do vertex shader program
}
void SomePixelFunction()
{
// Do pixel shader program
}

technique RenderScene
{
  pass P0
  {
    VertexShader = compile vs_1_1 SomeVertexFunction();
    PixelShader = compile ps_1_1 SomePixelFunction();
  }
}
```

Don't try to put this code into your program; it's just pseudo-code so you can see the basic layout of the shader programs. You'll be writing your own shader programs in a short while, so don't get too anxious. The main thing for which you will use the effects system (at least in the short term) is to maintain and modify the preceding variables and then to compile and use the shader programs it allows you to access.

If you look at the code that already exists for this application, you'll notice that the effect variable is used for a number of things and that a file is already created for you to hold the shader code, `KartRacers.fx`. You can see the code it contains in Listing 20.1.

LISTING 20.1   The Empty Shader File

```
//------------------------------------------------------------------------
// File: KartRacers.fx
//
// The effect file for the KartRacers sample.
//
// Copyright (c) Microsoft Corporation. All rights reserved.
//------------------------------------------------------------------------


//------------------------------------------------------------------------
// Global variables
//------------------------------------------------------------------------
float appTime;  //App's time in seconds
float4x4 worldMatrix;  // World matrix for object
float4x4 worldViewProjection;      // World * View * Projection matrix


//------------------------------------------------------------------------
// Techniques
//------------------------------------------------------------------------
technique RenderScene
{
    pass P0
    {
    }
}
```

As you can see here, this has the basic layout that the preceding example did,
with the exception that there are no shader functions defined here. That's what
you'll be doing later in this chapter. For now, the things to notice are where the
effects variable is used within the program. Once in the `OnCreateDevice` method,
the object is created within the resource cache:

```
string path = Utility.FindMediaFile("KartRacers.fx");
effect = ResourceCache.GetGlobalInstance().CreateEffectFromFile(e.Device,
    path, null, null, shaderFlags, null);
```

Then later, within the `OnFrameRender` method, the values of the global variables
are set:

```
// Update the effect's variables.  Instead of using strings, it would
// be more efficient to cache a handle to the parameter by calling
// Effect.GetParameter
effect.SetValue("worldViewProjection", camera.WorldMatrix *
    camera.ViewMatrix * camera.ProjectionMatrix);
effect.SetValue("worldMatrix", camera.WorldMatrix);
effect.SetValue("appTime", (float)appTime);
```

Because there is nothing going on in the current techniques, this approach is fine
for now, but to use the programmable pipeline, you need to change this.

Writing a Vertex Shader

Before you write your first vertex shader program, you need something to render other than the blank screen that currently is displayed after you click one of the new game type buttons. Your first object rendered with the programmable pipeline might as well be the go-kart because that will be the focus of the game. Add the following variables to your class now:

```
// Kart mesh
private Mesh kartMesh = null;
private Texture[] kartTextures = null;
```

You've been using meshes and textures throughout this book, so this code shouldn't be that surprising. You might have noticed that the materials you normally create when you load the mesh are nonexistent, though. The materials are used by the fixed-function pipeline to determine how to blend the colors between the light and the textures, and they are not necessary for the programmable shaders you will be writing this chapter.

You also need a place to create these objects. You don't want to create them at startup because the application might just quit right away; instead, you create them when the user clicks one of the new game buttons to start playing the game. Find the OnNewGame method in your class and add the following code to load the kart mesh:

```
ExtendedMaterial[] materials = null;
// Create the kart mesh and textures
kartMesh = Mesh.FromFile(MediaPath + "kart.x", MeshFlags.Managed,
    sampleFramework.Device, out materials);

if ( (materials != null) && (materials.Length > 0) )
{
    // Create the textures
    kartTextures = new Texture[materials.Length];
    for(int i = 0; i < materials.Length; i++)
    {
        kartTextures[i] = ResourceCache.GetGlobalInstance().CreateTextureFromFile(
            sampleFramework.Device,  MediaPath +
            gameUI.GetComboBox(PickKartControl).GetSelectedData() as string);
    }
}
```

Loading the mesh happens the same way as always here, with the only exception being the material loading code. Three things stand out:

▶ The material structures themselves are ignored.

▶ The resource cache is used to load the textures.

▶ The texture filenames are also ignored, and the combo box data (which stored the texture filename you would be using) is used instead.

With the mesh and textures loaded now, you're ready to start writing your shader. Open the KartRacers.fx file and replace the code with that in Listing 20.2.

LISTING 20.2 The Empty Shader File

```
//--------------------------------------------------------------------------
// Global variables
//--------------------------------------------------------------------------
float4x4 worldMatrix : WORLD;  // World matrix for object
float4x4 worldViewProjection : WORLDVIEWPROJECTION;
// World * View * Projection matrix

float4 Transform(in float4 pos : POSITION, out float4 Position :
                 POSITION) : COLOR0
{
    // Transform position
    Position = mul(pos, worldViewProjection);

    return 1.0f;
}

//--------------------------------------------------------------------------
// Techniques
//--------------------------------------------------------------------------
technique RenderScene
{
    pass P0
    {
        VertexShader = compile vs_1_1 Transform();
        PixelShader  = NULL;
    }
}
```

You'll notice that one of the variables (appTime) has been removed, a function has been added, and new things have been added to the P0 pass. The variable was removed because it isn't required for this application, but you should take a closer look at this new function.

It takes a single parameter in, a float4 called pos. This is the position of the vertex being computed currently. Notice that the second parameter is an out parameter, also of type float4. This parameter will be the transformed vertex after the shader executes. Last, notice that the function itself also returns a float4, which will be the final color of the vertex.

The only thing this shader does is transform the vertices from model space. In the fixed-function pipeline, this transformation happens by setting the three

Transform variables on the device, namely, World, View, and Projection. Because you're not using the fixed-function pipeline, you are required to do this transformation yourself, by multiplying each vertex by the combined world/view/projection matrices. Notice that you are required to use the mul intrinsic: the combined matrix is a float4x4, but the vertex is only a float4. The result is stored in the out parameter specified in the function prototype.

You might also be wondering what the things after the colon (:)mean, such as pos : position. They are called **semantics**, and they are simply extra information for you to use to clarify what types of data the variables hold. In the preceding case, it means that the pos variable holds position data.

Declaring Variables in HLSL and Intrinsic Types

You will notice that we are using some intrinsic types that don't exist in the C or C# languages, namely, float4 and float4x4. The scalar types that HLSL supports are

bool	true or false
int	A 32-bit signed integer
half	A 16-bit floating-point value
float	A 32-bit floating-point value
double	A 64-bit floating-point value

A variable of one of these types will behave just as it would in the C# language, a single variable of that type. However, adding a single integer value to the end of one of these scalar types will declare a vector type. These vector types can be used like a vector or like an array. For example, look at a declaration similar to one we used:

```
float4 pos;
```

This declares a Vector4 to hold a position. If you want a 2D vector instead, you could declare it as

```
float2 someVector;
```

You can access the members of this variable as an array; such as

```
pos[0] = 2.0f;
```

You can also access this type much as a vector in your C# code, such as

```
pos.x = 2.0f;
```

You can access one or more of the vector components in this way. This technique is called **swizzling**. You may use the vector components of xyzw as well as the color components of rgba; however, you may not mix and match them in the same swizzle. For example, these lines are valid (even if they don't do anything):

```
pos.xz = 0.0f;
pos.rg += pos.xz;
```

However, this line is not:

```
pos.xg = 0.0f;
```

The xg swizzle isn't valid because it's mixing both the vector and color components.

Variables can also have modifiers much as they do in C and C#. You can declare constants much as you would normally:

```
const float someConstant = 3.0f;
```

You can share variables among different programs:

```
shared float someVariable = 1.0f;
```

See the DirectX SDK documentation if you want more information on the HLSL language.

You might notice that the function here will always return a color of 1.0f (which happens to be pure white). Although this isn't the desired final effect, it will help you get started enough to see something onscreen.

The changes to the technique and pass are actually minor. These two lines are simply telling the effects system that you are going to be using a vertex shader (the 1.1 model) and that the Transform method will be the shader in use, but you will not be using a pixel shader at all. The effects system handles the rest.

Now you need to add some code to get the mesh rendered. Find the OnFrameRender method, look for the if statement determining the current game state, and add the else clause in Listing 20.3 to it.

LISTING 20.3   Rendering Your Effect

```
else if (currentState == GameState.Gameplay)
{
    // Update the effect's variables. Instead of using strings, it would
    // be more efficient to cache a handle to the parameter by calling
    // Effect.GetParameter
    effect.SetValue("worldViewProjection", camera.WorldMatrix *
        camera.ViewMatrix * camera.ProjectionMatrix);
```

LISTING 20.3   Continued

```
    effect.SetValue("worldMatrix", camera.WorldMatrix);

    effect.Technique = "RenderScene";
    int passes = effect.Begin(0);
    for (int pass = 0; pass < passes; pass++)
    {
        effect.BeginPass(pass);
        for (int i = 0; i < kartTextures.Length; i++)
        {
            kartMesh.DrawSubset(i);
        }
        effect.EndPass();
    }
    effect.End();
}
```

Make sure to remove the calls to SetValue outside of the if statements because they're no longer required (and will throw a runtime exception because you removed that variable). What's going on in this code snippet? Obviously, the first thing you do is set the values for the variables declared in your shader file, just as the code did before. But what do you need to do then?

First, you tell the effects system which technique you want to be running; in this case, you want to run the RenderScene technique (of course, because it's the only one there). With the technique set, you want to then render some objects using it, so you call the Begin method, which returns the number of passes that this technique has. Although you happen to know that this technique only has one pass in it currently, it's still best to start the loop in this way so if you ever want to add passes to your techniques later, you could without any code changes.

Once inside the loop, you call the BeginPass method, passing in the index of the pass you're currently on. This is Direct3D's cue to ensure that all shader data and state are set up correctly on the device so the device is ready to render your data with the appropriate shader. You should do all the drawing you plan on doing in between the BeginPass and EndPass calls. You'll notice that this code snippet does exactly that by calling the DrawSubset member of the mesh for each texture in the list. After all the passes are finished, you call the End method on the effect to let the effects system know you've completed your work.

You probably noticed you haven't used your texture yet (such as through a call to SetTexture). I address textures later in this chapter during the pixel shader portion. Although the PixelShader member is set to null, the mesh is rendered without any shading from lighting. In this case, it is pure white because that's the color you returned in the vertex shader.

Construction Cue

Running the application now and choosing a new game option will just show you a big blob of white (because the default camera is too close). Find the `OnResetDevice` method and add this line to the end of it:

```
camera.SetRadius(30.0f, 30.0f, 200.0f);
```

This code zooms the camera out some and allows you to see the model. You can drag using the mouse buttons to rotate the model around (and the wheel to zoom in and out). See Figure 20.1 for an example of the program up to this point.

FIGURE 20.1
Your first shader output.

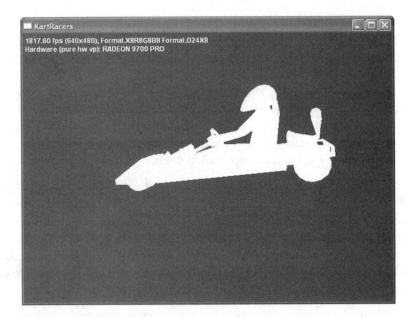

Adding Realism Using Shading

You don't need to be a graphics designer to realize that doesn't look all that great. It's just a big white blob that vaguely resembles a go-kart. The problem here is that your shader returned 1.0f (pure white) for every vertex, so naturally the entire model is colored pure white. You need to fix this problem, which you do by emulating a directional light from the fixed-function pipeline.

You've been using directional lights throughout this book as a way of making things appear more realistic, and now you implement the same directional light using a shader and the programmable pipeline. Back in the KartRacers.fx file, replace the Transform function with the one in Listing 20.4.

LISTING 20.4 Directional Lighting Shader

```
float4 Transform(in float4 pos : POSITION, in float3 normal : NORMAL,
out float4 Position : POSITION) : COLOR0
{
    // Transform position
    Position = mul(pos, worldViewProjection);

    // Transform the normal
    float4 transformedNormal = mul(normal, worldViewProjection);

    return dot(transformedNormal, lightDirection);
}
```

You'll notice here the parameters have changed. Rather than a single in parameter that is the position, now a second parameter is the normal of the vertex. This parameter is required for the directional light calculation. The first part of the shader code is the same; the position is transformed and returned via the out parameter. However, you are not simply returning a solid white color from this function. First, you take the normal of the vertex, transform it just as you did the position, and store that in a new local parameter transformedNormal. You then return the dot product of the transformed normal and a light direction variable you haven't yet defined. You should define it in your .fx file with the rest of your variables:

```
float4 lightDirection;   // Direction of the light
```

Now, you just update your C# code to take advantage of this new shader. The only change required is a call to set the value of the light direction variable. To make it easier, first, declare a new "constant" to hold the light direction:

```
// Light direction
private static readonly Vector4 LightDirection = new Vector4(0, 0.1f,
    -1.5f, 1.0f);
```

Then, find the two calls to SetValue in the OnFrameRender method and add the new one directly after that:

```
effect.SetValue("lightDirection", LightDirection);
```

Running the application now and selecting the new game will show you a shaded version of the go-kart, much as you see in Figure 20.2.

FIGURE 20.2
Shading added.

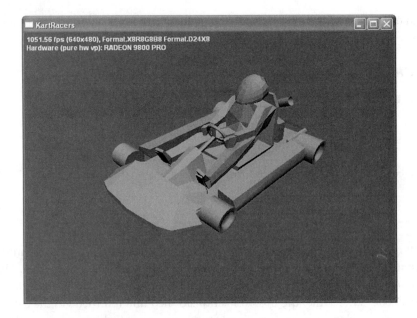

Adding the Pixel Shader

Once again, this screen is better, but it's still not perfect. What about the texture you have loaded? To use the textures, you have to write a pixel shader. Pixel shaders are just as easy to use as a simple vertex shader. Replace your KartRacers.fx file with the code in Listing 20.5.

LISTING 20.5 Your Completed Mesh Shader

```
//--------------------------------------------------------------------------
// Global variables
//--------------------------------------------------------------------------
// World matrix for object
float4x4 worldMatrix : WORLD;

// World * View * Projection matrix
float4x4 worldViewProjection : WORLDVIEWPROJECTION;
float4 lightDirection;  // Direction of the light
texture SceneTexture;

sampler SceneSampler =
sampler_state
{
    Texture = <SceneTexture>;
};


float4 Transform(in float4 pos : POSITION,
in float3 normal : NORMAL, in float2 uv : TEXCOORD0,
```

LISTING 20.5 Continued

```
out float4 Position : POSITION, out float2 texcoords : TEXCOORD0) : COLOR0
{
    // Transform position
    Position = mul(pos, worldViewProjection);

    // Store uv coords
    texcoords = uv;

    // Transform the normal
    float4 transformedNormal = mul(normal, worldViewProjection);

    return dot(transformedNormal, lightDirection);
}

float4 TextureColor(in float2 textureCoords : TEXCOORD0,
 in float4 diffuseColor : COLOR0 ) : COLOR0
{
    // Get the texture color
    return tex2D(SceneSampler, textureCoords) * diffuseColor;
}

//--------------------------------------------------------------------
// Techniques
//--------------------------------------------------------------------
technique RenderScene
{
    pass P0
    {
        VertexShader = compile vs_1_1 Transform();
        PixelShader  = compile ps_1_1 TextureColor();
    }
}
```

I need to address a few new things here. First, you add two new variables to the file, namely, a texture and a sampler. The texture is naturally the one you've already loaded when you loaded the mesh, and the sampler is what the pixel shader uses to read the texture data. Notice that the sampler sets its internal value to the texture variable you've already created. You only need to modify the texture variable directly.

You also slightly modify the vertex shader program by adding two new parameters, each a texture coordinate but one marked in and the other marked out. Because the pixel shader requires the texture coordinates, you'll notice that the code simply passes it on here.

Next is the TextureColor method, which will be the pixel shader. It has two inputs, the texture coordinates from the vertex shader and the diffuse color, which was the return value of the vertex shader program. Notice that the pixel shader also returns a color, which will be the final color for each pixel in the scene. To get that color, the pixel shader has a simple formula: first, get the color of the pixel in the texture (the `tex2D` intrinsic), and then, multiply it by the diffuse color returned from the vertex shader. This formula produces an image that is the correct color as the textures show, but it is also shaded correctly, as you saw earlier in Figure 20.2.

Now, the only remaining item to cover is actually updating the C# code to ensure that the texture is being set correctly. Back in the `OnFrameRender` method, find the innermost loop right before the call to `DrawSubset` and add the following:

```
effect.SetValue("SceneTexture", kartTextures[i]);
effect.CommitChanges();
```

This change updates the effects system with the correct texture and allows it to render the go-kart correctly (as you see in Figure 20.3). Pay attention to the call to `CommitChanges`, though. This call is informing the effects system that you have changed one of the values used to render and you want the effects system to use this updated value now. Considering that you've only loaded a single texture, this call isn't exactly *required*, but it is good to get into the habit now before more complex things are rendered and it is required. It's also interesting to point out that depending on which kart you select on the main user interface screen, the resulting kart in the game play mode looks different.

FIGURE 20.3
Finally, the complete model.

Summary

During this chapter, you learned all about the basics of the programmable pipeline and how to write simplistic vertex and pixel shaders to get your code to render models in an interesting way.

With a basic understanding of the programmable pipeline, you can move on to something that all games need: good level-of-detail algorithms.

CHAPTER 21

Controlling the Level of Detail

In many modern games today, an artist (or more likely a group of artists) designs content. Most times, this content is quite large and has a significant amount of detail built into the model, which might be necessary to view when you're up close to the model. However, when the model is not close to the camera, having all that detail, which the user will never see anyway, is somewhat of a waste.

As they say, the fastest polygon to draw is the one that you don't. In this chapter, you will look at several techniques you can use to control this level of detail.

In this chapter, you'll learn

- ▶ How to simplify a mesh
- ▶ When to use a simplification mesh
- ▶ How to use a progressive mesh

Simplifying a Mesh

Now, imagine that the racing game you're creating has a model which sits to the side of the track. This model is quite detailed and has plenty of vertices in it; however, you don't want to waste time drawing the highly detailed model if you can't see it all. You could ask your artist to give you a second, less detailed model and swap out the models you're using, depending on the situation, but that implies that the artist has a lot of free time to make these low-resolution models.

It is easier to simply take the meshes you already have (the high detailed ones) and use the built-in Simplify method on the mesh object. **Simplifying** a mesh is the act of taking an existing mesh and using a set of provided weights to remove as many faces or vertices to achieve a lower detail mesh. However, before a mesh can be simplified, it must first be cleaned.

You clean a mesh by adding another vertex where two fans of triangles share the same vertex. Let's look at the overload you use for the Clean method:

```
public static Microsoft.DirectX.Direct3D.Mesh Clean (
    Microsoft.DirectX.Direct3D.CleanType cleanType ,
    Microsoft.DirectX.Direct3D.Mesh mesh ,
    Microsoft.DirectX.GraphicsStream adjacency ,
    Microsoft.DirectX.GraphicsStream adjacencyOut ,
    System.String errorsAndWarnings )
```

The first parameter of this method tells the runtime what type of operations should be performed to clean the mesh. See Table 21.1 for the possible values for this parameter.

TABLE 21.1 Possible Clean Type Flags

CleanType.BackFacing	This option merges triangles that share the same vertex indices but have face normals pointing in opposite directions (commonly called back-facing triangles).
CleanType.BowTies	This option splits a shared vertex if it is at the apex of two triangle fans and mesh operations affect one of the fans.
CleanType.Skinning	This option uses the BackFacing flag to prevent infinite loops during skinning operations.
CleanType.Optimization	This option uses the BackFacing flag to prevent infinite loops during optimization operations.
CleanType.Simplification	This option uses both the BackFacing and BowTies flags to prevent infinite loops during simplification operations.

It's pretty obvious the Simplification flag is the one that is required for the call to Simplify. The other parameters are the mesh that should be cleaned, the adjacency information, and an out parameter that gives you any errors or warnings that occurred during the cleaning operations.

Construction Cue

Remember, if you are using the overload with the out parameter for errors and warnings, ensure that no exception is thrown if an error occurs. You need to manually check the string to see if any error occurred in this case.

Now you should update your rendering code to clean your mesh, so find the OnNewGame method where you load the mesh and replace it with the one in Listing 21.1.

LISTING 21.1   Loading and Cleaning Mesh

```
private void OnNewGame(object sender, EventArgs e)
{
    ExtendedMaterial[] materials = null;
    GraphicsStream adj = null;
    // Create the kart mesh and textures
    using (Mesh tempMesh = Mesh.FromFile(MediaPath + "kart.x", MeshFlags.Managed,
             sampleFramework.Device, out adj, out materials))
    {

        if ( (materials != null) && (materials.Length > 0) )
        {
            // Create the textures
            kartTextures = new Texture[materials.Length];
            for(int i = 0; i < materials.Length; i++)
            {
                kartTextures[i] =
                ResourceCache.GetGlobalInstance().CreateTextureFromFile(
                sampleFramework.Device,  MediaPath +
                gameUI.GetComboBox(PickKartControl).GetSelectedData() as string);
            }
        }

        string errors = null;
        kartMesh = Mesh.Clean(CleanType.Simplification | CleanType.Optimization,
            tempMesh, adj, adj, out errors);

        if ( (errors != null) && (errors.Length > 0) )
            throw new InvalidOperationException("Error cleaning mesh: " + errors);

        // Now optimize the mesh in place
        kartMesh.OptimizeInPlace(MeshFlags.OptimizeVertexCache, adj);
    }

    currentState = GameState.Gameplay;
}
```

You'll notice a few changes to the underlying code here. First, you add the adj parameter to store adjacency information about the mesh. It is returned to you from the FromFile method on the mesh class. Notice also that you change and add that method into a using statement. Instead of getting the kartMesh directly from that method, you create a temporary mesh. The cleaning operation returns a new mesh, and that's the mesh that you want to use as the kart's mesh.

After the textures are loaded (same as in the last chapter), the mesh is then cleaned. The flags passed in are for both simplification and optimization because the mesh is optimized directly after this part. Notice that the method will throw an exception if any data in the errors parameter notifies you that the operation failed.

Now, your mesh is ready to be simplified. Look at the overload for the Simplify method:

```
public static Microsoft.DirectX.Direct3D.Mesh Simplify (
    Microsoft.DirectX.Direct3D.Mesh mesh ,
    Microsoft.DirectX.GraphicsStream adjacency ,
    Microsoft.DirectX.Direct3D.AttributeWeights vertexAttributeWeights ,
    Microsoft.DirectX.GraphicsStream vertexWeights ,
    System.Int32 minValue ,
    Microsoft.DirectX.Direct3D.MeshFlags options )
```

The structure of this method should seem similar. The mesh you want to simplify is the first parameter, followed by the adjacency, which you can specify as either an integer array or a graphics stream. Because you're using a graphics stream for your adjacency currently, it just makes sense to use this overload.

The AttributeWeights structure for the next parameter sets the weights for the various values used when simplifying the mesh. Most applications should use the overloads that do not take this member because the default structure only considers geometric and normal adjustment. Only in special cases would other members need to be modified. The default values for this structure, if you do not pass it in, would be the following:

```
AttributeWeights weights = new AttributeWeights();
weights.Position = 1.0f;
weights.Boundary = 1.0f;
weights.Normal = 1.0f;
weights.Diffuse = 0.0f;
weights.Specular = 0.0f;
weights.Binormal = 0.0f;
weights.Tangent = 0.0f;
weights.TextureCoordinate = new float[]
{0.0f, 0.0f, 0.0f, 0.0f, 0.0f, 0.0f, 0.0f, 0.0f };
```

The next member is a list of weights for each vertex. If you pass in null for this member, it is assumed that each weight is 1.0f.

The minValue member is the minimum number of faces or vertices (depending on the flags you pass in) that you want to simplify the mesh to. The lower this value, the lower the details of the resulting mesh.

> You should be aware that just because this call succeeds, it does not mean that your mesh has this exact number of vertices or faces. This member is intended to be a desired minimum, not an absolute minimum. It might not be possible to simplify your mesh to the desired level.

The final parameter to this function can be only one of two flags in the MeshFlags enumeration. If you want to simplify the number of vertices, you should pass in MeshFlags.SimplifyVertex; otherwise, you simplify the number of indices and use MeshFlags.SimplifyFace.

Although you don't need to simplify the go-kart mesh in this example, if you wanted to create a simplified version of the mesh, you could do so like this:

```
Console.WriteLine("Number of faces: {0} - Vertices {1}",
    kartMesh.NumberFaces, kartMesh.NumberVertices);
Mesh temp = Mesh.Simplify(kartMesh, adj, null, 1, MeshFlags.SimplifyVertex);
kartMesh.Dispose();
kartMesh = temp;
Console.WriteLine("Number of faces: {0} - Vertices {1}",
    kartMesh.NumberFaces, kartMesh.NumberVertices);
```

> Make sure you clean the mesh again after optimization to ensure that it is ready for simplification.

Using a Simplification Mesh

Although simplifying a mesh directly as you did here is feasible in a few situations, in most cases you have to store entirely too many meshes for it to be useful in a real-world situation with many levels of detail. (Each level of detail requires a separate mesh.) What you need is a way to do something similar but without the requirement of all these mesh copies.

You can use the SimplificationMesh object to encapsulate the process of simplifying a mesh. However, you can't actually use the object to do the rendering; you must first get an actual mesh from the simplification mesh. Creating the simplification mesh is simple; here is the overload:

```
public SimplificationMesh ( Microsoft.DirectX.Direct3D.Mesh mesh ,
    Microsoft.DirectX.GraphicsStream adjacency ,
    Microsoft.DirectX.Direct3D.AttributeWeights vertexAttributeWeights ,
    Microsoft.DirectX.GraphicsStream vertexWeights )
```

If you noticed that these are the same parameters as those in the Simplify method, with the exception of the minimum value and flags, you are quite observant. The object that is created is ready to simplify the passed-in mesh, but until you call one of the reduce methods on the object, it maintains a full set of vertices and faces.

If you were interested in reducing the amount of vertices and faces in the simplified mesh, you would use two methods, ReduceVertices and ReduceFaces, which reduce the number of vertices or faces, as the names imply. If you wanted to simplify the mesh to the lowest possible detail, you would call code such as the following:

```
SimplificationMesh simplifiedMesh = new SimplificationMesh(mesh, adj);
simplifiedMesh.ReduceVertices(1);
simplifiedMesh.ReduceFaces(1);
```

Assume that mesh is a loaded mesh and adj is the adjacency information for that mesh. However, there are no drawing calls located on the SimplificationMesh object, so drawing with this object is unsupported, as mentioned earlier. Instead, you need to use the Clone method from the SimplificationMesh object to get the real mesh. The overload looks like this:

```
public Microsoft.DirectX.Direct3D.Mesh Clone (
    Microsoft.DirectX.Direct3D.MeshFlags options ,
    Microsoft.DirectX.Direct3D.VertexFormats vertexFormat ,
    Microsoft.DirectX.Direct3D.Device device ,
    out int[] adjacencyOut , out int[] vertexRemap )
```

As you see here, this method returns a mesh and the mesh that is returned is the simplified version (that is, the result of any reduce calls). Although many applications don't use this overload (they use the overload without the adjacencyOut and vertexRemap parameters), the method itself is simple. An example of calling it using the preceding sample code is

```
mesh.Dispose();
mesh = simplifiedMesh.Clone(simplifiedMesh.Options.Value,
    simplifiedMesh.VertexFormat, device);
```

Notice here that the original mesh is disposed to clean up any resources and then reassigned to the newly cloned simplification mesh.

One of the first problems you might notice with this object type is that you can't seem to regain any of the lost vertices. Sure, you can simplify the mesh just fine, but what if you want to raise the level of detail in the model? There is no RaiseVertices method, and using the ReduceVertices method and passing in a larger number of vertices has no effect. The SimplificationMesh objects are designed to simplify meshes, and that is all: there is no going back. Progressive meshes were designed to handle this case.

Controlling the Level of Detail Using a Progressive Mesh

Naturally, in some cases you only want to simplify a mesh. For example, imagine a model for a rocket you've just fired. Unless you have really bad aim, more than likely this object will not return toward you. However, a more common case is where you need to progressively lower *or raise* the level of detail. I'm sure you can see where the name of the **progressive mesh** came from.

Unlike the `SimplificationMesh`, the `ProgressiveMesh` class derives from the `BaseMesh` class and can be used directly to draw the mesh onscreen. The `ProgressiveMesh` class is created in much the same way that the `SimplificationMesh` is. Look at the constructor:

```
public ProgressiveMesh ( Microsoft.DirectX.Direct3D.Mesh mesh ,
    Microsoft.DirectX.GraphicsStream adjacency ,
    Microsoft.DirectX.Direct3D.AttributeWeights vertexAttributeWeights ,
    Microsoft.DirectX.GraphicsStream vertexWeights ,
    System.Int32 minValue ,
    Microsoft.DirectX.Direct3D.MeshFlags options )
```

Notice that here, the constructor is almost a mixture of the constructor for the `SimplificationMesh` object and the `Simplify` method. The *minValue* parameter is the minimum amount you want to allow this mesh to be reduced to. After the object is created, you can set the number of faces or vertices to any number of faces or vertices between that minimum value and the `ProgressiveMesh.MaxFaces` or `ProgressiveMesh.MaxVertices`, depending on what you're modifying.

After the progressive mesh is created, it will be fully simplified. If you want to ensure that it is the high-resolution version of the mesh after creation, you need to use code such as the following:

```
using(Mesh tempMesh = Mesh.Clean(mesh, adj, adj))
{
    // Create our progressive mesh
    progressiveMesh = new ProgressiveMesh(tempMesh, adj,
    null, 1, MeshFlags.SimplifyVertex);

    // Set the initial mesh to the max
    progressiveMesh.NumberFaces = progressiveMesh.MaxFaces;
    progressiveMesh.NumberVertices = progressiveMesh.MaxVertices;
}
```

Construction Cue

After your progressive mesh is created, you can use it just as you would use your normal mesh, drawing it every frame. You can add and remove vertices and faces depending on how far away from the camera the object is, so you have complete control over the level of detail of your object.

Construction Cue

> It's common to store multiple meshes of varying levels of details rather than have one large progressive mesh controlling the entire range of details. If you look at the progressive mesh sample that ships with the DirectX SDK, you see an example of this implementation. You can use the `TrimByFaces` and `TrimByVertices` methods on the progressive mesh object to change the level of detail that any particular progressive mesh supports.

Summary

Throughout this chapter, I discussed various ways of controlling an object's level of detail. You learned two different methods for mesh simplification and another method of controlling a mesh's level of detail in real time. These routines can be powerful performance-saving methods for you later.

During the next chapter, you will learn about new methods for rendering your scene.

CHAPTER 22

Using Render Targets for Effects

Until now, you've been rendering everything you've done directly to the back buffer. In the vast majority of cases, this is the behavior you want, but what if you want to render somewhere else? What if you want to take the scene you've just rendered and use that as a texture somewhere else, say on a video screen inside your level?

In Direct3D, you accomplish this goal through the use of render targets.

In this chapter, you'll learn

▶ How to render a track and multiple karts

▶ How to create and use render targets

▶ How to implement a rear-view mirror

Rendering a Track and Multiple Go-Karts

Before you can do any of those things, first you need something interesting to be rendered. You currently have a single go-kart being rendered, which is all well and good, but it doesn't give you much opportunity to see anything if you render a scene into your texture. To change this situation, first you should set up your code to create and render multiple go-karts.

Find the declaration to your go-kart variables for the mesh and textures and replace them with these:

```
// Kart mesh
private const int NumberKarts = 5;
private Mesh[] kartMeshes = null;
private Texture[][] kartTextures = null;
```

```
// Track mesh
private Mesh trackMesh = null;
private Texture[] trackTextures = null;
```

Along with creating an array of meshes for the kart and textures, you also add a constant to describe the number of karts that will be rendered, plus a mesh and array of textures for the track. Because you changed the names and types of the parameters that you had previously declared, nothing will compile now. First, you can fix the creation of the meshes, so find the OnNewGame method in your class, and replace it with the one found in Listing 22.1.

LISTING 22.1   Creating Meshes

```
private void OnNewGame(object sender, EventArgs e)
{
    ExtendedMaterial[] materials = null;
    GraphicsStream adj = null;
    // Load an array of karts
    kartMeshes = new Mesh[NumberKarts];
    kartTextures = new Texture[NumberKarts][];
    for (int meshes = 0; meshes < NumberKarts; meshes++)
    {

        // Create the kart mesh and textures
        using (Mesh tempMesh = Mesh.FromFile(MediaPath + "kart.x",
                    MeshFlags.Managed, sampleFramework.Device,
                    out adj, out materials))
        {

            if ( (materials != null) && (materials.Length > 0) )
            {
                // Create the textures
                kartTextures[meshes] = new Texture[materials.Length];
                for(int i = 0; i < materials.Length; i++)
                {
                    kartTextures[meshes][i] =
                        ResourceCache.GetGlobalInstance().CreateTextureFromFile(
                        sampleFramework.Device,  MediaPath +
                        gameUI.GetComboBox(
                        PickKartControl).GetSelectedData() as string);
                }
            }

            string errors = null;
            kartMeshes[meshes] = Mesh.Clean(CleanType.Optimization,
                tempMesh, adj, adj, out errors);

            if ( (errors != null) && (errors.Length > 0) )
                throw new InvalidOperationException("Error cleaning mesh: "
                                                    + errors);

            // Now optimize the mesh in place
            kartMeshes[meshes].OptimizeInPlace(
                            MeshFlags.OptimizeVertexCache, adj);
```

LISTING 22.1 Continued

```
        }
    }

    // Now load the track mesh and textures
    using (Mesh tempMesh = Mesh.FromFile(MediaPath +
                gameUI.GetComboBox(PickLevelControl).GetSelectedData() as string,
                MeshFlags.Managed, sampleFramework.Device,
                out adj, out materials))
    {
        if ( (materials != null) && (materials.Length > 0) )
        {
            // Create the textures
            trackTextures = new Texture[materials.Length];
            for(int i = 0; i < materials.Length; i++)
            {
                if ( (materials[i].TextureFilename != null) &&
                    (materials[i].TextureFilename.Length > 0) )
                {
                    trackTextures[i] =
                        ResourceCache.GetGlobalInstance().CreateTextureFromFile(
                        sampleFramework.Device,  MediaPath +
                        materials[i].TextureFilename);
                }
            }
        }

        string errors = null;
        trackMesh = Mesh.Clean(CleanType.Optimization,
            tempMesh, adj, adj, out errors);

        if ( (errors != null) && (errors.Length > 0) )
            throw new InvalidOperationException("Error cleaning mesh: "
                                                + errors);

        // Now optimize the mesh in place
        trackMesh.OptimizeInPlace(MeshFlags.OptimizeVertexCache, adj);
    }

    currentState = GameState.Gameplay;
}
```

The big changes here are twofold: first, instead of creating a single mesh and set of textures for the go-kart, you're now creating an array of each. Notice that the textures have turned into an array of arrays because each mesh can have zero to many textures. Each mesh is loaded, each of the textures is loaded (based on the input from the user interface), and then each mesh is cleaned for optimization and optimized.

After that, the track mesh is created. It is also loaded from the data in the user interface screen. (track.x was loaded as the data of the pick-the-level combo box.) It too is cleaned and optimized before it is ready to be rendered. I hope you

noticed earlier that you never cleaned up the go-kart mesh and textures. In all
reality, cleaning up the textures isn't required because the ResourceCache class
handles that, but cleaning up the meshes is. Find the OnDestroyDevice method
and add the cleanup code from Listing 22.2 to that method.

LISTING 22.2   Cleaning Up Meshes

```
if (kartMeshes != null)
{
    // Clean up kart meshes/textures
    for(int i = 0; i < kartMeshes.Length; i++)
    {
        if (kartMeshes[i] != null)
        {
            kartMeshes[i].Dispose();
            kartMeshes[i] = null;
        }
    }

    // Clean up track mesh/textures
    if (trackMesh != null)
    {
        trackMesh.Dispose();
        trackMesh = null;
    }
}
```

If you want to just see what rendering the go-kart and track would be like (see
Figure 22.1), simply find the OnFrameRender method and update the two compile
errors left, by adding a [0] to the variables:

```
for (int i = 0; i < kartTextures[0].Length; i++)
{
    effect.SetValue("SceneTexture", kartTextures[0][i]);
    effect.CommitChanges();
    kartMeshes[0].DrawSubset(i);
}
```

You also need to render the track (this code before the EndPass call):

```
// Move the track up some
Matrix worldMatrix = Matrix.Translation(0, 4.5f, 0);
effect.SetValue("worldViewProjection", worldMatrix *
    world * view * proj);
// Render the track
for (int i = 0; i < trackTextures.Length; i++)
{
    effect.SetValue("SceneTexture", trackTextures[i]);
    effect.CommitChanges();
    trackMesh.DrawSubset(i);
}
```

You've moved (translated) the track up 4.5 units as well.

FIGURE 22.1
Go-kart and track.

That code isn't robust because it cannot render more than that one kart, so that's something you should address first. Because you'll be required to render the scene twice anyway (once for the main screen and once for the rear-view screen), you should encapsulate this rendering into a new method. Add the method in Listing 22.3 to your class file now.

LISTING 22.3 Rendering Your Scene

```
private void RenderScene(Matrix world, Matrix view, Matrix proj)
{
    // Update the effect's variables. Instead of using strings, it would
    // be more efficient to cache a handle to the parameter by calling
    // Effect.GetParameter
    effect.SetValue("worldViewProjection", world * view * proj);
    effect.SetValue("worldMatrix", world);
    effect.SetValue("lightDirection", LightDirection);

    effect.Technique = "RenderScene";
    int passes = effect.Begin(0);
    for (int pass = 0; pass < passes; pass++)
    {
        effect.BeginPass(pass);
        // Render the karts
        for (int kart = 0; kart < kartMeshes.Length; kart++)
        {
            Matrix kartMatrix = Matrix.Translation(kart * -5.5f, 0,
                                                    kart * -40.0f);
            effect.SetValue("worldViewProjection", kartMatrix *
                world * view * proj);
```

LISTING 22.3   Continued

```
                for (int i = 0; i < kartTextures[kart].Length; i++)
                {
                    effect.SetValue("SceneTexture", kartTextures[kart][i]);
                    effect.CommitChanges();
                    kartMeshes[kart].DrawSubset(i);
                }
            }

            // Move the track up some
            Matrix worldMatrix = Matrix.Translation(0, 4.5f, 0);
            effect.SetValue("worldViewProjection", worldMatrix *
                world * view * proj);
            // Render the track
            for (int i = 0; i < trackTextures.Length; i++)
            {
                effect.SetValue("SceneTexture", trackTextures[i]);
                effect.CommitChanges();
                trackMesh.DrawSubset(i);
            }
            effect.EndPass();
        }
        effect.End();
}
```

The method here is similar to the code you had within that if statement in the
OnFrameRender method earlier. Now, however, you also have a loop to render
each of the meshes for the various go-karts. Notice that each kart is offset some
by updating the matrix passed in to your vertex shader. Updating your
OnFrameRender method to remove the code you had in the else statement and
replacing it with the following line of code renders a scene much like you see in
Figure 22.2:

```
// Now render the scene normally
RenderScene(camera.WorldMatrix, camera.ViewMatrix, camera.ProjectionMatrix);
```

Construction Cue

You've created a new mesh for each kart you're rendering. This work isn't required
because you could have just re-used the same kart mesh/texture combination over
and over again. You did it so you can use *different* kart mesh/texture combinations
in the future, if you want.

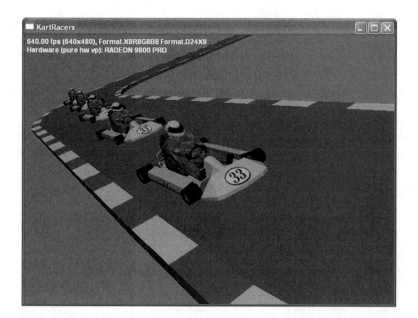

FIGURE 22.2
Go-karts and
track—spaced out.

Creating Render Targets and Surfaces

Now that you have a track and multiple karts being rendered, you can get your scene ready to create a rear-view mirror effect. To do this task, you need to create a texture that is a render target. As the name implies, a **render target** is the target of your rendering. Before you begin with that, though, you need to ensure that your device is capable of rendering to a render target of the appropriate type. Find the IsDeviceAcceptable method and before the final return true; line, add the following:

```
// Skip back buffer formats that don't support render targets format we want
if (!Manager.CheckDeviceFormat(caps.AdapterOrdinal, caps.DeviceType,
    adapterFormat, Usage.RenderTarget, ResourceType.Textures, Format.X8R8G8B8))
    return false;
```

Here you're checking whether the device can accept render target textures of type Format.X8R8G8B8, and if it cannot, you return false, signifying that this device isn't acceptable. Now, you need to declare these variables to continue:

```
// Rearview mirror
private const int RenderTargetSize = 256;
private RenderToSurface rearSurface = null;
private Texture rearTexture = null;
private Surface rearTextureSurface = null;
```

First, you have a constant that is the size of the render target you will be creating. (You will almost always want this number to be a power of 2, such as it is here.) Next, you declare the RenderToSurface object, which is a helper class that allows you to render your scene to a surface later. Next, you declare the texture that will be the render target and the surface that will be the underlying surface of that texture.

Because you're not entirely sure where you'll be using this texture and surface, you want to create these objects in the OnResetDevice method. While you're there, you might as well also add the support code for the RenderToSurface object. Add the following code to that method:

```
// Re-create the render target texture
rearTexture = new Texture(sampleFramework.Device, RenderTargetSize,
    RenderTargetSize, 1, Usage.RenderTarget, Format.X8R8G8B8, Pool.Default);
rearTextureSurface = rearTexture.GetSurfaceLevel(0);

if (rearSurface != null)
{
    rearSurface.OnResetDevice();
}
```

Here you'll notice that the texture is created first, using the render target size and a single mip level. The usage will be for a render target, and the format is what you checked earlier in your IsDeviceAcceptable callback. After the texture is created, you store the surface for that texture as well. Because there is only a single mip level, getting the first surface level is always correct for your scenario. For the rearSurface helper class, you simply call the OnResetDevice method if it has been instantiated so far.

Notice that the texture was created in the Pool.Default memory pool, which normally signifies video memory. For a render target texture, this *must* be the memory pool specified. You must also clean up the texture when the device is lost to ensure proper reset. Find the OnLostDevice method and add this code to the end:

```
// Clean up rear view mirror texture
if (rearTexture != null)
{
    rearTexture.Dispose();
    rearTextureSurface.Dispose();
    rearTexture = null;
    rearTextureSurface = null;
}
if (rearSurface != null)
{
    rearSurface.OnLostDevice();
}
```

Notice that only the rearTexture variable is checked for null here. Because the surface is created from the texture, it is assumed that if the texture is valid, the surface must be. Because these objects are in the default memory pool, they are required to be disposed now. They are also set to null so they cannot be used again (until the device is reset). Also notice that the appropriate helper method is called on the rearSurface member. Because you're on a cleanup kick anyway, add this code to the OnDestroyDevice method, even though you haven't written the code to create the surface yet:

```
if (rearSurface != null)
{
    rearSurface.Dispose();
    rearSurface = null;
}
```

Finally, the last thing you want to do is create your helper object. In the OnNewGame method, add this creation code to the end:

```
// Create rear-view mirror surface and texture
rearSurface = new RenderToSurface(sampleFramework.Device, RenderTargetSize,
    RenderTargetSize, Format.X8R8G8B8, true, DepthFormat.D16);
```

Notice that you've used the same render target size and format here.

Rendering a Scene to a Render Target

Now that you have your variables created, you are ready to render the scene into this render target texture you've created. Add the method from Listing 22.4 to your code now.

LISTING 22.4 Rendering a Scene into the Rear View

```
/// <summary>Renders the scene into the rear-view mirror texture</summary>
private void RenderRearViewMirror(Device device)
{
    if (currentState != GameState.Gameplay)
        return; // Nothing to do here

    // Render the scene into the surface for the rear-view mirror
    Viewport view = new Viewport();
    view.Width = RenderTargetSize;
    view.Height = RenderTargetSize;
    view.MaxZ = 1.0f;

    rearSurface.BeginScene(rearTextureSurface, view);
    device.Clear(ClearFlags.Target | ClearFlags.ZBuffer, 0, 1.0f, 0);

    RenderScene(Matrix.Identity, Matrix.LookAtLH(
```

LISTING 22.4   Continued

```
        new Vector3(0, 10, -8), new Vector3(0, 0, -30.0f),
        ModelViewerCamera.UpDirection), camera.ProjectionMatrix);

    rearSurface.EndScene(Filter.None);
}
```

Here you check to make sure that the scene is in the GamePlay state, and if it isn't, you simply exit out of the method because you have nothing to render. You'll notice that the BeginScene method takes the surface that will be rendered to as an argument. Because you are using the surface you retrieved from the texture, any updates to this surface are reflected in this texture. The EndScene method allows you to pass in a mipmap filter that you want to apply to the surface. Rather than worry about the device capabilities, simply use no filtering for this example. One last thing to notice is that the clear color for the scene was changed. You do so to show the obvious difference between the "real" scene and the rear-view mirror scene.

Aside from that, this rendering is basically the same as the rendering of the normal scene. You call Clear on the device, and then you call RenderScene with a different set of matrices. This step renders the scene (still using your shaders) to the texture. However, you haven't added a call to this method anywhere yet. Add a call to this method as the first line of the OnFrameRender method (before the Clear call):

```
// Before you do anything else, render the rear-view mirror
RenderRearViewMirror(device);
```

Construction Cue

> You are required to call this new method before the first call to BeginScene in the OnFrameRender method. The helper class will also call BeginScene on the device (when its BeginScene method is called), and you can only have one call to BeginScene before you call EndScene.

Displaying the Rear-View Mirror

Now that you have the scene rendered into your texture, it should be a simple matter to get that displayed onscreen. Because it is a single texture, you can reuse the sprite class you used for the background of the user screen to render the rear-view mirror. In the OnFrameRender method, find the call to RenderScene and add this code snippet, which should show you a scene similar to Figure 22.3:

```
// Render the rear-view mirror texture
backgroundSprite.Begin(SpriteFlags.None);
backgroundSprite.Draw2D(rearTexture, System.Drawing.Rectangle.Empty,
    new System.Drawing.Rectangle(0,0,256,128), new System.Drawing.Point(200, 0),
    unchecked((int)0xffffffff));
backgroundSprite.End();
```

FIGURE 22.3
A rear-view mirror.

Summary

In this chapter, you focused on getting a rear-view mirror created and rendered for your game. You were required to render multiple go-karts, the track, and finally the scene multiple times to render the scene to a texture. You then used that texture to display a rear-view mirror.

In the next chapter, you will look at more detailed shader programs.

CHAPTER 23

Understanding the High-Level Shader Language

A couple of chapters ago, I briefly introduced the High-Level Shader Language (HLSL), and you even got to write some basic vertex and pixel shaders using it. However, I scratched only the surface of this amazing technology. There are entire books dedicated to understanding the intricacies of the language and writing amazing shaders.

Because this book is only a beginner's book, an exhaustive look at this technology isn't feasible, but you should get a little more information on the subject to help you write the great games of the future.

In this chapter, you'll learn

▶ Why you should fully understand HLSL

▶ How to update lighting code to add specular highlights

▶ How to implement per-pixel lighting

Understanding Limits on Older Shader Models

Because you manipulate a pixel shader in this code, one thing you might notice is that the number of available instructions you can use in a 1.1 pixel-shader pass is extremely limited. For pixel shaders under version 1.4, you are limited to 12 instructions for the entire shader program, which obviously isn't much. For version 1.4, the limit is raised to 28 (in two phases), but that is still not much. You are also limited to 8 constants in these shader programs. Pixel shader versions 2.0 and higher have the ability to perform more complex operations and have higher instruction and constant counts. You can check the capabilities for your card to find out how many of each are supported.

For the first part of the lighting code here, you use the same pixel shader you had in the beginning, but once you move on to the per-pixel lighting, you will quickly realize that you've run out of instruction space. Although you could probably tweak the shader to fit within the limited space, it's probably easier to just force the 2.0 shader model (which is what you'll be doing).

Two things you also might not be aware of are flow control and looping, both of which are available in shaders. Older shader models do not natively support flow control, or branching. To facilitate this, when generating the actual shader code, the HLSL compiler might actually unwind a loop or execute all branches of if statements. This point is something you need to know, particularly if you are already writing a complex shader that is stretching the limits of the instruction count. Take a simple loop such as the following:

```
for(int i = 0; i<10; i++)
{
    pos.y += (float)i;
}
```

Even though there is only a single statement in the line, this shader code once unwound takes up a whopping 20 instructions (at least). When your instruction count limit is 12 (as for pixel shaders 1.1), this simple loop wouldn't compile.

With newer hardware coming out that supports the 3.0 shader models (and even current hardware that supports the 2.x shader models), these issues are less of a problem.

Adding Specular Highlights to Kart

With the background out of the way, you should take a bit of time to add some basic specular highlights to your car. A **specular highlight** is an area of glossiness on an object. That's the effect you are going for. To calculate this reflectivity, you not only need to know which direction the light is coming from, but you also need to know the location of the camera (or your "eye"). Add this declaration to your shader code (KartRacers.fx):

```
float4 eyeVector; // Vector for the eye location
```

Naturally, you update your rendering code as well, so find the OnFrameRender method in your C# class, and before the call to RenderScene, add the following line:

```
effect.SetValue("eyeVector",new Vector4(camera.EyeLocation.X,
    camera.EyeLocation.Y, camera.EyeLocation.Z,1));
```

This code ensures that the shader will know about the location of the camera when you're running the shader necessary for calculating the specular highlights. Of course, so far, you haven't even written that shader. Look at the code in Listing 23.1 and add that to your KartRacers.fx file.

LISTING 23.1   A Per-Vertex Specular Shader

```
//---------------------------------------------------------------------------
// Transformation with single directional light plus per vertex specular
//---------------------------------------------------------------------------

struct PER_VERTEX_OUT
{
    float4 Position : POSITION;
    float2 TexCoords : TEXCOORD0;
    float4 Color : COLOR0;
};

PER_VERTEX_OUT TransformSpecularPerVertex(float4 pos : POSITION, float3 normal
: NORMAL, float2 uv : TEXCOORD0)
{
    PER_VERTEX_OUT Output = (PER_VERTEX_OUT)0;

    // Transform position
    Output.Position = mul(pos, worldViewProjection);

    // Store uv coords
    Output.TexCoords = uv;

    // Transform the normals into the world matrix and normalize them
    float3 transformedNormal = normalize(mul(normal, worldMatrix));

    // Transform the world position of the vertex
    float3 worldPosition = normalize(mul(pos, worldMatrix));

    // Store the eye vector
    float3 eyeDirection = normalize(eyeVector - worldPosition);

    // Normalize the light direction
    float3 lightDir = normalize(lightDirection);

    // Store the diffuse component
    float4 diffuse = saturate( dot(lightDir, transformedNormal) );

    // Calculate the specular component
    float3 reflection = normalize( 2 * diffuse * transformedNormal - lightDir);
    float4 specular = pow(saturate(dot(reflection, eyeDirection)), 8);

    // Set the combined color
    Output.Color = diffuse + specular;

    // Return the data
    return Output;
}
```

Two big things should jump out at you right away. First, something that resembles a structure was declared, and second, this shader looks a lot more complicated than that last one. The structure is used as the output of the shader function instead of having a series of in parameters followed by a series of out parameters. The HLSL compiler is smart enough to use the output structure, and that is much easier to read than several out parameters. Take the Transform shader you wrote earlier. It had three input parameters, two output parameters, and a return value. This way, the same parameters and outputs are centralized, so you have three input parameters and a single returned structure.

Inside the shader code itself, things start out the same as they did in the last shader. You transform the position, you store the texture coordinates, and then you transform the normal. Here's where things start changing, though. Notice how you've transformed the normal against the world matrix, not the combined world, view, projection matrix? The specular calculation requires that the normal be transformed into world space but not into view or projection space, which is why this part is required.

You then transform the vertex into world space alone and calculate an eye direction (by subtracting the eye location from the transformed world position). Then, you calculate the diffuse directional light color (much as you did before) and combine that with a specular component, which is calculated by the reflection of the directional light and your eye.

After you have the calculations, you store the color (the diffuse added with the specular component) and return the output structure. Because this specular code is designed to run in a per-vertex lighting environment, you aren't required to change the pixel shader you have from earlier. It is perfectly valid still. You need to add a new technique to render this effect, so in your KartRacers.fx file, add the following technique to the end:

```
technique RenderSceneSpecular
{
    pass P0
    {
        VertexShader = compile vs_1_1 TransformSpecularPerVertex();
        PixelShader  = compile ps_1_1 TextureColor();
    }
}
```

To use this effect now, go to the RenderScene method and switch the technique being used to this new one:

```
effect.Technique = "RenderSceneSpecular";
```

Running the application now, you should see the specular highlights rendered on everything. Everything! You probably don't want to see these highlights being rendered on the road, so instead of rendering the entire scene with the same technique, you should split it between the two techniques you already have defined. Replace the RenderScene method with the one in Listing 23.2.

LISTING 23.2 Updating Your Rendering Code

```
private void RenderScene(Matrix world, Matrix view, Matrix proj)
{
    // Update the effect's variables. Instead of using strings, it would
    // be more efficient to cache a handle to the parameter by calling
    // Effect.GetParameter
    effect.SetValue("worldViewProjection", world * view * proj);
    effect.SetValue("worldMatrix", world);
    effect.SetValue("lightDirection", LightDirection);

    effect.Technique = "RenderSceneSpecular";

    int passes = effect.Begin(0);
    for (int pass = 0; pass < passes; pass++)
    {
        effect.BeginPass(pass);
        // Render the karts
        for (int kart = 0; kart < kartMeshes.Length; kart++)
        {
            Matrix kartMatrix = Matrix.Translation(kart * -5.5f, 0,
                                                    kart * -40.0f);
            effect.SetValue("worldViewProjection", kartMatrix *
                world * view * proj);
                for (int i = 0; i < kartTextures[kart].Length; i++)
                {
                    effect.SetValue("SceneTexture", kartTextures[kart][i]);
                    effect.CommitChanges();
                    kartMeshes[kart].DrawSubset(i);
                }
        }
        effect.EndPass();
    }
    effect.End();

    // Now render the track without specular highlights
    effect.Technique = "RenderScene";
    passes = effect.Begin(0);
    for (int pass = 0; pass < passes; pass++)
    {
        effect.BeginPass(pass);
        // Move the track up some
        Matrix worldMatrix = Matrix.Translation(0, 4.5f, 0);
        effect.SetValue("worldViewProjection", worldMatrix *
            world * view * proj);
```

LISTING 23.2 Continued

```
        // Render the track
        for (int i = 0; i < trackTextures.Length; i++)
        {
            effect.SetValue("SceneTexture", trackTextures[i]);
            effect.CommitChanges();
            trackMesh.DrawSubset(i);
        }
        effect.EndPass();
    }
    effect.End();

}
```

The important thing to notice here is that the effect's technique is switched after rendering the go-karts and before rendering the track. The code is similar between the two renderings other than that. With that, the specular highlights are only on the karts, but because the karts have many "flat" areas, it doesn't look as realistic as it should.

Making Specular Highlights Per Pixel

To address this issue, you can make the highlights appear per pixel rather than per vertex. Doing so requires a more complicated pixel shader. Back in your KartRacers.fx file, add the new shader functions in Listing 23.3.

LISTING 23.3 A Per-Pixel Shader

```
//---------------------------------------------------------------------------
// Transformation with single directional light plus per pixel specular
//---------------------------------------------------------------------------

struct PER_PIXEL_OUT
{
    float4 Position : POSITION;
    float2 TexCoords : TEXCOORD0;
    float3 LightDirection : TEXCOORD1;
    float3 Normal : TEXCOORD2;
    float3 EyeWorld : TEXCOORD3;
};

PER_PIXEL_OUT TransformSpecularPerPixel(float4 pos : POSITION, float3 normal
: NORMAL, float2 uv : TEXCOORD0)
{
    PER_PIXEL_OUT Output = (PER_PIXEL_OUT)0;

    // Transform position
    Output.Position = mul(pos, worldViewProjection);
```

LISTING 23.3 Continued

```
    // Store uv coords
    Output.TexCoords = uv;

    // Store the light direction
    Output.LightDirection = lightDirection;

    // Transform the normals into the world matrix and normalize them
    Output.Normal = normalize(mul(normal, worldMatrix));

    // Transform the world position of the vertex
    float3 worldPosition = normalize(mul(pos, worldMatrix));

    // Store the eye vector
    Output.EyeWorld = normalize(eyeVector - worldPosition);

    // Return the data
    return Output;
}

float4 TextureColorPerPixel(
 float2 uvCoords : TEXCOORD0,
 float3 lightDirection : TEXCOORD1,
 float3 normal : TEXCOORD2,
 float3 eye : TEXCOORD3) : COLOR0
{
    // Normalize our vectors
    float3 normalized = normalize(normal);
    float3 light = normalize(lightDirection);
    float3 eyeDirection = normalize(eye);
    // Store our diffuse component
    float4 diffuse = saturate(dot(light, normalized));

    // Calculate specular component
    float3 reflection = normalize(2 * diffuse * normalized - light);
    float4 specular = pow(saturate(dot(reflection, eyeDirection)), 8);

    float4 textureColorFromSampler = tex2D(SceneSampler, uvCoords);
    // Return the combined color
    return textureColorFromSampler * diffuse + specular;
};
```

You'll notice here that the code is generally the same as that in the per-vertex version, but this time, it is split across two methods. Because the pixel shader cannot retrieve much of the data that the vertex shader can, you'll notice that the only job the vertex shader has here is to pass the data on to the pixel shader in the form of texture coordinates. The pixel shader then takes that data and performs the same operation the pixel shader did earlier.

Once again, you need a new technique to access this new effect. Because this pixel shader is more complicated, you need at least a 2.0 shader to execute it:

```
technique RenderSceneSpecularPerPixel
{
    pass P0
    {
        VertexShader = compile vs_1_1 TransformSpecularPerPixel();
        PixelShader  = compile ps_2_0 TextureColorPerPixel();
    }
}
```

You'll notice that ps_2_0 is used to signify the updated shader required. However, currently you don't know whether your device even supports this shader model. Because you've already decided to support a minimum of vs_1_1 in the IsDeviceAcceptable method, and you already have techniques that use this version, you should only use the 2.0 version if it's supported. It's like an "added feature." Add a new variable to your C# code to decide when to use this version:

```
// Can the device use pixel shader 2.0?
private bool canUse20Shaders = false;
```

This line defaults to false, so the advanced shaders aren't forced on a user that can't support them. However, if the user can support them, you want them to be used, so find the OnCreateDevice method and add this check to the end:

```
if (sampleFramework.DeviceCaps.PixelShaderVersion >= new Version(2, 0) )
{
    canUse20Shaders = true;
}
```

Finally, you need to update the rendering method so the kart rendering uses the correct technique, depending on which model is available:

```
effect.Technique = canUse20Shaders ? "RenderSceneSpecularPerPixel" :
    "RenderSceneSpecular";
```

With that, you should be able to see your kart being rendered with per-pixel specular highlights, as shown in Figure 23.1.

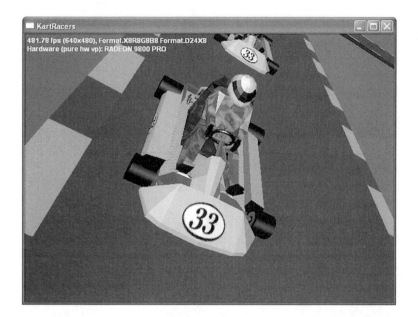

FIGURE 23.1
Specular highlights.

Summary

In this chapter, you focused on getting a rear-view mirror created and rendered for your game. You were required to render multiple go-karts, the track, and finally the scene multiple times to render the scene to a texture. You then used that texture to display a rear-view mirror.

In the final chapter, you will look at performance considerations for developing games.

CHAPTER 24

Performance Considerations

One of the most important parts of game development is considering performance. All the good game developers are concerned about the performance of the code they write, and they want to ensure it runs as fast as possible. This chapter will point out some easy things to remember.

In this chapter, you'll learn

- ▶ Whether Managed DirectX is fast
- ▶ The event model
- ▶ The horrors of boxing
- ▶ Native assembly generation

The Event Model and Managed DirectX

Managed DirectX has plenty of events that it captures and fires in a normal application. Every single managed graphics object hooks certain events on the device to ensure that it can behave correctly.

For example, when a device is reset (due to a window resize or a switch to or from full screen), any object stored in the default memory pool needs to be disposed. Many objects also have something to do after the device is reset. In the default case, each object that needs to be disposed before a reset hooks the DeviceLost event, and the items who also have post-reset work hook the DeviceReset event.

This scenario doesn't even consider the fact that each object hooks the device's Dispose event. In short, if events are being hooked, every Direct3D object will have a hook on the device. So why is this a problem?

Take this seemingly "safe" code as an example (assuming swapChain is a valid swap chain and device is a valid Direct3D device):

```
device.SetRenderTarget(0, swapChain.GetBackBuffer(0, BackBufferType.Mono));
device.DrawPrimitives(PrimitiveType.TriangleList, 0, 500);
```

Looks simple enough, just using the back buffer of the swap chain as the render target. However, if the events are being hooked, a lot more is going on here. The GetBackBuffer call returns a new surface representing the current back buffer of the swap chain. This object hooks the device lost and disposing events, which are at least three allocations (the actual surface, along with the two event handlers).

Worse than that, this object (which is only used for a brief period of time) is never collected, as long as the device is still alive, because it has hooked events on the device. This memory (and these objects) are never reclaimed. The objects eventually get promoted to generation two, and memory usage on your application will just as steadily rise. Imagine a game running at 60 frames per second, each frame calling this code.

To think, we haven't hit the end of the problems yet either! Imagine the game running at 60 frames per second that has been running for 2 minutes. The device's dispose event has 7,200 objects hooked, and the Dispose method is invoked because the application is shutting down. It takes a significant amount of time to propagate this event, so it appears that your application has locked up (when in reality it is simply notifying every object that the device is now gone).

A more efficient way of writing this code is something like the following:

```
using (Surface buffer = swapChain.GetBackBuffer(0, BackBufferType.Mono))
{
    device.SetRenderTarget(0, buffer);
    device.DrawPrimitives(PrimitiveType.TriangleList, 0, 500);
}
```

In this scenario, you get rid of the objects immediately. Yet you still have the underlying "problem" of the event hooking.

An even better solution is to turn off the event hooking within Direct3D completely. You can use a static property on the device to do this:

```
Device.IsUsingEventHandlers = false;
```

If you do this before you create your device, you completely turn off the internal event handling for Direct3D. Beware of doing it, though, because you need to manage the object lifetimes yourself. Remember from early in the book, the sample framework does this management automatically. Now you know the reason.

The default behavior of device hooks is extremely convenient, but if you want top performance, you might want to avoid the default event code. At least understand when and how the events are hooked, and structure your code to be as fast as possible (such as using the second code snippet over the first).

Native Assembly Generation

One of the first things that people might notice when they're running managed applications is that the startup time is slower than it is for a "native" application. The major cause of this slowdown is the actual compilation that needs to happen (just in time [JIT] compiling). Because the managed code must be compiled into native code before it's executed, this compilation provides an expected delay when starting the application. Because Managed DirectX is built on top of this system, code you write using the Managed DirectX runtime has this behavior as well.

Because the JIT compilation can do a lot of optimizations that just can't happen during compile time (taking advantage of the actual machine the code is running on rather than the machine it was compiled on, and so on) the behavior here is desired. The side effect (the slowdown) is not. It would be great to find a way to remove this cost. Luckily for us, the .NET Framework includes a utility called Native Image Generator (NGen), which does exactly that.

This utility natively compiles an assembly and puts the output into what is called the native assembly cache, which resides within the global assembly cache. When the .NET Framework attempts to load an assembly, it checks whether the native version of the assembly exists, and if it does, it loads that instead of doing the JIT compilation at startup time, potentially dramatically decreasing the startup time of the application using these assemblies. The downsides of using this utility are twofold. First, there's no guarantee that the startup or execution time will be faster (although in most cases it is so you should test to find out), and second, the native image is "fragile." A number of factors cause the native image to become invalid (such as a new runtime installation or security settings changes). After the native image is invalid, it still exists in the native assembly cache and is never used. Plus, if you want to regain the benefits, you need to NGen the assemblies once more, and unless you're watching closely, you might not even notice that the original native assemblies are now invalid.

If you've decided you would still like to NGen your Managed DirectX assemblies, here are the steps you would take:

1. Open a Visual Studio .NET 2003 command prompt.

2. If you do not want to open that command window, you could simply open a normal command prompt window and ensure that the framework binary folder is in your path. The framework binary folder should be located at `%windir%\microsoft.net\framework\v1.1.4322`, where `%windir%` is your Windows folder.

3. Change the directory to `%windir%\microsoft.net\Managed DirectX`, where `%windir%` is your Windows folder.

4. Go into the folder for the version of Managed DirectX you want to NGen from here (the later the version, the more recent the assembly).

5. Run the following command line for each of the assemblies in the folder:

```
ngen microsoft.directx.dll (etc)
```

If your command prompt supports it, you might also use this command line instead:

```
for /R %i in (*.dll) do ngen %i
```

If you later decide you do not want the assemblies compiled natively, you can use the `ngen /delete` command to remove these now compiled assemblies.

Construction Cue

Note that not all methods or types are natively compiled by NGen, and they still need to be "JITed." Any types or methods that fall into this category will be output during the running of the NGen executable.

The Horrors of Boxing

The .NET runtime and the C# language have changed the way people write code. It has opened up the world of programming to new developers and expanded the productivity of the ones who have been around for a while. It handles so many things for you that it's quite easy to forget how much some operations cost. Look at this real-world example.

The Billboard sample that shipped with the DirectX software development kit (SDK) in 2002 and 2003 (it was removed for the DirectX SDK Summer 2004 release) had multiple versions: an unmanaged version written in C++ and two managed versions, one written in C# and the other in VB .NET. Because each of the DirectX SDK samples includes the frame rate while you are running, you can easily tell which of the applications is running "faster" and by approximately how much. Comparing the C++ Billboard sample with the C# Billboard sample, you'd notice the C# version runs at approximately 60% the speed of the C++ sample, and that was about the best it could do.

Considering that the other samples run at similar speeds between the managed and unmanaged variations, there must be something special about this particular sample that causes this slowdown. Naturally, there is, and the culprit is boxing and unboxing.

The term **boxing** refers to what the .NET runtime does to convert a value type (such as a structure) into an object. The reverse of this process is obviously called unboxing. To perform this operation, the .NET runtime allocates a portion of the heap large enough to hold your value type and then copies the data from the stack (where the value type resides) to the newly allocated heap space.

When looking at the Billboard managed sample, you might notice that each tree drawn has a corresponding structure that maintains the information needed to draw the tree. Because the trees are alpha blended and need to be drawn in a certain order (from back to front), each tree is sorted every frame. This code was in the sample to do this:

```
trees.Sort(new TreeSortClass());
```

This class implemented IComparer, which is needed for comparison. If you look at the implementation of this class, you see quickly that the comparison method takes two objects as parameters, whereas we are using a structure. This structure must be boxed before it can be passed on to the compare method. Then, as soon as the compare method is started, the object is unboxed to be able to manipulate the data.

On average, the sort method was called approximately 4,300 times per frame. Each of these calls performs a total of two boxing operations, followed immediately by two unboxing operations. The structure itself was defined as such:

```
public struct Tree
{
        public CustomVertex.PositionColoredTextured v0, v1, v2, v3;
        public Vector3 position;
        public int treeTextureIndex;
        public int offsetIndex;
};
```

If you calculate the structure's size, you see that it is quite large, 116 bytes. So calculate the data that is being allocated and copied during a single sort operation. Multiply the number of bytes that need to be allocated per object (116) by the number of objects (2) by the number of calls per frame (4,300), and you come up with a whopping 997,600 bytes that need to be allocated for *every* frame. This number covers just the allocation for the boxing operation; it doesn't even consider the copy operation to get the data into the newly allocated object.

Even after the copy operation takes place, as soon as the method is entered, the first thing that happens is that it takes all the data that has just been boxed and unboxes it. The exact same allocation and copy need to be performed a second time, with the exception being that this allocation is performed on the stack.

In reality, for every frame the Billboard sample is running, 1,995,200 bytes on average are allocated between the stack and heap and then copied back and forth between them. This conclusion doesn't even consider the fact that this large amount of tiny allocations (because each allocation is 116 bytes) will cause the garbage collector to kick in quite a few times for a generation zero collection. No wonder that sample ran with such poor performance.

The point of this exercise is that many developers using managed languages don't understand the costs behind the code they are writing. The .NET runtime gives you enormous power and flexibility, but given the "newness" of the Application Programming Interface (API), it's still common to see people take advantage of these features without fully understanding the costs associated with them. I'm quite sure the average developer wouldn't realize that the simple sorting algorithm in the Billboard sample would be allocating and copying close to 2MB of data *per frame*.

The Speed of Managed DirectX

It seems that at least once a week I'm answering questions directly regarding the performance of managed code and Managed DirectX in particular. One of the more common questions I hear is some version of "Is it as fast as unmanaged code?"

Obviously, in a general sense, it isn't. Regardless of the quality of the Managed DirectX API, it still has to run through the same DirectX API that the unmanaged code does. There is naturally going to be a slight overhead, but does it have a large negative impact on the majority of applications? Of course it does not. No one is suggesting that one of the top-of-the-line polygon pushing games coming out today (say, Half Life 2 or Doom 3) should be written in Managed DirectX, but that doesn't mean there isn't a whole slew of games that could be. I get to that in a moment.

I'm also asked quite a bit, "Why is it so slow?" Sometimes, the person hasn't even run a managed application. He just assumes it has to be slow. Other times, he might have run numerous various "scenarios" comparing against the unmanaged code (including running the SDK samples from previous versions) and found that in some instances there are large differences.

As mentioned earlier, all the samples in the previous SDK used the dreaded DoEvents loop, which can artificially slow down the application due to allocations and the subsequent large amounts of collections. The fact that most of the samples run with similar frame rates as those for the unmanaged API was a testament to the speed of the API to begin with.

Many of the developers out there today simply don't know how to write managed code that performs well. This point isn't about any shortcoming of the developer, but rather the newness of the API combined with not enough documentation on performance and how to get the best out of the common language runtime (CLR). For the most part, we are all newbies in this area, but things will only get better.

It's not at all dissimilar to the change from assembler to C++ code for games. It all comes down to a simple question: do the benefits outweigh the negatives? Are you willing to sacrifice a small bit of performance for the easier development of managed code? The quicker time to market? The greater security? The easier debugging?

As I touched on earlier, certain games today aren't good fits for writing the main engine in managed code, but plenty of titles are. The top-10 selling PC games a short while ago included two versions of the Sims, Zoo Tycoon (+ expansion), Age of Mythology, Backyard Basketball 2004, and Uru: Ages Beyond Myst, any of which could have been written in managed code.

Anyone who has taken the time to write some code in one of the managed languages usually realizes the benefits pretty quickly.

Understanding the Cost of Methods

One of the most important ways to ensure that you write applications with the best performance is to always know the cost of any method you call. Although memorizing all the different permutations of APIs you can call and the performance they take is unreasonable, you should have at least a vague idea about the cost of any method.

Managed DirectX has a few cases where seemingly harmless code can cause problems. For example, any method that takes a string as an argument in Managed DirectX has the cost of allocating a new unmanaged string type and copying the string data over.

Take the case where you are using High-Level Shader Language (HLSL) to render your scene, and numerous times throughout each frame, you switch the technique being used, such as the following:

```
myEffect.Technique = "TransformWorldSpace";
//Render some stuff
myEffect.Technique = "TransformAndAddGlow";
// Render some other stuff
```

Each time you switch the technique, you are allocating some memory and copying the technique name over. A much better solution to this problem is to cache the handles returned:

```
// On device creations, cache technique handles
EffectHandle handle1 = myEffect.GetTechnique("TransformWorldSpace");
EffectHandle handle2 = myEffect.GetTechnique("TransformAndAddGlow");


// Later on, for every render
myEffect.Technique = handle1;
//Render some stuff
myEffect.Technique = handle2;
//Render some stuff
```

You should always know what an underlying method costs; I cannot stress this point enough.

Summary

Wow! Twenty-four chapters sure go by quickly. With this book behind you, you're well on your way to becoming the great game developer you hope to be.

Your next step should be to take the Kart Racers game you've been working on and make it the best racing game you can make.

Happy gaming!

PART VI

Appendix

Developing a Level Creator

In the first section of this book, you wrote a game called Blockers, a simple puzzle game. The code assumed you had a level creator that output files in the correct format. This level creator was included with the CD, and this appendix covers that program briefly.

Writing the Level Creator

Although you could create a fancy 3D graphics version of the level creator for the Blockers game, one thing any good tool developer realizes is that tools need to be functional and written quickly. Why spend all the time making a fancy 3D graphics version, when you can simply use the WinForms controls to get the job done easily? To get started, load the Blockers solution file, right-click on the solution in Solution Explorer, and click Add New Project. Choose a WinForms project, and call it LevelCreator.

This step automatically generates some code, so open the form1.cs file in code view (*not* in designer view), and replace the automatically generated variables with these:

```
private static readonly Color[] BoxColors = {Color.Black, Color.Red ,
        Color.Blue, Color.Green, Color.Yellow, Color.SandyBrown,
        Color.WhiteSmoke, Color.DarkGoldenrod, Color.CornflowerBlue,
        Color.Pink
    };

int playerIndex = 0;
private const int SquareSize = 13;

private System.ComponentModel.Container components = null;
private static readonly string MediaPath =
    ConfigurationSettings.AppSettings.Get("MediaPath");
private System.Windows.Forms.Label label1;
private System.Windows.Forms.Label label2;
private System.Windows.Forms.Label label3;
```

```
private System.Windows.Forms.Label label4;
private System.Windows.Forms.CheckBox chkWrap;

private System.Windows.Forms.Label label5;
private System.Windows.Forms.Label label6;
private System.Windows.Forms.TextBox txtTime;
private System.Windows.Forms.TextBox txtMoves;
private System.Windows.Forms.NumericUpDown levelNumber;
private System.Windows.Forms.Label label7;
private System.Windows.Forms.Button btnSave;

private System.Windows.Forms.Button[] levelButtons;
private byte[] levelIndices;
private System.Windows.Forms.Button[] mainButtons;
private int[] mainColors;
```

You'll notice that the box colors array matches the one you have in the Blockers game. If you change one, you need to make sure that you change them in both places. The same goes for the SquareSize constant. You'll also see a variable to maintain the starting location of the player (marked by an asterisk). Next, you'll see a series of controls that make up the user interface controls for the application.

Next, replace the constructor with the following one:

```
public Form1()
{
        //
        // Required for Windows Form Designer support
        //
        InitializeComponent();

    // Create the main buttons
    mainButtons = new Button[4];
    mainColors = new int[4];

    for (int i = 0; i < 4; i++)
    {
        mainButtons[i] = new Button();
        mainButtons[i].Tag = i;
        mainButtons[i].BackColor = System.Drawing.Color.Black;
        mainButtons[i].Location = new System.Drawing.Point(16 + (72 * i), 40);
        mainButtons[i].Size = new System.Drawing.Size(24, 24);
        mainButtons[i].TabStop = false;
        mainButtons[i].Click +=new EventHandler(OnMainButtonClick);
        mainColors[i] = 0;

        this.Controls.Add(mainButtons[i]);
    }


    levelButtons = new Button[SquareSize * SquareSize];
    levelIndices = new byte[levelButtons.Length];
```

```
    int index = 0;
    this.SuspendLayout();
    Font f = new Font(this.Font.Name, 10.0f);
    for (int j = 0; j < SquareSize; j++)
    {
        for (int i = 0; i < SquareSize; i++)
        {
            levelButtons[index] = new Button();
            levelButtons[index].Tag = index;
            levelButtons[index].Font = f;
            levelButtons[index].BackColor = System.Drawing.Color.Black;
            levelButtons[index].Location = new System.Drawing.Point(2 +
                                    (22 * i), 80 + (22 * j));
            levelButtons[index].Size = new System.Drawing.Size(20, 20);
            levelButtons[index].TabStop = false;
            levelButtons[index].Click +=new EventHandler(OnLevelButtonClick);
            levelIndices[index] = 0;

            this.Controls.Add(levelButtons[index]);
            index++;
        }
    }
    this.ResumeLayout(true);
}
```

After calling the `InitializeComponent` method (which you'll see in a moment), this code creates two sets of buttons: one set of four at the top, which are the level colors, and then a 13x13 array of buttons that make up the level itself. Each block in the level is one of the four main buttons or black, signifying that it's empty and doesn't exist in the level. When you choose the colors of the main level buttons, any corresponding button in the level itself should change colors. Before you define the event handlers you've used in the constructor, here is the `InitializeComponent` method:

```
private void InitializeComponent()
{
    this.label1 = new System.Windows.Forms.Label();
    this.label2 = new System.Windows.Forms.Label();
    this.label3 = new System.Windows.Forms.Label();
    this.label4 = new System.Windows.Forms.Label();
    this.chkWrap = new System.Windows.Forms.CheckBox();
    this.label5 = new System.Windows.Forms.Label();
    this.label6 = new System.Windows.Forms.Label();
    this.txtTime = new System.Windows.Forms.TextBox();
    this.txtMoves = new System.Windows.Forms.TextBox();
    this.levelNumber = new System.Windows.Forms.NumericUpDown();
    this.label7 = new System.Windows.Forms.Label();
    this.btnSave = new System.Windows.Forms.Button();
    ((System.ComponentModel.ISupportInitialize)(this.levelNumber)).BeginInit();
    this.SuspendLayout();

    this.label1.Location = new System.Drawing.Point(8, 8);
    this.label1.Size = new System.Drawing.Size(64, 23);
```

```
this.label1.TabIndex = 0;
this.label1.Text = "Color 1";

this.label2.Location = new System.Drawing.Point(80, 8);
this.label2.Size = new System.Drawing.Size(64, 23);
this.label2.TabIndex = 1;
this.label2.Text = "Color 2";

this.label3.Location = new System.Drawing.Point(160, 8);
this.label3.Size = new System.Drawing.Size(64, 23);
this.label3.TabIndex = 2;
this.label3.Text = "Color 3";

this.label4.Location = new System.Drawing.Point(232, 8);
this.label4.Size = new System.Drawing.Size(64, 23);
this.label4.TabIndex = 3;
this.label4.Text = "Color 4";

this.chkWrap.Location = new System.Drawing.Point(296, 40);
this.chkWrap.Size = new System.Drawing.Size(120, 16);
this.chkWrap.TabIndex = 4;
this.chkWrap.Text = "Wrap Colors?";

this.label5.Location = new System.Drawing.Point(296, 72);
this.label5.Size = new System.Drawing.Size(104, 23);
this.label5.TabIndex = 9;
this.label5.Text = "Number Seconds";

this.label6.Location = new System.Drawing.Point(296, 136);
this.label6.Size = new System.Drawing.Size(104, 23);
this.label6.TabIndex = 10;
this.label6.Text = "Max Moves";

this.txtTime.Location = new System.Drawing.Point(296, 96);
this.txtTime.Size = new System.Drawing.Size(96, 20);
this.txtTime.TabIndex = 11;
this.txtTime.Text = "180.0";

this.txtMoves.Location = new System.Drawing.Point(296, 168);
this.txtMoves.Size = new System.Drawing.Size(96, 20);
this.txtMoves.TabIndex = 12;
this.txtMoves.Text = "500";

this.levelNumber.Location = new System.Drawing.Point(296, 232);
this.levelNumber.Minimum = new System.Decimal(new int[] {
    1, 0, 0, 0});
this.levelNumber.Size = new System.Drawing.Size(104, 20);
this.levelNumber.TabIndex = 13;
this.levelNumber.Value = new System.Decimal(new int[] {
    1, 0, 0, 0});

this.label7.Location = new System.Drawing.Point(296, 208);
this.label7.Size = new System.Drawing.Size(104, 23);
this.label7.TabIndex = 14;
this.label7.Text = "Level Number";

this.btnSave.Location = new System.Drawing.Point(304, 320);
this.btnSave.Size = new System.Drawing.Size(104, 24);
```

```
this.btnSave.TabIndex = 15;
this.btnSave.Text = "Save Level";
this.btnSave.Click += new System.EventHandler(this.OnSaveLevel);

this.AutoScaleBaseSize = new System.Drawing.Size(5, 13);
this.ClientSize = new System.Drawing.Size(424, 382);
this.Controls.Add(this.btnSave);
this.Controls.Add(this.label7);
this.Controls.Add(this.levelNumber);
this.Controls.Add(this.txtMoves);
this.Controls.Add(this.txtTime);
this.Controls.Add(this.label6);
this.Controls.Add(this.label5);
this.Controls.Add(this.chkWrap);
this.Controls.Add(this.label4);
this.Controls.Add(this.label3);
this.Controls.Add(this.label2);
this.Controls.Add(this.label1);
this.FormBorderStyle = System.Windows.Forms.FormBorderStyle.Fixed3D;
this.MaximizeBox = false;
this.MinimizeBox = false;
this.Name = "Form1";
this.Text = "Blockers Level Creator";
((System.ComponentModel.ISupportInitialize)(this.levelNumber)).EndInit();
this.ResumeLayout(false);

}
```

With that code, you should be able to view the window in the designer now. It should look something like Figure A.1.

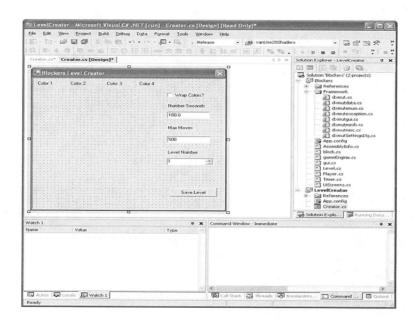

FIGURE A.1
Design view.

Now you can add the event handlers you declared in the constructor:

```
private void OnMainButtonClick(object sender, System.EventArgs e)
{
    Button b = sender as Button;

    int index = (int)b.Tag;

    mainColors[index]++;
    if (mainColors[index] >= BoxColors.Length)
        mainColors[index] = 0;

    ((Button)sender).BackColor = BoxColors[mainColors[index]];

    UpdateBoxColors();
}

private void OnLevelButtonClick(object sender, EventArgs e)
{
    Button b = sender as Button;

    int index = (int)b.Tag;

    if ((Form.MouseButtons & MouseButtons.Right) == MouseButtons.Right)
    {
        playerIndex = index;
    }

    levelIndices[index]++;
    if (levelIndices[index] >= 5)
        levelIndices[index] = 0;

    UpdateBoxColors();
}
```

In each of these methods, you take the button and update its color to the next color in the array. In the level buttons, using the right mouse button also has the effect of moving the player's start position to that point. You'll notice each of the methods also calls this UpdateBoxColors method, as follows:

```
private void UpdateBoxColors()
{
    for(int i = 0; i < levelButtons.Length; i++)
    {
        if (levelIndices[i] < 4)
        {
            levelButtons[i].BackColor = mainButtons[levelIndices[i]].BackColor;
        }
        else
        {
            levelButtons[i].BackColor = System.Drawing.Color.Black;
        }
        if (playerIndex == i)
        {
            if (levelButtons[i].BackColor == System.Drawing.Color.Black)
            {
```

```
                playerIndex++;
            }
            else
            {
                levelButtons[i].Text = "*";
            }
        }
        else
        {
            levelButtons[i].Text = string.Empty;
        }
    }
}
```

Finally, all you need to do is write the code to save the level out to a file. This code should look familiar because it is basically the inverse of the loading code you wrote for Blockers:

```
private void OnSaveLevel(object sender, System.EventArgs e)
{

    FileStream stm = File.Create(MediaPath + string.Format("Level{0}.lvl",
                                        (int)levelNumber.Value));

    float maxTime = float.Parse(txtTime.Text);
    int maxMoves = int.Parse(txtMoves.Text);

    stm.Write(BitConverter.GetBytes(maxTime), 0, sizeof(float));
    stm.Write(BitConverter.GetBytes(maxMoves), 0, sizeof(int));

    int numColors = 0;
    for (int i = 0; i < 4; i++)
    {
        if (mainColors[i] > 0)
            numColors++;
        else
            break;
    }
    if (numColors < 2)
        throw new InvalidOperationException("You need more colors defined.");

    BlockColor[] colors = new BlockColor[numColors];

    int numberColors = colors.Length;
    stm.Write(BitConverter.GetBytes(numberColors), 0, sizeof(int));

    for (int i = 0; i < colors.Length; i++)
    {
        colors[i] = (BlockColor)(mainColors[i] - 1);
        stm.WriteByte((byte)colors[i]);
    }


    BlockColor final = colors[colors.Length - 1];

    stm.WriteByte((byte)final);
```

```
stm.Write(BitConverter.GetBytes(chkWrap.Checked), 0, sizeof(bool));

int blockIndex = 0;
for (int j = 0; j < SquareSize; j++)
{
    for (int i = 0; i < SquareSize; i++)
    {
        if (levelIndices[blockIndex] < numColors)
        {
            stm.WriteByte(levelIndices[blockIndex]);
        }
        else
        {
            stm.WriteByte((byte)0xff);
        }
        blockIndex++;
    }
}

stm.Write(BitConverter.GetBytes(playerIndex), 0, 4);

stm.Close();
}
```

Because this code uses the sizeof keyword, you are required to turn on unsafe code. With that, you're free to make as many levels as you want for Blockers. See Figure A.2 for an example of the final level creator in action.

FIGURE A.2
The level creator in action.

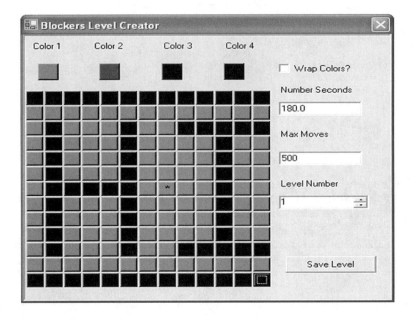

Have fun!

Index

Numbers

A

B

B

How can we make this index more useful? Email us at indexes@sampublishing.com

V-Z